ORNAMENTAL GARDENING IN INDIA

ORNAMENTAL GARDENING IN INDIA

DR. KAUSHAL KUMAR MISRA

BIOTECH

2011

BIOTECH BOOKS

ISBN 978-81-7622-231-0

Published by
BIOTECH BOOKS
4762-63/23, Ansari Road, Darya Ganj,
New Delhi-110002 (India)
Phone: 23262132
E-mail: biotechbooks@yahoo.co.in

Laser Typesetting by : Deep Graphics, Delhi

PRINTED IN INDIA

Dedicated
to
The Loving Memory of
My Beloved Uncles
Late Shri Bharat Prasad Mishra
(1912-1971)
and
Shri Shivgulam Mishra (1922-2000)
who had the great love for the nature

CONTENTS

PREFACE

The present book 'Ornamental Gardening in India' has sixteen chapters. The first chapter consists of importance and scope which deals with present status, scope, export potential of floriculture products and prospects of diversification in floriculture. The second chapter consists of history of gardening which deals with gardening in Persia, China, Greek, Rome, Italy, French, Holland, England, Japan and India. The third chapter deals with nursery management which consists of necessity of nursery, type of ornamental nursery, layout and planning of nursery, propagation techniques, insect-pests and diseases of nursery. The fourth chapter consists of plant growth regulators and their uses which deals with the type of growth regulators, its use in propagation, control of plant height, flowering, senescence, pinching, dormancy and vase life. The fifth chapter deals with flowering annuals and herbaceous perennials which consists of classification of annuals, herbaceous perennials, their cultural management and description of some important annuals and herbaceous perennials, flower seed production, herbaceous border and lawn management.

The sixth chapter consists of shrub, climbers and related structures which deals with classification of shrubs, cultural management and description of some important shrubs, climbers, shrubbery border, hedges, edges, topiary, arches and pergolas. The seventh chapter consists of trees which deals with selection, maintenance and care, description of some important trees and trees for bio-aesthetic planning. The eight chapter consists of bulbous and foliage plants which deals with cultural management and description of some important bulbous and foliage plants. The ninth chapter consists of cacti, succulents and ferns which deals with their management and description of some important cacti, succulents and ferns. The tenth chapter consists of orchids which deals with the cultivation and description of some important orchids. The eleventh chapter consists of palms and cycads which deals with importance, cultivation and maintenance, different types and utility of palms and cycads.

The twelveth chapter consists of Bonsai which deals with the classification, culture and management of bonsai. The thirteen chapter consists of principles and features of garden designs which deals with principles of garden design, styles of gardens and different features of garden like garden walls, fencing, steps, garden drives, paths, side drains, lovely pattern, wodden block, flower bed frames, garden adornments, bird bath, floral clocks, fountains, garden seats, Japanese lanterns, ornamental tubs, urns, vases, ornamental stones, plant stands, statues and sundials. The fourteen chapter consists of indoor gardening which deals with the selection of house plants, management of indoor plants, gardening in tubs and urns, hanging baskets, window gardens, troughs, bowls and trays, vertical garden, jar and bottle gardening and terrariums. The fifteen chapter consists of rock and water gardening which deal with the construction and management and plants suitable for rock and water gardens, marsh garden, sunken garden and gardening in the shade. The sixteen chapter consists of roof gardening which deals with what is green roof, history, type of green roofs, benefits of green roofs, roof conditions and suitability for greening and plants used in roof gardening.

Efforts have been made to describe the ornamental gardening in India in a systematic and comprehensive manner. The subject matter illustrated with figures, tables and photographs, wherever, felt necessary. The selected references presented at the end can be useful to obtain further information. Glossary containing related terms has been presented. In the last index has been presented. The book has been written keeping in view the requirements of the graduate, post graduate students, teachers and research scientists in ornamental gardening. The author is grateful to his professors particularly to Professor J. P. Singh, the ex-head, Department of Horticulture, Allahabad Agricultural Institute, Allahabad and his several students who assisted him in his scientific pursuit in Ornamental Horticulture during the last three and half decades at Govind Ballabh Pant University of Agriculture and Technology, Pantnagar. I am thankful to my wife Mrs. Manjul Misra who takes great pain in arranging the various chapters, My daughter Mrs. Kanan Kaushal Pandey for collection of plants from south India and my advisee Miss Shweta Uniyal for her help in typing and reference collection. I am also thankful to my Ph. D. students namely, Dr. Deepti Singh, Dr. Jyoti Kumari, Miss Meenakshi Basoli, Mr. Manish Kapoor and Mr. Himanshu Trivedi for their help in collection of material.

April, 2011

Dr. Kaushal Kumar Misra
Pantnagar

CHAPTER-1

IMPORTANCE AND SCOPE OF ORNAMENTAL GARDENING

Flowers have been associated with mankind since time immemorial. They have been used for garland making, self adornment, religious offerings and other social ceremonies. References to flowers and gardens are found in ancient Sanskrit classics like the Rig Veda (C 3000-2000 BC), Ramayana (1200-1300 BC), Mahabharata (prior to 4th Century BC), Shudraka (100 BC), Ashvagodha (100 AD), Kalidasa (400 AD) and Sarangdhara (1200 AD). The social and economic aspects of flower growing were, however, recognized much later. In past, these requirements were met from home-grown plants. In India, initially commercial floriculture industry grew because of increasing need for low-cost flowers by European cut flower market place. European flower traders identified commercial floriculture production in Southeast Asian countries; flowers were initially produced mainly for export, which has simply changed to opportunities for supplying to local markets. The potential for commercial floriculture expansion in India is unlimited, provided strength is capitalized and weaknesses are converted into opportunities through strategic planning, infrastructural development and regional cooperation. Marketing strategies linked with production and business management having horizontal and vertical integration would lead to the development of commercial floriculture in India. Attempt should be made to examine the scenario, identify the constraints in development of floriculture in India and develop strategies for promotion of marketing for flowers in an integrated manner.

Present status

Floriculture in India is still in infancy. Goverment of India identified floriculture as a sunrise industry and accorded it 100 per cent export oriented status. The liberalization of industry and trade policies paved the way for development of export oriented production of cut flowers. The new seed policy had already made it feasible to import planting material of international varieties. The government of India offers tax benefits to new export oriented floriculture companies in the form of income-tax holidays and exemption from certain import duties. Agricultural and Processed Food Products Export Development Authority (APEDA), responsible for export promotion and development of floriculture in India, grants subsidies for establishing cold storage, precooling units, refrigerated vans and green houses and air freight subsidy to exports. It has been found that commercial floriculture has higher potential per unit area than most of the field crops and is, therefore, a lucrative business. According to National Horticulture Board, the total area under flower crops during 2007-08 was estimated around 1.61 thousand hectares, concentrated mostly in Maharashtra, Karnataka, Tamil Nadu, Andhra Pradesh and West Bengal. India is the second largest flower grower after China. Tamil Nadu is leading producer of loose flowers closely followed by Karnataka both in terms of area and production. The production of loose flowers during 2007-08 was recorded as 870.4 MT, while number of cut flower produced during this period was 43417.5 millions. The productivity of flowers was 5.4 MT/Ha and had highest in Bihar (17.05/ha) followed by Haryana (11.55/ha.), Madhya Pradesh (10.59/ha). In India total export of floriculture products was Rs. 340.14 Crore in 2007-08 (APEDA). The major export destination of India includes USA, Netherlands, UK, Germany and Japan. Still India is a marginal player in the world floriculture trade indicating a strong potential that can be exploited in this sector.

Table 1.1: Major loose flower producing states in India (2007-2008)

States	Per cent share
Tamil Nadu	25
Karnataka	19
Andhra Pradesh	14
Punjab	9
Maharashtra	8
Haryana	7
Gujarat	6
West Bengal	6
Others	3

Table 1.2: Major cut flower producing states in India (2007-08)

States	Per cent share
West Bengal	45
Maharashtra	13
Karnataka	13
Gujarat	12
Utter Pradesh	9
Uttaranchal	3
Delhi	2
Others	3

Table 1.3: Area and production of flowers in India

Years	Area (In 000' HA)	Production	
		Loose (In 000' MT)	Cut (Million numbers)
1993-94	53	233	555
2001-02	106	535	2565
2002-03	70	735	2060
2003-04	101	580	1793
2004-05	118	659	2071
2005-06	130	656	2921
2006-07	144	880	3716
2007-08	161	870	434

Source: NHB Database 2008

With the declaration of floriculture as an "extreme focus area" by the Ministry of Commerce and Industry, Government of India, floriculture sector has acquired a special status in the horticulture basket of India. India produces a wide variety of floricultural products which inter alia include flowers and foliage, both fresh flowers and dried, like roses, carnations, chrysanthemums and orchids. With world's fastest growing retail market, second largest consumer base and unlimited opportunities for growth, Indian Floriculture is today a force to recon with. The domestic industry is growing at an annual growth rate of 10-20% per annum. Floriculture industry is targeting an annual $ 1-billion in export of floricultural products by 2010. Currently, flower trade has attracted the largest demand from an estimated 300 million middle-class flower-loving people with consumption in the cities and major towns at 40 per cent per annum. Flower retail shops have mushroomed all over the place from major metros to market shops and flower boutiques. Further, super-market/ hypermarket retail chains have fuelled the growth in the consumption. Cashing is on this trend, the Minister of the State for Commerce also feels that floriculture is all about creating new employment opportunities in far flung areas rather than talking about Dollars, the focus should be on million jobs. Six Agri Export Zones on floriculture have been set up in Sikkim, Tamil Nadu, Uttarakhand, Karnataka and Maharashtra. The APEDA has taken a number of measures to facilitate floriculture exports. Some key Indian airports like New Delhi, Mumbai, Hyderabad, Bangalore, Chennai, Thiruvananthapuram and Cochin now have cold storage and cargo handling facilities. More airports will have these facilities in the future. Among other things, flower auction centres are coming up in Bangalore, Mumbai, Noida and Kolkata. These are readymade market facilities for trading and price discovery for a variety of flowers, both for export and domestic markets. India has to achieve the ambitious export target of Rs 1000 crore per annum over the next 5 years, a paradigm shift is required. The key issues that need to be addressed in the Indian context are: economic of scale, product range/ latest varieties, year round exports, quality control and certification, cold chain management. The APEDA has been addressing these issues through various forums on a concerted basis given its mandate to promote floricultural exports from India.

Scope

The scope of floriculture in India has increased tremendously which is evident from the increase in area from 53,000 ha in 1993-94 to 1,61,000 ha during 2007-08. There is cent per cent increase in area and more than 230 per cent increase in loose flower production and 480 per cent increase in cut flower production. There is high competition as floricultural economy has shifted to consumer-driven enterprises rather producer-driven economy. In this scenario of consumer-driven market, producer of all sizes have to focus on marketing with lookout for national brands to boost their sales. Growers have to look for niches and value-added products. There is a trend for direct marketing besides marketing through super markets and wholesale markets. Business management is becoming important in this scenario of global competition.

Export Potential of Floricultural Products

India is endowed with proximity to market in Japan, Russia and South-East countries. The Government allows subsidy on air freight for export to Europe, West Asia and South East Asia. Import duties have been reduced on cut flowers, flower seeds and tissue-cultured plants. Floricultural exports from India comprise fresh cut flowers (to Europe, Japan, Australia, Middle East and USA), loose flowers, cut foliage (to Europe), dry flowers (to USA, Europe, Japan, Australia, Far East and Russia) and potted plants (limited to very few countries). Out of these components, dry floricultural exports registered a phenomenal growth during the last decade. The floriculture exports which stood at Rs 63 crore during 1996-97, increased almost five times to Rs 340.40 crores during 2007-08. Indian exports mostly target the major floriculturally important events like Christmas day, New Year Eve, Valentine day and Mother's day. The major factors are the unfavourable weather conditions during winter in major production centres in the Northern Hemisphere that limit the production. Therefore, markets are open to produce that comes from more favourable climates from the Southern Hemisphere. India, therefore, finds itself competing with other equally favourable countries like Kenya, Ecuador and Morocco during such events. The export basket comprises dry flowers (71%), fresh cut flowers (18%), live plants (9%), fresh bulbs (1%) and foliage (1%). Indian exports of cut flowers into Europe stand at £ 2.6 million (0.1% of the £ 3 billion imports into the EU), out of which 94% comprise rose imports. In terms of value, the rose export from India is in the range of £ 2.4 million (0.3% of total EU rose imports from outside the EU). Ornamental foliage exports from India are worth £ 10.5 million (2% of total EU exports) while the exports value of ornamental plants from India stands at £ 2.2 million (0.1% of EU plant imports). India exports small quantities of cuttings and young plants valued at £ 1.6 million (less than 1% of total EU imports) to markets in Europe. In terms of volumes, India exported 17 million stems of cut flowers and 5 million cutting and slips during 2005.

Prospects of diversification in floriculture

Traditional flower cultivation

The domestic consumption of loose flowers, especially of Marigold, China aster, Jasmine, Crossandra and Barleria has been increased tremendously. It is clear that area under traditional flowers has increased significantly (>90% of total flower crops). This sector, in spite of its potential, is still an unorganized and often does not get proper importance. Research is required on developing high yielding cultivars, year round production of chrysanthemum, China aster and marigold and in promotion of crops like annual chrysanthemum and desi rose.

Hi-tech/Protected Cultivation

The cut flowers which are being exported from India are from these hi-tech floricultural units. Protected cultivation although is in limited area (5% of total flower crop area), its contribution to total floricultural exports is significant. At present, there are about 110 export-oriented floricultural units (EOUs) in operation, covering an area of 500 hectares. These units are growing mostly roses but can be diversified into orchids, anthurium, gladiolus and tuberose as the demand for tropical flowers is increasing worldwide. India has several advantages and great potential to increase the hectares under intensive production and ultimately to increase the floricultural exports provided the units should be opened in ideal locations with sound technological back-up.

Dry Flowers

Dry flowers constitute more than two-thirds of total floricultural exports. For making dry flowers and plant parts can be collected from wild sources or some flower crops like Dahlias, marigold, jute flowers, wood roses, wild lilies, helichrysum and lotus pods. Some flowers that are air-dried and used include Dahlias (*Dahlia hortensis*), poppy seed heads (*Papaver somniferum*), roses, Delphinium, larkspur, lavender (*Lavendula augustifolia*), African marigold (*Tagetes erecta*), strawflower (*Helichrysum bracteatum*), globe amaranth (*Gomphrena globosa*) and lotus pod. Dry flowers constitute nearly 15 per cent of the global floriculture business and form the major share in Indian floricultural exports. At present, the industry is not well organized and depends on plant material available in forests and no systematic growing of specialized flowers exists anywhere in the country. The demand for dry flowers is increasing at an impressive rate of 8-10% and, therefore, there is a great scope for the Indian entrepreneurs.

Flower Seed Production

Seed production of seasonal flower crops is a lucrative business and practiced in considerable area in Punjab and Haryana. This offers higher returns from unit area. Of late, demand is increasing in domestic markets. Research work is required to develop high-yielding cultivars including F1 hybrids and agro-techniques for producing uniform seed with higher certification standards.

Nursery Industry

Lack of quality planting material is the major hindrance for not realizing the full potential of floriculture in India. Plant material of various kinds (seedlings, budded plants, rooted cuttings, bulbs, tubers, corms and annual seeds) is required for commercial flower production, potted plant production for adding to home garden and for landscaping (corporate landscaping and bio-aesthetic planting).

Pot Pourri

Pot pourri is mixture of dried, sweet-scented plant parts including flowers, leaves, seeds, stems and roots. The basis of a pot pourri is the aromatic oils found within the plant. A significant component of dry flower export comprises pot pourries. In the recent past, floriculture has been considered as a viable option of diversification in agriculture. Now within floriculture itself, there are in a number of options a flower grower or a floriculturist can take up.

Essential Oils

Essential oils and perfumery from natural sources are in great demand. In India, flower crops grown for essential oil production are limited and include mainly rose, jasmine and tuberose. *Rosa damascena* is exclusively cultivated for extraction of essential oils, rose water, attar and gulkhand in certain pockets of Rajasthan and Uttar Pradesh. Research should be focused on development of cultivars with higher oil content and standardizing distillation methods for higher oil recovery. Further, identification of more crops and standardization of production technology needs to be included in the research agenda. Promotion of this sector encourages ancillary industries like steam distillation and use of indigenous technical knowledge (ITK) for making value-added products.

Natural Dyes

Marigold pigments are widely used in the poultry industry to enhance the colour of the meat and yolk of the eggs and used in food and textile industry. So far, isolation of xanthophylls from marigold has been standardized. More crops can be identified and procedures can be standardized for full exploitation. Technology development in all the areas mentioned above not only improves the situation of respective sub-sector of floriculture but these become important avenues for diversification of floriculture, sources of income generation and means of employment to the youth.

Import of Floricultural Produce

India imports a wide range of floricultural produce from different parts of the world. India's major imports are from Netherlands followed by China, Thailand and USA. The imports to India peaked during 2005-06 with an overall import of Rs 1,796.33 lakhs followed by Rs 1,137.80 lakhs during 2004-05.

Strategies for Marketing of Floricultural Products

Rapid technological agri-business, international economic integration, saturated markets and free market mechanism have provided opportunity but also the challenges. Retailing on markets will be more complex. Service, quality and reliability would be an essential factor for securing position in international market. Producers have to organize the production so as to supply the necessary quantities according to the required quality standards. Any parties in the chain which do not contribute to higher added value, will disappear. The advantages of large-scale market could be found for efficient purchasing process and also in terms of logistics and use of information technologies. Accordingly, our efforts have to be directed to harness the potential through strategic promotion of market. Strategies could be for policy support, infrastructural development, professionalism in market management, networking of markets and quality assurance. All these developments provide opportunity for production and marketing. This would need strategic marketing approach having backward and forward linkages coupled with horizontal and vertical integration. By providing sufficient attention and support, attaining the goal of reliable production of high-quality product consistent in quantities could be attained. Resultantly, Indian flower sector would soon become a major player in the region as well as in European flower market. Moreover, given the rapidly increasing rate of spending among Asian consumers for cut flower industry will soon surpass consumption rates for cut flowers compared to other regions.

Cooperation and commitment, in terms of education, research, funding and communication in India would be a driving force to become a leader of commercial floriculture worldwide, in years to come. The strategies have been chalked out to meet the challenges and to make floriculture a most viable activity in India to ensure employment with enhanced farm income. The challenges are to capture emerging trend in marketing through innovation and skilled professional management. Therefore, strategies to promote effective marketing should include, quality assurance, transportation, hub development for effective delivery, institutional support for information and training, speciality production, reducing cost and widening products, developing domestic market, promoting indigenous plants and flowers, developing professional skill and knowledge management, promoting uses of flowers and providing policy support product and delivery. Therefore, there is a need for quality products and delivery and to develop quality certification system as developed in Holland which ensures the quality for the brand.

CHAPTER-2

HISTORY OF GARDENING

The flowering plants which are the main ornaments of garden, originated in the cretaceous period about 110 million years ago. During that period the predominate animals were dinosaurs and other giant reptiles. Mammals have their humble origin at that time but there were no human beings to admire the flowers. *Homo sapiens*, the true men, emerge about the pleistocene period. The Neanderthals who occupied cave in Iraqi kurdistan between 100,000 and 60,000 years ago buried their dead with flowers. Cave paintings of France clearly show the aesthetic sensibility of Cro-Magnan men. History of gardening extends across at least 4,000 years of human civilization. It is connected with the history of people and their culture, which includes their science, art and literature. When men began to build shelter for himself and cultivated the surrounding land, they conceived the idea of a garden with a utilitarian purpose to grow edible or useful plants in their neighbourhood. However, garden for pleasure and enjoyment appear to have come into existence much later elsewhere in the Middle-East and these gardens were suppose to have been developed by the rich and mighty people of those days.

The imaginary Garden of Eden perhaps marks the genesis of garden and gardening where Adam was the first gardener or horticulturist while Eve supplied information about the trees and its fruits and thus become the first horticultural scientist. Egyptian tomb paintings of 1500 BC are some of the earliest physical evidences of ornamental horticulture and landscape design. They depict lotus pond surrounded by symmetrical rows of acacias and palms. However, the early Egyptian gardens seemed to have no flowers. They were mainly concern with the cultivation of fruits and vegetables. Gardens were enclosed first within thorn fences and later brick walls. Gardens were mainly developed around temples and many exotic trees were introduced. Thus Egyptian gardening added to the art of gardening, making new species and formal and architectural styles. Another ancient gardening tradition is of Persia. Many of the ideas of early Egyptian gardens were taken to Persia where the gardens become more decorative. The first Persian gardener mention in literature is Cyrus I who was founder of the Achaemenid dynasty and captured Babylone in 539 BC. According to Xenophon, Cyrus I laid out a garden at Lydia and had set the design of Chahar Bagh that Persian garden had followed ever since. Darius, The Great was said to have had a "Paradise Garden". The hanging gardens of Babylone were renowned as a wonder of the world. These were built by Nebuchadnezzar in about 600 B.C. and were square, with sides about 120 metres in length. A series of terraces was formed one above the other, each narrower at the back than the front so that the whole formed the shape of a pyramid. Vast stone beams and stone pillars were used as supports and the floors of the terraces were made waterproof with reeds and bitumen or pitch to prevent moisture from oozing downwards. Soil was spread on the terraces and trees and flowers were planted in it. Nizami's poem on the love tale of Layla and Majnum throw some light on Persian gardens of 12 century which mention about red tulips, yellow roses, narcissus and pomegranates.

Gardening in Persia

The ancient Parisians paid much attention to the beauty of gardens. They planned them with many avenues and thought it especially beautiful to have a long chain of pools in which fountains played. Invasion of Arabs greatly influence the gardens of Islamic Iran. They were rectangular, enclosed, architectural and formal with fountains, partitions and have many large fruit trees. By far the most important flower in Islamic Persian garden was the rose. Fruit trees were the first in all Arab gardens. In parts of Persia they include citrus, principally the orange. The Islamic gardens early realised that few trees are more ornamental than fruit trees and made their apples, pears, plums, apricots and peaches serve a dual purpose. The design of the Arabian gardens based on the aridity of their countries preferred architectural geometrical gardens based on the exigencies of irrigation. The Moors, as the Arabs were called, made a great impact on the life of the people of Spain. Spain was under Mohammedan rule during 7th to 11th centuries. During this period, the rulers left their mark on the architecture and gardens of Spain. It is the architecture which gave the individuality to the palaces and gardens of Moorish Spain. The dome and the horseshoe arch are distinct contributions of the Arabs to the architecture of Spain. The Moorish gardens of Spain were mainly designed to treat patios of large mansions and were formal and geometrical like Persian gardens. The trees mainly consisted of palms, olives, oranges and other Mediterranean species.

Gardening in China

When Europe was, still in the age of barbaric ignorance, Chinese started agriculture around 2700-2400 BC. The art of gardening reflected a high level of perfection. The Chinese know how to acclimatise plants from warmer climates and hasten their growth. They used shelters, forcing frames and heated glasshouses. They knew about pruning and grafting of trees. Ornamental gardening in China had largely developed along the line of idealisation of natural scenery. Buddhism reached China in 64 AD and has a profound effect on the life and environment of the Chinese, their architecture, literature, painting and above all on the art of gardening. The floral art of China was already quite advanced in the T'ang dynasty (618-900 AD). Tray gardens were frequently depicted in paintings of the Sung dynasty (960-1279 AD). The Chinese valued plants for their distinctive habit and grace rather than for their colour, scent and form. They preferred white flowers with the exception of chrysanthemum which was yellow. China has the largest flora of any temperate zones of the world and gave many ornamentals to the gardens of other countries.

Gardening in Greek

The Greeks are supposed to have occupied the gardens of the Persians but although those of Athens are said to have been very beautiful, few of the other Greek cities had public gardens. At that time wealthy people chose to live outside the cities in houses standing in their own gardens. In Homer's Odyssey there is a description of the wonderful gardens. Greek gardens were above all utilitarian in that they were meant for growing vegetables and fruits for eating. The idea of a garden for enjoyment came after the Persian conquest under Alexander (330 BC). The first park of Greece was dedicated to Diana, the Goddess of Hunting at Scillus. It was laid out by Xenophon (434-356 BC), the historian and soldier, on his return from Persian expedition. In this park fruit trees were symmetrically planned around the temple, an inspiration from Persian gardens. The almost total absence of ornamental garden plants is a notable fact and indicates that the Greeks did not have gardens in the sense that they are known to us. The contribution of Greeks to the world of gardening is more in their architecture and art rather than in plants.

Gardening in Rome

The Romans planned their gardens even more carefully, sometimes levelling hills, making artificial ones, building terraces and making lakes. They combined the best ideas of the Egyptians, Persians and Greek. The Romans were the first who built houses with small gardens usually enclosed by trellis- work and decorated with climbing plants. Within the garden were stone ornaments, vases and urns and window boxes and plants in tubs were normal decoration. The heartland of Roman Empire, Italy, is the most beautiful country in the world. It is the smiling land of vineyards, olive orchards, villas and gardens. In the 2nd century BC, parks, fish ponds and villas spread over the countryside. Two early authors gave a great deal of information about the plants and gardens of Rome at about the time of the coming of Christianity. Pliny (23-79 AD) produced his *Historia Naturalis*, which include the natural history of plants, while his nephew, Pliny the younger was a writer and Orator and it is from his letters that we learn about the design of Roman gardens. The first garden of medicinal plants owned by Antone Castor, the famous Roman doctor, at the time of Pliny.

Gardening in Italy

After the fall of the Roman Empire, it was left to the monks to continue the art of gardening in their monasteries and examples of their skills are still to be found in the Vatican Gardens of the Pope. Herbs used in medicine were of especial interest to monks who grew them in herb gardens. Gradually an Italian style of garden was developed with long walks bordered by small trees, the branches of which intertwined overhead. The flower beds were laid out in patterns. The renaissance gardens were mainly characterised by terraces linked by magnificent staircases often decorated with statues and green walls or rooms of clipped evergreens. Sometimes, an entire hill side was terraced and separated from its surroundings by belts of evergreens. The design and planting of parterres become a highly developed art and scented herbs were used for creating knots. The covered walks were shaded by clipped myrtle or cypress. Rome was the centre of the Catholic world, visiting bishops and cardinals brought bulbs and seeds of exotic plants as gifts and this lead to the enrichment of Italian gardens. Garden of Renaissance, Italy had a profound effect not only on garden architecture of France and England but also on the formal architectural gardens of every part of the world.

Gardening in French

French gardening has long been famous, particularly the gardens of the Palace of Versailles. These were designed by Andre Le Notre, a famous French landscape architect and are a masterpiece of layout and design. Trees, shrubs and other plants are all fitted into a pattern and magnificent fountains and cascades very often lit up made such use of water as had never been thought of before. Le Notre designs were copied in England at Melbourne Hall in Derbyshire and Birmingham Park in Yorkshire.

Gardening in Holland

Holland was much influenced by France in garden art. From the engravings of the artist Vredemann de Vries published in 1548 AD, the idea is getting of 16th century gardens of Holland. These gardens were formal, rectangular, enclosed in hedges, with summer houses. Hyams observed that water played a very insignificant part in most Dutch gardens. It may be that people of a water-logged country like Holland, intersected by canals and water ways, do not want features in their gardens which they see all around in their daily life. The Dutch were the head of the rest of Europe in horticultural botany which made difference to their gardens. The Dutch contribution was in new bulbs, in plants from the southern hemisphere and the Far East and in the art of topiary which the Dutch first learned from the French and then carried to extraordinary lengths. The Dutch finally carried European horticulture to other parts of the world.

Gardening in England

Gardening in England had seen a phasic change and ultimately reached to its evolutional zenith. Early English gardens (during 1066-1500 AD) were purely utilitarian. The principle gardeners were monks who planted kitchen gardens for supplying vegetables to monasteries and developed herb gardens for medicinal purposes. Not till the later 12 century were there references to flowers being used to adorn gardens; roses were probably among the first. During beginning of 16th century and between middle of 18th century Elizabethan gardens dominate in the England. By the time of Henry III (1509-1597 AD), gardening had received a great stimulus and in England, it reached the age of symmetry. In the middle of 16th century, flower beds, knot gardens, topiaries and terraces were introduced in the English garden from the continent. Through the reigns of James I (1603-1625 AD) and Charles I (1625-1649 AD), the love of gardening and flowers were introduced from the Netherlands. In the early 18th century many people rebelled against formal gardens and preferred a more natural style. Cardinal Wolsey at Hampton Court made the first garden on a magnificent scale in the new manner. William Kent, Lancelot Brown and Sir Humphry Repton removed all traces of formality. The terraces, stately parterres, yew hedges and regular shaped beds were abolished and the ground laid out in entirely new line. Towards the end of 19th century, Gertrude Jekyll introduced a vigorous new approach which has exerted a great influence on garden design in England. She was pioneer in the art of adopting an arrangement of living plant material on site. The royal botanical garden, Kew was founded by Richard Bennet at the resident of Sir Henry Capel. It became the true botanical garden in 1759 with the appointment of Willin Aiton as

Superintendent. The prime maker of famous Kew garden was Sir Joseph Banks. Gardening in America, France and Germany were entirely transformed by English style. It is certainly not too much to claim that between 1750 and 1850 the English garden conquered the world of garden art and garden science.

Gardening in Japan

The Japanese have made an art of gardening, with waterfalls and streams, lakes with islands and bridges and hills, rocks and trees, all carefully arranged. There are special Japanese gardens designed for drinking tea in and tiny gardens made in bowls with minute trees which speak of the art of bonsai. Japanese garden art was greatly influenced by Chinese and were brought by Buddhist monks in about 500 AD. At first, gardens were crude and consisted of only a pond with an island after the Chinese prototype but later they developed their own design. The early gardens had the principal features of a mountain, a pond and a bridged island. During the period of Empress Suiko (592-628 AD) this sort of garden art was originated in Japan. In the Nara period (646-794 AD) and in the period of Heian (794-1185AD), the art and craft of Chinese gardening influenced further the miode of living of the Japanese. The typical features consisted of an open space, a pond with an island, a hillock on the south of the pond and a stream of water. The usual style was to divide the water into two channels, one leading to the pond and other to form a waterfall from a hill. The following Kamakura period (1186-1393 AD) saw the Buddhist priests designing their own gardens and many grand gardens like Tenryuji, Saihoji, Ginkakaji and Ryoajni were constructed, these Zen gardens were more substantial, more reposeful and were based on good landscaping rules. The prominent features of these gardens were water, stones and evergreen plants. They were selected in such a manner that the garden would not undergo major changes during the four seasons of the year. The most notable of the Zen gardens is the moss garden of Saihoji temple in Kyoto which was designed by a priest Muso Kokushi (1275-1351 AD). Under the shades of maple and pines, different kind of mosses were grown, resembling a green carpet.

During the reign of Muromachi (1392-1573 AD), gardening in flat was introduced. Around 1480-1490, greatest of all gardens, Ryuan-ji was built. From this time onwards, more thought was given to ornamental superficial aspects of landscaping rather than expressing philosophical ideas. In the Momoyoma period (1573-1603) more and more stones of diverse nature were incorporated in ornamental gardens. During the Edo period (1603-1867), stroll gardens, came into existence. These gardens consisted of larger lakes with islands surrounded by paths leading to various garden features. The present day designs of the gardens of Japan belong to the Meiji period (1862-1912). In that time, foreign influences were apparent. Flower beds, lawns, gravel paths, bronze statues and other such ornaments together with many of the super-facilities of the west were taken over and incorporated into the traditional gardens with the result that very few maintained their unspoiled Japanese character. Despite the brilliance of the Japanese in floriculture, pure botanical gardening has not long been practised in Japan. It started in Japan after World War II with such impetus that during these years some 60 such gardens were planted. The oldest true botanical garden is Koishikawa established in 1684 which turned out to be the Botanical garden of Tokyo University from 1877 and spread over 16 hectares with arboratum, systematic garden, fern garden and psycic garden.

Gardening in India

Origin of gardening in India has been intricately bound up with the origin of civilisation. The first recorded history of civilisation back to 2500 BC before the Aryans came. The Aryan civilisation dates back to about 1600 BC. The epics of the Aryans, the *Ramayana* and *Mahabharata*, believed to have been compiled during 500 BC, mentioned gardens, trees and flowers. Reference has been made about the beautiful gardens of the city of Indraprastha in the Sabha Parva of the Mahabharata. "Ashokavan" where the Sita was kept in captivity is known to all. In Ramayana, it has been mentioned that the palaces had beautiful gardens with numerous flowers and shady groves and the lakes were full of lotus flowers. As early as 233 BC, King Ashoka planted banyan and mango trees along the roads. This planting of roadside avenue trees was known as " Margeshuvrikha". Sudraka, in 100 BC, has given the account of flowers and garden in "Mrchakalikam". About 57 BC Kalidas in his play Abhigyana shakuntal, referred tom pleasure gardens with beautiful ornamental trees and climbers. In 1300 AD, Sarangadhara in his "Upavana Vinoda" and "Sarangadhara Paddhati" has describe the art of gardening. Vatsyana (300-400 AD) has rendered interesting account of four kinds of gardens namely Pramadodyan, Udyan, Vrikshavatika and Nandanyan.

During the Buddhist period, gardens were laid out around the monasteries and stupas and there were beautiful gardens in Nalanda and Taxila. From about 300 BC onwards, the greatest gardens in India were built by Buddhist monks. The murals in the Ajanta caves, the quintessence of buddhist art which date back to 700 AD not only show the high level of art that was attained in that period but also give us a glimpse of the life of the common people in those times. Some of these pictures show wreaths of flowers in the hair of women, garlands around their neck and bracelets of flowers around their arms. Shakuntala, clad in tree bark and decked with garlands of flowers, meet her lover Dushyanta under the shade of an amaltas tree laden with golden yellow flowers. The custom of use of flowers in worship was borrowed by the Chinese and Japanese from India. Since time immemorial some trees were considered sacred in India. It appears from the literature that there are two type of gardens existed in India. One type is followed in royal palaces and other type built up around the ashrams of Rishis and Munis.

During the reign of Maharajas, the Mughal and the British, many gardens were laid out in India and many ornamental plants were introduced from Africa, China, Japan, Europe and America. Beginning with the invasion of Muhammad Bin Quasim in 712 AD, India suffered continuously at the hand of foreign invaders which included the powerful and ruthless Ghaznavi (1001-1024 AD), Shahabuddin Gauri (1176-1196 AD) and others. This disturbing era was not conductive to any permanent garden development in spite of the fabulous wealth of the country. The early Islamic gardens in India were designed by persians and very much resembled the gardens of Iran. The first glorious period of islamic gardening in India was under the rule of Feroz Shah (1352-1388) AD. Many gardens were established around Ferozabad as Delhi was known in that days but the greatest Islamic gardens in India were those planted by the Mughal emperors. Babar (1508-1530 AD) was the first Mughal emperor who introduced the gardening techniques in central Asia, Iran and India. He built the Ram Bag and Zora Bag at Agra, besides the two gardens "Bag-i-Wafa" and "Bag-i-Kilan" near Kabul, Afghanistan. Only one garden in Delhi bears the neme of Emperor Humayun (1531-1556 AD) later known as Humayun's Tomb. This was built by his widow, Haji Begum. This garden is on Char Bag pattern and persian in character. Gardens at Fatehpur Sikri, Sikandra in Uttar Pradesh; Hari Parbat and Nasim Bagh in Kashmir were established during Akbar's reign (1556-1605).

The zenith of this school of garden art came in the reign of Jahangir (1605-1627) and his garden loving Persian wife Nurjahan. He laid out many gardens all over his kingdom including the famous "Shalimar" and less known Achabal and Verinag gardens in Kashmir, the tomb of I'timad-ud-Daula in Agra, Khusroo Bag in Allahabad and the Lake Palace in Udaipur. Apart from this, he also laid out Wah Bag, Hassan Abdal in Rawalpindi and Dil-khush Bag and Shahadara gardens at Lahore. The Nishat Bag, one of the most beautiful and picturesque terrace gardens amongst those of the Mughals, was constructed on the Dal Lake of Kashmir by Asaf Khan, father-in-law and minister of Shahjahan. This garden presents a graceful and unique picture of high terraces, gurgling waterfall and grand panoramic view towards the hills and along the Dal Lake. Shahjahan (1628-1658), the most romantic of Mughal Emperors and husband of Mumtaz Mahal, constructed Darasukon and

Pari Mahal, Chasma Shahi and Char Chenar Island in Kashmir; Shalimar Bag and Red Fort garden in Delhi; Agra Fort and Tajmahal at Agra; Shalimar Bag and Lahore Fort at Lahore. Aurangzeb (1658-1707), being a religious bent of mind, laid out a garden in the Badshahi mosque in Lahore besides constructing Cho Burj Bag and Nawa Kot. He had laid out a beautiful terrace garden in the plains of India, known as the Pinjore Garden. Roshanara Begam, the sister of Aurangzeb was well known both for her garden and personality. She had laid out the Roshanara garden in the northwestern suburbs of Shahjahanabad. As a memorial to his first wife, Aurangzeb, made a Mausoleum at Aurangabad. It is based on the design of the Tajmahal.

The gardens at small places like Jaipur and Jodhpur were modelled on the old gardens of the Mughals and Udaipur in Rajasthan. In Gwalior and other States of Central India and Deccan, some of the old Maratha and Mohammadan Kingdoms followed the Mughal style of gardening for their palaces with suitable changes to maintain local identities. In the old city fort of Shanwar Wada at Poona, around the old ruins of Bijapur in Kolhapur and in other parts of the country, traces of Mughal style of gardening are apparent. At one time, Rajput Gardens in India were famous. The palace of Amber was built on barren rocks by Raja Man Singh (1590-1695 AD) and was completed by Jai Singh II (1699-1743 AD). Below the palace; there is a large lake with a beautiful garden with three terraces and parterres of different shapes. The city of Jaipur was founded by Jai Singh II in 1727 AD. In the heart of the city is the Raja's Palace with a lovely garden. In the garden runs a canal with fountains which in the past spurted coloured water. Another city famous for garden is Jodhpur which was founded by Rao Jodha in 1459 AD. Raja Abhai Singh (1724-1749 AD) was a builder of palaces and gardens. This pleasure-loving king started digging a lake which is named after him as Abhai Sagar and laid out gardens at Jodhpur and Mandore. Mandore is a fragrant garden and its most interesting feature is an octagonal garden pavilion of red sandstone with projecting windows. Another famous garden in Rajasthan is at Deeg in the erstwhile Bharatpur State. In the Deeg palace, the garden is 132.5m long and 105m wide and in the centre is an octagonal pond. Eastern Rajasthan is the land of red hills and lakes which includes Udaipur, Bundi, Kota and Kishengarh. Rana Udai Singh built a new capital on the Pichola lake in 1559 AD which was named after him as Udaipur. Apart from the palace, the Udaipur, gardens are noteworthy. Bundi is another place with its lakes, gardens, forests and palaces. Bundi developed a style of painting of haunting beauty of glorifying nature. Apart from this, Kota and Kishengarh are known for their palaces and gardens.

The Ovadh rulers laid out beautiful gardens between 1753-1856 AD. Shuja-ud-Doulah (1753-1775 AD) constructed a magnificent mausoleum at Faizabad, around this Gulab Bari was developed. The Safdarjang tomb in Delhi was also built by him, in memory of his father in 1754 AD. It was laid out on the Char Bag type, surrounded with high walls. Saadat Ali Khan (1798-1814 AD) built the Farhat Baksh, the place of delight, at the bank of Gomti. The next ruler of Ovadh, Nasir-ud-din Haidar (1827-1837AD) developed Dilkhusha park, filled with antelopes, tigers and peacocks, to enjoy the wild life. The last king of Oudh, Wajid Ali Shah (1847-1856 AD) developed a garden named Hyder Bag. There were two pretty canals on two sides of the garden, Chashma-i-Shirin and Chashma-i-Faid, both contained fountains with sprays.With the frequent visits and settlement of Western powers on the Indian coast line, a new turn was on the anvil regarding garden making. The Portuguese, who arrived in India in the 14th and 15th centuries followed by early English and French traders in the 16th century, did not influence garden art noticeably. Nevertheless, the impact of their western civilisation was being felt even in the capitals of the old kingdoms. Eventually, when the English were firmly entrenched in India, the garden art of the west began to establish itself.

Several great gardens were established by the British people in India. The oldest Botanical Garden in India is Lalbagh, Bangalore, which was founded by Hyder Ali, the ruler of Mysore (1760). After Tippu's fall in 1779, the garden was taken over by the English. As the years rolled by, the garden was embellished and enriched and at present the total area is about 96 hectares. It is the guiding centre for all horticultural extension, training and developmental activities in the southern states of India. Among the botanical gardens in India, the Indian Botanic Garden, Howrah is the largest of its kind in Asia and was established in 1787. The garden was founded by Lieut. Col. Robert Kyd and occupies an area of 109.4 hectares on the bank of river Hooghly. It has been a centre of excellence for botanists and horticulturists for more than two centuries. The botanical garden at Saharanpur, is another old garden originally established by Intizam-ud-Doulla and taken over by East India company from Marathas in 1817. There are two important and interesting botanical gardens in the hills of India. The Llod Botanical Garden, Darjeeling, West Bengal was laid out in 1873 at an elevation of 2,100 metres under the expert supervision of the famous botanist, Sir George King. The garden is spread over an area of 16 hectares comprising different sections. Another most beautiful and picturesque botanical garden in the southern hills is the Botanical Gardens of Udhagari. The garden was established in 1847 at an altitude of 2,200 to 2,300 meters above sea level on 20.4 hectares of land. The National Botanical Research Institute, Lucknow known as Sikandar bag. The garden is spread over 30 hectares of land on the south bank of the river Gomti. The Botanical Garden of the Forest Research Institute is the youngest botanical garden in India, established in 1934 at an altitude of 663 meters. Planting in the New Forest Estate in which the garden is situated was started in 1925 by R.N. Parkar. It occupies about 8 hectares out of the 445 hectares area of the New Forest Estate of Dehradun. Another young botanical garden is the Botanical Garden, Coimbatore, Tamil Nadu which was established in 1908 by the department of Agriculture, Madras. Rastrapati Bhavan Garden, New Delhi was laid out in 1929 on the patterns of Mughal gardens with the conventional arrangements of squares, terraces, water channels, etc. The main garden area is roughly 134 sq.m. and is bounded from all sides by a paved red stone path.

Apart from these, there are several other beautiful and old gardens.The Agri-Horticultural Society Garden, Alipore, Kolkatta is one of the best of its kind in India. Though the Society was initiated much earlier by Dr. William Carey, the Society could lay out a garden of its own in 1872 only on 10 hectares of land at Alipore Road, Kolkatta. This is considered one of the best laid out gardens in India. Brindavan Garden, Mysore, founded in 1927, is a garden famous for its illuminated running water and innumerable fountains decorated by coloured lighting. Sim's Park, Coonoor, Tamil Nadu, is a park established in 1874 by J.D. Sim. The park is spread over an area of 15 hectares at an altitude of about 1,740 metres in the Nilgiri hills and is the centre of attraction of the people of Coonoor and Wellington. In Tamil Nadu, there is another old park, Bryant Park, Kodaikanal, established in 1909 in an area of 10 hectares. Sayaji park at Baroda, Gujrat is named after its founder, the former Maharaja Sayajirao III who established it in 1879 over an area of 40 hectares. It is an attractive pleasure garden with a large collection of ornamental plants, toy train, children's park museum and zoo with rare animals. The Rose Garden at Chandigarh is situated in the centre of the city on a 15 hectare plot which was started in 1966 for making a Rose museum. Rock garden is under establishment by Mr. Nek Chand Saini in Chandigarh. Cactus garden is situated in Panchkula (Haryana) with more than 2500 species under the chief architect, Dr. J. S. Sarkaria. There was several Japanese style gardens of recent origin like Roshanara Park, Delhi, the garden at the official residence of the Prime Minister at Sadarjung Road, New Delhi, the garden at the residence of the Lt. Governor of Delhi, Kamala Retreat at Kanpur and at the residential complex of Gurudeva Rabindranath Tagore at Santiniketan. Other notable parks are Cubbon Park, Bangalore; Buddha Jayanti Park, New Delhi; Maitri Bag, Bhilai, M.P. and Lamaya Park, Burnpur, West Bengal. With the effort of the horticultural departments in several states, big industrialists and industrial establishments, many new parks and gardens are being constructed incorporating different concepts and ideas to catch the eye of onlookers.

CHAPTER-3

NURSERY MANAGEMENT

Nursery is the cradle of plants. Nursery is a place where plants are cultivated and grown to usable size. Now-a-days nursery management gained a status of commercial venture Floriculture in India is growing at the rate of 7-10 per cent per annum. The area under flowers is around 1,16,000 ha, concentrated mostly in Andhra Pradesh, Karnataka, Maharashtra, Tamilnadu and West Bengal. The success of floriculture industry mainly depends on the quality of seed and planting materials. Because of the diversity in floriculture products, production and distribution of both vegetatively propagated plant material and also seed propagated plant materials have emerged as the most important and powerful business all over the world. In India, major constraint in growth of floriculture is lack of good planting materials. It became a basic need of a grower. The quality refers to genuine and diseased free material. Good quality planting material will boost productivity. Seeds or any other planting materials are the carriers of genetic potential for higher crop production. The floriculturists are less sensitive to price when they are sure of quality planting material, its exclusiveness and the monetary compensations that will accrue from higher production. In case of problems caused by virus and virus like diseases, use of virus free planting materials becomes mandatory. Viability and good germination are of paramount importance in case of seed propagated ornamental crops (Marigold, Aster, Zinnia). In ornamental crops very little have been achieved in the production of genuine planting materials free from the diseases. It is perhaps lack of infrastructure facilities and trained manpower. Cultivation of flower crops for planting material production (seed, bulbs production) requires constant attention, in-depth knowledge, skill and specialization.

Necessity of Nursery

Seedlings not only reduces the crop span but also increases the uniformity of the crop and thus, harvesting as compared to direct sown crops. Transplanting of seedlings also eliminates the need for thinning and provides good opportunities for virus free vigorous and off-season nursery, if grown under protected conditions. Following are some of the advantages of nursery.

1. It is easy and economical to manage seedlings under small area.
2. Effective and timely plant protection measures are possible with minimal efforts.
3. Nursery provide favourable climate to emerging plants for their better growth and development.
4. The effective utilization of unfavourable period by preparing nursery under protected conditions.
5. Effective input utilization for crop production by reducing initial stage crop infestations and interferences.
6. Nursery production help in maintaining effective plant stand in shortest possible time through gap fillings.
7. Raising of seedlings or saplings in nursery provide more time for pre-planting preparations.

Type of ornamental nursery

Field grown nursery

Field production requires soils with good fertility, high Organic-matter content (3-5%), and fine tilth, sandy-clay to clay-loam soil which will hold together in a ball are ideal.

Container plant production

Container production does not necessarily require good soil on site. Container growing medium can be brought from remote locations. However, good soil on site as a resource in media construction may be useful. A firm surface, which allows for the placing of containers and insures surface drainage, is a must.

The advantages of containerized production include:

1. High plant densities,
2. Use of land unsuited for field production,
3. Planting times independent of the weather,
4. Lower transportation costs because of lightweight media and less root loss and a greater chance of survival than with field-grown plants.

The disadvantages are also numerous like

1. Small containers need frequent watering,

2. Nutrients are rapidly depleted,
3. Plants easily become root-bound,
4. Containers are costly,
5. Labour costs to pot up plants are high and
6. The roots are stressed by temperature extremes.

There are several factors to keep in mind when deciding which containers to use: cost, design features that control root growth, how the container affects growing medium moisture content and temperature, availability, how the container suits the particular needs of the nursery, durability, and shipping capacity. Round black plastic pots are the norm but they can cause root constriction, leading to plants with poorly developed root systems. There are other kinds of containers that promote better root systems. For instance, copper-lined, white, and light-coloured containers produce more root growth and square and stair-step pots help keep plants from becoming root-bound.

Seedling Production using Seedling Trays or Plug Trays

Plug trays are also called as pro-trays (propagation trays). The most commonly used are 98-celled trays. The dimensions of the trays are generally 54 cm in length and 27 cm in width with a cavity depth of 4 cm. These trays are made of polypropylene and are re-usable up to five to six times depending on the care with which they are handled. Before using every time it is necessary that these trays are thoroughly washed and disinfected with a fungicide. The holes at the bottom of the cells control the moisture properly. Equal spaced cells facilitate equal growth of the seedlings. Coir dust (Coco peat) Well decomposed and sterilized commercial growing medium is better as the incidence of seedling diseases is less or nil and it contains in it right amount of moisture to support seed germination. The most commonly used growing medium is coir dust (coco peat), which is steam sterilized to prevent nursery diseases. Coco peat is a by-product of coir industry and it has high water holding capacity. It should be well decomposed, sterilized and supplemented with major and micro nutrient sources before using it as the growing medium. Neem cake enriched with Trichoderma (100:1) is applied @ 100 kg per tonne of the medium to prevent seedling diseases.

Advantages of growing seedlings in plastic trays under protected structures:

1. Seeds germinate properly.
2. Mortality of seedlings is very rare.
3. There is no loss of expensive seeds of hybrids.
4. There is adequate space for each seedling to grow properly.

5. Equal and healthy growth of each seedling.
6. Damage due to pests and diseases are very rare.
7. Seedlings do not wither during transport.
8. Promotes better root growth.
9. Damage to roots is very rare during shifting and planting.
10. Hassle free planting.
11. Facilitates uniform maturity of the crop.

Lay out and Planning of nursery

For the establishment of ornamental plant nursery on scientific base the following points have to be considered.

A. Selection of site Location:

1. The selected site for establishing a nursery should be located in an established nursery area. By doing so, one can share the experiences of fellow nurserymen and thereby many mistakes can be avoided in planning, management and marketing of the nursery stock.
2. The selected site should preferably near a highway or atleast connected with a good motorable road, which facilitates easy and economic transport of inputs and nursery plants to the users, orchardists and fruit growers.
3. The selected site should also have electricity and other communication facilities. These facilities will improve the production as well as marketing.
4. The nursery area should be near the water source.
5. It should be well protected from animals.
6. Proper drainage facility should be provided.

Soil:

The success of any nursery depends mainly upon the quality of soil and abundant supply of good quality potable water. Before selecting the site for nursery, the soil and water analysis must be done, since most of the fruit and ornamental plants cannot tolerate salinity and alkalinity. The soil should be light to medium in texture with good fertility and sufficient water holding capacity along with good drainage. A soil pH of 6.0 to 7.0 is most suitable for any nursery. Salinity in soil or irrigation water leads to salt injury resulting in nutritional deficiencies, marginal browning of leaves and in acute cases death of grafts, layers and nursery seedlings especially in summer months. Therefore, a careful selection of soil with good quality irrigation water supply is of paramount importanance for the nursery.

Topography:

The topography of the selected land should be plain with one per cent slope. The slope facilitates smooth flow of irrigation water.

B. Planning and layout of a nursery

After selection of site for the establishment of a nursery, planning may be done in consultation with an experienced horticulturist or nurserymen. By doing so the cost on establishment, production and marketing can be reduced substantially, besides performing various nursery operations most efficiently and economically. While planning and layout are being done, the following components are to be taken care and provision should be made for these.

1. Fence:

Prior to the establishment of a nursery, a good fence with barbed wire must be erected all around the nursery to prevent tress pass of animals and theft. The fence could be further strengthened by planting a live hedge with thorny plants like Koranda.

2. Roads and paths:

A proper planning for roads and paths inside the nursery will not only add beauty, but also make the nursery operations easy and economical. This could be achieved by dividing the nursery into different blocks and various sections. But at the same time, the land should not be wasted by unnecessarily laying out of paths and roads.

3. Progeny block/Mother plant block:

The nursery should have a well-maintained progeny block or mother plant block/ scion bank planted with those varieties in good demand. The grafts/layers/ rooted cuttings/ seedlings should be obtained preferably from the original breeder /research institute from where it is released or from a reputed nursery. One should remember that, the success of any nursery largely depends upon the initial selection of progeny plants or mother plants for further multiplication. Any mistake made in this aspect will result in loss of the reputation of the nursery. A well managed progeny block or mother plants block will not only create confidence among the customers but also reduces the cost of production and increases the success rate of grafting/ budding/layering because of availability of fresh scion material throughout the season within the nursery itself and there will not be any lag period between separations of scion and graftage.

4. Wells, pump, pipelines, generators etc:

Fruit and ornamental nursery plants require abundant supply of water for irrigàtion, since they are grown in polybags or pots with limited quantity of potting mixture. Hence sufficient number of wells to yield sufficient quantity of irrigation water is a must in nurseries. In areas with low water yields and frequent power failures, a sump to hold sufficient quantity of water to irrigate the nursery plants is also very much essential along with appropriate pump for lifting the irrigation water. In areas where electricity failure is a problem which is more common, an alternate power supply (generator) is very essential for smooth running of pumpset. Since water scarcity is a limiting factor in most of the areas in the country a well laid out PVC pipeline system will solve the problem to a greater extent. An experienced agricultural engineer may be consulted in this regard for layout of pipeline. This facilitates efficient and economic distribution of irrigation water to various components in the nursery.

5. Office cum stores:

An office-cum-stores is needed for effective management of the nursery. A store room of suitable size is needed for storing polybags, tools and implements, packaging material, labels, pesticides, fertilizers and so on.

6. Seed beds:

In a nursery, this component is essential to raise the seedlings and rootstocks. These are to be laid out near the water source, since they require frequent watering and irrigation. Beds of 1-meter width of any convenient length are to be made. A working area of 60cm between the beds is necessary. This facilitates ease in sowing of seeds, weeding, watering, spraying and lifting of seedlings. Irrigation channels are to be laid out conveniently. Alternatively, sprinkler irrigation system may be provided for watering the beds, which offers uniform germination and seedling growth.

7. Nursery beds:

Rising of seedlings / rootstocks in polybags requires more space compared to nursery beds but mortality is greatly reduced along with uniformity. Nursery beds area should also have a provision to keep the grafted plants either in trenches of 30cm deep and 1 m wide so as to accommodate 500 grafts / layers in each bed. Alternatively, the grafts/ layers can be arranged on the ground in beds of 1 m wide with 60cm working place in between the beds. Such beds can be irrigated either with a rose fitted to a flexible hosepipe or by overhead micro sprinklers.

8. Potting mixture and potting yard:

For better success of nursery plants, a good potting mixture is necessary. The potting mixtures for different purposes can be prepared by mixing fertile red soil, well rotten FYM, leaf mold and oil cakes in different proportions. The potting mixture may be prepared well in advance by adding sufficient quantity of superphosphate for better decomposition and solubilization. The potting mixture may be kept near the potting yard, where potting/pocketing is done. Construction of a potting yard of suitable size facilitates potting of seedlings or grafting/ budding operations even on a rainy day.

C. Structures for nursery

Shade houses:

Shade houses in nurseries in tropical and sub-tropical regions offer many advantages like raising of seedlings in bags directly, protecting the grafts from hot summer months, effective irrigation through upside down overhead micro-sprinklers. The shade houses made with shade nets (50% or 75%) for regulation of shade are particularly very useful in arid regions where the humidity is very low during summer months.

Greenhouses/Polyhouses :

Greenhouse is a covered structure which protects plants from wind, precipitation, excess solar radiation, temperature extremes and considerable pest and disease attack. Greenhouse or polyhouse cultivation may be undertaken for hardening tissue cultured plants or for growing foliage ornamental plants and cut flowers to achieve optimum levels of production. There are number of types of greenhouse namely low cost green house and commercial green houses.

Hotbeds:

The hot bed is often used for the same purpose as a green house but in a smaller scale. Amateur operations and seedlings can be started and leafy cuttings root early in the season in such structures. Heat is provided artificiallv below the propagating medium by electric heating cables, pot water pipes or hot air blows. As in the green house, in the hot beds attention must be paid for shading and ventilation as well as temperature and humidity control.

Cold frames:

A cold frame is a transparent-roofed enclosure, built low to the ground, used to protect plants from cold weather. The transparent top admits sunlight and prevent heat escape via convection that would other wise occur, particularly at night. Essentially, a cold frame functions as a miniature greenhouse.

Lathhouses:

A structures consisting of a frame supporting strips of wood which are spaced to provide about 50% shade. These structures are very useful in providing protection from the sun for container grown nursery stock in areas of high summer temperatures and high light intensity. Well established plants also can require lath house protection including shade loving plants Lathhouses construction varies widely depending on the material used. Aluminium prefabricated lathhouses are available but may be more costly than wood structures. Shade is provided by appropriate structures and use of shade nets of different densities allow various intensities of light in the lathhouses.

Mist chamber:

This is a structure used to propagate soft wood cuttings, difficult to root plants and shrubs. Here the principle is to spray the cuttings with a minimum quantity of water. This is achieved by providing the cuttings a series of intermittent sprayings rather than a continuous spray. The intermittent spraying can be done easily by means of a high pressure pump and a time switch. The pump leads to a pipeline system inside the propagating structure. The mist nozzles are fitted to these pipelines and suitably spaced over the propagating material.

Nursery bed/boxes:

These are raised beds or boxes made of brick and mortar, provided with drainage holes at the bottom. The dimensions of the boxes are 60 cm high, 120 cm broad and length as required preferably not exceeding 10 m. Roof structures for planting on both sides and forming ridges at the centre are constructed on the top of the nursery beds. These structures may be made permanent with angle iron or may be made of wood. Moveable bamboo mats, palm leaf mats are placed over these structures to protect the seedling from hot sun and heavy rains. Even shade roofing can be used for this purpose for raising see dings.

Fluorescent light boxes:

Young plants of many species grow satisfactorily under artificial light from fluorescent lamp units. Although adequate growth of many plant species may be obtained under fluorescent lamps but not up to the mark compared to good green house conditions.

Propagating cases:

Even in green house, humidity conditions are often not sufficiently high for rooting. The use of enclosed frames or cases covered with glass or plastic materials may be necessary for successful rooting. In using such structures, care is necessary to avoid the build up of disease organisms due to high humidity.

Various nursery operations

Solarization for nursery bed sterilization

It is a method of heating soil through sunlight by covering it with transparent polythene sheet to control soil borne diseases including nematodes. Other additional beneficial effects include control of weeds, insect-pests and release of plant nutrients resulting in increased crop growth. Solarization is a non chemical alternative for diseases, insect-pests and weed controls.

Rooting and Growing Media

Potting Media

Media for plant growth and seed germination have great significance in nursery business. Propagating medium plays an important role in raising of successful plant material in nursery production. Propagating medium is the substance, be it peat, sand, cocopeat, vermiculite or other material, into which the unrooted cuttings are inserted or seeds are sown for germination. The material for rooting and growing media may be used either alone or incorporated with one or more products in combination. The materials used for rooting media may be naturally occurring or max; be manufactured artificially. In many cases, the waste or surplus products from the industries viz., saw dust is used for this purpose.

Qualities of an ideal rooting media:

- The substance must have appropriate physical and chemical properties.
- They must retain sufficient water and air and allow sufficient drainage.
- The substance must be free from weed seeds, nematodes, fungi, bacteria and insect-pests.
- The acidity or alkalinity should be in optimum for different species.
- The medium must be sufficiently firm and dense to hold the cuttings or seeds in place during rooting or germination.
- Its volume must be fairly constant when either wet or dry. It must be capable of being sterilized. The rooting media should support the cuttings to avoid lodging. This is particularly important whenever larger level cuttings are used under mist chamber conditions.

Selection criteria for media:

- ❑ Always consider utilizing local products to save transportation costs.
- ❑ An optimum pH for the rooting medium should be 5.5 - 6.5, with a range of 4.0 - 5.0.

Propagation Techniques

1. Seed Propagation:

Propagation by seeds is the major methods by which many ornamental plants are perpetuated. It is one of the most efficient and widely used propagation methods. Various types of seasonal shrubs and ornamental flowering and avenue trees are also multiplied by the seeds.

Nursery preparation and sowing of seeds:

The seeds can be sown in seed pans, seed frames, pots or in baskets. For larger requirements, permanent seed frames could be constructed for sowing the seeds. Adequate drainage facilities should be provided in the sowing media in order to drain out the excess moisture. The soil for sowing seed should be light and porous. A mixture made up of one part in each of loam and sand and two parts of leaf mould is ideal for sowing. The seeds should be sown in the nursery beds evenly and thinly. The seedlings in the thickly sown seed bed will be weak due to competition for nutrition and also subject to damping of disease easily. After sowing the seeds they should be covered with fine sand or leaf mould twice the thickness of the seeds. As a general rule large sized seeds should be sown a bit deeper.

2. Cutting:

Propagation by cutting is a simple and less expensive method. Cutting is a process by which a plant is produced by severing a vegetative portion from the plant and rooting it in a favourable medium under optimum conditions. Plant parts such as stems, roots, leaves and modified stems such as corms, rhizomes, tubers, runners and bulbs are used for this purpose. The stem cutting can be categorized into 3 types.

Softwood cuttings:

These types of cutting can still be sub-divided into two groups. In the first group comes those cuttings which are taken from herbaceous plants such as coleus, carnation, dahlia and chrysanthemum. The second group consists of cuttings taken from the unripened tips of woody plants, such as most of the ornamental shrubs and some trees. The cuttings should be detached from the mother plant from below a node.

Semi-hard- wood cuttings:

Semi-hard-wood cuttings are those which have passed the soft-wood stage but yet to ripen fully. Jasmines and Hydrangeas are example of plants from which such cuttings are taken for propagation.

Hard-wood cuttings:

The cuttings which are taken from the mature growth, as in some shrubs and trees. While in the first two categories of cuttings, the length of cutting remains 10 cm and 15 cm respectively, but in case of hardwood cuttings, the length depends upon the nature of plants and prevailing climatic conditions. Normally, for many hard-wood cuttings, the length varies between 25 and 30 cm. The stem cuttings are further categorized into 3 groups.

i) *Terminal cuttings*: Such cutting are obtained from terminal portion of a shoot. The leaves from the lower portion of the cutting are removed by nipping (and not by tearing off), while 2-4 leaves are retained in the apex. If the size of the leaves is very larger, these may be cut into halves. Most of the cuttings are to be inserted in the rooting media as early as possible, after being detached from the mother plant. But in case of cacti and some other succulent plants these are air-dried for 2-4 days before inserting in the rooting media.

ii) *Heel cutting*: When lateral shoots are pulled off from the stem with a portion of the stem attached to it, these are called heel cuttings. Heel cuttings root more easily. If needed, the basal end could be smoothened off with a sharp knife. Sometimes carnation cutting are prepared in this way.

iii) *Node cuttings*: Plants like Dracaena and Dieffenbachia are propagated from single or multiple node cuttings. Such cuttings are normally placed horizontally on the rooting media.

iv) *Root cuttings*: Root cuttings should be taken from young roots of average thickness and the length may vary from 2.5 to 15 cm with one or a few buds. The cuttings are placed horizontally or vertically in light soil or sand. The horizontally placed cuttings are covered sufficiently. The adventitious buds give rise to new shoots and roots to grow from the base of these buds or from the cut sections of the old roots.

v) *Leaf cuttings*: In this method the leaf stalk when notched and placed in rooting medium, they produce individual plants.

Factors affecting rooting in cuttings:

Age and nutritional condition of the stock plant, position of the shoot on the parent plant, maturity of the tissue at the base of the cuttings and presence of leaves and buds on the shoot are the internal factors affecting the rooting of cuttings. Light, temperature, humidity and rooting medium are the external factors affecting the rooting wounding and defoliation treatment with growth regulators are used especially in ornamental like Bougainvillea (2000 ppm of IBA+NAA mixture by quick dip method) and Ixora (IBA 200 ppm).

3. Layering:

Layering is done when a clone cannot be rooted through stem cutting. It is an important method of commercial propagation in ornamental like Jasmine, Hibiscus, Ixora and Mussanda. Generally the plants, which are difficult to multiply by cutting, can be raised by one or other method of layering. In this method, since the twigs are attached to the mother plant, the supply of food and water supply are not discontinued, this helps in rooting in layer than cuttings. Rooting of layering is encouraged by etiolating. Presence of sufficient oxygen, moisture and temperature and application of root promoting substances at the time of layering help to get profuse roots in a short time. Root promoting substances are applied as powder or in lanolin.

Simple or ground layering:

It is the common and simplest form of layering. Majority of the variegated plants which are difficult to root from cuttings could be rooted through this method of layering. Some clumbers are also rooted through this method.

Air layering:

Air layering is one of the most widely used method of layerage in ornamental plants. A large number of shrubs, foliage plants and even ornamental trees are raised by this method. Generally terminal portions are used for air layers. The mature branch is slit or notched below a node at the desired height. The part of the wounded stem, as well as 5 cm on either side of the wound, is covered with damp sphagnum moss and this is covered over by polythene sheat and secondly tied at both ends the polythene paper around the moss to form a bag and fold the ends several times inwards to prevent the moisture in the moss from coming out. The two ends are tied firmly on the two sides of the stem layered.

4. Grafting:

Grafting is the method of propagation used for perpetuating clones that cannot be readily maintained by several methods of propagation. It is used for obtaining special forms of plan growth etc. This method of propagation is limited for plants. Sometimes approach grafting is done for propagation of delicate Hawaiian cultivars of Hibiscus.

5. Budding:

In budding, a single bud, as against a scion wood containing a number of buds in the case of grafting, is inserted on the rootstock in a manner that both will unite and continue to grow as a single plant. Three to five weeks after the budding operation, the portion of the rootstock about 3-5 cm above the union, is cut off. Mostly 'T' budding is employed for propagation of most of the ornamental plants. The patch budding is generally not popular. This method is sometimes used for multiplication of hibiscus hybrids. The optimum time of budding is when the stock plant is actively growing and the bark separates easily from the wood.

6. Others

Suckers:

In some plants new stems are produced from the adventitious buds on their roots. Such new growths are called suckers. These suckers can be perpetuated as individual plants. (e.g. gerbera, chrysanthemum).

Division:

This type of propagation is the simplest method of propagation for increasing the number of stock plants. It involves simply dividing the plants into small pieces each of which must contain a portion of the rootstock with leaves or buds or as a few roots. Division must be carried out during the dormant season. The clumps are lifted with a fork and are divided by separating them into suitable sized portions. Each portion shows contain about 3 or 4 buds or stems and the outside portions of the clumps should be selected, as these are the most vigorous. Some of the clumps are easy to divide by pulling them apart after shaking of the loose soil, others are more difficult, and the rhizomes or rootstocks have to be separated with or without knife or through with a spade. The divided portions must be planted firmly and well watered within an hour or two. Majority of herbaceous ornamentals can be increased through this method. (e.g., Alstroemaria, Delphinium and Campanula)

Rhizomes:

Rhizomes are subterranean stems that arise from a lateral bud from the main stem at ground level and extend underground near the surface horizontally. The aerial shoots develop from the laterial buds. Generally rhizomes are cut into small pieces having one or more buds and planted for multiplication (e.g. Canna).

Stolons:

A slender branch, which normally produces roots and bears a bud at this extreme, this forming a new plant e.g., Chlorophytum.

Tubers:

They are short, thickned part of subterranean branches, which store large quantities of plant food, mainly starch. Tubers contain buds in the axils of reduced leaves. (e.g., Tuberose)

Corm:

These are underground stem with a short, fleshy, vertical axis covered with dried leaf bases. (e.g., gladiolus).

Watering:

Watering should be done according to the need of plants. The nursery should have a water source of its own. For this model, digging a well (12 m deep × 3 m dia) and installation of a 2.0 HP kerosene pumpset with accessories are considered. Sprinkler and Drip system of irrigation could be installed if, economy permit.

Weeding:

Weed control is extremely important. Weeds not only compete for water and nutrients but they can also hinder sales of nursery stock. Weed control efforts should focus on two areas: in the pot and under the pot. Sanitation is the least costly and most effective method for controlling weeds. To prevent weed seeds from blowing into pots, attention to a vegetation-free zone both on and surrounding the production bed is critical. Hand weeding is costly but it may be appropriate in a small nursery setting. Weeds must be removed when they are still small, since large quantities of media are lost when big weeds are pulled out of containers. Herbicides, on the other hand, are widely used in container nursery production. Even though weed-free media is used to establish nursery plants, wind and birds and surface irrigation water are sources of weed seeds that get deposited onto the pot surface. Thus, pre- and post-emergent herbicides are commonly used in commercial nursery production to control these freeloaders.

Fertilization:

When the plant have produced 3-4 leaves, they are manured with a mixture of NPK (2:1:2) and sand at 1:9 ratio. One teaspoonful of this mixture should be applied per plant at 3-4 weeks interval during the growing season. If required, foliar application of nutrients can be started when the cuttings have produced 6-8 leaves. Manuring is to be done very carefully. Vigorous growth of plant is always attractive to the buyer. Heavy manuring is not beneficial for storage of plants.

Diseases and Insect-pests management

Insect-pests, diseases are critical factors in the process of multiplication of plant material under open as well as controlled conditions. Control of insects and diseases are integral part of the nursery plant production.

Insect-Pests

Scales

Scales are serious pests on many plants. These remain covered inside a hard coating which looks like a waxy scale and infest lower surface of leaves and veins of branches. These insects suck plant sap and as a result plants become weak. The affected leaves turn yellow, deformed while the branches and the plant may die in severe cases. Plants with green shade or semi shade are more prone to attack. If tender annual flowerings crops are attacked, it is necessary to eradicate them immediately.

Selection of scale free planting material prevents early build up of pests. Cutting and burning of infested parts reduces further spread. Sprays of dimethoate, etheon and chlorpyriphos at 0.05% provides effective control of scales. Application of 10% pongamia oil to pruned shoots completely controls rose red scale within 3 weeks. Natural enemies viz., *Aphytis* spp. *Chilocorus nigritus* and *Pharasymnus horni* are common enemies of red scale in nature. Spraying of fish oil resin soap at 0.5 kg/30 litres of water dimethoate 0.05% provides effective control of scales on orchids. Rogor (0.2%), metasystox (0.2%), sevin (0.2%) and nuvacron (0.05%) are most effective for scale insects, thrips and aphids.

Thrips

Thrips are minute insects and mainly attack tender leaves and growing buds. These are sucking insects which affect a large number of plants. Both nymphs and adults can affect plant parts. As a result of sucking nature of the pest, plants become weak and the affected parts develop brown streaks, with burnt appearance. The tender twigs, foliage, flower buds get distorted and dry.

Sprays of oxydemeton methyl or dimethoate or oxydemet on methyl or acephate given at 0.05% at 10 days interval provides significant control of thrips. A predatory wasp, Polistes hebraeus preys on *R. cruentatus*. Soil application of phorate @ 1 kg a.i./ha also reduces thrips damage. Drenching soil with chlorpyriphos 0.1% also helps in reducing population.

Aphids

Aphids are sucking insects which are blackish or brownish or green in colour and suck sap from tender shoots, leaves and flower buds. The aphids excrete honey-dews on the foliage causing sooty mould to grow over the foliage. Shoots or foliage get deformed. Affected plants become weak and retard in growth. In case of ornamental plants, ornamental look may be affected.

Spraying of dimathoate 0.05% or oxydemeton-methyl 0.05% or malathion 0.1 % at 10-15 days interval controls aphid population effectively. To prevent recurrence of the pest granular insecticides like phorate @ 1.0 kg a.i/ ha should be applied to soil. Application of 4% alcohol extracts of *Solanum indicum* and *Erythrina indica* provides good control of rose aphid. Water extract of pongamia kernel 4% or pongamia oil 2% sprays cause significant mortality of aphids on chrysanthemum. Application of neem oil 1% also reduces aphid population effectively. Grubs and adults of coccinellid beetles and maggots prey upon the aphids and effectively wipe out their population in nature.

Mealybugs

Mealybugs are small fleshy insects which remain covered in a white, wooly and waxy secretions. Generally older plants are affected. The insects suck the sap as a result of which plants weaken, leaves turn yellow and get deformed. In severe cases affected plants may even die. Mealybugs secrete honey dews which stick to the foliage and as a result of which sooty mould cover the leaf surface impairing the normal activity of the leaves.

Prompt collection and desctruction of infested parts reduces spread of the pest. Crawling of ants on plants is the sign of beginning of mealybug infestation. Spraying should be taken up at this stage. Sprays of methyl parathion (0.05%) or dimethoate (0.05%) or acephate (0.1 %) at 15 days interval effectively controls mealybug infestation. Application of pongamia oil (2%) provides good control of mealybugs, if plant is not sensitive to oil sprays. Release of coccinellid predator,

Cryptolamus montrouzieri and a parasitoid, *Leptomastridia abnormis* reduces mealy bug population in glass house grown ornamentals.

Whiteflies

Whiteflies are tinny insects, white in colour and are very active. Excessive dampness and dark conditions should be avoided for crops grown under protected conditions. Removal and burning of heavily infested leaves check multiplication of the pest. Clean cultivation, using of insect screening nets and Proper closing of doors help in preventing incidence of whiteflies. Spraying of phosphamidin (0.05%) alternated with triazophos (0.05%) at an early stage of infestation effectively contains pest build up. Sprays of methomyl and acephate at (0.05%) significantly reduce nymph and pupal population. A management package of spraying dichlorvos (0.05%) for adults, triazophos or Spark at (0.05%) alternating with pongamia oil 1% for nymphs and soil application of carbofuran @ 1 kg a.i./ ha provides effective control of whitefly on gerbera. Release of a parasitoid, *Encarsia formosa* (6 adults/m^2), and use of yellow sticky traps gives significant control of whiteflies on green house ornamentals.

Mites:

The mite is a minute dot sized pest red in colour almost invisible to the naked eyes, resembling the spider but not a true spider. This is a sucking type of pest if established once, they may become a serious problem. The tender shoots affected by mites develop spots and turn yellow, dry and drop.

Cutting and burning of severely infested plant parts reduce further multiplication of mites. Proper ventilation, irrigation and clean cultivation are essential to keep the pest population under control. Acaricides like dicofol (0.05%) and wettable sulphur (0.3%) sprays (2-3) at 15 days interval gives considerable control of mites. Commercial neem formulation (3500 ppm azadirachtin) application against *T. urticae* causes mortality, growth retardation, reduction in egg hatchability and egg laying. Methyl parathion 0.05%, fluvalinate (0.012%) and ethion (0.05%) also offer significant control of mites that infest various ornamentals. Use of dicofol (0.05%), protenofos (0.05%) and wetlable sulfur (0.05%) brings down mites population considerably on ornamental crops. Release of predatory mite, Amblyseivs sp @ 20/plant successfully contains *T. urticae* population on Rose.

Leaf Eating Caterpillars

Caterpillars feed on foliage. They damage leaves by feeding. Collection and destruction of egg masses and leaves infested with early larval instars of hairy caterpillar and *S. litura* reduces pest build up. Setting up of light traps attracts adult moths and helps in monitoring pest population. Spraying of quinalphos 0.05% or chlorpyriphos (0.05%) gives protection to foliage from semiloopers, hairy caterpillars and *Spodoptera litura*. Application of *Bacillus thuringiensis* dust and spray (3 × 106 spores) gives effective control of these caterpillars on rose. Spraying of plant derivatives like neem oil (1 %) or neem kernel extract (4%) checks damage by early instar larvae.

Leaf Beetles and Weevils

Soil application of phorate or carbofuran @ 1.0 kg a.i./ ha controls grubs. Setting up of light traps help in collecting adults and monitoring pest incidence. Fortnightly sprays of quinalphos (0.05%) or methyl parathion (0.05%) or chlorpyriphos (0.05%) taken up in the evening protects foliage from beetles and weevils on rose. Ethanol extract of neem kernel at (2.5%) or neem oil (1%) inhibits feeding by chafer beetles on roses.

Cut Worms

These are essentially found in a nursery. The insect remains in the soil and attacks the seedlings at ground level. Use of light traps collects adult moths. Poison bait consisting of carbaryl or malathion at 0.1% , wheat bran and mollasses scattered in the field, controls larvae. Sprays of methyl parathion (0.05%) or quinalphos (0.05%) provides protection to foliage from cut worms. Application of granulosis virus causes 90-94% mortality of cutworm on ornamentals.

Leafminers

The larvae of the insects mines into leaves between epidermal layers leaving excreta on leaf surfaces. The affected leaves become brittle turn brown and dry. Removal and destruction of severely mined leaves reduces further damage. Sprays of deltanethns (0.05%) triazophos (0.06%) and pongamia oil (0.5%) causes significant mortality of larvae. Drenching of soil with Margosan (0.33%) and spraying with same chemical at 0.94 and 1.25% effectively reduces number of pupae and adults. Three sprays of Rogor (0.2%) at the interval of 6 days is most effective. Use of yellow sticky traps coated with chlorpyriphos or permethrin reduces adult population. Release of eulophid parasitoid. *Diglyphus intermedius* @ 1000 at weekly intervals gives considerable reduction of leaf miner population on chrysanthemum.

Snails and Slugs

Snails are one of the important pests found in nursery. They cut the young plants at general level and damage seedlings during rainy season. Hand picking and killing by putting them in 5% salt solution is the most effective method to bring down the population. Spreading of 'Snail kill' (3% metaldehyde pellets) in the field kills snails and slugs. Spraying of neem oil 1% and water extract of soapnut (5%) protects foliage from snail damage.

Diseases

Damping off

This is a major disease of germinating seeds which is caused by three separate fungi mainly species of *Pythium, Rhizoctonia* and *Phytophthora.* The disease is expressed either by the failure of the seedling to emerge or by the death of the seedling soon after emergence. A common symptom is the girdling of young seedling stems at the soil surface. Damping off usually occurs only in young, succulent seedlings during or shortly after germination but older plants may be affected in severe cases. Control measures involve direct control by use of Captan (0.2%) or Bavistin (0.15%) or Kavach (0.2%), drenching or use of organomecuerials such as Cersan or Thiram or Agrosan as seed treatment chemicals at rate of 2g/ kg of seed. Regulation of environmental conditions such as excess humidity is necessary. Water also plays an important role in spread and control of disease.

Anthracnose

This is a kind of leaf spot formed in young plants and spots are circular, slightly raised concentric and are studded with large number of raised black or red bodies. The infection spreads rapidly under high humid conditions, spraying with copper fungicides (0.2%) or Bavistin (0.15%) will control the disease.

Blights

These also sometimes causes damage to the nursery stock in high humid areas. The blights are kept under control by constant and timely spray of copper fungicides (0.2%) or Dithane M-45 (0.2%).

Dieback

This is serious in some of the grafts/buddlings at the young stage. The disease may be due to fungi. The symptoms are drying up of the margin of the leaf and drying slowly spreads to young shoots in severe cases. Control measures involves dipping of scion sticks in Bavistin or Benlate (0.2%) solution and prophylactic sprays with Topsin M (0.15%) or Bavistin (0.15%).

Leaf spots

The disease is very common in grown up plans and number of fungi as well as bacteria is involved. The leaf spots vary in size shape colour and extent of damage. The symptoms vary according to the pathogen involved. Spraying with Copper fungicide (0.2%) or Bavistin (0.15%) or Dithane M-45 (0.2%) will control the disease.

Powdery mildews

This is a common malady in most of ornamental crops during dry cool weather and when plants produce new flesh. The powdery mildews are easily recognised by the presence of scattered areas showing powdery growth mostly on the young leaves. Spraying with wetable sulphur sulfex (0.2%) or Calixin (0.15%) will control the disease. Precautions for handling plant protection equipment. Dusting or spraying should never be done against the wind and it is preferable to have them done in cool and calm weather.

Packing and Handling

Seeds are cleaned and stored in close bottles or tins. Before packing, they are dried first in shade for 2-3 days and finally in the sun for a couple of days. In husked seeds, the husks are removed before packing. It is important to see while packing the plants that the container is neither over-packed nor loose enough allowing the contents to move about. All space should be filled up by some packing materials like straw and dried grass. For long distance destinations, the ball of earth should be soaked in water and covered with a thick layer of wet moss. Only plants having a well-developed root system should be selected for such destinations. They are packed in bamboo-matted boxes in between layers of straw. Rhizomes of water-lily and lotus are wrapped in moist sphagnum moss and polythene to keep them moist during transit and then packed in baskets or cardboard cartons.

Storage

Seeds are stored in a cool, dry place or kept in desiccator. Living plants should be kept in shade. Bulbs, corms and tubers are stored in single layer over dry sand, flat wooden trays or racks in a well-aerated store room with low temperature and low humidity. Before storing, they may be treated with fungicides and insecticides such as 0.1% benlate or 0.1-0.2%, captan and seven (0.2%).

Marketing

Export potentiality of nursery products is also very high. Seeds, bulbs, tubers, cactus, flowering plants, foliage plant, unrooted cuttings and cut flowers are exported from India to many countries such as Australia, Netherlands, UAE, Japan, UK, Singapore, Germany, New Zealand and so on. With increasing income and living standard, local demand take new edge.

Assistance from Government for establishing a nursery

NABARD provides refinance assistance for a broad spectrum of investment and production oriented activities in the rural sector. NABARD has been extending refinance support for the promotion of all kinds of nurseries in appreciation of this important need. The wide range of nurseries covered by the umbrella of refinance support include those of ornamental crops, fruit srops, plantation crops, tissue culture laboratories and green houses. NABARD provides its services to this sub-sector by the following means:

- Extends refinance support to the commercial and cooperative banks.
- Appraises commercial nursery projects to be financed by the banks.
- Prepares model schemes and guidelines for the benefit of the bankers in particular.
- Publishes a quarterly scientific journal namely "Technical Digest" covering technical and economic aspects of different activities including nursery development.
- Support R&D projects on technological improvement in production of quality planting materials by providing assistance from R&D grant.
- Providing the technical support to the bankers.
- Organising the workshops and seminars for the benefit of the bankers.

Credit support for promotion of nurseries

The activities and items related to nursery development for which credit support is available through the banks be enumerated as under:

- Land development- land levelling, bunding, terracing, preparation for raising the nursery and so on.
- Raising the mother plants and the nursery- their maintenance and upkeep.
- Irrigation-well, pumpset, pipeline, water storage tanks and sprinkler system.
- Civil structures such as green house, laboratory, godown/storage, watchmen's quarter and work-sheds.

- Erection of fencing.
- Procurement of all kinds of machinery, equipments and tools necessary for raising the nursery.

Each project, however, needs to be technically feasible, financially viable and bankable to be eligible for bank finance and NABARD's refinance support.

Table: 3.1: Methods of propagating foliage plants:

Botanical names	Common names	Air layers	Cane cuttings	Offset divisions	Leaf cuttings	Seeds	Eye cuttings	Spores	Tip cutting
Aechmea spp.	Bromeliad			*		*			
Adiantum spp.	Maidenhair fern			*				*	
Aglaonema	Aglaonema		*						*
Aphelandra squarosa	Zebra plant						*		*
Araucaria excelsa	Australian pine	*				*			
Ardisia crenata	Coralardisia					*			*
Asparagus spp	asparagus					*			*
Aspidistra elatior	Cast-iron plant			*					
Begonia spp	Rex begonia				*				
Brassia actinophylla	Schefflera					*			*
Calathea spp.	Calathea			*					
Chamaedorea elegans	Parlor palm					*			
Chlorophytum comosum	Spider plant			*					
Cissus antarctica	Kangaroo vine						*		*
Cissus rhombifolia	Grape ivy						*		*
Codiaeum variegatum	Croton	*							*
Coffea arabica	Coffee					*			

Contd...

Table: 3.1 ...contd.

Cordyline terminalis	Ti		*			*			*
Crassula spp.	Jade plant				*				*
Diffenbachia spp.	Dumb cane		*						*
Dizygotheca elegantissima	False aralia					*			*
Dracaena fragrans	Massangeana		*						*
Dracaena godseffiana	Dracaena								*
Dracaena marginata	Marginata		*						*
Dracaena sanderiana	Sanderiana								*
Episcia spp.	Episcia			*	*	*			*
Epipremnum spp.	Pothos						*		*
Ficus elastica	Rubber plant	*					*		*
Ficus lyrata	Fiddle leaf fig	*					*		
Hoya carnosa	Wax plant						*		*
Kalanchoe spp.	Kalanchoe				*				*
Maranta spp.	Maranta								*
Monstera deliciosa	Monstera	*				*	*		*
Nephrolepis exaltata	Boston fern			*					
Palm spp.	Palms			*		*			
Pepromia spp.	Pepromia				*		*		*
Philodendron florida	Florida philodendron	*					*		*
Philodendron hastatum	Hastatum	*					*		*
Philodendron micans	Micans						*		

Contd...

Table: 3.1 ...contd.

Philodendron scandens oxycardium	Heart-leaf philodendron						*		
Philodendron panduriforme-on	Panduriforme						*		*
Philodendron selloum	Selloum					*			
Pilea cadierei	Aluminium plant								*
Platycerium spp.	Staghorn fern			*				*	
Podocarpus macrophylla	Podocarpus					*			*
Polyscias spp.	Aralia		*						*
Pteris spp.	Pteris fern			*				*	
Saintpaulia spp.	African violet				*				
Sansevieria hahnii	Hahnii sansevieria			*	*				
Sansevieria trifasciata	Sansevieria			*	*				
Spathiphyllum spp.	Spathiphyllum			*		*			
Syngonium spp.	Nephthytis (var.)						*		
Zygocactus spp.	Christmas cactus								*

CHAPTER-4

PLANT GROWTH REGULATORS

Some chemicals occurring naturally within plant tissues have a regulatory role, rather than a nutritional role in growth and development. These organic compounds other than plant nutrients, which when used in minute quantities can inhibit, stimulate or alter growth are termed as *Plant hormons*. There are five primary classes of plant hormones: auxins, gibberellins, cytokinins, ethylene and abscissic acid. Plant growth regulator is a broad term which includes natural and synthetic plant hormons and retardents. Ornamental crops find extensive use of growth regulators for modifying their developmental processes. In fact these have become integral component of agro-technological procedures of a few cultivated ornamental crops. Since the regulation for usage of chemicals in ornamental crops are less stringent unlike those in food crops, their application in these crops extended to alter a variety of responses. The limitation of their usage has been almost entirely the consideration of economics, such as cost benefit ratio. The major areas where growth regulators have successfully played their roles in ornamental plants are in vegetative propagation, inhibition of abscission, prevention of dormancy, growth control and promotion of flowering, prolonging vase life of flowers and retarding their senescence. Besides five classical hormones categories, there are some chemicals which are considered as new age plant growth regulators. These include:

- Brassinosteroids: It helps in pollen tube growth, stem elongation, orientation of cellulose microfibrils and enhanced ethylene production.
- Jasmonic acid: It promoted antifungal proteins, growth inhibitor, inhibit seed and pollen germination and induce fruit ripening.
- Salicylic acid: Blocks ethylene synthesis, induce flowering in long day plants, antifungal property and thermogenesis in voodoo lily.
- Polyamines: Tuber formation, root initiation, flower development and fruit ripening (may not have truly hormonal role but participate in metabolic pathways for cellular functioning).

Some common uses of plant growth regulators in floriculture are described below:

Plant Propagation

Seed germination: Gibberellins, cytokinins and morphactins can play a great role in the regulation of seed and bulb production. GA_3 is used as an alternative to cold stratification, to promote germination of seeds of some shrubs and trees. Cytokinins are found to promote bulb formation in lilies.

Vegetative propagation: A large number of ornamental plants are propagated by vegetative methods such as stem and leaf cuttings, by bulb, corms and tubers. The use of plant growth regulators have revolutionised the modern propagation techniques. The use of auxin in adventitious rooting is most widely acknowledging phenomenon. The most commonly and widely used auxin in promoting rooting is Indolebutyric acid (IBA). Next in importance are Naphthaleneacetic acid (NAA) and Indoleacetic acid (IAA). But NAA and IAA are less uniformely effective compared to IBA. It has been observed that often mixtures of two auxins are much more effective than when applied singly. Some chemicals are found to enhance the effect of IAA, NAA and IBA in forming roots of the cuttings in a number of ornamental shrubs. These compounds are known as synergists. Some commonly found synergists are, p-hydroxybenzoic acid, salicylic acid, tannic acid, gallic acid, etc. There are generally three techniques of auxin application-(i) prolonge soak treatment for 24 hrs at low concentrations (25-100 ppm), (ii) quick dip method; dipping the basal portion for 5 to 2 minutes in high concentrations (1,000-10,000 ppm) depending upon nature of cutting and (iii) application of auxin through talc or lanolin paste. It was found that not only high percentage of rooting but also large numbers of roots in many difficult-to-root shrubs, climbers and trees by treating these with IBA and NAA in talc. However, this method has a limitation as when in commercial propagation a large number of cuttings are dipped in talc, the cuttings in the centre of bundle may not get the talc uniformly.

The success of rooting depends upon some environmental and physiological factors. The environmental factors include season, photoperiods, light, temperature, aeration and humidity. Rainy and spring seasons appear to be the best time for rooting of cuttings or layers. Photoperiods, either long or short, influence rooting depending upon the species. The optimum photoperiod appears to be that which helps in the accumulation of carbohydrates in the cutting prior to its detachment from the mother plant or at the time of rooting process. It has been observed that though callus formation may be favoured under a cool condition, root growth is promoted by higher temperatures. Proper aeration near the root zone is also necessary for root formation. Since a cutting has no sucking organ, a high humid atmosphere is favourable for root formation. The physiological factors that influence rooting are polarity, presence of leaves, active buds in the cutting, nutrient status of the cutting, and auxin level in the cutting. Cuttings placed upside down will not root as the movements of auxins are from the apex to the base of the original position of the cutting in the mother plant. The leafy cuttings root much better than leafless cuttings as the leaf provides some nutritive materials beneficial for root formation. Presence of active bud in cutting helps rooting and this effect is ascribed mainly to the production of auxins in the buds. But, in certain species, the flower buds have antagonistic effect on rooting. Occurrence of comparatively low level of soluble nitrogen in the cutting and presence of traces of boron in the rooting media are beneficial for root formation. The total absence of boron may result in complete failure in root formation. Relatively high level of nitrogen in the cutting inhibits roots formation, especially when the carbohydrate level is low.

Micropropagation: This method of propagation has a potential of being the rapid and cheaper method of producing the ornamental plants. The procedure of manipulation through tissue culture techniques rely on mass production of shoots, either adventitiously from explant or by enhance auxillary branching of excised shoot tips and their rooting. All the success has been accomplished with media supplemented with suitable growth regulators. It is found that higher concentration of BAP (10 mg/l) was effective for explant establishment while moderate concentration of BAP (5 mg/l) and kinetin (0.2 mg/l) concentration produces higher number of shoots per culture in gerbera. High frequency (92.78 %) for callus induction from leaf disc of gerbera was obtained for MS medium supplemented with BAP (1 mg/l) and 2,4-D (2.5 mg/l). While maximum somatic embryo induction (64.56%) from callus clumps was obtained with BAP (0.5 mg/l) and NAA (1mg/l) supplements.

Control of Plant Height

Growth retardents which reduce plant height, either slow down cell division or inhibit cell elongation. The growth retardents are specific to the plant species in their action. A particular retardent may dwarfen only a particular plant species while it may not be effective on others. Foliar sprays of daminozide (SADH) are commonly used on chrysanthemum, azalea, bedding plants and kalanchoe, whereas, chlormequat (ccc) sprays or drenches are used on begonia, calceolaria, geranium and poinsettia. Ancymidol is active on many monocots (lilies, tulips and hyacinth). Ethophon controls the elongation of the scope of the narcissus and lily stem but can induce flower abortion in lily.

There are only a few floricultural crops on which growth regulators are applied for purpose of enhancing growth. GA_3 has been of considerable use for growth promotion. The cases in which growth promotion by growth regulators can be helpful are those where environmental factors delay or inhibit growth or where problems are encountered due to excessive application of retardents. GA_3 in 1-6 ppm can be used in chrysanthemum to promote growth if growers are concern about excessively short stems. GA_3 is applied 1-3 days after planting and can be repeated in three weeks later for this purpose. Tuberose plant sprays with GA_3, 40 days after planting and African marigold at 22 days after planting increases spike length and plant growth.

Control of Flowering

Now-a-days flower forcing to obtain flowers during desire period is a common technique. Growers alter temperature and photoperiod to control flowering time. This process basically alters the balance of endogenous growth and flowering regulators. Artificial application of plant growth regulators can also enhance, hasten, or delay the flowering time in some species. Auxins may slightly hasten or strongly inhibit flowering in many species, particularly to plants which are sensitive to photoperiodism and vernalisation. GA_3 in the concentration range of 5-25 ppm can be used for early flowering in antirrhinum. Application of 100-200 ppm GA_3 in dahlia induces early flowering. Application of gibberellin induces flowering in some long day plants under non-inductive short photoperiods but gibberellin spray fail to induce flowering in short day plants under long day conditions. Cytokinins could possibly be used to improve flowering in pansy grown in nutrient poor conditions (which causes calcium deficiency in the terminal meristem) by opening up the stomata. Cytokinins help with other nutrient deficiency problems such as tulip stem topple. Alar and Cycocel induce flowering on smaller plant under short day condition in bougainvillea. It was found that cytokinins help to reduce the delay in flowering in poinsettias caused by heat or cold or to reduce splitting caused by high night temperature.

Senescence

Consumer acceptance of any flowering plant would increase if flower senescence is delayed. Premature loss of flower and/ or foliage is a problem to the grower, retailer and flower lover. Improper practices that cause flower abscission must be controlled but the inherent behaviour of some crops to lose leaves or flowers earlier than desired are not easily regulated. Ornamental plants, *Impatiens* and *Hibiscus* are plagued with excessive accelerated floral abscission. GA_3 and BA are reported as the strongest inhibitors of senescence in hibiscus whereas cycocel and IBA have mild response towards senescence inhibition. Delay in senescence caused by BA is due to rise in sugar content, acidity and rate of respiration for several days and maintained chlorophyll, potassium and nitrogen contents. It is found that cytokinins are used to prevent lower leaf yellowing and flower senescence in of easter lily during cold storage. Cytokinins prevent leaf yellowing of turf under heat stress condition. Cytokinins help delay the senescense of ethylene sensitive flowers and leaves in the cut flower industry by delaying the onset of the climateric rise in respiration and ethylene production that occurs when senescense begins.

Pinching

In many floricultural crops pinching is a common practice to encourage lateral shoots. It is found that ant-auxins can easily overcome apical dominance. Application of TIBA on marigold in 25ppm concentration at 5-leaf stage produce more branches than pinching.

Dormancy

Maintaining dormancy: The prevention of sprouting in nursery stock of trees and shrubs are utmost important. Plant growth regulators have a practical utility in this area. It has been found that auxins applied as an emulsion, spray and dip treatment have potential to reduce bud sprout in storage of several ornamental plant species, provided these are applied in proper concentration. The optimum effective concentration varies from species to species. The efficacy of auxins in this direction depends much on time of application and stomatal temperature. Early foliar application just before the storage has been promising for such practice. Maleic hydrazide prolongs dormancy in woody plants.

Breaking dormancy: Growth regulators have been successfully used for breaking dormancy. GA_3 and cytokinins are potential growth regulators for this purpose. Besides these, thiourea at 500 ppm found most suitable for breaking dormancy in fresh corms of gladiolus.

Vase life

Prolonging the vase life of cut flowers has been a task of great importance for helping the commercial growers. Single growth regulators may not play a significant role in flower senescence but interaction among different growth regulators may determine the potential life of cut flowers. Cytokinins play an important role in delaying senescence of many flowers. Growth retardants such as B-9, cycocel,

MH and cyclohexamide are also known to prolong vase life of various species. SADH (0.2%) with sucrose (0.4%) were found to increase the vase life of tuberose spike.

Methods to apply plant growth regulators in floricultural crops:

1. **Foliar spray:** The most common method of applying growth regulators is spray applications. When using plant growth regulators as a foliar spray, it is important to achieve thorough, consistent and uniform coverage. Failure to apply these chemicals properly can lead to inconsistent results.
2. **Drenching:** Drenching is the second most common method of applying plant growth regulators. Effective method of applying growth regulators to rooted plants as they are absorbed through the roots and will be transported via xylem. Drench applications usually provide longer lasting, more uniform control of plant height than spray applications and typically use a larger, more diluted volume of solution than sprays. Drenches are primarily applied to the top of the media of a growing plant, and for most chemicals, 60 ml. of final solution is applied to a 10 cm pot or 120ml to a 15cm pot.
3. **Sprench method:** The sprench method is a hybrid of the spray and drench methods. When using this technique, a higher volume of spray is applied, achieving more of a drenching effect than that of a spray application. Typically, sprench volumes are two to four times that of a spray. The chemical concentration being applied is usually less than a spray but more than a drench.
4. **Pre-plant bulb soaks:** Bulb dipping or bulb soaking is another innovative method that has been developed to help growers to achieve height control for certain bulb crops. This method involves dipping or soaking bulbs in a growth regulator solution prior to planting. The concentration of the chemical and the soak time depends on the woodiness of the bulb.
5. **Seed soaking:** Seeds are soaked in growth regulators mainly GA_3 to improve germination.
6. **Sub-irrigation or hydroponic application:** Occur at almost every irrigation via drip method or to plants grown hydroponically.
7. **Paint:** Mixing PGR into latex paint and painting it onto the bark of young trees or onto buds to improve branching.
8. **Pre-plant dip:** Many growers are using a pre-plant dip of cuttings to obtain height control. This method can be used on either rooted or unrooted cuttings of some plant varieties. To achieve results, the cuttings are placed in a growth regulator solution just long enough to thoroughly wet all of the leaves and stems and then they are removed and planted.

9. **Controlled residue technique:** This is the innovative approach many growers are trying. This application technique involves applying the growth regulator directly to the container prior to filling it with media. As the roots grow and come into contact with the container, they take up the chemical and height control can be achieved.

Before determining an application method, the grower must know how the PGR is taken in by the plant. B-9 and Cycocel are primarily taken up by the leaves whereas Bonzi, Piccolo and Sumagic are primarily taken up by the stems and petioles or through the root system. Concentration may vary widely with plant species. Start with a lower concentration if active concentration is unknown. Timing of PGR applications must be matched to the proper plant stage of development to achieve the desired goal. For example GibGro (GA_3) is being used to partially substitute for cold storage of azaleas, plants should be at stage of floral development (style elongated and open). Applying prior to this stage could result in abnormal flower development. In general growth regulators should be applied late in the evening or early in the morning to avoid transpiration. Plant should not be wilted or stressed at the time of application. A turgid plant is more able to absorb and translocate a PGR than a wilted plant. Number of application is likely to be species dependent and the time required for its metabolic consumption.

Constrains

- Misapplications lead to lower plant quality.
- **Common problems:** Phytotoxicity, delayed flowering and stunted growth. For example overdose of Florel (ethephon) causes delayed flowering and under stress condition (temperature or water) result in leaf yellowing.

For enhanced crop production, plant growth regulators have a very exciting and positive future with today's floriculture producers. Growers are developing many new application methods for the chemicals currently available and will continue to discover many new uses and new chemicals for plant growth regulators in the future.

CHAPTER-5

FLOWERING ANNUALS AND HERBACEOUS PERRINIALS

Flowering Annuals

Annuals are those plants which complete their life cycle in one season. These are genetically programmed to flower seed and die in one season or year. All food and energy of annuals goes to flower and seed production. Most of flowering annuals complete their lifecycle within 3-6 months.

Classification of annuals

1. *Based on growing season*

a) **Winter annuals** – Antirrhinum, China aster, ageratum, arctotis, brachycome, carnation, calendula, comanula, cineraria, dimorphotheca, dianthus, larkspur, lupin, mignonette, nasturtium, nigella, pansy, petunia, phlox, salvia, stock, sweet pea, verbena and viola.

b) **Summer annuals** – This include cosmos, coreopsis, gaillardia, portulaca, sunflower, tithonia and zinnia

c) **Rainy seasons annuals** – Balsam, cockscomb, gomphrena and marigold.

2. *Based on tolerance to frost*

a) **Hardy annuals** – These annuals are tolerant to frost e.g., calendula, cornflower and so on.

b) **Half-Hardy annuals** – These annuals are intermediate to hardy and half-hardy annuals e.g., marigold, ageratum and so on.

c) **Tender annuals** – These annuals are least tolerant to frost e.g., wax or fibrous bigonia.

3. ***Based on colour of blooms***

a) **Blue, Purple and Lavender flowered annuals** – *Ageratum mexicanum, Anchusa, Browallia elata, Callistephus chinensis, Centaurea cyanus, Clitoria ternatea, Convolvulus minor, Delphinium ajacis, Delphinium hybridum, Echium plantagineum, Gilia capitata, Heliotropium arborescens, Iberis umbellate, Ipomoea rubro-caerulea, Lobelia erinus, Myosotis, Petunia hybridia, Salvia farinacea, Viola tricolor hortensis* and *Verbena hybrida.*

b) **White Flowered annuals** – *Alyssum, Callistephus chinensis, Convolvulus major, Dianthus, Nigella, Phlox, Papaver* and *Zinnia.*

c) **Yellow and orange flowered annuals** – *Cacalia lutea, Calendula officinalis, Dimorphotheca aurantiaca, Eschscholzia californica, Tagetes, Tropaeolum* and *Zinnia.*

4. ***Based on Fragrance***

a) **Fragrant Annuals** – *Alyssum, Cheiranthus cheiri, Centauria moschata, Dianthus caryophyllus, Heliotropium, Lathyrus odoratus, Mathiola, Phlox* and *Reseda odoratta.*

b) **Non fragrant annuals** – *Amaranthus, Cosmos, Clitoria ternatea* and so on.

5. ***Based on soil moisture content***

a) **Moisture loving plants** – *Nelumbo lutea, Nelumbo nucifera* and *Victoria regia.*

b) **Plants grown on normal moisture** - *Antirrhinum, China aster, carnation, calendula, cineraria, dianthus, larkspur, nasturtium, nigella, pansy and so on.*

c) **Plants grown on dry soils** – *Ageratum, Alyssum, Brachycome, Phlox* and *Tropaeolum.*

6. ***Based on Light requirement***

a) **Shade loving plants** – *Ageratum, Alyssum, Calceolaria, Calendula, Delphinium, Impatiens, Lupin, Phlox, Salvia* and *Verbena.*

b) **Plant grown on sunny situation** – *Dianthus, Petunia hybrida*, sunflower and so on.

Herbaceous Perennials

There are some plants with soft stems that cannot be included in the shrub group. They are termed as herbaceous perennials. They live year after year, whereas, annuals completed their life cycle within one season. Among the many herbaceous perennials available for cultivation, only a few do well in tropical climate. The majority of others thrives best in temperate climate. The one distinct advantage of this group is that, unlike the annuals, no pains are to be taken to raise them again and again every year or every season. Under temperate climate, some of them need only heading back to the ground level for rejuvenation. The herbaceous perennials are propagated through seeds, offsets, divisions or cutting. The plants, being comparatively hardier than the annuals, are easy to grow and some of them bloom for a considerable part of the year, if not throughout.

Cultural Management

Soil

The annuals thrive best in deep, well drained and well cultivated soil which is not acidic in nature. If the soil is acidic, addition of lime will be necessary to make it neutral as far as possible. In clay soil, the addition of lime will break up the stiff soil and an application of sufficient organic matter will make the soil porous. In sandy soil, a lot of organic matter should be added and wherever possible this should be improved upon with the addition of clay as it is costly to improve the texture of such soil with manure. The beds should be worked up thoroughly to a depth of 30 cm but the digging work should not be undertaken in a very wet soil. The digging should be repeated 2-3 times and the soil pulverized thoroughly to obtain the best results. Before planting, the surface should be firmed by drawing a light roller.

Sites

The seasonal flowers do best in full sun. But many of the annuals such as ageratum, sweet alyssum, calendula, clarkia, forget-me-not, larkspur and salvia can be grown in semi-shade, although the quality and quantity of the flowers may suffer.

Layouts

It is advisable to locate the beds with a strip of lawn in front and between two beds having enough running and turning space for the lawn mower to work. While situating beds in the midst of the lawn, care should be taken that the annuals flowers do not have to compete with the invading roots of the grasses. This is ensured by running a sharp spade deep into the ground around the edges of the bed every two or three weeks. Another precaution in this regard is to make the beds at least one metre wide. In the shrub border, this precaution is not needed where the intention is only to cover the vacant spaces with the annuals. The beds may be formal or informal. For mixed borders, large informal beds are better. In smaller beds, only one kind of annual with attractive colour and profuse blooming habit is grown. For the mixed borders, the taller growing plants such as hollyhock and sunflower are put in groups in the background. The intermediates such as antirrhinum, poppy, salvia and lupin are put in middle rows. The third clump may be made up of aster, dianthus and calendula and the edge may consist of the dwarf types such as sweet alyssum, pansy and candytuft.

Sowing

It is the general practice to raise the seedlings in nursery and then transplant them in beds or pots. The only exceptions are those which have either bold seeds such as sweet pea, sunflower, morning glory and so on or those annuals which are difficult to transplant such as Californian poppy and linaria. These are sown directly at places where they are to be grown and later thinned out to proper spacings depending upon the type. The seeds can be sown in earthen seed pans or pots, wooden seed trays, raised nursery beds or seed frames which are generally 1 to 1.2m broad, 60 cm deep and of a convenient length. The compost for the seed beds or pans consists of one part sifted garden soil and one part of finely sieved leaf mould and if needed ½ part of sand may be added, especially for clayey soil. The compost should be sterilized before sowing to eliminate soil borne fungi, especially those causing "damping off". Before filling up the pans or the trays, adequate drainage facility is to be ensured by providing holes at the bottom. The seeds are sown in raised beds for this purpose. The bottom layer in the pans is filled with broken bricks or rocks to prevent the possibility of the drainage holes getting clogged. The compost is filled and made firm with the help of a rammer made of a flat wood fitted with a handle at the centre. Before sowing, the seeds are treated with a little of fungicide such as captan, arsan or cersan to prevent the seedlings from getting fungal diseases. The seeds are sown in the pans in rows placed 3-6cm apart made with the help of a pencil or a stick of similar thickness at 0.3 to 0.6 cm depth. Small seeds such as petunia may be fixed with a little quantity of fine silver sand to get uniform sowing. Before sowing the seeds, the compost should be made slightly moist as the water applied after sowing will not be readily absorbed and the seeds may float. Immediately after sowing the seeds watering is done carefully with a fine rose-can. The pots are then covered with glass pans or newspaper sheets and kept in partial shade. Further watering is done, if needed, keeping in mind that over-watering is harmful. After germination, the seedlings are exposed to sunlight. Otherwise, they may become weak and lanky. The exposure to sunlight is gradually increased, starting from a couple of hours a day, till transplanting time when these should become sufficiently strong to withstand the full sun.

Pricking

This is the term given to the operation of transferring the young seedlings to another pan or tray. As soon as the seedlings are sufficiently large to handle, these are pricked with the help of a pointed stick or a metal label, at 5-7 cm apart in previously prepared holes and the compost around the collar and the roots of the seedlings is firmed carefully. The compost in this case will be a little richer than that of the seed pans. This operation ensures healthy growth of seedlings. The whole operation should be carried out with extreme care so as not to damage the very fragile stem and roots. Often the seedlings are pricked singly in small nursery pots (7.5 cm) and transplanted in permanent beds at 4 to 6 leaf stage along with the compost which comes off intact when the pot is inverted with a little jerk, if the compost is just sufficiently moist. While inverting the pot the outcoming compost is to be supported with the fingers of the left hand to prevent cracks in the compost. This method eliminates the chances of mortality in transplanting as the roots are not disturbed.

Transplanting

The time of transplanting the seedlings is generally one month after sowing when they have developed four leaves. A day or two before the actual transplanting operation, water is withheld to harden the seedlings. This operation reduces the chances of mortality. Transplanting is done on a cool cloudy day or in the evening which enables the seedling to get established during the cool night. The bed for transplanting should be prepared thoroughly to depth of 30-45 cm and the soil pulverized to a fine texture. The soil should be enriched with the addition of 4-8 kg of well rotten cow dung or horse manure or any other good compost and four table spoonfuls of super phosphate or bone meal per square metre area. A small hole is made at the place where the seedling is to be inserted and the soil around the seedling. To get the seedlings established, light watering every day in the early morning and the late afternoon will be required for about a week.

Irrigation and Nutrition

The most common mistake done by the amateurs is daily watering of the established seedlings. This is extremely harmful. Daily light watering is needed only for about a week after transplanting. Thereafter, the correct method is to flood the bed first and then weeding and hoeing are done after a couple of days when the soil is just moist. The soil is then allowed to dry before the next flooding. It has already been mentioned that the ground should receive at the time of soil preparation sufficient organic matter which is vital for plant growth and development. The chemical fertilizers are added in small doses during this time. During vegetative growth, a mixture of chemical fertilizers and organic manure in the form of a week solution is given once in a fortnight. About 4-5 kg of fresh cowdung manure or oil cakes such as neem, groundnut, mustard and a handful each of ammonium sulphate and super phosphate are dissolved in about five litres of water and allowed to ferment for few days, it is diluted to tea colour and then applied at the rate of 3-4 litres per square metre area followed by flooding with water. Alternatively, a dry mixture is prepared with ammonium sulphate, super phosphate and potassium sulphate in the proportion of 2:1:1, respectively and added at the rate of 60 g per square metre and forked in followed by flooding of the beds. If the fertilizer mixture comes in direct contact with the foliage, it may cause scorching. When the flower buds appear, a fertilizer mixture consisting of super phosphate and potassium sulphate in the proportion of 2:1, respectively applied at the same rate as the above mixture.

Staking, Pinching and Disbudding

The plants with weak, slender or straggling stems will need staking when they are 15-20 cm tall. Creepers such as sweet pea, morning glory, nasturtium and so on will also need necessary supports. Stakes prepared with split bamboos are painted green. Painting of the sticks with green helps conceal them among the green plants. Jute, cotton and pigeon pea sticks are useful as stakes. Many seedlings such as carnation, marigold and dianthus need pinching at this stage. Aster, cosmos and zinnia develop flower buds as early as when these are 5-10 cm high and are pinched off. The number of buds per stem is reduced by disbudding the axillary buds if large are desired.

Description of some important annuals and herbaceous perennials

Arbronia umbellata: Common Name: Sand verbena; Family: Nyctaginaceae

This seasonal flower is most suitable for the rockery. It takes about 3-4 months from sowing to flowering. This is a climbing or trailing annual growing up to a height of 45 cm and trailing up to 90-150 cm. The flowers are rosy lilac, sweet scented during night and somewhat resemble verbena.

Achillea filipendulina: Family: Asteraceae

It is a robust perennial plant, growing to a height of 150 cm, with pinnately lobed, toothed and pungent foliage. The bright yellow flowers are densely borne in somewhat convex heads which sometimes measure 12 cm across. The plants need staking.

Achillea millefolium: Common Name: Milfoil; Family: Asteraceae

The plant is 30-90 cm tall, perennial and bears white flowers in flattish heads.

Acroclinium roseum: Common Name: Everlasting flower; Family: Asteraceae

The plants are 45-60 cm tall bearing double daisy like flowers of pure white, pink and shades of rose with bright golden yellow and dark coloured centers. The flower are borne singly at the end of long stems and papery in texture. It is useful for cutting and last long when cut and dried. The leaves are narrow and glaucous green.

Adonis aestivalis: Common Name: Pheasant's Eye; Family: Ranunculaceae

Branching annual and perennial rock plants which are 25-30 cm tall and suitable for cultivation in mixed borders, open woodland and wild gardens. The plant has a deep green, finely cut, fern like foliage and bears small dark crimson buttercup like flowers of about 2.5 cm across.

***Ageratum* spp.:** Common Name: Floss Flower; Family: Asteraceae

The plant height ranges from 15 to 45 cm. The dwarf types are especially suitable for beds, borders or rockeries. The branches are covered with fluffy heads of flowers with colour ranging from pale lavender to deep mauve. Some cultivars bear white flowers.

Agrostemma githago: Common Name: Corn Cockle; Family: Caryophyllaceae

This is a hardy annual, tall, slender plant growing to a height of 60-90 cm. The large *Viscaria* like flowers are 5 to 7.5 cm across and pale lilac in colour with radial lines of dark dots in each petal. They are useful for mixed border and pots.

Althaea rosea: Common Name: Hollyhock; Family: Malvaceae

In temperate countries and in hill stations, this is treated as a perennial, whereas, in the plains, it behaves like an annual. It is a majestic plant, attaining a height of 1.5 to 2.5 m or more under favourable conditions, with rough, large, round and kidney shaped leaves. The large, single, semi-double or double flowers are borne in the axils of the leaves all along the length of the stem.

Alyssum maritimum: Common Name: Sweet Alyssum; Family: Cruciferae

This forms a low-growing, spreading plant with narrow grey foliage. The plant branch freely and each branch ends in a spike of usually white flowers which are honey scented. When in flowering, the compact plant looks like a carpet of flowers.

They are suited for beds, borders, window boxes, hanging baskets and as the first row in a herbaceous border.

***Amaranthus* spp.:** Common Name: Amaranth; Family: Amaranthaceae

This group comprises some useful garden annuals with bright foliage or blooms or both. It grows to a height of 1 to 1.5 m. It bears tail-like, often with knots at short intervals, drooping flower spikes, white, pale green or crimson in colour.

Anchusa capensis: Common Name: Cape Forget-me-not; Family Boraginaceae

The plant grows as a biennial or a perennial but can also be grown as an annual in gardens. It grows well in the hills and in plains having a long and cool winter. The plant is compact and grows to a height of 30 to 45 cm. The flowers are deep blue with a white centre and 0.6 to 0.7 cm across.

Angelonia grandiflora: Common Name: Angelonia; Family: Scrophulariaceae

A very popular, hardy, dwarf perennial which bears terminal racemes of sweet scented purple or white flowers.

Antirrhinum majus: Common Name: Snapdragon; Family: Scrophulariaceae

This is a branching perennial plant, 30 to 90 cm tall, with numerous spikes, mostly of crimson and white colour. The colour of the flower varies widely in all the types ranging from white and cream to yellow, shades of pink, scarlet, red, orange, brick red, mauve, rose, maroon and so on.

Aquilegia vulgaris: Common Name: Columbine; Family: Ranunculaceae

These are pretty perennials plants about 60 cm tall, with handsome fer-like foliage consisting of three leaflets in a leaf. The flowers are double or single and large, 10-12 cm across with a long spur. The flower colour ranges from white to red, yellow, pink, crimson, blue and lavender.

Arctotis grandis: Common Name: African Daisy; Family: Asteraceae

The species is vigorous growing and bushy in habit. The flower stem attains a height of 45-60 cm and thus suitable for cutting. The colour of the flower is white with a lilac centre and the backside of the petals is steel grey.

Aster amellus: Common Name: Perennial Aster; Family: Asteraceae

It grows to a height of 60 cm. the single flowers are small, 2.5-5 cm across, daisy-like, borne in large heads (30-45 cm) of corymbose panicle and are white, lavender, mauve, deep blue, lilac and pink.

Bartonia aurea: Common Name: Gloden Star; Family: Loasaceae

An easy to grow, hardy and showy annual, 45 to 60 cm in height. The flowers are large buttercup like and glistening orange in colour with a central mass of feathery stamens. It is useful as a bedding plant.

Bellis perennis: Common Name: English Daisy; Family: Asteraceae

It is a perennial plant but can be best grown as biennial in the hills and as annual in the plains. It is a dwarf plant, 20-30 cm in height. The leaves are strap-shaped, tapering towards the tip and form into tuft at the base. The flowers are 2.5 to 5 cm across and the flower stalk is about 15 cm long. The flowers are 2.5 to 5 cm across and the flower stalk is about 15 cm long. The flowers are single or double and the petals may be flat or quilled. The flat type is available in white, crimson and pink. The quilled in a beautiful salmon-pink shade and in crimson.

Berbenia cordifolia: Common Name: Elephant Ear; Family: Saxifragaceae

The plants are 30 cm tall, with large heart-shaped foliage and rose-pink flowers measuring 2 cm across which are borne on medium stalks above the foliage. It is a perennial plant.

Brachycome iberidifolia: Common Name: Swan River Daisy; Family: Asteraceae

It is a beautiful dwarf annual with a slender stem and finely divided leaves. The flowers are 2.5 cm across, borne in profusion and are white, blue, pale blue, mauve or purple. It is an appropriate plant for rock gardens and herbaceous borders.

Browallia demissa: Common Name: Amethyst flower; Family: Solanaceae

It is a plant of medium size, rather moderately tall, attaining a height of 30-45 cm. flowers resemble Lobelia, 1 cm long and are borne in the axils of narrow, oval, green leaves. There are two colours blue and white.

Cacalia coccinea: Common Name: Tassel Flower; Family: Asteraceae

A hardy annual 30 to 45 cm tall. The leaves are thin, long, oval and remain attached to the wiry and hairy stem. The small flowers which are 1.5 cm across are borne in clusters on the wiry stems and look like a tassel. Flowers are commonly orange-scarlet or dull red in colour but there is one variety *Cacalia lutea* with golden-yellow flowers.

Calceolaria: Common Name: Slipperwort; Family: Scrophulariaceae

The plants are remarkable for their brightly coloured flowers and a peculiar shape as that of circular pocket purses. *Calceolaria* includes many species of annuals and perennials. They may be herbaceous or shrubby in habit.

Calendula officinalis: Common Name: Pot Marigold; Family: Asteraceae

One of the most commonly cultivated seasonal flowers. It flowers almost throughout the year. The flowers measure 4-5 cm across and their colour varies from straw colour to deep orange. The flower may be single or double. Calendula is useful for bedding, cutting, potting and for window boxes.

Campanula medium: Common Name: Canterbury Bells; Family: Campanulaceae

It is a biennial, bearing bell shaped flowers of white, blue, pink, mauve or violet colour. The flower are single or double. The species *Campanula ramosissima* is an annual, 22-45 cm tall. *Campanula pyramidalis*, commonly called 'Chimney bell flower' is another biennial species. *Campanula persifolia* and *Campanula carpatica* are two perennials.

Celosia argentea: Common Name: Cockscomb; Family: Amaranthaceae

A very popular and easy to grow annual, 25-50 cm in height but it may grow up to 150-180 cm during rainy season. It has branching growth habit and produces feathery flower spikes in a pyramidal fashion resembling Ostrich-plumes, in various colours of silver, yellow, golden-yellow, red and orange.

Centaurea cyanus: Common Name: Cornflower; Family: Asteraceae

A hardy upright annual. The plant is slender and 60-90 cm tall. The original blue flower colour sported to a multiple range of colours such as white, pink, maroon and purple. It is useful as cut flowers and can be grown in annual and mixed borders.

Centaurea moschata: Common Name: Sweet Sultan; Family: Asteraceae

Bears fragrant flower heads of white, delicate mauve, deep mauve, purple, yellow or deep red on long stems. Plants are about 90 cm to 1 m tall. The flowers are excellent for cutting and look like powder puffs.

Cheiranthus cheiri: Common Name: Wallflower; Family: Cruciferae

Wallflower is a medium tall shrubby biennial or perennial. There are some early flowering annuals. They are popular for spring bedding and cutting because of their wide colour range and sweet scent.

Chrysanthemum coronarium: Common Name: Crown Daisy; Family: Asteraceae

It is taller and more vigorous plant. The flower shade is yellow and white. *Chrysanthemum carinatum* or tricoloured Chrysanthemum is the best of the annual types. The flower colour is rich crimson but the mixture of colours is available.

The plant grows to a height of 60 cm. The large flowers, about 7 cm across, show a bright coloured ring at the base of the petals and a dark coloured disc at the centre, thus producing triple ring effect.

Clarkia elegans: Common Name: Clarkia; Family: Onagraceae

It is hardy annual with slender but graceful branches and grows to a height of 60 to 90 cm. The single or double flowers are borne in the axils of the leaves and the petals are beautifully ruffled.

Cleome spinosa: Common Name: Spider plant; Family: Capparidaceae

It is a tall plant, with sharp spines all over including the leaves. The large clusters of four petalled flowers have long prominent stamens and these give the plant its name. The flowers are scented and may be pink, light purple, rose or white in colours.

Clianthus dampieri: Common Name: Glory Pea; Family: Leguminosae

It is one of the most showy winter annuals. The plants are branching and grow upto a height of 80 cm. The flowers are quite large, 6-8 cm across and are borne in clusters of 4-6 flowers. The flowers are pendulous and dark crimson colour with a raised black base which resembles the eyes.

Collinsia bicolor: Common Name: Collin's Flower; Family: Scrophulariaceae

An easily grown beautiful hardy annual of branching habit. Plants are slender and grow upto 40 cm. The flowers are borne in long spikes and are lilac, white and salmon in colour. The plant is suitable as a pot plant and woodland garden.

Coreopsis: Common Name: Tick seed; Family: Asteraceae

There are two commonly grown species, *Coreopsis tinctoria* and *Coreopsis drummondii*. In *Coreopsis tinctoria,* the flower colour is mainly yellow and crimson brown. In *Coreopsis tinctoria* var. *marmorata* the flowers are curiously marbled and striped. The plants may be tall or dwarf. *Coreopsis drummondii* has yellow flowers with dark crimson centre. The plants are medium tall.

Cosmos bipinnatus: Common Name: Cosmos; Family: Asteraceae

A delightful annual, mainly grown in the rainy season. The plant is 50-120 cm tall and bears rose, pink, crimson, purple, lavender and white flowers with yellow centre on long stalks. Flowers are large, 10-15 cm across and may be single or double including some tetraploids.

Cuphea ignea: Common Name: Cigar Plant; Family: Lythraceae

A dwarf, bushy annual, having unusual shaped scarlet flowers with a dark ring at the base resembling a cigar. *Cuphea miniata* is another species with open scarlet flowers having purple bases and white mouth.

Cynoglossum amabile: Common Name: Chinese Forget-me-not; Family: Boraginaceae

A hardy perennial, about 30 cm tall but is grown as an annual. The tiny blue flowers are borne in clusters and are sweet scented. A white cultivar is available.

Delphinium ajacis: Common Name: Rocket Larkspur; Family: Ranunculaceae

This species include white, blue, mauve-purple, pink and red shades. The plant grow up to 90 cm in height. It is popular as cut flower and for growing as a background or in front of a tall hedge or a border and in pots.

Delphinium consolida: Common Name: Imperial Larkspur; Family: Ranunculaceae

They are usually tall, 90-150 cm and branching.

Delphinium hybridum: Common Name: Perennial Delphinium; Family: Ranunculaceae

Perennial Delphinium thrives best in hills and can be grown as annual in northern plains in and around Delhi with long cool winter. It is a robust, 150-180 cm tall plant with flowers in several colours including pure white, deep bright blue and sky-blue, which come true from seed. The other flower colours are purple, lavender, lilac and mauve.

Dianthus barbatus: Common Name: Sweet William; Family: Caryophyllaceae

This is a biennial plant but an annual strain is available. Some of the early flowering biennials can be grown as annuals. Sweet William is closely related to pink. The plant is about 30-45 cm tall with double or single fragrant flowers borne at the apex of the branches in rounded clusters. The flowers which are white, scarlet, dark red and in different shades of pink are self coloured, edged, mottled or with prominent white eyes.

Dianthus Caryophyllus: Common Name: Carnation; Family: Caryophyllaceae

It is a flowering annual but in reality it is treated as biennial and succeeds well as such. There are different types of carnations and each of these can be grown successfully in cooler parts of the plains and at medium to high elevations.

Dianthus chinensis: Common Name: Chinese Pink; Family: Caryophyllaceae

The plants are 30-45 cm tall and bear brightly coloured scented flowers. The flowers are self coloured, exquisitely marked, edged or bloctched. Some of them have petals beautifully fringed. There are cultivars in which blooms are borne in upright stems. The flowers colour ranges from white to red, scarlet, pink, lilac, violet, maroon black and mauve.

Digitalis purpurea: Common Name: Foxglove; Family: Scrophulariaceae

It is a biennial, rarely perennial but sometimes treated as annual. It is grown in the hills. The plant, 60-150 cm tall, is cultivated for the production of digitalin, a medicine. The flowers are bell-shaped, slightly drooping and open at mouth which is sometimes spotted.

Dimorphotheca sinuata: Common Name: Cape Daisy; Family: Asteraceae

The plants are about 30-60 cm tall, branching and bearing daisy like large flowers of various shades of colour such as white, bluish white, shades of yellow, salmon, rose and reddish-purple. The plants are free-flowering and the flowers remain open during day time only.

Echium plantagineum: Common Name: Tower of Jewels; Family: Boraginaceae

It has both tall and dwarf cultivars. The small bell shaped flowers have a wide range of petal shades of blue, mauve, purple, rose-pink and white. It is useful for mixed borders, rock gardens and for edging.

Eschscholzia californica: Common Name: Californian Poppy; Family: Papaveraceae

In its natural home, the plant is a perennial but is grown in the garden as an annual. The plants are 30-45 cm tall, with blue-green, finely cut foliage and slender stem somewhat resembling a carrot. Some varieties are dwarf, 20-30 cm tall. The flowers are large, about 10 cm in diameter, saucer shaped, single, semi double or double and have shades of bright yellow, lemon, orange, crimson, cream, creamy white. Some are bicoloured, outer side bronze and inner side orange.

Euphorbia heterophylla: Common Name: Annual Poinsettia; Family: Euphorbiaceae

It is a hardy annual growing to a height of 60-90 cm. The flowers orange-red in colours, are borne in clusters at the end of branches. The leaves surrounding the flowers get attractively coloured during the hot season and resemble Poinsettia.

Felicia bergeriana: Common Name: Kingfisher Daisy; Family: Asteraceae

A dwarf (15-20 cm), useful annual, bearing numerous small, bright metallic blue flowers resembling daisy. Plants are useful for rock gardens, for front position in borders and pots.

Gaillardia pulchella: Common Name: Blanket flower; Family: Asteraceae

A free flowering annual which blooms in succession for quite some time. This is very easy to grow and most popular. The plants are medium, 40-45 cm tall. The flowers are large, 5-7 cm across, single or double and are available in many pretty colours and their combinations such as yellow, lemon, yellow-purple, cream, orange and maroon.

Gazania splendens: Common Name: Treasure flower; Family: Asteraceae

A dwarf, trailing plant with narrow, long, pointed, silvery and hairy leaves. The flowers are in shades of red, pink, orange, yellow and white and are daisy like in shape. It is grown in rock gardens, in front rows of borders and for edging.

Gerbera: Common Name: African Daisy; Family: Asteraceae

It is a dwarf perennial herbaceous plant. The plants are stemless, dwarf, 30-45 cm tall and are hairy throughout. The leaves are 12-20 cm long, 5-7 cm broad, deeply lobed with a fairly long petiole. The flowers are daisy like, 7-10 cm across but in certain hybrids these may be as large as 15 cm across.

Geum coccineum: Family: Rosaceae

A herbaceous perennial, suitable for medium and high elevation. The plant flower freely. The flowering is from summer to autumn. The colour of flower is brick red.

Gilia capitata: Common Name: Ipomopsis; Family: Polemoniaceae

The plants are 45-60 cm tall with very finely cut foliage, small and lavender-blue flowers. It is suitable for growing in front rows in borders and rock gardens.

Godetia grandiflora: Common Name: Satin Flower; Family: Onagraceae

It is a dwarf plant with large flowers produced in clusters.

Gomphrena globosa: Common Name: Globe Amaranth; Family: Amaranthaceae

It is a rugged looking annual and does not require any special attention. The plants are bushy in nature and may be tall or dwarf. The flowers are round and clover like or button like in shades of white, orange, magenta, purple, violet, rose and pink and are everlasting.

Gypsophila elegans: Common Name: Chalk plant; Family: Caryophyllaceae

A dwarf, slender, lance-shaped, grey-leaved annual, bearing clusters of small, white or pink flowers. It is grown in beds, borders, rock gardens and for covering open spaces in beds of bulbous plants.

Helianthus annuus: Common Name: Sunflower; Family: Asteraceae

The giant, common yellow sunflower is a coarse looking plant with rough textured leaves. The flowers are 20-30 cm across and are single or double.

Helichrysum bracteatum: Common Name: Strawflower; Family: Asteraceae

It is a commonly grown plant, 50-80 cm tall, bearing everlasting flowers of 7-10 cm diameter. The flowers last long and give a papery feeling when touched with hand. The plant flowers without inhibition.

Heliotropium arborescens: Common Name: Heliotrope; Family: Boraginaceae

It is a perennial plant but can be grown as an annual. The plants are branching and compact, 30-45 cm tall. The small tubular flowers are borne in long trusses well above the foliage. The plants flower freely and the flower colour ranges from white to blue, purple and various shades of purple. The flowers are vanilla-scented.

Heuchera sanguinea: Common Name: Crimson Bells; Family: Saxifragaceae

A perennial herb, 30-45 cm high, with heart-shaped or roundish, much lobed leaves. The flowers are small, bell-shaped and numerous borne on long stalks. These are suitable for table decoration.

Hunnemannia fumariifolia: Common Name: Mexican Tulip; Family: Papaveraceae

A perennial plant, grows to a height of 40-90 cm and bears yellow flower which are 5-7 cm across.

Iberis umbellata: Common Name: Candytuft; Family: Cruciferae

The plant is 15-30 cm tall and small flowers are borne in broad clusters, Known as Umbels, with a wide range of colours including white, pink, carmine-rose, purple and lilac.

Impatiens balsamina: Common Name: Touch-me-not; Family: Balsaminaceae

The plant are 22-60 cm tall, bearing Camellia like double or single flowers with varying colours such as rose, pink, scarlet, red, violet, salmon pink, purplish red, lilac, blue, mauve and white.

Kochia scoparia* var. *trichophila: Common Name: Summer Cypress; Family: Chenopodiaceae

It is a dense bushy symmetrical, oval or round annual foliage plant, 60-90 cm tall and 30 cm across. The whole plant is covered with finely cut and narrow pea green ornamental foliage. On maturity, the plant turns into rich coppery red and red flowers also appear giving the plant the look of burning bush.

Lathyrus odoratus: Common Name: Sweet pea; Family: Leguminosae

Sweet pea is valued and widely cultivated for its range of flower colours, elegant form, fragrance and utility as a cut flower. Sweet peas are commonly used as temporary screens to hide unsightly objects or to separate the kitchen garden from the flower garden or alongside a path.

Limonium sinuatum: Common Name: Sea Lavender; Family: Plumbaginaceae

The species is actually a biennial but is generally grown as an annual. The plants grow to a height of 45 to 60 cm and the stems are hardy and angular. The foliage is grey-green and deeply cut. The flower stalk is winged and the calyx is toothed and straw like. The flower colours are available are white, rose, mauve, lavender and dark blue.

Linaria maroccana: Common Name: Toad Flax; Family: Scrophulariaceae

A commonly grown annual, with small pretty flowers. The plants are 20-35 cm tall, bushy having erect branches. The leaves resemble Flax. The mini antirrhinum like flowers are produced in abundance. The flowers are white, yellow, pink, purple, lavender, rose, blue, mauve and bicoloured having blotches of different colours on the lip.

Linum grandiflorum* var. *rubrum: Common Name: Scarlet Flax; Family: Linaceae

The plants are 30-60 cm tall with narrow pointed foliage. The scarlet flowers with dark centres are 2.5-3.5 cm across and are borne in loose panicles. The variety rubrum is the best. This showy annual can be used in annual borders or beds for a fine display.

Lobelia erinus: Common Name: Lobelia; Family: Campanulaceae

A low growing, 15-30 cm tall, exceedingly beautiful and profusely flowering plants of great garden value. The small flowers are white, different shades of blue, crimson and purple in colour, with a yellow or white eyes. The plant may be either compact or trailing in habit.

***Lupinus* spp.:** Common Name: Lupin; Family: Leguminosae

The plants are 45-75 cm tall with foliage deeply-lobed and the long flower spikes growing well above the foliage, bear numerous small pea like flowers of white, pink and pale blue colours.

Matricaria eximia: Common Name: Feverfew; Family: Asteraceae

The plant is a perennial, 30 cm tall but when raised from seed can be grown as an annual. The flat heads of small double flowers may be ivory white or yellow in colour.

Matthiola incana: Common Name: Gilliflower; Family: Cruciferae

It is a genus of annual, biennial and perennial flowers. The small, rosetted and rounded single or fully double, scented flowers are borne on long spikes. There is wide range of flowers colours from white to crimson, dark red, pink, rose, mauve, lavender and blue.

Mesembryanthemum criniflorum: Common Name: Fig Marigold; Family: Aizoaceae

A handy, spreading, 10 cm tall annual, bearing daisy like flowers, 2.5-3.5 cm across, with a wide range of colours including white marked with crimson, pink or buff at the edges of petals or self coloured types in shade of yellow, crimson, apricot, orange, redand white.

Mimulus tigrinus: Common Name: Monkey Flower; Family: Scrophulariaceae

Although they are perennial, they could be conveniently grown as annuals. The plant are 30-45 cm tall and moderately branched. The flowers with two lips are gloxinia like, open mouthed hence known as monkey flower. Flowers are 2.5 – 5 cm across with many colours including crimson, pink, yellow and other intermediate shades and spotted and blotched generally with brown or maroon.

Mirabilis jalapa: Common Name: Four O’Clock; Family: Nyctaginaceae

A tall, bushy perennial, though generally grown as an annual. The flowers are fragrant, five lobed and 2.5 – 5 cm across with colours of red, yellow or white and often striped. The plants flower in the afternoon or in cloudy weather.

Molucella laevis: Common Name: Bells of Ireland; Family: Labiatae

Plant grows to 60-90 cm in height. The small white flowers which are inconspicuous are produced in successive whorls in the axils of leaves. This is useful for table decoration.

Myosotis alpestris: Common Name: Forget-me-not; Family: Boraginaceae

A perennial plant is generally grown as an annual. Both Dwarf and tall types are available. The tiny flowers are borne in clusters and are white, sky-blue, dark blue or pink in colour with a small yellowish eye and fragrant in afternoon.

Nemesia strumosa: Common Name: Nemesia; Family: Scrophulariaceae

The flowers are white, rich blue, primrose, yellow, orange, scarlet or crimson in colour and are marked with contrasting colours. The large flowered varieties are good for cutting and last as long as 2-3 weeks when kept in low bowls and cut at bud stage. They are good for bedding and borders. The dwarf types can be used with advantage in rock gardens, edgings and window boxes.

Nemophila menziesii insignis: Common Name: Californian Blue-Bell; Family: Hydrophyllaceae

A slender growing and spreading plant, 15-20 cm tall. The plants get covered with numerous small bell shaped and sky blue flowers with a white eye. There are some cultivars having deep purple, pure white and spotted flowers.

Nicotiana alata grandiflora: Common Name: Tobacco Plant; Family: Solanaceae

It is a perennial species, but is best grown as an annual. The plants are 60-90 cm tall, branching with large, coarse and hairy foliage. The flowers are large tubular or trumpet-shaped and white, blotched with various shades such as violet, lavender, yellow, crimson, pale green, maroon and so on and are sweet scented.

Nierembergia caerulea: Common Name: Cup Flower; Family: Solanaceae

A dwarf perennial plant, but grown as annual. The small petunia like or cup-shaped, flattish flowers are violet-blue in colour with a yellow eye and are produced in abundance.

Nigella damascena: Common Name: Fennel Flower; Family: Ranunculaceae

A pretty, upright, 30-45 cm tall plant with finely cut foliage and attractive semi double white, deep blue or rose coloured flowers which remain surrounded by the leaves.

***Oenothera* spp.:** Common Name: Evening Primrose; Family: Onagraceae

It is 60-120 cm tall. It is a biennial but can be grown as an annual. The flowers are yellow, tubular in shape up to 15 cm across and open in evening.

Orthosiphon stamineus; Family: Labiatae

A herbaceous perennial, 30-60 cm tall, bearing pale lilac blue flowers, 2.5 cm across and the stamens are much exerted giving the appearance of a cats whiskers. It is generally grown as a house or greenhouse plant. The plants are grown in semi-shade.

Paeonia officinalis: Common Name: Peony; Family: Ranunculaceae

It is a perennial herb grown in beds, borders and shrubberies. Flowering season is during the summer.

Papaver rhoeas: Common Name: Corn Poppy; Family: Papaveraceae

It is about 60 cm tall and bears cup-shaped single or double flowers with frilled silken petals. The flower colour may be white, all shades of pink including salmon, pale mauve, blue and dark maroon, all with a white base and many have attractive picotee edging.

Pelargonium: Common Name: Geranium; family: Geraniaceae

Geraniums are herbaceous perennials, mostly grown as potted plants for their handsome flowers borne in clusters. The leaves are showy.

Penstemon: Common Name: Beard Tongue; Family: Scrophulariaceae

It is a perennial but very often grown as an annual. It is suitable for beds and borders.

Petunia hybrida: Common Name: Petunia; Family: Solanaceae

The height of the plant may vary between 20-30 cm and 30-45 cm depending upon the type. The flowers are single or double and the petals may frilled and ruffled in various ways and may be veined or marked beautifully. The flower colours available are pink and red, pale blue, violet, yellow, cream, purple and mauve and some cultivars are bicoloured. Petunia is free flowering plant.

Phacelia camanularia: Common Name: Phacelia; Family: Hydrophyllaceae

A hardy annual, 20-25 cm tall, having attractive grey toothed foliage. It bears clusters of small, bell shaped, deep gentian-blue flowers with conspicuous anthers which are primrose coloured.

Phlox decussata: Common Name: Border Phlox; Family: Polemoniaceae

It is mostly unbranched and 45-120 cm tall perennial plant. The leaves are oblong lanceolate and flowers are like those of common phlox with white, pink, mauve, violet, purple, crimson and red colours.

Phlox drummondii: Common Name: Annual phlox; Family: Polemoniaceae

It is easy to cultivate, free flowering and ranges in height from 15 to 45 cm. The flowers are delicately scented with a wide range of colours such as pure white, several shades of pink, vermilion, crimson, violet and purple.

Pimpinella monoica: Common Name: Lady's Lace; Family: Umbelliferae

A tall annual with deeply cut foliage bearing numerous white flowers in large spray on a long stem. The umbels resemble the carrot or the fennel. The plants is grown in the borders and sometime in the shrubbery.

Platycodon grandiflorum: Common Name: Chinese Bellflower; Family: Campanulaceae

It is 30-60 cm tall, bearing bell-shaped flowers of blue or white shade, single or semi-double and about 7 cm across. The shoots die after each flowering but sprout again from the thick roots which survive a number of years underground.

Portulaca grandiflora: Common Name: Rose Moss; Family: Portulaceae

This is a low growing annual with a trailing habit. The leaves are cylindrical and fleshy. The flower colours are brilliant and available in shades of white, purple, sulphur-yellow, lavender-pink, salmon, scarlet, crimson and orange. The flower may be single or double.

Primula malacoides: Common Name: Baby Primrose; Family: Primulaceae

A herbaceous perennial, 30 cm tall with a rosette of large broad leaves at the base. The flowers, single or double are borne on a long slender stalk in trusses. This plant is good for growing in pots, beds, shrubbery and for cut flowers.

Pyrethrum roseum: Common Name: Pyrethrum; Family: Asteraceae

The plants are 30-60 cm tall with finely cut leaves and big flowers resembling daisies in colours of white, lilac, rose and red. Sometimes flowers are tipped yellow and the disc is yellow.

Reseda odorata: Common Name: Mignonette; Family: Resedaceae

The plants are 30-40 cm tall and bear small flowers of bronze, white, red, crimson and yellow shades. The cut flowers last long and emit an agreeable perfume.

Rudbeckia bicolor: Common Name: Cone Flower; Family: Asteraceae

It is a very attractive annual, 30-60 cm tall, bearing large flowers resembling daisies. The flowers are borne on long stalks and are yellow shades having a mahogany-crimson central zone and a dark brown central disc.

Saintpaulia ionantha: Common Name: African Violet; Family: Gesneriaceae

African violets are stemless, hairy perennial with ovate or subcordate leaves having many small and a few long hairs on both surfaces. The flowers are of violets shape but larger in size.

Salpiglossis sinuata: Common Name: Velvet Flower; Family: Solanaceae

A tall growing beautiful annual, bearing petunia like tubular flowers, white, crimson, shades of pink, gold, golden-yellow, chamois, scarlet and gold, blue and gold and rich violet in colour. The plant flowers profusely.

Salvia: Common Name: Sage; Family: Labiatae

There are five species of Salvia which are grown as annuals:

Salvia coccinea: It is an annual. The plants are 30-60 cm tall and sometimes up to 70 cm. The flower spike is long, erect and bears small crimson and scarlet flowers.

Salvia farinacea: It is a perennial species but is grown as annual. The plants grow to a height of 60-90 cm with shinning green leaves, bearing long spikes of lavender-blue flowers.

Salvia horminum: Often known as Blue Beard. It is 30-45 cm tall with small purple blue, pink or white flowers.

Salvia patens: This is another perennial species but is best grown as annual. The plant is 30-75 cm tall, bearing long spikes of bright blue flowers.

Salvia splendens: The plants may be tall or dwarf and bushy. The long terminal spikes with their tubular bright scarlet flowers are borne above foliage. There are cultivars with salmon, pink and violet flowers.

Saponaria calabrica: Common Name: Soapwort; Family: Caryophyllaceae

It is a dwarf annual, bearing in abundance sprays of starry pink or white flowers. It is grown in beds as background, in rock gardens and as edging. The flowers are good for cutting.

Scabiosa atropurpurea: Common Name: Egyptian Rose; Family: Dipsaceae

A colourful branching annual, growing to a height of 60-90 cm. There are dwarf growing varieties. The plants bear handsome globose or rounded heads of flowers borne on stiff stalks and are available in beautiful shades of pink, pale mauve, blue, scarlet, dark maroon and white.

Schizanthus hybridus: Common Name: Butterfly Flower; Family: Solanaceae

The plants are vigorous, branching and grow upto 90 cm or more. The colour range of the flower is wide and varying and mostly blotched, veined and spotted exquisitely in contrasting colours thus earning the name of butterfly flower. The small flowers are borne in abundance, measuring 2.5 cm across, resembling orchids.

Senecio cruentus: Common Name: Cineraria; Family: Asteraceae

It is one of the best shade-loving annuals. The large dark-green heart-shaped leaves are most attractive. Plant grow to a height of 30-60 cm and the daisy like brightly coloured flowers are borne in clusters and may be self coloured or with contrasting centres of white or prominently marked or circled with various shades.

Silene pendula: Common Name: Catchfly; Family: Caryophyllaceae

A bushy dwarf annual, bearing single or double flowers in sparse clusters and in colours ranging from white to rose, pink, purple, crimson and salmon.

***Solidago canadensis*:** Common Name: Golden Rod; Family: Asteraceae

Solidago comprises a number of perennial species of which *Solidago canadensis* is most commonly grown. The plants are hairy, 90-180 cm tall, stout and with much branched stems. The pretty golden-yellow flowers are feather like and crowded in a long terminal panicle.

***Streptocarpus* spp.:** Common Name: Cape Primrose; Family: Gesneriaceae

These are perennial stemless herbs suitable for medium and high elevations with one leaf or a rosette of several leaves, more generally prostrate and a single leaf may measure from 7.5 cm to 15.0 cm. The showy blooms are borne in erect scapes and the shades include blue, lilac, mauve, pink and white.

***Tagetes* spp.:** Common Name: Marigold; Family: Asteraceae

The Marigolds are one of the easiest annual flowers to cultivate and have wide adaptability to different soil and climatic conditions. The plants, with their attractive flower colours bloom for a considerably long period and the flowers keep remarkably well when cut.

Tithonia rotundifolia: Common Name: Mexican Sunflower; Family: Asteraceae

A free flowering tall growing plant with rough, large, heart-shaped foliage and large single flowers, resembling single dahlia. The flower colour is orange with tufted yellow centre.

Torenia fournieri: Common Name: Wish-borne Flower; Family: Scrophulariaceae

This is an erect, much-branched, glabrous annual growing to a height of 30 cm. the flowers, looking somewhat like antirrhinum in form are violet and pale blue in colour with a blotch of golden yellow in the throat.

Trachymene caerulea: Common Name: Lace Flower; Family: Umbelliferae

The plants are 45-60 cm tall, with finely divided leaves and small lavender blue flowers which are borne in umbrella like clusters on long stalks.

Tropaeolum majus: Common Name: Garden Nasturtium; Family: Tropaeolaceae

There are four main garden types of nasturtium are: a) Tall Climbing Singles which trail or climb to a height of 180-250 cm, b) Dwarf Single (25-30 cm), c) Semi-Double Gleam, which are semi climbing in nature and the flowers are scented delicately and d) the Dwarf Double. The nasturtiums have wiry stems, large attractive rounded leaves and spurred flowers, 6-7 cm across. The flower colours include orange, primrose, salmon, orange-red, scarlet and deep mahogany.

Ursinia anethoides: Common Name: Jewel of the Veldt; Family: Asteraceae

A medium tall shrubby plant with deeply cut foliage and beautiful daisy like flowers of glowing orange colour with crimson centre and borne on the long stalks. The flowers are produced for a long duration and are excellent for cutting, bedding and pots.

Venidium fastuosum: Common Name: Namaqualand Daisy; Family: Asteraceae

A bushy showy annual, 60 – 90 cm tall, bearing large, about 10 m across, deep orange flowers with a black zone and a shining black centre, borne on long stalks. The whole plant is covered with white hair.

Verbena x hybrida: Common Name: Verbena; Family: Verbenaceae

The garden Verbenas are compact bushy plants, 20-30 cm tall, with a little tendency to trail. The plants are perennial but treated as annual. The flowers are borne in cluster above the grey-green foliage having toothed margins.

Vinca rosea: Common Name: Periwinkle; Family: Apocynaceae

The plants are 30-60 cm tall perennials and covered with bright green smooth oblong leaves. The flowers are rosy purple or white, the latter with or without a very small reddish eye. The plants are free flowering and bloom round the year.

Viola tricolor hortensis: Common Name: Garden Pansy; Family: Violaceae

Pansy is an all time favourite perennial bushy trailing herb, 15-22 cm tall but treated as an annual in the plains and as biennial in the hills. The flowers are delicately scented especially during the early hours and the size may be upto 10-12 cm across in giant cultivars.

Viola cornuta: Common Names: Tufted Pansy; Family: Violaceae

The plants are tufted and the flowers are smaller in size. The flowers borne on short stalks are self coloured and include white, blue, violet-blue, yellow, apricot and ruby.

Viola odorata: Common Names: Sweet Violet; Family: Violaceae

These are small herbaceous perennials prized for their sweet-scented flowers. The plants are trailing in habit with round leaves and bear single or double flowers in shades of white, blue and purple.

Zinnia elegans: Common Name: Zinnia; Family: Asteraceae

It is a popular garden annual and varies in height from very dwarf to tall types. As a result of intensive breeding various flower forms-single, semi-double and double varying in size from 2.5–15 cm across, have been obtained in various colours such as white, cream, primrose, golden-yellow, orange, scarlet, crimson, pink, lilac, purple and chocolate.

Zinnia linearis: Common Name: Zinnia; Family: Asteraceae

This is a perennial zinnia with neat, bushy erect habit, up to 30 cm tall, producing bright golden-yellow flowers, 3-5 cm across with a dark centre and stripes of lighter shade. There plants flower during the summer and the rainy season.

Flower Seed Production

Flower seed production has better returns. Seed production of flowering annuals requires constant attention, in-depth knowledge, skill and specialization. Developing flowers in new attractive forms and colours are possible. With such an advancement, production and marketing of flower seeds have assumed international importance. In U.S.A and Europe, the climatic conditions during winters in open are unfavourable for seed production. Therefore, many seed companies from the USA, UK, Holland, Germany and France have started their flower seed production in India which in turn are getting the seeds produced on contractual basis from farmers in different regions having favourable climate conditions. Mostly open-pollinated cultivars have been adopted by the growers. In India about 600-800 ha area is under seed production. Of the total production, Punjab alone contributes for 45-50% Sangrur, Ludhiana and Patiala are being major seed producing centres. The rest is contributed by Karnataka (Bangalore and Ranebennur), West Bengal (Kalimpong and Tarai area), Jharkhand (Ranchi), Maharashtra (Pune), Haryana (Panipat and Sirsa), Himachal Pradesh (Kulu Valley) and Jammu and Kashmir (Srinagar Valley). Since production of seasonal flowers is mainly labour dependent, surveillance is absolutely necessary to ensure good returns. The production of flower seeds is divided into 3 climatic zones. They are:

a) Mild areas: *Antirrhinum, Calendula, Chrysanthemum, Clarkia, Godetia, Phlox* and *Viola.*

b) Subtropical area: *Portulaca, Petunia, Celosia, Dianthus.*

c) Tropical areas: *Ipomoea, Tagetes, Zinnia, Salvia.*

For successful flower seed production, the pollination behaviour of a particular crop is necessary. On the mode of pollination there are three type of flowers :

a) Self pollinated flowers: The isolation distance for this type of flower is 2 m. Flowers which comes under this group *are Dianthus chinensis, Dianthus caryophyllus, Dianthus barbatus, Lathyrus odoratus* and Lupins.

b) Often cross-pollinated: The isolation distance for this type of flower is 100 m. Flowers which comes under this group are *Antirrhinum, Godetia, Larkspur, Linaria, Lobelia, Petunia, Phlox, Salvia, Verbena* and *Viola tricolor.*

c) Cross-pollinated: The isolation distance for this types of flower is 400 m. Flowers which comes under this group are *Althea rosea, Alyssum, Calendula, Celosia, Centaurea, Chrysanthemum, Clarkia, Cosmos, Coreopsis, Gaillardia, Gomphrena, Helianthus, Helichrysum, Iberis, Impatiens, Portulaca, Tagetes, Nasturtium* and *Zinnia.*

Climate and Soil

The flowers can be cultivated in a variety of climatic conditions. They can be grown in a variety of soil but sandy-loam soils with medium fertility and adequate water holding capacity are ideal for seed production. In heavy and clay soils, the root system does not develop vigorously. Sandy and clay soils are not ideal. Water carrying various plant food materials in solution from a root to stem may drain out too soon from sandy soils, creating a drought.

Cultivation

Raising nursery: The most popular and practiced method to grow annuals is from seeds. Some annuals and perennials treated as annuals can be propagated from cuttings. They are *Ageratum, Coleus, Petunia* and marigold. Some annuals such as sweet peas, balsam and sunflower are sown directly. Their seeds are sown in 1 m wide and 20 cm raised nursery beds prepared after mixing equal quantity of garden soil, sand, well-decomposed farmyard manure and powdered leaf mould. The seeds should be sown in lines 4-5 cm apart. Cover them with a fine leaf-mould mixture upto a half to 1 cm. The water should be applied with a sprinkler, using a fine hose till the establishment of seedlings. The seeds germinate 3-4 days in summer and 5-8 days in winter. The seedlings having 2-3 leaves become ready for transplanting 20-30 days after sowing in summer and 30-40 days in winter. The plants like *Vinca* require pricking. This is the operation in which the seedlings are thinned out from nursery bed and again planted in another bed before planting in the field.

Planting: Well-rotten farmyard manure should be mixed @ 50 tonnes/ha, 1 month before transplanting of seedlings in the field. After proper ploughing and leveling the field, the seedlings should be planted preferably during late evening or on cloudy days. The distance for tall annuals should be 60 cm × 45 cm, for medium height annuals 45 cm × 45 cm and dwarf annuals 25 cm × 25 cm.

Aftercare: Generally crops require 3-4 and 4-6 hoeing during winter and summer seasons respectively. The flower crops need light and frequent irrigations. Irrigation should be given after 4-5 days during summer and 7-10 days in winter. The irrigation should be restricted at the time of seed ripening. Regular visits at different periods of the days are required to ensure good health of plant and better yields. The application of N@ 100 kg/ha is beneficial in improving the seed yield in *Coreopsis, Gaillardia, Helichrysum* and *Balsam*. The full dose of urea should be given in 2 splits, first at two months after transplanting followed by irrigation and second about one month after the first application.

Insect-Pests and Diseases

Common insect-pests of annuals are *Heliothis* spp. and aphids. The *Heliothis* spp. generally attacks *Helichrysum, Antirrhinum, Coreopsis, Dianthus* and *Cosmos*. The caterpillars can be controlled by spraying of Thiodan 35 EC/litres/ha. The common host plants for aphids are stock, *Nemesia, Calendula* and *Alyssum*. Spraying of Rogor 30 EC or Metasystox 25 EC 2.5 ml/litre is effective to control aphids.

The diseases caused by viruses are incurable. Only regular check and removal of affected plant parts control their further spread. The diseases caused by fungi and bacteria can be controlled to a great extent if they are diagnosed properly. Damping off is most common disease at the seedling stage. Seed dressing with Bavistin (1g/kg) or Captan (3g/kg) controls it. Drench the infected nursery beds with Captan (0.2%) or Bavistin (0.1%). Stem-rot of many plant tissues caused by fungi and bacteria is another common disease.

Postharvest Management

Generally rainy and summer season annuals bloom 50-60 days after planting. Their harvesting starts 20-30 days after flowering. However, in winter season annuals, the juvenile phase is longer, the plants bloom 90-120 days after transplanting. This time slightly varies from crop to crop and region to region depending on climatic conditions. Harvesting is a very critical stage in flower seed production. The pods are harvested individually by hand with sickle when the pod colour changes from green to dark brown and when it shows the signs of slight splitting and drying. The flowers are produced in a succession of about 30-60 days or even more. They mature at different times, resulting in seed harvesting at different intervals. The pods are spread over tarpaulin in a well-ventilated room for a week and reshuffled daily. The seeds are sieved with different types of sieves of iron mesh/plastic mesh and finally cleaned by hand winnowing or using a table fan to separate out light seeds and dust particles. The yield of flowering seed depends mainly on cultural and management practices. The returns from their seed production are quite remunerative compared to traditional crops. Net returns range from Rs 25,000-75,000/ha depending on the nature of crop, skill of management and seed collection. The seeds after proper cleaning are packed in HDPE bags and kept in shady and well-ventilated rooms.

The techniques of seed production of some of the annuals are given below:

Alyssum saritimum: The blooming in Alyssum continues till April-May in the plains of North India. In its annual growth, flowering and seed set run concurrently. Because of bushy and dwarf nature, this is ideal for planting in pots and beds. For better seed production, planting during October end to first week of November improves seed yield. The plants should be planted 30 cm × 20 cm apart in flat beds in sandy soils or on raised beds of 60 cm width and 10 cm height in heavy soils. The peak flowering period is February end to mid March. The seeds should be harvested during first fortnight of April only once or twice. The lower branches of plant mature early. They should be harvested when the branch colour is green. The second harvesting is done at the maturity of seeds. The harvested branches are placed in shady and well ventilated place for a week. Regular reshuffling is done to hasten drying of seeds. Simple crushing with hands and winnowing help separate their seeds. The seeds are passed through a muslin cloth to remove their dust. Thus the seed yield of 125-150 kg/ha is obtained.

Coreopsis lanceolata: Seed production of tall varieties are preferred due to ease in collection. The height and spread of well grown plants at seed harvesting stage varies from 90-100 cm and 70-80 cm. Generally one plant produces 15-20 primary/main branches, producing 4-5 flowers each. The seedlings should be planted in flat beds at a spacing of 60 cm × 45 cm during second fortnight of November till December end. The plants planted in December do not grow so vigorously compared to those planted in November, ultimately reducing the seed yield. The flowering starts from first week of April and continues till May end. Flowers are continuosly produced afterwards. Due to more temperature by June end, the flower size becomes very small and cross-pollination is not so effective. The seed is ready for harvesting in last week of April. The harvesting continues till first week of June during clear weather. The seeds are produced in a cup shaped pods which at early stage of development is tightly closed. It advances towards maturity, it loses the quality. The individual pods are picked by hand in the beginning (till May), but in June, the plant are harvested and staked in shade over tarpaulin. The seed shattered in the field is collected with broom. The seed yield varies from 5-5.5q/ha.

Coreopsis tinctoria: The flower size in this species is smaller than *Coreopsis lanceolata*. Flowers are produced in a group of 20-25 on the terminal of a branch. Dwarf varieties are used for garden displays and tall ones for seed production. Its plant bears 18-25 branches which produce secondary branches bearing flowers. A fully mature plant attains a height of more than 1 m. the plants bloom by March end and remain in blooming till mid June. The flowers produced after that period set low seed and that too of poor quality. The inflorescence is harvested with a sickle when it matures, petals drop down and pods give a dry look. Harvesting duration is longer than *Coreopsis lanceolata* which usually goes till June end and delays the planting of other rainy seasons crops. However, rainy season annuals for seed production can be best planted after this crop. The yield of clean seed varies 5-6.25 q/ha.

***Cosmos* spp.:** These are planted as rainy season annuals. The plants bloom 40-50 days after transplanting. Seeds of *Cosmos sulphureus* are mature for harvesting after mid September and harvesting continues till October end. However, in *Cosmos bipinnatus*, the flowering starts in September end and continues till November. The seed setting occurs from October to mid November. The harvesting continues till first week of December. The seeds are bold and oblong. They are individually fixed on the receptacles. They are picked by hand when seed colour changes to dark brown and flower stalk gets dry. The seed lot containing inert matter is blown off by a fan or hand winnowing. The seed yield ranges 187-375 kg/ha depending on time of planting and climatic conditions.

Escholzia californica: The seeds are directly sown by November end in lines 45 cm apart on raised beds. First hoeing is done to remove weeds and extra plants 15-20 days after planting, maintaining plant to plant distance of 30 cm. Flowering starts during February end, the peak flowering being in March end. The seeds are enclosed in a legume of size 5-7 cm. At harvesting, the legumes turn yellowish-green having some moisture. The seeds turn black. Slight delay results in an immediate splitting. The legumes are harvested individually with a sickle from March end to April end. The cleaning of seed is very simple. The harvested legumes are placed in shade for 3-4 days and reshuffled with hand everyday. It results in splitting of legume and seed shattering. Then seeds are cleaned with a hand sieve. Finally seeds are cleaned by winnowing. The seed yield ranges from 130-175 kg/ha.

***Gaillardia* spp.:** A constant succession is produced from May-July when planted during November end for seed production. The plant attains a height of 70-80 cm at flowering stage. For its commercial cultivation in heavy and clay soils, the plants should be planted on ridges 70 cm apart from the top level, maintaining plant to plant spacing of 60 cm but in sandy loam soils, planting is done in flat beds. The harvesting of seed starts from May end to July or before the onset of the monsoon. The seed collection should be done by wearing gloves at 6-7 days interval. There is no shattering problem. The seeds are kept under shade for one week. A light roller is rolled over seed balls to break them. Then this plot is sieved with a wire mesh of 1.7 × 1.7 cm to separate stalk from seeds. After that they are winnowed to remove the dust and dead light seeds. The yield of clean seeds are 5-6 q/ha, depending on the collection accuracy and weather conditions.

Helichrysum bracteatum: Tall and erect varieties are grown for seed production. For higher seed yield an early winter season crop is preferred. The seedlings should be transplanted during October end to first week of November 60 cm × 40 cm apart. The plants flower in the beginning of March, the duration of flowering being about 45 days. The receptacle containing seeds turn grayish brown at harvesting. The seeds from central line of disc begin to shatter on touching. The mature pods are plucked with hand daily from March end to April. The seeds carry hairy wings at the top. These wings help them fly away with the wind in April when stormy winds are expected almost everyday, leading to decreased seed yield. Hence daily harvesting is advised. The highest seed yield of 70-80 kg/ha may be obtained.

Impatiens balsamina: It is cultivated as rainy season annual in north-western plains of India. The first week of July is ideal time of its transplanting. The plants are planted in flat beds at a spacing of 30 × 30 cm in sandy loam soils. However, the raised beds should be prepared in heavy soils. The plants usually bloom 50-60 days after planting. The pods containing seeds are harvested when green pods turn yellowish green with pinkish tinge and the pod loses the moisture content. October is the harvesting time. Since seed pods are very susceptible to splitting due to delay, they should be harvested after every third day to ensure good yield. The seed yield varies from 250-310 kg/ha.

Monarda citriodora: It is long duration crop compared to other annuals used for seed production. It responds to single harvesting unlike other annuals. The transplanting of seedlings is done during November 45 cm × 45 cm apart. Plants grows vegetatively till mid April. The flowering starts in April and lasts up to mid June. The complete plants are harvested by June end before the onset of monsoon. The shape of flower is such that it holds moisture which reduces seed germination and also increases the labour cost for seed cleaning. For seed extraction, bunches of plants are held in an inverted position in hands after cutting. They are slightly shaken over a sheet of cloth to spread out the seeds. The seeds are cleaned with a hand winnower or a fan, the seed yield being 250-310 kg/ha.

Petunia hybrida: The plants bloom after mid March which lasts up to mid June. The seed harvesting starts from first week of April and continues till last week of May. This crop is very susceptible to seed shattering. Delay in picking may lead to even 100% loss. To collect the seed, pods are harvested individually when their colour changes to light brown and sepals are still green. This practice is followed for first 15 days. After that during peak harvesting period, the iron or aluminium trays are kept below one or two plants and the plant is slightly shaken once or twice a day on the tray so that fully ripe seeds may shatter on them. After the harvesting is over, the seeds are cleaned with a plastic sieve of a suitable size. Petunia seeds are cleaned from dust with the help of a fan or a cooler. Its seed yield varies from 150-175 kg/ha.

Phlox drummondii: The transplanting should be completed by mid-November to get the highest seed yield. The seedlings are planted at 45 cm × 45 cm spacing. First flower appears in beginning of March, the peak flowering being by the March end. The plants attain a height of 60-70 cm. A maturity, the seed pods arranged on the terminal of a branch, turn light brown. The branches are dried but still have some moisture content. This stage is visible during April-May. The branches are harvested with a sickle twice or thrice depending on their maturity. After one week, the pods are slightly crushed to separate seeds which are sieved with a wire-mesh. The entire seed lot is flown under a fan to remove dust particles. The seed yield is 375-480 kg/ha.

Tagetes species: *Tagetes patula* is usually preferred by the farmers because of the single type of flowers, bearing true to type seeds, whereas, in *Tagetes erecta,* a mixture of single and double flowers is obtained. The seedlings of *Tagetes patula* transplanted during July end complete their vegetative phase by September end. The plants remain in flowering from November to March. The seed harvesting starts from November. At this stage, the flowers and cypsela are dried. The seed cup contains black seeds. After keeping the seed stock under the sun daily for a week for a few hours and then in shade for one to two weeks, the seeds are cleaned by simple crushing, sieving and winnowing. Its seed yield is 375-500 kg/ha.

Verbena hybrida: Being a commercial flower for seed production, the nursery is transplanted during first week of November to fetch good returns. The flowering starts by March end. It is at its peak in April. The plants continue to bloom till mid June. These flowers do not have any significance since they do not set seed due to high temperature. Therefore, harvesting should be completed till mid May without any delay. It is different from other winter season annuals for seed harvesting. It needs only 3-4 harvestings depending on the maturity of flowers. The collected seeds are crushed by hand and winnowed to separate seeds. The yield of clean seed varies from 250-375 kg/ha, depending on plant health and harvesting.

Viola tricolor: Mid October is ideal planting time because maximum seed set occurs from March end to mid April. This species does not set seed on selfing. Therefore, flowers are cross pollinated by hand with the help of small camel hair brush when flowers are half to fully opened. The capsule containing 40-50 seeds is a united form of 3 boat-shaped valves which easily split at full maturity. So capsules are harvested with small stalk at yellowish green stage. The seeds turn light brown by that time. After that the pods are kept in shady places on a cloth sheet for about one week. The seeds are cleaned with a hand winnower, the yield being 60-75 kg/ha depending on the success of hand pollination and seed collection. The cultivation of this species is restricted only to a limited scale because of the high labour cost for hand pollination and seed collection. However, open pollinated species of Viola have been adopted by the growers for seed production. Its yield is 200-250 kg/ha if planted at a spacing of 25 cm × 25 cm.

Herbaceous Border

This is containing hardy perennial herbaceous plants which die down to ground level after flowering but put up new growth from the roots in the next season. In actual practice, it is quite common to include bulbous plants and annuals in the herbaceous border. Herbaceous border needs a good depth of soil and a sunny situation. The border may be placed against a wall, a fence, shrubs, a hedge or form a double border one behind another divided by a grass path. A border may be put to mark a division between one part of garden and another. It is always desirable to have a living background such as a hedge or a shrub but care must be taken to see that the roots do not interfere with the border plants. Therefore, shrubs and hedges having limited root spread should be preferred. If an informal design is desired, the border should have curved margins provided they are justified under the prevailing circumstances and is not just some thoughtless curves.

a) **Frontage:** The best frontage is a stretch of neatly kept lawn because this provides a good generally be not less than 2 m across. For a larger border, it may be 3 m. a paved brick or stone walk is considered the best. The edging, 30-45 cm of width between the border and grass may be constructed of paved stone or brick ground colour.

b) **Height and arrangement:** In a wide border, plants of all heights are recommended provided the grower can give enough attention on the staking of tallest plants. For a narrow width or double faced border, the maximum height should be limited to 3 m.

c) **Grouping and colour:** In a herbaceous border plants are arranged in bold groups. In an average sized border each group will come of 4-5 plants while in large borders it may vary from 5-7 plants. Planting a large numbers of plants in one group, particularly those which grow vigorously, should be avoided. Each group should be planted in drifts of irregular shapes than being put in box or round shaped drifts. Though generally the gradation in herbaceous border is from dwarf to taller placed towards the back. It can be broken here and there to avoid monotony or to formal look.

There are two extreme views regarding colour schemes. One group of gardeners feels that colour schemes should harmonize i.e., light shades leading to dark shades while dark shades leading to light shades while the other prevailing opinion is that nature never clashes. In olden times, the English garderns used to have exclusive borders of red, blues, yellows, pinks or even whites but today, with the problem of space very few gardeners can afford to have such a luxury. The arrangement of different colours varies with the taste of individuals but basically it is an artistic job. A basic study of the natural colours will be helpful in formulating colour schemes in the garden. The three basic colours are red, yellow and blue while the secondary colours are orange, green and violet. Red, orange and yellow are considered as hard or warm colours, whereas blue, violet and green are considered soft or cool. White, black and grey are accepted as neutral colours. The basic arrangement of colours in annual beds may be classified as:

1. **Monochromatic:** It is arranging different tones of the same colour either of the same species or in combination with different species.
2. **Analogous:** This can be achieved by using closely related or harmonious colours such as violet with blue and light blue with green and yellow with green or yellow with yellow orange. This may be done using either soft or warm analogous colours.
3. **Complementary or Contrasting:** Two opposite or contrasting colours-blue and orange, red and green, violet and yellow are called complementary. This can be sub divided further to split complementary colours (violet with yellow green and yellow orange) and triads such as red, yellow and blue or violet, pink and yellow. A contrast may be soft or warm.

The proper combination of colours is very important in annuals and the same is true in the case of plant height and time of flowering. The tall plants such as hollyhock, sunflower, tithonia and marigold are put in the background, antirrhinum and larkspur are coming next in order, phlox, dianthus (pink), sweet alyssum and Pansy are arranged next in accordance with their height while arranging the annuals in a herbaceous border, the time of flowering should be kept in mind. The late flowering types such as hollyhock should be sown atleast a month earlier than the early flowering sweet alyssum, otherwise, a part of the bed will look patchy if all are sown together. The annual beds should also harmonize with the other plants of the garden such as shrubs, trees, hedges and so on.

d) **Planting:** It is always desirable to draw actual planting plan on a paper according to scale and the scale should not less than 1:15. The drifts should be drawn showing the shape and size with the names of the plants for each drift inserted along with their height, colour of flower and time and duration of flowering. The plan is then taken to the site to form an idea by imagination how the plan will lock. Pegs and canes of same height as the plants to be grown may be placed in position and a rough idea made as to how they will look. After this, the final plan is made and actual planting is undertaken.

e) **Choice of plants:** The main aim of a herbaceous border in a temperate country is to have colour in the garden throughout the summer and the autumn, although in practice it is not feasible to have a mass of flowers during all that period. With careful selection it is possible to have a sufficient number of flowers throughout this period.

Annual mixed border

A border consisting of mixed annual flowers are called annual mixed border. There is hardly any difference in principle between a herbaceous border and an annual mixed border except that latter is annual in duration.

Mixed border

A mixed border generally includes herbaceous shrubs, sub shrubs, herbaceous perennials, bulbous plants and annual flowers which are arranged against the background of walls, ornamental trees or fencing.

Lawn

A lawn can be defined as the green carpet for a landscape. It is a basic feature for home ground development and an essential feature for any other type of garden. In a home garden a lawn improves the appearance of the house, enhances its beauty, increases conveniences and usefulness thus adding monetary value to the real estate. The lawn provides a perfect setting for a flower bed, a border, a shrubbery or a specimen tree or a shrub. Besides the material value, a lawn has its spiritual value, too. A lawn is the source of charm and pride and reduces tension of the mind after a day's hard work in the materialistic world. The view of lawn should be uninterrupted from the house or from the entrance. If the lawn is spacious, seasonal beds, herbaceous borders, beds of canna, attractive specimen trees or shrubs such as *Aruacaria cookie, Thuja, Callistemon lanceolatus* and *Brya ebenus* may be planted. Some bulbous plants such as Zephyranthes may be planted in groups in the lawn.

Preparation and Management

Lawns are generally prepared for ornamental and recreation. They vary in size from small green patches of home garden to large expensive turf of public park and botanical gardens.

1. *Selection of site and soil*

Sites having sunny situation and free from constant shade are more suitable sites for lawn. The soil should be fertile, friable, loam, well drained and atleast 7.5-12.5 cm deep. It should have deep moisture retentive sub soil. Clay soils can be improved by application of F.Y.M. without this treatment, clay soils should never be used for preparation of lawn. Water logged condition, alkaline and acidic soils should be avoided.

2. *Preparation of soil*

In the month of May and June, the ground is dug up upto depth of 45-60 cm and exposed to bright sun atleast for a week and if possible for a fortnight. This treatment helps in better aeration and inactivation of inert material, weeds and soil borne insect-pests and diseases. The soil should be turned over 2-3 times, every time breaking down clods and removing pieces of stone and inert material. A rough leveling is done simultaneously. The soil is mixed with F.Y.M. and watered 2-3 times at monthly intervals followed by weeding. The ground must be finally leveled either by using spirit level or by using level pegs (which are 30 cm long with pointed lower ends and 5 sq. cms. at the top. A straight wooden plank which is about 21.25 cm long and 12.5 cm wide, all the pegs are marked at 15 cm from the top).

3. *Manuring*

Before final leveling of ground about 30 cart load of well decomposed F.Y.M. or compost per hectare is to be incorporated in the soil and forked.

4. *Selection of Grass*

The most suitable grass for most parts is the doob grass (*Cynodon dactylon*) also known as hariali, arukampillu and durba in the vernacular. This goes by the names Bahama-grass or Couch grass or Bermuda grass. The grass thrives well under hot, sunny weather. This grass will not grow under shade. In Europe and America many grasses are used for the lawn, some of which may suit for our hill stations. The finer varieties are *Agrostis tennuis, Agrostis canina, Festuca ovina* and *Festuca rubra,* while the cheaper mixtures consist of perennial rye grass (*Lolium perenne*) and crested dogs tail (*Cynosurus cristatus*). The world meadow grass (*Poa nemoralis*) grows well under shades of trees. The 'Kentucky bluegrass' is one of the most sought after lawn grasses in the western countries which goes by the nomenclature *Poa pratensis.* This is also known as June grass. The grass is of very fine texture and gives a soft carpet like feeling when laid as lawn. The colour is blue-green. This grass may go dormant in the hot summer and to keep it green and nice heavy watering will be needed. This grass grows best in full sun. It makes a soft and superb lawn, especially in mild climates and can be tried at other places.

5. *Planting of lawn*

Seeding: This method is followed where grass is not available in the locality. The seed is purchased from a reliable firm. Before sowing the seeds, ground should be initially prepared, watered well and a final dressing of 4 cm thick with equal parts of garden soil and finally shifted leaf mould is evenly spread over the surface 12.5-20 kg of seeds per hectare, mixed with equal quantity of river sand or finally shifted garden soil is broadcasted evenly at anytime of year avoiding danger of severe rain but the best time is either before or immediately after the rains. After this the soil is raked gently for covering of the seeds. Seeds sown within two days of full moon produces better germination and growth of grass. After seeding, watering is done daily by a fine nozzle to keep the surface moist. After first watering a light rolling should also be done. The seeds start germinating 3 weeks after seeding. If the germination is poor reseeding should be done.

Turfing: It is quickest and most satisfactory method of lawn farming in tropics. The grass is selected from a place where it is short, compact and free from weeds. This grass is cut into fine turf or small pieces and spread on the ground where lawn is to be developed. The entire turf area is thoroughly rolled and watered.

Turf plastering: Mud plaster with chopped grass stem is commonly used for planting lawns. The grass root and stems are cut into bits of 5-7 cm long. Two parts of these bits, one part each of well decomposed horse manure and fresh cow dung + one part of loam soil are thoroughly mixed and prepared into a form of paste by stirring it with the necessary quantity of water. This mixture is spread evenly over the surface to be developed as lawn and leveled with the wooden board or block. After spreading this mixture, the surface is kept moist with frequent watering. The grass will start sprouting within 15 days and will be ready for mowing after 3 months.

Dibbling: The most common method of lawn planting is dibbling of grass roots. The grass used for dibbling should be selected from sunny situation. Well ripened grass with short internodes is lifted with the help of khurpi and dibbled erect on prepared soil having holes 7 cm apart. The soil is pressed thoroughly around the grass so that after watering grasses remain erect. After planting very light roller is passed over the surface and light watering is done at short intervals. The grass will take roots and will be ready for cutting after about a month.

6. *Management of Lawn*

Irrigation: The frequency of irrigation depends upon weather conditions. No damage is caused by irrigation while it is hot but less irrigation is required when it is cooled. Irrigation at 2-3 days intervals during summer and 8-15 days intervals during winter is sufficient. In rainy season watering is avoided. A rubber hose attached with municipal water pipe is a very efficient way of watering and is always preferred over flooding.

Rolling: Before first mowing, the lawn is rolled with light roller to depress the hard substances present over the soil surface. Except two rolling, the use of roller is discarded.

Mowing: Lawn should be mowed frequently enough to permit the clippings to remain, get decomposed and thus add nutrients to the soil. In addition, the clipping provides light mulch and has the tendency to permit the growth of weeds. The average lawn can be set to cut 3.75 cm long which is a right height for most of the grasses. Lawn should always mowed at the interval of 8-10 days and grasses should never allowed to form seed stock.

Manure and Fertilizers: The continuous loss of nutrients at regular interval due to the constant and regular mowing with removal of clipping requires manuring. A combination of both organic and inorganic manure is more suitable. A mixture of ammonium sulphate, super phosphate and potassium sulphate in ratio of 2:3:1@ of 6 g/m^2 once a month and 3-4 times from December and onwards should be applied. Ammonium sulphate is applied @ 3 g per 30 sq. cm. at bi weekly intervals at 3-4 times from February onwards.

Mulching: The practice of covering lawn with manure, leaves or straw in the fall to reduce winter killing in temperate region do more harm in tropical parts. Therefore, in tropical parts a 2-3 cm thick layer of equal decomposed, sieved composed and F.Y.M. should be spread as a mulch and this is done twice before the grasses are mature.

Weeding: One of the main aspects of maintenance is the control of weeds. Without close attention or care a time will come when weeds will overcome the lawn grass, the soil will become sick. Weed is common in both new and old lawns. Therefore, as soon as a lawn is established weeding should start and continue at regular intervals or whenever the weeds come out. The motha (*Cyperus rotundus*) is the most difficult weed to eradicate because of its deep root system. In freshly prepared lawn, the growth of motha is profuse and unless this growth is checked the weed will smother and hamper the growth of doob. This should be removed with the roots as deep as possible with a long narrow bladed (1-1.5 cm) Khurpi. It is almost impossible to eradicate motha completely. But, once the lawn is well established with regular mowing the growth of motha is kept in check.

Resting: Resting of lawn is necessary especially in winters. Most of the cricket pitches, hockey and football ground are given resting atleast for a fortnight in 3 months. Resting not only provide the greenness of grasses but it also helps in maintaining evenness and thick cushion appearance.

Control of Insects and Diseases: Some pests like earthworm, ants, moles and fungal diseases damage lawn in one or the other way and hence they must be controlled by suitable means. Earthworm can be controlled by application of 15-28 g of potassium permanganate crystals dissolved in 4.5 l of water for 1 square metre lawn area. Ants can be controlled by putting one tea spoon carbon bisulphate in each hill. Lead arsenate 2.3 Kg per 93 square metre is used for fungal control.

CHAPTER-6

SHRUBS, CLIMBERS AND RELATED STRUCTURES

Shrubs

Shrub is any woody, perennial, bushy plant that branches into several stems or trunks at the base and is smaller than a tree. It is different from tree in lacking a single trunk. Shrubs provide fragrance at nose level and beauty at eye level. Shrubs are an important feature of permanent landscape planting, being used for formal decorative groups, hedges, screens, and background plantings, to which they contribute pattern, colour, fragrance, or utility. In the natural style of landscape gardening they are simply allowed to grow untended but in many gardens they are pruned in the spring or winter for greater shapeliness and to induce more compact growth. The selection of different species and varieties of shrubs should be done according to the region, soil, climate and situation of planting. A large number of species and varieties of shrubs are available with a wide range of variations in shape, size, growth habits of plants and diversified types of flowers with different colours.

SHRUBS FOR TEMPERATE REGION

1. Temperate flowering shrubs: *Camellia japonica, Cestrum elegans, Fushsia hybrida, Hypericum ovalifolium, Weigela florida* and so on.
2. Temperate foliage shrubs: *Duranta* spp., *Euonymous japonica, Juniperus horizontallis, Spiraea japonica* and so on.

SHRUBS FOR TROPICAL REGION

1. Tropical flowering shrubs: *Ixora singaporensis, Tabernaemontana coronaria, Buddleia madagascariensis, Caesalpinia pulcherrima* and *Cestrum nocturnum.*

2. Tropical foliage shrubs: *Excoecaria bicolour*, Acalypha, Graptophyllum and so on.

SHRUBS FOR SUB-TROPICAL REGION

1. Sub-tropical flowering shrubs: *Bauhinia acuminata*, Bougainvillea, Clerodendron, *Gardenia jasminoides*, *Hamelia patens*, *Hibiscus rosa sinensis* and *Lagerstromia indica*.
2. Sub-tropical foliage shrubs: *Codiaeum variegatum*, *Ficus elastica*, *Fortunella japonica* and *Hibiscus variegata*.

Cultural and Management

Planting

Before shrubs are planted, the soil should be thoroughly prepared to ensure satisfactory rooting and growth of the plant. The size of pits should be approximately 60 cm × 60 cm × 60 cm spacing should be decided with due regard to the size of the shrub. A shrubbery border should be manured with a mixture of well decomposed cowdung and leaf mould, just after pruning and atleast once a year.

Training

Shrubs may be trained to a single stem and allowed to branch out and form a good head at a desired height. These are known as standards. *Lantana, Tabernaemontana, Lagerstroemia* and *Allamanda* are some of the common shrubs that can be so trained. Favourite budded rose varieties make excellent flowering standards. Standard and half standard shrubs prove very useful for the decoration of terraced lands.

Description of some important shrubs

Acalyha wilkesiana: It has copper coloured leaves. The plant is vigorous in growth.

Acalyha hamiltoniana: This species has green foliage with pale yellow or cream coloured edges.

Acalyha godseffiana : It is a small shrub with pale yellow leaf edges.

Acalyha illustris: This species has large, green and blotched leaves.

Acalyha macrophylla: This species is having red brown foliage.

Acalyha macrostachya: This species has deep brown leaves with deep pink streaks.

Acalyha sanderiana: This species has green leaves with very long, red flowers, borne on a drooping spike.

Adenium obesum: A very interesting plant from East Africa. The plant is unique in its growth habit. As the shrub grows the base of the plant becomes swollen. The leaves which are fleshy, have a pink mid-rib. The flowers which are pink bloom from March to December.

***Aralia* spp.:** Many species commonly known to the gardener as 'aralias' can be conveniently used under shady locations. The shrubs grow straight and produce few branches if left uncut. The leaves are small and round with wavy edges.

Asclepias curassavica: This is known as Blood flower. It is a small shrub producing interesting, small, yellow scarlet flowers. The foliage is thin and long. The plant grows well under shady positions.

Azaleas: They are small shrubs with few leaves on thinly spread branches. The flowers are large, having white, pink, scarlet, purple and other hues. This shrub thrives in cold climate and at high altitude.

Bauhinia variegata: This is a shrub of medium height. The leaves are pretty green with a double lobe, growing on thin, scanty branches. The flowers are white and appear during June.

Bauhinia acuminata: This is an erect shrub. The lobes of the leaves are pointed. The white flowers, which appear during March are very pretty.

Bauhinia galpinii: This is plant of low and thick growth. The flowers are brick red and attractive against dark green foliage.

Beloperone oblongata: This is known as Shrimp plant. It is a small shrub with angular branches. The dull green leaves are scanty but the long sprays of flowers with salmon-red bracts are very attractive. The shrub flowers throughout the year.

Breynia nivosa: This is a medium sized shrub with small, round thickly set leaves. The tender shoots have white blotches at the tip of the new branches.

Brunfelsia latifolia: This is known as Yesterday Today and Tomorrow. The medium size flowers appear almost all the year round but more profusely during summer. The blooms are dark blue or light violet when they appear but turn white the next day. The shrub prefers shade but grows well in open sunshine.

Brunfelsia americana: This species has white flowers that turn yellow when about to fade.

Brya ebenus: it is commonly known as Jamaica ebony. It is a tall shrub or medium sized tree with evergreen, small, shiny leaves and bright orange yellow flowers. It flowers from March onwards. When in full bloom it becomes an object of beauty in any garden.

***Buddleia* spp.:** They are noted for the ornamental quality of the foliage and flowers. They are good for creating thick shrub berries. The branches are long and drooping with pointed, narrow leaves which are green above and dull white underneath.

Calliandra haematocephala: This is a beautiful dwarf shrub with thin and narrow pointed leaves. The pretty flowers are delicate, resembling puffballs. The colour of the flowers is scarlet.

Calliandra houstoniana: This a taller shrub with scanty growth of branches. The colour of the flowers slightly differs from that of *Calliandra haematocephala*.

Camellia japonica: This is a tall shrub with thick growth of branches and leaves. The leaves are dark green and smooth. The flowers are double, waxy in appearance, with white or pink hues. They are suitable for high hills and cold regions and do not thrive well in the plains.

Carissa carandas: This is known as Karonda. It has a bushy habit. The plant is slightly thorny and has small pointed leaves. The garden variety produces small, rounded and pointed fruits. The white or cream and red colour of the fruits makes them very attractive. It is very hardy plant, useful as a hedge or screen and stands pruning and cutting well.

Cassia didymobotrya: This is a very attractive medium sized plant, with upright growth. The large, dark green leaves have broad, oblong and rounded leaflets. The yellow flowers appear on tall stalks. Their beauty is enhanced by the large, brown bracts. The plant flowers in winter.

Cerbera fruticosa: This species does not grow vigorously nor does it have any extensive branching system. The pale pink flowers shine out of the few green leaves and adorn the plant in almost all seasons. It is suitable for shady places.

Cestrum nocturnum: It is one of the most popular shrubs of the garden. The sweet fragrance of its tiny flowers pervades the night during the monsoon. It flowers three or four times a year and stand pruning well.

Cestrum diurnum: It is similar to *Cestrum nocturnum* with the exception that the sweet scent of the flowers does not pervade the night but spread during the day.

Cestrum aurantiacum: This species has orange flowers.

Cestrum elegans: This species produces purple flowers. It is better suited for cold climate.

Clerodendrum indicum: This species has very pretty white flowers with red base. When they bloom during the monsoon, hanging like tiny lamps on long strands, the shrub is at its best. This can be grown at shady position.

Clerodendrum thomsonae: This is a pretty shrub with a trailing habit and limited growth. The flowers are red and white, appearing during rainy season.

Clerodendrum inerme: This has a vigorous growth habit. Under the gardeners shears it remains in control and produces an evergreen, thick well set hedge.

Clerodendrum squamatum: This species produces red flowers in large clusters. Even the fruits look pretty after the flowering is over in March-April. It grows vigorously under shade.

Clerodendrum fragrans: This species has large, very green, smooth and shining leaves. The white bouquet of innumerable double flowers, slightly dark red at the tips, appears during the monsoon. It is a vigorus plant and grows in partial shades.

Codiaeum variegatum: This is known as Croton. It is a handsome plant with colourful foliage. The large leaves have blotches of red, brown, green, yellow, cream, pink and innumerable other colours blended artistically. There are forms with twisted, thin leaves, narrow leaves or very broad bluntly tipped leaves. These shrubs when grown in pots and arranged in porches or verandas, create a delightful display. They thrive luxuriantly in humid climate in partial shady locations.

Coffea bengalensis: This is a small shrub with white flowers. When the plant is in bloom during February, it produces a picturesque effect.

Crossandra infundibuliformis: This produces orange red flowers almost all the year round. It is a small shrub of hardy character with straight growth and small leaves. It stands partial shade and sunshine.

Datura suaveolens: This is a medium sized shrub with pretty long, tubular flowers. The trumpet shaped white flowers hang down artistically. The plant grows well under partial shade.

Dodonaea viscosa: This species has small, dark, shining leaves. It is a medium sized shrub useful for hedges. When the plants are closely grown and clipped well, they form one of the most beautiful hedges.

Dombeya spectabilis: This is a tall shrub with a large spreading head, with sparse foliage near the ground. The leaves are large and dull green. The pretty, pink flowers bloom in clusters during the cold weather. When in flower, the shrub is very attractive.

Dombeya natalensis: This produces large, white, fragrant flowers. The other white variety is known by the trade name 'Alba Magnifica', 'Lancasteri' and 'Gagiana' have blooms with pink shades.

***Dracaena* spp.:** It grows tall and straight and bears large, broad and pointed, colourful leaves on a single stem. The foliage develops a range of fine colours. The plant is suitable for pot culture and planning under shade.

Duranta repens: This is very popular as a hedge plant. When thickly planted, it makes an excellent hedge suitable for trimming and cutting. The small leaves and branches have a tendency to grow quickly when cut. The shrub is suitable for many types of climate and soil. There is a garden variety with variegated leaves.

***Eranthemum* spp.:** This consist of a group of shrubs which are valuable for their foliage as well as flowers. The variegated leaves have irregularly marked green, yellow, red or white blotches. The flowers may be brick-red, purple or maroon. These go by the names of 'Bicolour', 'Grandifloum' and 'Laxiflorum'.

Eranthemum nervosum: This is a hardy shrub of medium height. The blue flowers appear in spikes.

Eranthemum azureum: This species has flowers of deep blue colour. The plants bloom in winter.

Euphorbia pulcherrima: This is known as Christmas flower. It is well known for its beautifully coloured bracts. The shrub is of scanty growth with long, pointed leaves. The bright red bracts appear at the end of the branches during November. They continue to grow for two months or more.

Euphorbia mili: This is a dwarf thorny shrub with sharp spines growing all over its branches. The flowers are small and sparkling red. The leaves are tiny and green. The plant is suitable for dry places.

***Fuchsia* spp.:** They are medium sized plants, not very bushy in growth. The leaves are thick and green. The flowers are pink or pinkish white and red with single or double formation. These are suitable for cold regions and hills. They do well in pots. Many species of *Fuchsia* have extremely ornamental flowers.

Galphimia gracilis: This species bears a profusion of small, yellow flowers, practically all the year round but the blooms are at their best during the rainy seasons. The small, green leaves on the dark red, tender stems make the plant attractive even when it is not blooming.

Gardenia jasminoides: This grows to a good height if not distributed by unnecessary pruning. The waxy-white, scented, double flowers appear from March onwards. The dark green leaves are shiny and thinly set on the branches. The plant is useful for a shrubbery.

Hamelia patens: This a very vigorous shrub of spreading habit. The small leaves and orange-red, orange and green colours. The small, red fruits appear during winter. The quick growing, hardy shrub needs heavy pruning to keep it under reasonable control. It is useful for planting in a distant shrubbery.

Hibiscus mutabilis: This is a large shrub with large, green leaves. The flowers are double, white or pink. The plants bloom in October. It is a hardy plant for a hedge.

Hibiscus schizopetalus: This is known as Coral hibiscus. It is a hardy shrub having long branches clad thinly with dark green leaves of moderate size. The flowers are red with fringed petals and a well elongated central staminate tube. The drooping and hanging position of the flowers is an interesting feature of this plant. It is good for hedges and for live screens and it stnds cutting and pruning well.

Hibiscus rosa-sinensis: This is known as Rose of China or Shoe flower. It has dark green leaves and single or double, large flowers. The flowers have many colours ranging from deep red, bright red, yellow and red with white stripes. They appear throughout the year. The plant is excellent for a shrubbery, hedge and as a single specimen on the lawn.

Hibiscus syriacus: This species has white or purple blue flowers with single or double forms. Other colours include violet red, pink and deep purple hues.

Holmskioldia sanguinea: It is known as Cup and Saucer plant or Parasol creeper. It is a very interesting plant with trailing growth. The small circular flower red in colour has a peculiar formation. The plant blooms during October-December when the flowers fill up all the branches with their bright red waxy hue.

Hydrangea macrophylla: It is a vigorous shrub growing successfully in the hills and in cool climates. If grown in the plains, the plants do not attain any degree of perfection. Its large clusters of pale-pink or blue flowers are well set off against the broad, green leaves.

Ixora coccinea: This is called as Scarlet ixora or Rookmini. It is a shrub of medium height, with pointed, long leaves. The small, red flowers appear in large heads or clusters at the end of branches. The monsoon is the best season for flowers.

Ixora rosea: This species has pink flowers which bloom during the rainy season.

Ixora barbata: This species with white flowers blooms in summer.

Ixora undulate: This species has white flowers. These are scented and bloom in March-April.

Ixora fulgens: This species has large red flowers.

Ixora lutea: This species produces large clusters of yellow flowers.

Jacobinia carnea: It is a small shrub with very long leaves. The clusters of carmine-red flowers are borne on the top of the branch well above the leaves.

Jasminum sambac: This is known as Arabian jasmine, Bela, Motia or Mogra. It is small trailing shrub with white scented flowers with single or double forms. It flowers during summer and the early monsoon and is a good shrub for planting at a distance.

Jasminum multiflorum: It is known as *Jasminum pubescens* or Kund. It is a shrub of trailing growth. It usually flowers during summer and the monsoon. Pubescens is a trade variety which has pink colour under its white petal. All jasmines are hardy and can be easily cultivated in many localities.

Jatropha hastata: It is called as *Jasminum pandurifolia.* It is a hardy, medium sized shrub with scanty growth. The leaves are smooth, green and spatula shaped with tiny red flowers appearing in all seasons.

Jatropha podagrica: It is a small shrub with a curiously shaped stunted stem which is disproportionately thick at the base and thin at the growing points. The leaves are deeply cut. The cluster of bright red, small flowers appear mostly in the monsoon. It is very interesting plant for pot culture.

Jatropha gossypifolia: It is a medium sized plant, very hardy and suitable for growing under adverse conditions of climate and soil. The leaves and branches are dull red or dark purple turning to green under favourable conditions.

Lagerstroemia indica: It is a tall shrub, with scraggy branches and small rounded leaves. The purple crinkled flowers bloom from May to August.

Lagerstroemia rosea: This species has pink blossoms.

Lagerstroemia candida: This species produces white flower and suitable for shrubbery planting when other shrubs are used to hide the bare bases of these plants.

Lantana camara: It is a very hardy shrub, generally considered a weed in many gardens. The small leaves with cut margins and the tiny flowers borne in clusters are pretty. The flowers are yellow, orange, red, white, pink, purple or mauve. The varieties with yellow, red and white flowers are more attractive than others.

Lantana sellowiana: This is a trailing plant with purple flowers.

Lantana depressa: This is a semi trailing plant with yellow flowers.

Lawsonia inermis: It is called as Mehndi and is well known plant grown for its quality as a good hedge plant. The small green leaves and thick branches stand pruning well. To enjoy the sweet fragrance of its pale yellow or cream white flowers, it may be grown away from the main garden and left to bloom by itself without much inference. The horticultural variety Rubra has pale pink flowers.

Lochnera rosea (Vinca rosea): It is known as Periwinkle, Baramasi or Sadafuli. It is very dwarf shrub bearing flowers throughout the year. The small, pink or pink violet flowers fill up the dwarf bush with a profusion of colours. There is a white flowered pretty variety with a red dot in the centre.

Magnolia mutabilis: This is known as Jahuri Champa. It is a small shrub with large green leaves. The flowers are yellow and delightfully scented.

Magnolia coco or Magnolia pumila: This plant has white blooms. The plants are suited for cool places and for pot cultures.

Malpighia coccigera: This species has tiny green, shiny leaves with spines on them. The very small, pinkish white flowers blossom during the rainy season. If the plant is kept in shade, it may be flower any time of the year. It is dwarf plant useful for planting at the edge of shrubbery.

Malvaviscus conzattii: It grows to a medium height. The leaves are bright green and thinly set on the branches. The bright red flowers do not open but hang artistically from the plant in long buds. There is a variety with pale pink flowers. The plant is very hardy, grows well as a hedge and stands severe pruning.

Manihot esculenta: It is called as Tapioca or Cassava plant. It produces starch in its bulbous roots but the garden variety 'Variegata' is a very pretty plant with knotted yellow stems and deeply cut green and cream yellow leaves. It is hardy plant useful for pot culture and mass planting.

Murraya paniculata: This is also known as *Muraya exotica* or Kamini. It is an evergreen, tall shrub. The small, shining leaves and white scented flowers make it very desirable plant especially as a hedge or a screen. The shrub stands clipping well and grows well in sun or shade.

Mussaenda glabrata: This is known as Paperchase tree. It is a medium sized shrub of scanty growth. The dark green leaves contrast well with tiny yellow flowers, perched on a long white sepal resembling a leaf.

Mussaenda luteola: This plant has yellow leaf sepals.

Mussaenda erythrophylla: This plant has small yellow flowers, with bright red, leafy sepals. This plant is more attractive than the above two species. The flowers having coloured sepals appear during summer and the monsoon.

Myrtus communis: This is known as Vilayati mehndi. It is hardy shrub of very slow growth. The tiny leaves, not unlike mehndi emit fragrance when crushed. The shrub produces small white flowers and is useful for low hedge.

Nyrium indicum: This is also known as *Nerium odorum*, Oleander or kaner. It is one of the most common and hardy garden plants found all over the country. The thin straight branches have leathery, dull green and long leaves. The single or double, scented flowers appear in bunches on top of the growing branches, practically throughout the year. The flowers may be red, deep pink, pale pink or white. The tall shrub is useful for planting near the fence or as the screen.

Ochna squarrosa: An indigenous plant with tall growth habit also known as golden champaka in some localities, is a very attractive plant with bright yellow flowers. It is deciduous plant producing new leaves in March. The scented flowers open almost simultaneously. The fruits, which are small and black appear in clusters.

Oncoba spinosa: This is very tall evergreen shrub from Arabia is so called because it produces thorns at the leaf axils. The small leaves are reddish when young. The large flowers which are white are produced from April to August. The plant is useful as a screen or backdrop ion of any garden.

Osmanthus fragrans: This is also known as *Olea fragrans*. It is small shrub with scented flowers. The leaves are dark green and the small flowers are cream yellow appearing at the beginning of the cold season.

Pandanus sanderi: It is allied to the common Kevda except that it has long, green and creamy variegated leaves. It is very ornamental in pots and for mass effect when grown at a distance from the house. It thrives in poor soil and drought conditions.

Pedilanthus tithymaloides: This is known as slipper plant. It has varieties with green and variegated leaves. The latter is more attractive on account of its foliage streaked with pale yellow and green hues. Very desirable in a low hedge. It can be grown easily indoors.

Pentas lanceolata: This is also called as *Pentas carnea*. It is a small shrub with profusion of pale blue and pink flowers. Alba has white, Kermesina has crimson and Lilaciana has mauve blooms borne in large clusters.

Plumbago auriculata: This is also known as *Plumbago capensis*, Leadwort or Chitrak. It has trailing habit. The shrub grows very thickly, with thin twining and intermingling branches. The small leaves are dull green. The tubular, delicate flowers are borne in clusters of pale blue hue.

Plumbago indica: This species has red flowers.

Plumbago zeylanica: This species produces white blooms. It flower most of time but the blooms appear more profusely from October onwards.

Poinciana pulcherrima: This is also known as *Caesalpinia pulcherrima*, Peacock flower and Chhota gulmohar. It is a shrub or small tree of medium height with fine Gulmohar like leaves and leaflets. The plant has erect habit. It stands pruning well. The flower are deep orange, delicate and feathery. The buds and open blooms make a fine sight from May onwards. The shrub is at its best during the rainy season.

Punica granatum: This is called as ornamental pomegranate. It has double red flowers borne on straight branches. The leaves are small and shiny. The plant is fairly tall and bushy and is suitable for a screen which should be left uncut and undisturbed. The dwarf type is hardly more than 60 cm tall. It is grown as a curiosity in the pot.

Quassia amara: It is a tall shrub with thin branching habit. It is admired for its scarlet flowers, borne on long stalks at the end of the branches. The plant blooms practically all the year round.

Rondeletia odorata: It is a low shrub appreciated in our gardens for its small, deep orange and tubular flowers. They grow in compact, showy clusters at the top of the small branches during summer and in the rainy season. It is hardy shrub with slow growth.

***Rosa* spp.:** These are delightful plants bearing a variety of colourful flowers, distinguished by their forms and scent. There are some grown as standards and some thrive better as bushes. A few have trailing habits and are used as climbers on walls, pillars and arches.

Russelia equisetiformis: This is also known as *Russelia juncea* or coral plant. It is very graceful, dwarf, hardy shrub grown for its attractive red tubular flowers. The leaves are dark green, very small and thin growing on thin strand like branches which hang down. The flowers appear on the tender twigs almost from the base.

Russelia coccinea: This is also known as *Russelia sarmentosa*. It has larger leaves and smaller flowers. These are red or scarlet. The plant is erect.

Sophora tomentosa: It is a shrub of medium height. The foliage is green and delicate. The yellow flowers generally appear in the cold season. They are borne on long stalks at the end of growing branches.

Sophora secundiflora: It has violet or purple blue flowers.

Sophora viciifolia: This species has violet white flowers appearing in March-April.

Tabernaemontana divaricata: This is also known as *Ervatamia coronaria*, *Ervatamia divaricata* or Tagar. It is an evergreen, ever blooming plant with dark green, shiny leaves. The white double flowers are more profuse during summer and the monsoon. The plants are extremely hardy, would grow in any climate and soil conditions and are suitable for planting as a hedge.

Tecoma stans: This species is also known as *Bigonia stans*. It grows vigorously in many localities. The tall shrub has bright green leaves, thickly set on thin branches. The cut margins of leaves with their pointed ends bring a graceful form to this almost wild plant. The bright yellow, tubular open mouthed flowers impart a gay appearance to the tall hedge where the plants are most suitably planted as a screen.

Thunbergia erecta: This is also known as *Mayenia erecta*. It is a hardy shrub with small, thin and pointed leaves. The plant is in flower almost all the year round but bears more profusely in summer and in the rainy season. The funnel shaped tubular blue flowers are very handsome although their beauty is marred as they do not contrast well with the green foliage. The shrub can be grown as a hedge as it can be trimmed and cut without injury to the plant.

Climbers

There is hardly a garden that does not have a climber. A climber has to have a support if it is to display its charm of form, foliage and flower. An unsuitable or unsightly support can make the outlook of any attractive climber. A climber can be trained on a single, straight, durable post of wood, iron or masonry. It can spread its long and trailing limbs over an arch made out of any good material. A climber may make a walk under a pergola, shady and cool or it may cover a nice little bower. It may break the monotony of a bare wall of the house or become a screen and provide contrasting colours of foliage and flowers. In the absence of any support a climber may entwine its affectionate arms around any nearby tree even a babul tree. Posts, arches, pergolas, screens and other supports for climbers if erected without a definite plan would appear very much out of place. Their purpose should not be merely to support climbers but to add to the architectural features of any garden besides being functional. If the climber has to be trailed on a post, it should not occupy a central place and obstruct the view from the house. A series of well placed posts of wood and square or round columns of brick or stone 213 to 224 cm high along a path at the far end of the lawn or the garden supporting brightly coloured climbers would be delightful to the eye.

There are times when on requires a quick growing climber to screen an undesirable spot or enclose a garden area from prying eyes or perhaps to cover a trellis along a verandah. The popular, quick growing, blue, white or scarlet *Ipomoea*, the blue violet *Facquemontia*, the hardy *Quisqualis* and some species of Jasmine are suitable climbers for covering a bamboo or wooden trellis work. As these climbers grow quickly they require strong and durable supports. There cannot be an uglier sight than a rickety trellis bending and creaking under a heavy and unruly evergreen climber. There are two or three very fine climbers suitable for wall coverage *Ficus pumila* which sticks to rough or smooth walls and the *Bignonia* varieties which climb to great heights by means of their claws or hooked tendrils. Though *Ficus pumila* does not produce flowers, it tiny deep green leaves and dark brown branches weave an exquisite pattern against walls. The bright orange or light yellow clusters of *Bignonia* flowers create cheery surroundings around the house. There is hardly any picture that can be more attractive than a rose climber covering the front wall of a cottage.

All climbers become unruly consequently unsightly. Pruning of all climbers or creepers at least once a year is essential. The motto spare the secateur and spoil the climber should be the rule if one desires to grow well arranged attractive climbers in a well planned garden.

Description of some important climbers

Adenocalymna alliaceum: It is a climber of luxurious growth. The flowers, pale mauve in colour when blooming on a well grown climber present an admirable sight. The plant flowers all the year round.

Allamanda cathartica: It is one of the very common attractive climbers. The shining, green, pointed, thinly distributed leaves are a suitable background for the large, yellow and bell shaped flowers. This hardy plant can be easily grown as a climber on arches and as a shrub on lawns.

Antigonon leptopus: This species is also called as Coral creeper or sandwich Island climber. It is well known for its long spray of pretty pink flowers. Though small, they have a good mass effect. The long pointed crinkled leaves fall off at the beginning of the cold season. The flower along with the green leaves appear with rains. It is useful as a ground cover as it puts forth fresh shoots year after year from its bulbous roots.

Aristolochia elegans: This is called as Calico flower. It is the best of the many species of *Aristolochia* in cultivation. The brown green yellow flowers are among the most curiously shaped flowers of the world. The vine products flowers during the rainy season. A vigorous climber, *Aristolochia* is easily grown in any climate or soil.

***Arrabidaea magnifica*:** This is also known as *Bignonia magnifica*. It is climber of great charm. The small leaves are dull green but the flowers which bloom in the cold season are tubular and pale violet. They turn crimson when old. It is useful climber for arches and pergolas.

Asparagus plumosus: It is a very graceful climber suitable for growing in shade and in protected places. The network of pretty lacy leaves on the slender branches is very attractive. There are many species of Asparagus, all suitable for greenhouse planting and for growing in pots.

Banisteria laevifolia: This species has very curiously shaped yellow flowers. When it flowers during the hot and rainy seasons the effect is very impressive against the small, shining leaves which grow densely on heavily intermingling branches.

Beaumontia grandiflora: This is also known as Nepal trumpet flower. It is a climber of great vigour. When allowed to grow on high walls, straight tree trunks and garden lamp posts and the beauty of its foliage and flowers is well displayed. The climber has large and pointed leaves. The lily like white, tubular and large flowers are faintly scented. They generally appear from January to March. This is a picturesque hardy climber.

***Bougainvillea* spp.:** It is one of the most spectacular, hardy and easily grown trailing shrubs of the garden. The innumerable hues and tones of red, magenta, pink, orange, white as well as a variety with variegated leaves create a sensation in the garden.

Bougainvillea buttiana: It is a climber of vigorous growth with tender twigs, shoots and leaves which are hairy. The bracts are crimson coloured.

Bougainvillea glabra: As the name suggests is almost without hairs on its shoots and leaves. The bracts are magenta coloured. They are in bloom practically throughout the year. One of the old bougainvilleas it grows vigorously and is cultivated extensively in gardens.

Bougainvillea peruviana: It has mauve pink bracts. The twigs and shoots are not as woody as in other species. The foliage drops off in the early cold weather. This is one of the oldest species.

Bougainvillea spectabilis: It is a vigorous climber growing to great heights. The bract are purple or rose purple.

Campsis grandiflora: This is also called as *Campsis chinensis* or *Tecoma grandiflora*. It belongs to the large group of tecomas which have many beautiful vines and shrubs. It produces large, pretty, deep orange flowers in late summer and the monsoon. In certain localities it sheds its foliage during winter. It is useful climber for growing against the walls and on tree-trunks.

Campsis radicans: This is also called as *Tecoma radicans, Tecomaria capensis* or Trumpet vine. It is a shrub with trailing or climbing habits. The clusters of orange red, tubular flowers are very pretty against the dark green leaves of the plant.

Chonemorpha fragrans: This is also called as *Chonemorpha macrophylla*. It is a vigorous climber with woody stem. The leaves are leathery, broad, round and deep green. The flowers are creamy yellow turning to deep yellow when they are about to fade. They resemble *Plumeria* flowers and are heavily scented. The climber blooms during the hot months. It can be grown against tree trunks or on garden lamp posts. When grown on arches and pergolas need severe pruning.

Clematis paniculata: This is also called as Virgins bower. It becomes delightful vine when it is full of delicate pale white flowers. It blooms in summer and in monsoon the profusion of white, lacy, faintly scented flowers sometimes completely hides the small green leaves of the climber especially when it is grown in pots or trained low.

Clematis flammula: It has strongly perfumed white flowers. There are innumerable species of clematis more suitable for higher altitudes.

Clerodendrum splendens: It grows thick and produces dark green shining foliage. The leaves are broad and pointed and appear very ornamental when produced profusely. The large scarlet bunches of thin and long flowers appear in winter and often during the rains. *Clerodendrum* is a suitable creeper to grow over white coloured porches and pergolas. On arches it become unmanageable if not pruned from time to time.

Clytostoma callistegioides: It is also called as *Bignonia speciosa.* It is a climber with profuse growth. It supports itself along rough walls and other surfaces with the help of tendrils or leaf hooks. The leaves are not very large. The flowers are pale rose or lilac. This handsome climber blossoms in March-April and is ideal for covering large open surfaces or growing over a fence.

Doxantha unguis-cati: This is also called as *Bignonia gracilis, Bignonia tweediana* and *Bignonia unguis-cati.* It is a very vigorous climber reaching great heights over tall trees and high walls. The tiny hook like tendrils help this thin wiry climber in its great ascent. The yellow flowers appear during April and May and often in rainy season.

Ficus pumila: It is known as *Ficus repens* or Indian Ivy. It is a woody and hardy climber with small dull green leaves. It spreads along walls without any support. The aerial rootlets cling to the rough surface of the buildings. The plant does not flower but its beauty is in softening the architectural harshness with its dull green closely attached branches and leaves.

Hedera helix: It is known as English Ivy. It is a fast growing vine with many dark green pointed leaves. It grows well in the open in hills and also in conservatories or green houses on the plains but does not thrive under humid and hot climate. It does not flower but is useful in covering walls.

Hiptage benghalensis: It is also called as *Hiptage madablota* or Madhavi lata. It is well known for its sweet scented silky white small flowers. The long pointed leaves are green and shiny above with a dull green colour on its under surface. This hardy and woody semi climber blooms in February-April. It would grow wild and go out of control if not pruned occasionally. It is suitable for cultivating as a shrub away from the main garden or lawn.

Ipomoea tricolour: It is also known as *Ipomoea rubro-caerulea*, Morning glory or Heavenly blue. It is very vigorous climber that covers extensive areas in a short time with light purple branches. The leaves are large pointed and dark green. The azure blue or purple flowers appear in September-November. They fill up the whole area covered by the vine into a blue starred curtain. The flower fades in the late afternoon.

Ipomoea leari: It is a climber similar to *Ipomoea tricolour* in many respects. The leaves have three points. It is generally in flower during the rainy season.

Ipomoea carica: It is also called as *Ipomoea palmata*. It is the common hardy creeper popularly known as Railway creeper with purple flowers.

Ipomoea crassicaulis: Also called as *Ipomoea carnea*. It has flowers with pale mauve hue.

Ipomoea horsfalliae: It is one of the prettiest *Ipomoeas*. The five pointed, smooth, shining, dark green leaves growing on the profusely entwinged branches are very pleasant to look at even when this vine is not in flower. The deep pink small tubular flowers in clusters appear from September to December. It is very ornamental climber for pergolas and arches.

Jacquemontia pentantha: This is also called as *Jacquemontia violacea.* It grows very fast under many adverse conditions. The tiny, bell shaped, blue flowers and small pointed leaves combine to form an attractive plant material suitable for hiding rocks and trailing on wooden screens or white fences.

Jasminum officinale var. grandiflorum: Also known as Spanish jasmine or Chameli. It is a vigorous climber with pretty, green leaves, divided into small pointed leaflets. The white flowers with slightly tinged pink edges bloom like stars against the deep green of the foliage. The faint sweet scent of the flowers is pleasant. The climber blooms during the hot and rainy season. It turns wild if not pruned often and kept bounds.

Jasminum officinale: It is hardy climber with white, fragrant flowers. The flowers are produced in May-June and during the rainy season.

Jasminum auriculatum: It is also known as Jai. It is perhaps the most fragrant of all the jasmines. The flowers are smaller than of any other jasmine. When the plants bloom from July to October. The strong scent pervades the entire garden in the evening.

Jasminum primulinum: It is also known as Yellow jasmine or Suvarna Chameli. It is a hardy trailing climber with woody branches. The leaves and leaflets are dark green. The flowers are semi double and bright yellow, produced singly or in pairs along the entire length of the young branches during April-May and often during the rainy season.

Jasminum humile: It is yellow flowered plant of trailing habit. The single flowers are produced at the end of the branches. These are faintly scented.

Lonicera japonica: It is also called as Japanese honeysuckle. It is a hardy climber of medium growth. The branches are woody and covered with small, green leaves not very thickly set. The pale white, delicate, tubular, fragrant flowers appear in the cold season. The vine is good for arches and walls where light screening is needed.

Lonicera sempervirens: It has orange-red flowers without any scent.

Monstera deliciosa: It is also known as *Philodendron pertusum*. It is a shade loving climber or twiner of heavy growth habit. The leaves are very large and often perforated having cut edges. The aerial roots are thick protruding straight toward the ground. The plant produces a cream white longish fruit.

Monstera dubia: It is also known as *Marcgravia paradoxa*. It is similar to *Monstera deliciosa* in growth habit but the leaves are entire when young and deeply cut when plant becomes old.

Passiflora caerulea: It is also known as Passion flower or Krishna Kamal. It is a vigorous plant with extensive growth. The thin branches entwine extensively with the dark green shiny leaves. The leaves are five pointed. The flowers are blue purple or pale lilac with a very curious formation of all the floral parts. They are mildy fragrant. The climber blooms in the rainy season.

Passiflora racemosa: It is climber with red flowers. It is very ornamental when the strings of red buds and opened flowers hang gracefully from a pergola or a tree.

Petrea volubilis: This is called as purple wreath. It is a straggling, woody climber with rough ash green long leaves. The star shaped flowers are pale blue borne as long graceful sprays. It is a beautiful sight when the dark blue or purple corollas of the flowers shed all round the climber during March- April and at the end of the monsoon when the climber is generally in bloom.

***Philodendrons* spp.:** They are plants of climbing or trailing habit. The leaves are large, smooth and dark green. There are many species with attractive foliage.

Porana paniculata: It is also called as bridal bouquet when in full bloom covered with feathery sprays of white flowers. It is most fascinating during December. The large pale green leaves on the woody twines are completely covered when the vine has burst into a white lace curtain of fragrant flowers. This climber can be trained on tree trunks or on pergolas with great ease.

Porana volubilis: It is also called as Snow creeper. It is a climber with leaves and flowers smaller than those of *Porana paniculata.*

Pothos aureus: It is also known as *Scindapsus aureus*. It is a vigorous climber often reaching great heights when grown on the tree trunks. The leaves are very large blotched with yellow on green surface. A good greenhouse plant, it thrives well in shade and may be grown as an indoor plant in tubs or pots.

Pothos nitens: It root easily in water. They are often trained on indoor walls and windows and are erroneously known as money plants.

Pyrostegia venusta: It is also known as *Bignonia venusta* or Golden shower. It is one of the most spectacular garden climbers. The fiery orange curtain of tubular clusters of its innumerable flowers envelops pergolas and other features with a glow unparalleled in any colour scheme of a garden. The climber is in full bloom during January-February but it hardly attracts any attention when not in flower. It is hardy and is adaptable to any situation.

Quisqualis indica: It is also known as Rangoon creeper or Madhumalti. It is a very common hardy climber with fragrant flowers grown with ease throughout the country. The long green pointed leaves contrast well with clusters of white pink long tubular flowers. It is quick growing vine suitable for walls and arches.

Quisqualis indica var alba: This species has white flowers.

Quisqualis densiflora: This species has deep red larger flowers.

***Rosa* spp.:** Climbing roses are useful in training along the walls, pillars on pergolas, bowers and arches. There are innumerable varieties of climbing roses that grow with varying degree of success in various parts of the country.

Solanum wendlandi: It is also known as Giant potato vine. It is truly gigantic in its growth provided the right type of conditions is available. The climber with green branches spreads far and wide when planted near a shady tree or a pergola.

The many pointed, large, smooth, glossy leaves give an aura of everlasting freshness to the climber. The plant booms during the rainy season. The pale blue flowers are large, star shaped, turning dull white when fading.

Solanum seaforthianum: It has smaller, purple coloured flowers appearing in delicate clusters.

Solanum jasminoides: It is a small climber with small white flowers.

Stephanotis floribunda: It is also called as Creeping tuberose. It has small, thick, glossy leaves with white tubular waxy fragrant flowers. It is an interesting climber where light covering is desired. It growth is limited.

Strophanthus gratus: It is also known as *Roupellia grata* or Cream fruit creeper. It is a trailing shrub easily trained as a climber on a column. The thick green leaves offer a good contrast to the large white rose tinted flowers. The plant blooms during summer and the monsoon.

Thunbergia grandiflora: It is a climber with vigorous and extensive habit. Once it takes rot the rapidly growing creeper spreads thickly on the ground. The angular shoots produce bright green, large pointed leaves. The flowers are pale blue or whitish blue, large and attractive. The plant blooms from March onwards and is very good for growing on trees and for screening ugly sites.

Thunbergia mysorensis: This species produces yellow-red-purple flowers.

Thunbergia laurifolia: It is also called as *Thunbergia harrisi* and produces pale blue white flowers.

Trachelospermum jasminoides: It is also called as *Rhynchospermum jasminoides* or Star jasmine. It is a hardy vine of limited growth. The leaves are small and shiny green. The white flowers are few but fragrant and star shaped. They appear in March-April.

Vallaris solanacea: It is also called as *Vallaris heynii*. It is a very hardy climber or shrub with vigorous trailing habit. The leaves are small, green and thickly set on the entire plant. The flowers are tiny, bell shaped, white and scented. The climber blooms from December to April. It is most suitable for trailing on a wire fence and compound walls and for covering the greenhouse.

Vernonia elaeagnifolia: It is a very hardy quick growing climber. The small, dull green leaves or long strands land like a screen when grown on tall walls and wire fences. The flowers are inconspicuous and green white. The climber is very useful for growing on tall trellis and is used to ensure privacy. Other species are *Vernonia blanda* and *Vernonia scandans.*

Wisteria sinensis: It is a handsome climber producing violet blue or purple flowers. The long graceful strings of flowers cover the vine completely justifying its more common name, blue rain. It is suitable for cold climates and hill stations.

Shrubbery Border

Shrubbery is defined as woody or semiwoody perennial plants and grow upto height of about 0.5-4m. The plants are usually erect and bushy but some are decumlent or prostrate. These are the most important for gardens not only because of the large number of cultivated species but also due to their wide range of variation in shape and size of the plants, leaves, growth habit and size, shape and colour of the plants. Shrubs show great variation in height. Tall shrubs usually reach a height of 3-4 m e.g., *Hibiscus rosasinensis*. Dwarf shrubs are 0.4-1m in height.

Selection of shrubbery plant:

It depends on availability and duration of sunlight at the site of planting. Maximum height and spread of the plant, utility of plants and colours of flowers and season of flowering. Some important plants are *Ammonium magnifera, Calathea lindenian, Helicona, Musa coccinea* and *Pitcairnia.*

Principles of Planting:

In the planting of shrubbery following points should be remembered:

1. The shade of trees should as far as possible avoided. Very few shrubs well in shade. Therefore, to have the shrubbery at least 4.5-6 m in front of the boundry line of trees.
2. If the shrubbery line is kept in front of and clear of the boundry trees a very pleasing effect will be obtained which will give an amazing idea of space.
3. The best results are to be found in shrubs facing east and south.
4. Allow greater width where greater height is wanted.
5. Greater height is necessary in shrubberies, a good distance away from the house.
6. Use the shrubbery to hide ugly land marks such as vegetable gardens, tennis court.
7. Use the shrubbery to limit gardens in large compounds which cannot for any season be entirely brought under cultivation.

8. The width of a shrubbery should invariably be dictated by the height that is required. A reasonably good effect with a height of 5m can be obtained with two or three rows of shrubs planted in a bed of average width of 4 m.
9. Having determined a good width, a simple way to secure outline is to determine the line of compound boundary but should be at least 1 m clear of the boundary wall.
10. It is always safe to plant shrubs during early monsoon. In the two or three months of rain, it will not only establish but also start new growth and such plant thrives much better in the hot months of the year. Water logging for few days or very wet soil adversely affected growth of most of the garden plants and a well grown shrub plants can not be obtained in such a place. *Hibiscus, Plumbago* etc. do not even survive in a poor drained soil. Bougainvillea produce only vegetative growth in such conditions. In a line two or more plants of same variety adjacent each other. Grouped in this way, the shrubs stand out more clearly and their beauty and colour are more imprecise. Plants which will grow above 15 metres, it is recommended to dig pits 0.7 to 0.7 m and mix 4.5-6 kg of well rotten manure and raise the soil of the pit to about 20 cm from the ground level.
11. In Shrubbery, plants are planted on a long sturb of land where taller shrubs are grown at the back with the medium sized more to the middle and dwarf ones at the front. In this design upper portions of all the plants in the shrubbery bearing flower become visible. Colour of flowers and time of flowering are also considered so that the shrubbery remains colourful throughout the year with bloom and foliage.
12. Distance of planting in a shrubbery depends on the size of plants. Tall and bushy shrubs are generally planted at a distance of 1.5-2.5m shorter plants with less spreading habit can be grown at a distance of 0.37 m before planting the whole site for the shrubbery should be thoroughly dug and a few baskets of rotted cattle manure or compost added to the pit for each shrub. This distance between tall and intermediate shrubs should be about 45 cm. Method of preparation of beds are made according to colour e.g., First bed is of red flower, second is of blue or white flower. Tall shrubs are planted in front. Behind the tall shrub, medium and the dwarf shrub are planted.

Pruning

The removal of any part of a plant is termed as pruning. This includes cutting of small and large branches, dry flower spikes and cutting of root etc. Pruning encourages growth of new healthy shoots which bear more flowers and fruits that on an old branch. A shrub not only grows unusually tall and bushy due to constant production of week interlocked shoot which do not bear flower. It also become suitable home for insects. Shrubbery require constant pruning to keep them neat and in desired form. The purpose of the pruning will not be served if it is not done at the using time. Spring and summer flowers are usually produced in one year old shoots, therefore, be pruned after flowering. Shrubs which produce very quick growth during a particular period of the year usually stand heavy pruning. Varieties of Poinsettia and *Lagerstroemia indica* should be cut to about 30 to 40 cm and will produce shoots 1.5-2m in four to five months. Poinsettia should be pruned in early March just after the bracts have folded. If a smaller plant is desired they can be pruned second time in July. Varieties of *Lagerstonoemia indica* should be pruned in July after the leaves have fallen.

Plant Propagation

There is a large number of species and varieties of shrubberies plant. They can be propagated by different method.

Seeds: Several species and varieties of shrubs which produce seeds and the seedling flower with in a year or two without changing the character e.g., *Cassia, Glauca, Cassia bicerpoulain, Thrvallis glauca* and *Tecoma slans*. Though these shrubs requires a longer time to produce flower are propagated from seeds as they do not root easily from cuttings and layerings. These shrubs are slow growing and it has been found that root injury at the time of transplanting adversely affects the growth. It is thus suggested to sow one seed in a 10 cm pot and after the seedlings have grown about 10-15 cm high they are planted in a ground or in a bigger pot. *Barleria, Duranta* and *Dodonoea viscosar* are grown both from seeds and cuttings.

Stem cutting: A large number of shrubs root from stem cutting. Survival of stem cutting depends on the quality of the root system. *Abutilon, Angelonis, Cestrum* and *Buddlea* are easily propagated through stem cutting.

Layering: Both air layering and ground layering are practiced. *Tecona gaudichaudi, Randiamar cronta, Pootia grandipra* and *Quassia miniva* are propagated by air layering. Shrubs which have thin bark and rough wood and do not root well from stem cutting are usually propagated by ground layering e.g., *Daffordil* and *Hibiscus rosasinensis*.

Grafting: *Petrea arberea*, a large blue flowering shrubs does not root easily from layers and the percentage of survival is also low. It is grafted on the *Petrea volubilis* and the union takes place in a month. Budding has also been successful in several varieties of Bougainvillea.

Hedges

A hedge is a series of a plant grown in a straight line or a smooth curve to serve as a barrier or screen. It provides a natural background to a garden like a frame to picture. It may be external or internal. An external hedge is tall and may replace the compound wall. It also serves as a wind protection. It may be 1.5-2.5 m high. The internal hedge would separate one part of the garden from the others and is not so tall. It may vary from 30 to 90 cm. Hedges may be of deciduous or evergreen plants. They may be flowering plants also. Where a hedge is required immediately as a screen or windbreak, it should be quick growing, tall and evergreen.

Essentials of a good hedge

The essentials of a good hedge are that it should be thick and dense. It should have foliage from the bottom to top. It should be trim and neat and if it is a flowering hedge its bloom should not clash with the general colour scheme.

To achieve a shapely, attractive hedge fulfilling its role the following cultivation practices are recommended:

a) Soil may be dug at least two spits deep and 60 cm wide. In case of tall hedges of 2.7 m, the soil may be dug three spits deep and 90 cm wide. It should be well drained. The soil mixture should be rich with organic manure and leaf mould. Top dressing of bone meal is helpful. Deep placement of manure encourages deep growth of roots which allow hedge plants to grow erect and vigorous.

b) Soil may be enriched annually by adding organic manure and bone meal.

c) If placed along the fencing, it should be at a distance of atleast 45 cm from it to provide room for its side growth.

d) It may be planted closely subject to cost limitations. A double hedge in which the plants are staggered diagonally is preferable to single rowed one. Plant 20 per cent extra cuttings or retain extra seedlings in a corner for replacement. It prefers a spacing of 15-20 cm for cuttings and 20-30 cm for rooted plants.

e) Frequent pruning prevents the hedge from becoming thin and woody. Frequent light pruning is better than hard pruning done seldom. In the growing season it may be necessary to clip it at least 3-4 times till full growth is reached. Pruning is mainly for encouraging bushy growth. After it attains the desired height pruning is mainly for shape. The type and frequency of pruning will depend on the variety. A fast growing variety needs more frequent and hard pruning than slow growing ones. Do not prune until plants are well established.

Some important hedge plants

Acalypha: Many species are used as hedges but species such as *Acalypha tricolour* does not stand pruning well. *Acalypha hamiltoniana, Acalypha wilkesiana* var. *musaica* and other small leaved species can be trimmed regularly to form ornamental hedges. The tall species can be used as protective hedge. Cuttings are planted 25-30 cm apart.

Aralia: Different species are used as ornamental hedges.

Barleria: Different species with their beautiful flowers subject themselves to be trimmed to beautiful hedges. Plants are 60-100 cm high. Rooted cuttings are planted 20-25 cm apart.

Bauhi:ia acuminata: It can be trimmed to a nice hedge which looks more beautiful with its white flowers.

Bougainvillea: *Bougainvillea spectabilis, Bougainvillea glabra,* Mrs. Fraser and Partha and some other cultivars form good protective as well as ornamental hedges withstanding frequent trimming. Planting is done at 60-90 cm spacing and the plants are trained against barbed wire or wire trellis and the shoots including side shoots are trimmed to form bushy appearance. Plants without support can also be trained but supported hedge looks neat.

Caesalpinia pulcherrima: It should be pruned tall, harder pruning forces it to ageing faster. The plant flowers freely.

Carissa carandas: A throny bushy shrub which is used as an effective protective hedge. Seeds are sown 60-75 cm apart in single row. Cuttings also root easily.

Casuarina equisetifolia: This is a tree of Casuarinaceae family with very fine feathery branches resembling thin long leaves. This hardy and graceful tree, if left by itself grows to a great height. When its seedlings are planted about 60 cm apart in rows and at a distance of 60-90 cm, they make an excellent hedge capable of being trimmed to many shapes and forms.

Casuarina coriaria: It is a leguminous tree with graceful spreading habit and is useful for making garden hedges. The flowers of this tree resemble small puffballs. Young plants taken out of the nursery are planted about 60 cm apart in single or double rows. They are clipped every now and then to make a thick hedge.

Clerodendrum inerme: This is a indigenous hardy shrub which is easy to grow and stands severe cuttings or pruning throughout the year. It can be grown by cutting all the year round except when the climate becomes too hot and dry. If left uncut for a long time, it produces a large number of semi trailing branches which get entwined and form a strong barrier. The delicate white flowers of this verbenaceous plant borne on the branches rather sparsely are not so attractive.

Daedalacanthus nervosus: It forms an ornamental hedge which is generally 30-45 cm high. Cuttings are planted 20-30 cm apart in double rows separated by same spacing.

Dodonaea viscosa: It is a medium sized shrub of the Sapindaceae family, with shiny, simple leaves and woody branches is a plant which is grown from seeds for planting new hedges. The seed is sown *in situ* as the plant does not stand transplanting. It forms a well clippers, dark grey background to flower beds full of colourful plants. The only serious defect of this plant is that it is susceptible to a soil borne disease which dries out well established plants in a short time leaving an ugly gap in an otherwise well tended hedge. If it remains uncut for some time produces small flowers and winged seeds.

Duranta repens: It is also called as *Duranta plumieri.* It belongs to verbenaceae family, is equally good for growing as a garden hedge. This plant, if left by itself as an individual shrub or as an uncut hedge produces small golden orange fruits after the flowers fade out. The fruit contains a few hard seeds which should be planted as freshly as possible to obtain new plant. Some varieties of *Duranta* have white flowers or spines on their branches like *Duranta repens* var. *alba*. Some produce variegated leaves i.e., *Duranta repens* var. *variegata*. The shrub which is grown as a garden hedge is the easily cultivated variety. The white flowered variety of *Duranta* is also often used.

Eranthemum: Several species are used as ornamental hedge. Cuttings are planted 15 cm apart in double rows.

***Erythrina* spp.:** Many species of this genus can be trained into a good hedge by pruning and shearing.

Galphimia gracilis: A beautiful plant with yellow flowers which form a good hedge. The plant are planted 30 cm apart.

Grevillea robusta: An ornamental tree which forms a good hedge when planted closely and trimmed low.

Hamelia patens: A beautiful shrub which stands trimming and attains a height of 75-90 cm. It is planted 30 cm apart.

Lantana camara: This species make excellent hedges if planted judiciously. This trailing shrub of the verbenaceae family has many good qualities. It is very hardy and is able to resist drought. It grows quickly and without any special effort. This plant strands any amount of clipping and the rough prickly stems are deterrent to animals. It has pretty tiny flowers of various hues i.e., white, yellow, orange, scarlet and lilac are the more important among them. The yellow flowered *Lantana* with dwarf habit is suitable for hedges along roads or garden paths. The white flowered variety is suitable for growing as a background to many flower beds or as live screen. Its response to clipping is amazing. Even after severe pruning and trimming, *Lantana* produces flower in no time practically during the entire year.

Lawsonia inermis: This is also called as *Lawsonia alba* or Mehndi. It is very hardy and easy to grow shrub. The tiny shining leaves of this plant which belongs to Lythraceae, appear trim when grown as a hedge. If this plant is left uncut for some time it develops fine long sprays of dull white or pale yellow flowers which fill the atmosphere with a faint sweet fragrance. The small, round berries when dry give out plenty of tiny seeds which are often used to raise plants.

Murraya exotica: It also forms a good tall attractive hedge when properly trimmed.

Parkinsonia aculeata: It is a good hedging plant for the dry localities. It has ornamental foliage and nice yellow flowers.

Pithecellobium dulce: This is also known as *Inga dulcis* or Madras thorn. If grown singly, it grows into a big hardy tree bearing curiously shaped twisted thin green fruits with a white and pink pulp.

Poinsettia pulcherrima: It can be used as a beautiful ornamental hedge.

Polyalthia longifolia: It is one of the best among the trees which subject itself to be trained and pruned into a good hedge especially for screening and protection against winds.

Pongamia glabra: It is used as hedge especially in south India. The seeds are sown *in situ* or seedlings are planted 60 cm part.

Putranjiva roxburghii: It is another tree with ornamental foliage which is used as hedge.

Tecoma stans: It forms an attractive tall hedge within a span of two years with attractive yellow flowers.

Thevetia nerifolia: It forms good hedge especially for screening. It has beautiful flowers. Sometimes this plant is included in shrubs.

The other common flowering hedges are *Beloperone amherstia* with the perpetual rust coloured bracts overlapping small white flowers, *Buddleia asiatica* with grey green foliage and conical fragrant clusters of off white flowers, *Hibiscus* with its trumpet like bright flowers, *Nerium indicum, Plumbago auriculatum* and *Tabernaemontana.*

Edges

Lining of borders of flower beds, paths, lawn and shrubbery with brick, concrete and living plant is known as edging. Edging may be formal, made of stone, bricks and tiles or informal consisting of living plants. There are certain plants which are very suitable for edging purposes and these are known as edge plant. Edge plants, unlike hedges should grow very low as the purpose is not for screening but to provide a lining only for the purpose of decoration or demarcation.

Some important edge plants are:

Aerva sanguinolenta: A herb with leaves dark red above and paler beneath.

Alternanthera: The most commonly used herbaceous plant for edging. The species commonly used are *Alternanthera amabilis, Alternanthera amoenga, Alternanthera bettzichiana* var. *spathulata* and *Alternanthera versicolor.* The last two are very colourful, shaded red, bronze and pink. These are low growing and stand trimming very well. Cuttings are planted 3-5 cm apart in double rows spaced at 5 to 10 cm *in situ.*

Asystasia coromandeliana: A straggling herb which forms a good edging for shrubberies. It grows in shade. Flowers are white to pinkish. It should be trimmed to keep within bounds.

Cineraria maritima: A sub-shrub with a woody base, the whole plant is densely white woolly. This is good edge for red *Acalyphas* or similar shrub in shrubberies.

Coleus: Some dwarf coleus can also form edging to ornamental shrubs.

Echeveria: In the hill stations some species of *Echeveria* are used for edging rockeries.

Eupatorium cannabinum: A herbaceous erect plant which can be trimmed even to 15 cm. It forms a good green edge.

Iresine: The leaves are colourful differing in species from rose-carmine, red to deep blood red. The species are *Iresine herbstii* var. *brilliantissima* which has rich crimson leaves. *Iresine lindenii* in which the leaves are deep blood red.

Pilea muscosa: This species and some other species of *Pilea* are used for edging. *Pileas* are useful for edging rockeries. These are suitable for semi-shade but can be grown in the open in cool climates.

Topiary

The art of shaping a hedge in ornamental forms and figures is known as topiary. The figures may be of animals, fountains, pyramidical, cone shape and human shape such as a farmer with a pair of bullocks. It is an interesting garden feature but it needs a lot of labour in training of plant and after maintaining it. For this a skilful hand is necessary. Selection of plant for topiary plant should be perennial, slow growth rate, small leaves having multiple branches does not like by animals and less affected by plant diseases.

With the help of nails, stakes and wires the selected plant can be shaped.

Plants used for different shape

A. For plains:

1. For all shape such as animal, human beings and birds – *Clerodendron inermi, Duranta plumarai, Murraya exotica* and *Inga edulis.*
2. For Birds – *Gajurina* and *Poincerus trifolita* on chinese hajara.
3. For Umbrella shape – *Citrus mendurensis, Citrus arantium*
4. For round shape – *Diaspias embriopteris*
5. For pillars shape – *Thuja orientalis, Thuja compada, Cupresus* spp., *Polialthiya pendula* and *Polialthiya longifolia.*
6. For writing – *Aerua sanquinolenta, Alternanthera amabilis* and *Malpaighia coccigera.*

B. For hills:

Juniper, *Yew buxus* and *Cupressus macrocarpa.*

For shade – *Lingustrum privet.*

Arches

A garden may need some arches for training climbers or ramblers. Arches are generally constructed near the gate or over paths in the garden. An arch should be atleast 2 to 2.5 m high, so that the branches of creepers hanging down should not interfere with access. The breadth depends upon the path over which it is constructed but should not be less than 1 m. A general rule is to have the same width as the height provided space permits. The cheapest though not very durable method is to construct this supported on wooden poles. Over the poles longitudinal rails are placed and cross rails are fixed over these at intervals of 45-60 cm. The rails are fixed with the poles by driving in sturdy nails. The best method is to use angle iron support firmly grouted in the soil by concrete. The roof made of angle irons of different sections may be flat, arch type or angular with slopes on either side. The support can also be made of 7-10 cm diameter galvanized pipes fixed in similar way. On the top of each pipe a galvanized or steel plate (22.5 × 22.5 cm) with holes should be welded which facilitate the fixing of the longitudinal angle irons with the help of nuts and bolts or clamps. Galvanized wire nettings may be fixed on the sides of the arches to help the creepers to climb up. The portion of the wooden support going underground is painted with coal tar to prevent damage by termites. The angle iron and G.I. pipes are also coated with rust proof paints. The portion above ground should be painted green.

Pergolas

For growing creepers in a row pergolas are ideal structures on which these may be trained. A pergola may be defined as a series of arches joined together. Pergolas are generally constructed over pathways which add beauty to a garden. Like arches the support can be made of wooden or stone or brick pillars, angle iron and G.I. pipes. The supporting pillars may be connected together by wooden rafters or m.s. rods may be welded to the pillars. The roof may be made of angle irons of different sections with longitudinal and cross rails. Over this base strong galvanized wire mesh or welded mesh may be placed for the creepers to spread easily. The width of pergolas is kept generally within 2-2.5 m and the height is also the same but preferably on the higher side. The width may be increased or decreased a little, if necessary. The length will depend upon the area to be covered, the number of creepers available and of course the budget. The roof of a pergola may be flat or in the shape of an arch. As in the case of an arch, the pergola is also painted green to merge with the colour of the foliage. A pergola is a useful resting place during the summer months in a tropical country. The path below remains cool due to the creepers growing above. If the pergola, is wide enough concrete or wooden benches may be constructed for sitting. In broad pergolas it may also be possible to keep shade loving plants to protect them against sun but this may not be desirable all the time.

CHAPTER-7

TREES AND BIO-AESTHETIC PLANNING

Trees are considered as "the lungs of Earth". They are the botanical entities with perennial, tall and a conspicuous trunk. Trees come into existence about 50 million years ago and have a close association with mankind evolution. In different biotic zones different types of trees dominate which describe existing climatic conditions. Trees mostly bear the brunt of increasing population. Forests have been cleared for human settling and agricultural activities. Unjudicious felling of trees resulted into ecological imbalance, climate change, desertification and deterioration of soil conditions. Trees play important role in providing total living of this planet. They maintain balance between oxygen and carbon dioxide which is essential for the life of flora and fauna. Trees serve as natural air conditioner especially in hot and dry climates by increasing humidity around them through increasing transpiration, lower down temperature and thus change microclimate of surroundings. Trees regulate the rainfall and check the spread of desert. They are also the guardian of soil and check soil erosion by binding the soil particle with their roots. They improve the fertility of soil by adding organic manure in the forms of litter every year. To check the air pollution due to gases, dust, smoke, planting of trees is highly advantageous. Besides ecological importance, their economic significance cannot be overlooked. Trees provide us fruits, shelter, shade, fuel wood and timber wood for making furniture, ships and paper. Other economic products like rubber, gum and resins are also obtained from trees. Different plant parts of trees are used for medicinal purposes since Vedic time. Apart from all these virtues, trees have immense beauty from aesthetic viewpoint. They bring the change in skyline on account of variation in their height, shapes, foliage texture and flower colour. They are used in landscape plan for aesthetic and functional purposes. Trees are used in garden as specimen, avenue plantation, wind breaks and screening. A judicious planting of trees enhances the beauty of surroundings. As the trees are the framework of the garden, they should be easy growing, hardy and requiring little attention.

Planting of trees alongside the roads has a long history and Buddha Bhikshu was pioneer. Emperor Ashoka and Shershah Suri were well known arborculturists. Now a days increase in vehicular traffic made it compulsory to plant more trees.

Selection of Trees

This depends upon many factors which should be kept in mind when selection is done.

1. Purpose of Growing

A. Specimen tree: Such trees are planted singly for their attractive shape, beautiful foliage or for drooping branches which reflect humbleness, for example: the **unusual and attractive trunks** in *Adina polycephala, Acacia seyal, Barringtonia spicata*; **unique branching** in *Terminalia catappa*; **wild and vigorous root system** in *Ficus bengalensis, Sterculia alata*; **strange or unusal leaves** in *Ficus krishnae*; **twisted flowers** in *Couropita guinensis, Parkia filicoidea*; **strange fruits and nuts** in *Artocarpus heterophylla, Bixa orellana, Couropita guinensis* and *Kiglia pinnata*; all these peculiarities have a place in landscaping which can create focal point.

B. Flowering trees: These trees produce colourful and spectacular flowers and are planted for their beautiful flowers, for example:

Spectacular and rare flowering trees: *Amherstia nobilis, Baikiaea minor, Brownea grandiceps, Caesalpinia cacalaco, Colvillea racemosa, Gustavia angusta, Saraca thaipingensis.*

Ever Blooming Trees: The following trees produce flowers almost throughout the year, though there are seasons when the blooms come out in greater profusion.

Acacia auriculaeformis
Averrhoa carambola
Bauhinia monandra
Callistemon lanceolatus
Kleinhovia hospita
Melaleuca leucadendron
Mimusops elengi
Muntingia calabura
Plumeria acuminata
Solanum grandiflorum
Solanum macranthum
Thespesia populnea
Thevetia peruviana

Winter Blooming Trees: Some of the beautiful winter blooming trees are:

Bauhinia purpurea
Butea monosperma
Monodora grandiflora
Parkia africana

Caesalpinia cacalaco
Crataeva nurvala
Feronia limonia
Pithecollobium dulce
Protium serratum
Sesbania grandiflora

Spring Blooming Trees: The arrival of spring brings with it joy and elation. A large number of flowering trees bloom profusely, splashing the skyline with a riot of brilliant colours, for example:

Adenthera pavoniana
Amherstia nobilis
Bombax ceiba
Brownea grandiceps
Careya arborea
Ceiba pentandra
Cochlospermum gossypium
Elaeocarpus sphaericus
Erythrina blakei
Garuga pinnata
Gliricidia sepium
Grevillia robusta
Guaiacum officinale
Haematoxylon campechianum
Jacaranda rhombifolia
Mesua ferrea
Millettia ovalifolia
Moringa oleifera
Pachira insignis
Pterospermum acerifolium
Pterygota alata
Saraca asoca
Saraca cauliflora
Saraca declinata
Schinus molle
Schizolobium excelsum
Schleichera oleosa
Spathodea campanulata
Spathodea nilotica
Sterculia acerifolia
Tabebuia chrysantha
Tabebuia rosea
Tecomella undulata
Wrightia coccinea

Summer Blooming Trees: A large number of beautiful trees burst into attractive blooms with a wonderful array of varying colours during fierce hot condition of summer. Here are few examples:

Adansonia digitata
Albizzia lebbek
Barringtonia acutangula
Bauhinia tomentosa
Bauhinia variegata
Brownea ariza
Caesalpinia coriaria
Erythrina corallodendron
Erythrina cristagalli
Fillicium decipiens
Gardenia latifolia
Gustavia angusta
Holarrhena antidysenterica
Jacaranda acutifolia

Cassia fistula	*Lagerstroemia speciosa*
Cassia grandis	*Madhuca indica*
Cassia javanica	*Magnolia grandiflora*
Cassia nodosa	*Melia azedarach*
Castanospermum australe	*Peltophorum acerifolium*
Crataeva roxburghii	*Plumera acuminata*
Dalbergia lanceolaria	*Poinciana regia*
Dillinia indica	*Pongamia glabra*
Paterocarpus indicus	*Putranjiva roxburghi*
Syzygium cuminii	*Terminalia arjuna*
Terminalia bellerica	*Thespesia populnea*
Tipuana speciosa	*Wrightia tomentosa*

Rainy season flowering trees: As the earth gets quenched, the grounds gets covered with a carpet of green vegetation. Some of the handsome trees that bloom during the rainy season include:

Alstonia macrophylla	*Colivillea racemosa*
Anthocephalus indicus	*Couroupita guinensis*
Azadirachata indica	*Diospyros peregrina*
Brringtonia racemosa	*Lagerstroemia thorelli*
Brownea coccinea	*Oroxylum indicum*
Calophyllum inophyllum	*Plumeria alba*
Cananga multijuga	*Plumeria rubra*
Cassia marginata	*Samanea saman*

C. Trees for fragrant flowers: A flower without fragrance is like the sky without the moon, a man without learning or a woman without grace, says an indian proverb. Some important trees that bear scented flowers are:

Alstonia scholaris	*Melia azedarach*
Azadirachta indica	*Mesua ferea*
Bauhinia purpurea	*Michelia champaka*
Calophyllum inophyllum	*Millettia ovalifolia*
Cananga odorata	*Mimuspos elengi*
Cassia fistula	*Millingtonia hortensis*
Citharexylum quadrangulare	*Parkinsonia aculeata*

Erythrina blakei	*Plumeia acuminata*
Gardenia latifolia	*Plumeia alba*
Gustavia angusta	*Pterospermum acerifolium*
Haematoxylon campechianum	*Tectona grandis*
Holarrhena antidysenterica	*Terminalia bellerica*

D. Trees for checking air pollution: Industries are the major source of pollution and hence in such areas deciduous trees or trees having thick shining leaves will be more successful, for example: *Morus* sp., *Poplar hybrida*, *Plumeria acutifolia* and *Ficus infectoria*.

E. Trees for noise reduction: Trees decrease sound by 10 dB for every 30 m distance. Plants having thick and fleshy leaves with petiole flexible and capacity to withstand vibration are suitable for checking noise pollution. For example: *Acer negunda*, *Alstonia scholaris*, *Azadirachta indica*, *Butea monosperma*, *Betula pendula*, *Grevillea robusta*, *Juniperus chinensis*, *Madhuka latifolia* and *Terminalia arjuna*.

Trees for screening purpose: When tall upright trees are planted very close to give an ultimate look of curtain or screen. Such trees are planted to hide some objects or sides. For example: *Grevillea robusta*, *Eucalyptus* species, *Poplar* sp., *Polyalthia longifolia* and *Poliathia pendula*.

2. Climatic Factors

Selection of tree will depend upon prevailing climatic conditions of the locality and trees of other climatic conditions may or may not do well or later on decline. This depends upon the individual tree type.

Trees for Tropical climate: *Castanospermum austarle*, *Chorisia speciosa* and *Samanea saman*.

Trees for Temperate climate: Below is a list of temperate trees for the use in landscape work.

Acer palmatum	*Halesia caroliniana*
Amelanchier canadensis	*Koelreuteria paniculata*
Betula nigra	*Magnolia stellata*
Betula paperifera	*Malus floribundus*
Carpinus betulus	*Malus sargentii*
Celtis occidentalis	*Pinus bungeana*

Cercis canadensis Cornus kousa	*Pinus parviflora*
Crataegus cristagalli	*Prunus serrulata*
Crataegus viridis	*Sorpus aucuparia*
Ginkgo biloba	*Syringa reticulata*

Trees for arid climate: *Acacia* sp., *Crataeva religiosa, Albizzia lebbek, Butea frondosa, Prosopis juliflora, Melia azedarach* and *Casuarina equisetifolia.*

3. Soil factors: Trees are hardy species and are adaptable to varying soil conditions but needs specific conditions for their proper growth.

Salt resistant trees: *Azadirachta indica, Butea frondosa, Bassia latifolia, Phoenix dactylifera* and *Thespesia popunea.*

Trees for swamps and marshy areas: *Eucalyptus rostrata, Salix tetrasperma* and *Salix babylonica.*

Planting of trees

Preparation of field: Trees are perennial and will live for several years in the same place, so proper preparation of field is necessary. According to the landscape plan, a pit of 60 × 60 × 60cm size is dug out and should be left one fortnight for solar treatment. Soil should be well mixed with10-15 kg well rotten farmyard manure, 20-25g of 5% chloropyriphos which is essential to check the attack of termites. Refilling of pit should be done which is followed by immediate watering. After setting down the soil, planting of tree is done in the centre of pit.

Planting time: The time of planting vary from place to place. In general, the best planting time is during rains in June to August. If irrigation is assured, planting can also be done during February-March. In the hills, planting should be started in spring and continued through the rainy season. In mild climatic condition like Bangalore, planting can be done almost throughout the year. Dwarf trees are planted 5m apart in the rows and the taller and the spreading ones are planted 9-10m apart. But a tree with huge canopy such as banyan or the rain tree can be planted farther apart.

Maintenance and care of trees: After planting the trees, constant care is necessary to get the desired effect. Different necessary operations are:

1. **Staking**: Staking is necessary to prevent the tree from rocking in wind and thereby loosening its root hold, to provide some resistance to petty vandalism, damage and to prevent distortion of tree through lack of support. It should be carried out as inconspicuously as possible, compatible with its

effectiveness. Stake should be such that it suits the size of the tree and should be strong enough to provide the support. For this mostly, straight bamboos or iron bars can be used. It should be placed about 5 cm away from the main trunk so that it does not harm root system.

2. **Fencing and tree guards**: Young trees need protection against grazing by animals, human carelessness and adverse weather conditions until they are fully established. The type of fencing depends upon the factors like cost involved and availability of material. Most common and cheap fencing is obtained by putting thorny bushes around the tree. Other materials like bricks, perforated bitumen drum and wire netting are also used. These all materials make poor aesthetic effect and hence, cemented architectural structures or fabricated iron tree guards though little costly can be used.
3. **Weeding**: Weeding is important to prevent the shadowing and suffocation of young trees by vigorous growing weeds until these trees outgrow surrounding vegetation. Two to three weeding are sufficient in a year.
4. **Irrigation**-Irrigation in first few years must be done regularly and according to requirement. Watering during hot and dry period is necessary.
5. **Gap filling**: Replacement of dead tree is also very important and replanting should be done at the earliest with the tree of same age so that it does not disturb the uniformity of the trees.
6. **Training and pruning**: All dead wood, misshapen or dangerous branches hanging over roads and building. should be cut. Damaged or decayed branches should be cut away. All cuts more than 5 cm should be painted with Bordeaux mixture against the attack of pathogens.

Description of some important trees for temperate region

Prunus campanulata (Rosaceae): Common name- Taiwan cherry, Formosan cherry

It is a glabrous tree, 7-10 m tall and bears very ornamental flowers in a leafless condition. Flowers are pendulous, bell shaped and deep red in colour. *Prunus campanulata* is a slender, small tree densely branched but graceful. It grows up to 7.5 m high and wide. It produces single, drooping, striking rose flowers in clusters of 2 to 5. Leaves are simple, lustrous dark green, oval to obovate and alternate. In fall they develop a bronze-red color. Early bloomer and good for warmer areas.

Prunus sargentii (Rosaceae): Common name- Japanese flowering cherry, Sargents cherry.

Prunus sargentii is a deciduous tree that grows 6-12m in height. Its crown spreads to a width of 6-12m. New growth is a reddish or bronze in colour, which changes to shiny dark green. The leaves are obovate and have serrated margins. Leaves are 7.5 – 12.5 cm in length and are arranged alternately. In fall the leaves turn red, orange or yellow. It grows single pink flowers during March-April. The fruit is a favorite of birds.

Prunus subhirtella (Rosaceae): Common name- Spring cherry, Rosebud cherry

It is small tree with drooping and crooked branches. It produces rose-pink flowers during March-April.

Abies webbiana (Pinaceae): It is large handsome tree growing to a height of 30-45 m and a girth of 6-9m. The tree is admired for its beautiful needle-like foliage. It is suitable for growing at high altitudes only and is propagated from seeds obtained from female cones. It is generally planted singly in parks and botanic gardens.

Araucaria cookii (Coniferae), Common name: Monkey puzzle

It is native of South America. This genus contains most handsome evergreen gymnosperm. It provides a visual treat to garden lovers. It is always in demand due to its attractive shape and soft foliage. The branches which are horizontal and well placed on the main trunk are covered with needle like soft and dark green leaves. The plants need protection from severe cold in winter and from scorching heat during summer. Artificial rain by sprinkling water helps proper growth.

Cedrus deodara (Pinaceae): Common name-Indian cedar, Deodar

It is a large evergreen conifer growing up to 60m tall with a girth of 11m. It is suitable for hills only. It has a conical appearance when it is young and attains round shape in old age. Deodar tree can live up to 600 years. The leaves are needle like, mostly 2.5–5 cm long, occasionally up to 7 cm long, slender (1 mm thick), borne singly on long shoots and in dense clusters of 20-30 on short shoots. They are bright green to glaucous blue-green in colour. The deodar tree is the national tree of Pakistan. Among Hindus, it is worshipped as a divine tree, particularly in Kashmir and Punjab villages. It is widely grown as an ornamental tree much planted in parks and large gardens for its drooping foliage.The timber is used for making railway sleepers and the woods yields a fragrant essential oil.

Cryptomeria japonica (Pinaceae): Common name-Japanese cedar, dhup

It is a tall, evergreen, handsome, coniferous tree of conical shape, native of Japan and China. It thrives well only at 1,500m or above. It is good for avenue planting or for growing single in large parks and gardens.

Cunninghamia lanceolata (Cupressaceae) : Common name-Chinese fir

The tree is 50 m tall with conical or pyramidal, dark green crown. Cunninghamia bears softly spined, leathery, stiff, green to blue-green needle-like leaves that spiral around the stem with an upward arch.They are native of China, Taiwan and northern Vietnam. It is a prized timber tree in China, producing soft, highly durable scented wood. It is used in particular for manufacture of coffins and in temple building where the scent is valued.

Cupressus funebris (Cupressaceae) : Common name- Mourning Cypress or Chinese Weeping Cypress

It is a medium-sized coniferous tree growing to 20-35 m tall, with a trunk up to 2 m diameter. The foliage grows in dense, usually moderately pendulous sprays of bright green, very slender, slightly flattened shoots. The leaves are scale-like, 1-2 mm long, up to 5 mm long on strong lead shoots; young trees up to about 5-10 years old have juvenile foliage with soft needle-like leaves 3-8 mm long.

Cupressus macrocarpa (Cupressaceae) : Common name- Monterey Cypress

It is a medium-sized evergreen tree which often becomes irregular and flat-topped. It grows to heights of around 10-25 m and its trunk diameter reaches 0.6 m, rarely up to 1 m or more. The foliage grows in dense sprays, bright green in colour. The leaves are scale-like, 2-5 mm long and produced on rounded (not flattened) shoots. It is a hardy species which can be grown as avenue tree in many parts of the country. It may also be planted as specimen tree in garden. It forms good hedge but needs support at young stage.

Cupressus sempervirens (Cupressaceae) : Common name- Mediterranean Cypress, Italian, Graveyard Cypress or Pencil Pine.

This species is native of eastern mediterranean region. It is a medium-sized evergreen tree to 35 m tall, with a conic crown with level branches and variably loosely hanging branchlets. It is very long-lived, with some trees reported to be over 1,000 years old. The foliage grows in dense sprays, dark green in colour. The plant has a very stiff outline, so can be used as avenue tree. Its fragrant wood is utilized for cabinet making.

Cupressus torulosa (Cupressaceae) : Common name- Bhutan cypress

This species is native of Western Asia and Northern India. It is a tall tree with pyramidal shape crown at young stage, but forms a wide spreading crown with age. This plant occurs naturally in limestone formations. The wood is fragrant and resistant to decay. It forms a beautiful formal avenue.

Juniperus bermudiana (Cupressaceae) :

This densely branched, pyramidal tree is native of Bermuda. The leaves are bluish green and of two distinct types-needle like and arranged in threes on young trees and scale like and overlapping in old trees. In transition stages, the two kinds may be found on the same tree. A beautiful tree for planting and rows and in parks. Another species which is *Juniperus chinensis*, native of China and Japan.

Picea smithiana (Pinaceae) : Common name-Himalayan Spruce.

This plant looks like living herbarium since it gives shelter to so many orchids and other epiphytes. It is a tall (50 m or more), majestic tree of West Himalayan origin. It has wide spreading branches and long pendulous branchlets. The leaves are thick and dark green in colour. It is generally planted as specimen tree in large parks or botanic gardens at high altitude.

Pinus longifolia (Pinaceae) : Common name-Indian Pine or Chir

This is most commonly grown pine of Himalayan origin. It can grow to a height of 30m or more with round topped symmetrical head. The light green, long, pendulous, needle like leaves looks very attractive. It can be grown as a specimen tree in garden or parks.

Thuja occidentalis (Cupressaceae) : Common name- America or Common Arbor-vitae, Morpankhi (Hindi)

This is a pyramidal shape, handsome tree of North America origin. It can grow up to a height of 20m. The foliage is fern like and bright green above and yellowish-green below. During winter season the colour changes to dull brownish-green. The plant can tolerate trimming well and can be used for topiary. Their pyramidal and majestic look make them perfect for lining paths and garden. At young stage, it can be used as pot plant. Another species *Thuja orientalis* (Chinese Arbor-vitae) is of Chinese origin.

***Acacia* spp.** (Leguminosae): This genus is native of arid zone of central Australia and has large number of species. The tree of this genus grows luxuriantly in dry climate. Profuse flowering and heavy seed set help in their propagation. *Acacia arabica*, *Acacia fernesiana* and *Acacia modesta* are used to plant in unproductive land to protect soil from wind erosion. Animals are grazed on their leaves.

Acacia auriculiformis (Australian wattle): It is a dwarf species. The tree is popular in the garden for its attractive shape, foliage and produces typically spiral legume shaped fruits.

Acacia cyanophylla (Golden acacia): It is also dwarf but possess brittle branches. This handsome tree produces beautiful golden colour flowers.

Albizzia lebbek (Leguminosae): Common Name: Siris, Lebbek tree, Woman's tongue tree.

It is handsome, deciduous, spreading tree, native of tropical Asia and Africa. The tree is somewhat resistant to drought. This is quick growing tall tree having pinnate leaves of light green colour. Tree makes growth of an umbrella shape. Flowering occurs in April-May and flowers are pale greenish yellow in colour and mildly fragrant. This is a good tree for roadside plantation and its pods of straw yellow colour hang on tree for long time which makes it more attractive.

Albizzia procera (Leguminosae): Common Name: Safed Siris

This is native of Indo-Malaya region and is large quick growing tree. Trunk is tall and colour is greenish yellow white. Leaves are bipinnate of light green colour. Tree produces profuse flower in July-August. Flowers are small heads of yellowish white in colour. It is good tree for roadside plantation and for big parks.

Alstonia scholaris (Apocyanaceae), Common name: Devil's tree, Sapt parni or Satpattia.

It is native of Indo-Malaya region. In the beginning, it is a slow growing tree but later on grows fast. It is a tall tree. Leaves are shining green and produced in a whorl of 5-7. Flowers are produced in July-August in clusters which are greenish white. It is suitable for planting alongside the roads, groups or as a specimen in parks for shade purpose.

Azadirachta indica (Meliaceae), common name: Neem

It is native of Indo-Burma region. Tree is tall with brown stem. Leaves are pinnate, dark green and bitter in taste. Flowers are small, white and sweet scented which appear in the end of April to middle May. Fruits are drupe, oval in shape and golden yellow in colour at maturity. This is a medicinal tree and new emerging leaves are eaten for keeping away from many blood diseases. Leaves are hanged in the house and rooms of patients to repel harmful insects. Semi hardwood shoots are used as bruish to clean teeth. Margosa oil is prepared from fruits and seeds which is used in making soaps or medicines. Neem cake is used as a fertilizer which kills harmful insects, termites and nematodes. It is a good tree for roadside plantation and in big compounds for shade and in hospitals as a medicinal plant and for shade.

Bassia latifolia* syn. *Madhuka indica (Sapotaceae), Common name: Mahua

It is an indigenous tall growing tree with rounded crown. Leaves are large which fall in April and reappear in bright red colour in May. Flowering occurs in the end of April to first fortnight of May. The flowers are light yellow in colour which are not very showy. They bloom in the night and fall in the morning. Fruits are consumed in tribal area of central India and used to make a delicious brew. It is easily propagated by seeds. It should be planted in groups or singly in parks for shade.

Bauhinia (Leguminosae)

The genus is comprising of flowering trees and most of them are native of India. The generic name is given after twin brother, John and Casper Bauhin-famous botanists of 16th century. Plants of this genus are easily identified on account of peculiar leaves which are composed of two oval shaped leaflets united in the centre. Flower buds are cooked as vegetable. Easily propagated through seeds which are produced in abundance. Following species are very common:

Bauhinia variegata: This is tall tree producing flowers of rose coloured variegated with red and yellow which appear in mid of March. Most ideally suited for planting as specimen or in groups in gardens and in big parks and as avenue tree alongside the road.

Bauhinia alba: This is a medium tree bearing white flowers during middle of March. It is suitable for specimen or group planting.

Bauhinia triandra: It is a medium tall tree producing purple colour flower in mid of November. It is good for roadside plantations and group plantings.

Bauhinia blakena: This species is introduced from Hong Kong and is very handsome flowering tree. It is a medium tall tree with round top producing large purple flowers in the end of December to February. It is propagated through air layering. It is highly suitable for specimen and group planting.

Bauhinia sulphureus: It is a slow growing dwarf to medium tree which produces yellow flowers during rainy season.

Koelreutaria panniculata (Spaindaceae), Common name: Golden rain tree

It is native of Korea and China. It is a winter deciduous, medium sized and spreading tree. The emerging leaves are coppery to pink colour. It produces small yellow flowers on long panicles in late summer and is followed by development of ball/ bladder like red flushed fruit capsules. It is highly suitable for planting alongside the road for shade or flowers or in group planting in large parks.

Bombax malabaricum (Bombaceae), Common name: Semal, Simble or Red cotton silk

It is native of Indo-Burma region. It is considered as a sacred tree and is associated with Goddess Kali. It is a fast growing, tall, stately upright tree which is deciduous during February-March. Trunk has spines. Leaves are compound. Flowers are large, bright red or yellowish red in colour which appear in mid of March. Fruits contain silky floss which is used in stuffing pillows and cushions. Iι is highly suitable for boundary plantation of bigger compounds, national highways and in parks.

Butea monosperma (Leguminosae), Common name: Flame of forest, dhak, palas or tesu.

It is native of India. It is tall tree but does not look attractive due to crooked and distorted stem. Leaves are large, trifoliate and are used to prepare plates for community functions. It blooms in deciduous condition during end of March when whole tree covered in scarler orange crescent shaped flowers. When planted in groups, from distance, it gives appearance as if there were fire and hence, it is called as 'Flame of the Forest'. Lac insects are reared on its branches. Temporary dye is extracted from its flowers and in ancient days during Holi festival this colour was used to play.

Callistemon lanceolatus (Myrtaceae), Common name: Bottle brush.

It is native of Australia and is well naturalised under Indian condition. It produces bright red colour flowers during March-April at the end of branches, which resembles brush used for cleaning bottles, hence called as 'Bottle brush': It is well suited for planting at the gate of house, in the corner of lawn as a specimen tree and near water bodies. It is also highly suitable for grouping, screening and to be planted in the shrubbery. Its drooping branches are symbol of welcome on which dark green lanceolate leaves are nicely laced. *Callistemon polandii* is another species which produces yellow flowers.

Callistemon salignuso (White bottle brush or willow bottle brush): It is a very handsome erect to spreading type of small tree having thin branches and fragrant, narrowly lanceolate pale green leaves. It produces white flowers in the end of March to middle of April which attracts lots of honey bees. It is very suitable for small compound gardens as a specimen or group planting.

***Cassia* spp.** (Leguminosae)

This is important genus which has many colourful species and beautifies the surroundings with spectacular flowers in leafless condition. Following are important species:

Cassia fistula (Amaltas, golden laburnum or tree of prosperity): It is native of India. It is a tall tree having white stem. Leaves are pinnate and leaflets are larger than other species. Colour of emerging leaves vary from copper red to light yellow. Colour of flower is deep yellow which fades to light yellow in later stages. Flowers are well arranged on long drooping rachis which appears in middle of May when tree is in leafless condition and flowering continues up to July. It is an excellent specimen tree and for avenue or group planting. Fruits are used to prepare medicine. Tree grows well in dry region.

Cassia grandis (Pink Shower, Horse cassia), origin-Tropical America: The rose-coloured flowers are borne in long drooping racemes in leafless condition during March-April. This is an elegant, spreading and quick-growing tree.

Cassia javanica (Java cassia): It is native of Java, Malayasia and Sumatra. It is a medium tree, with a straight trunk and spreading crown having horizontal branches. The drooping branchlets with feathery leaves are very ornamental. The tree is deciduous during April-May and flowering starts from May which continues upto July. Flowers are deep pink to rose pink and well intermingled with leaves. The tree has brittle branches which may break due to strong wind, hence should be planted in sheltered position. A good tree for avenues and parks.

Cassia marginata : It is a medium sized tree with drooping and spreading habit. Flowering occurs during March-June and again in August-September under certain climatic conditions as of Bangalore.

Cassia nodosa: It is native of Mayanmar, Malaysia and India (mostly Assam). It is a comparatively large tree with a short gnarled trunk. The tree has pink flowers which appears in bunches from the nodes all along the branches, hence species called *nodosa*. The tree flowers in a leafless condition between May and June. It is one of the best flowering tree. The tree is most suitable for planting in parks, gardens and avenues.

Cassia renigera (Burmese Pink Cassia): It is native of Mayanmar. This tree is commonly found in Maharastra and Tamilnadu. It is a medium size deciduous tree. Its leaflets are leathery glossy and pointed. A large kidney shaped bract remains attached to the base of the young leaf-stalks and drops later on. The plant produces bright pink or rose flowers in leafless condition during April-June. It is suited for planting in large home gardens and parks.

Cassia siamea (Kasod tree): It is native of Indo-Malaya region. It is a medium, quick growing, evergreen tree with columnar to spreading crown. Yellow flowers start appearing in July and continue upto January. It is good for boundary plantation and for demarcation of large areas.

Cassia spectabilis : It is a beautiful, medium sized, umbrella shape tree native of Tropical America. The large (4 cm across), cup-shaped, golden-yellow flowers are borne in 30-60 cm long erect racemes of a beautiful appearance. It flowers during July-August when the whole plant gets covered.

Castanospermum australe (Leguminosae): Common name- Moreton Bay Chestnut, Black Bean

It is a slow growing, evergreen tree native of Australia. It reaches a height of 40 m at maturity. Flowering occurs during March in racemes of large orange-crimson flowers. The stout brown pods contain 2-4 large chestnut like seeds which are edible when roasted.

Chorisia speciosa (Bombaceae) : Common name- Silk floss tree, Resham Rui (Hindi)

Floss Silk Tree is often rated among the most beautiful trees in the world. This deciduous tropical tree from Brazil and Argentina is a large tree rated to over 18 m. The trunk becomes bottle shaped as it ages and it is covered with stout spines, more decorative than really frightening. It has pale green leaves palmately divided into 5-7 pointed leaflets. The young trees start out growing fast, straight and narrow, then slowly develop broadly spreading umbrella canopies as they age. Silk floss trees typically drop their leaves just before they put on their spectacular autumn display of large five-petaled flowers. The petals vary from pale pink to rose to purple or burgundy at the tips and grade into ivory with brownish spots or blotches at the base. After blooming, pear shaped fruits appear which have a silky floss on the seeds, hence the name. It is propagated by seeds.

Citharexylum quadrangulare (Verbenaceae) : Common name- Fiddle wood tree

This evergreen, medium to small size tree is a native of the West Indies. The leaves are lanceolate to about 10 cm long and branches are smooth and quadrangular. It is a beautiful tree with long tassels of richly scented white flowers. Flowers are pendant and cover the tree from March to October. Foliage is dark green, shiny, ornamental. Easy to grow and nice landscaping tree. Great butterfly and bee attractor. The wood has been used to make musical instruments.

Cochlospermum gossypium/C. religiosum (Chochlospermaceae) : Common name- Yellow silk cotton tree, Buttercup tree, Golden silk cotton tree, Galgal (Hindi)

Buttercup Tree is very common and conspicuous tree characteristics of the hottest, driest and stoniest slope. It is native to India, Myanmar and Thailand. It is a small tree growing upto 7.5 m. The bark is smooth and pale grey. It is sparsely clothed with leaves and sheds them at the height of the flowering season. The leaves appear at the tips of the branches and are palmately lobed. The flowers of the Butter cup tree are the most conspicuous part of the tree. They are large, growing upto about 10 cm, buttercup shaped and bright yellow. The stamens are orange. The flowering season is between February and April, particularly after the leaves are shed. The fruits are brown and oval shaped. They come in the form of a capsule made up of five segments. The capsule splits open to release the seeds which are embedded in the silky cotton contained within. This silky cotton is said to induce sleep when stuffed into pillows. *Cochlospermum* because the seed resembles a snail. *Religiosum* because the flowers are used in temple offerings.

Colvillea racemosa (Leguminosae) : Common name-Colville's glory (in honour of Sir Charles Colville), Whip tree, Kilbili (Hindi)

Colville's Glory is a beautiful, large tree from Madagascar with large pinnate leaves and very conspicuous cylindrical or cone shaped clusters of bright orange flowers that are bright red in bud. The tree grows to a height of 10-12m. Its grape-like clusters of velvety buds, varying from chameleon green to blood orange, are a sight to behold during August to September. Leaves a double-compound, very similar to those of Gulmohar. Its genus is named for Sir Charles Colville, a former Governor of Mauritius. It likes moist weather. Since the tree bears at the end of branches it should never be prunned.

Cordia sebestena (Boraginaceae): Common name-Geiger tree, Scarlet cordia, Bhokar (Hindi)

It is a dwarf tree of deciduous habit originated from American tropics. It is commonly named Geiger tree after Key West wrecker John Geiger. It is widely planted through tropics and sub-tropics for its ornamental flowers. The bell-shaped orange or scarlet flowers are borne almost throughout the year in terminal clusters but in more abundance during January to March. It has dark green oval shape leaves and oval shaped fruits that are edible. The dry wood when brunt emits a good perfume.

Couroupita guianensis (Lecythidaceae): Common name-Canon Ball Tree, Nagalinga, tope gola (Hindi)

The cannon ball tree is one of the more spectacular South American trees to be planted in subtropical and tropical botanical gardens throughout the world. This large deciduous tropical tree, 30-35 m tall, is listed as a rare tree and flower in India. The leaves, up to 15cm long are simple with serrate margin. It flowers in racemes which is cauliflorus; the yellow, reddish and pink flowers are stunning fragrant. These are 7.5cm to 12.5cm waxy aromatic smelling, pink and dark-red flowers growing directly on the bark of the trunk. The tree bears, directly on the trunk and main branches, large globose woody fruits; they look like big rusty cannonballs hanging in clusters, like balls on a string. Cannon ball trees usually carry 'CAUTION' signs posted on the trunks to advise people not to stand close to and directly under the fruits as one can get hurt as they drop off by themselves. The fruit contains small seeds in a white, unpleasant smelling white jelly, which are exposed when the upper half of the fruit goes off like a cover. The long dangling fruity branches give the tree an unkempt appearance. The hard shells are used to make containers and utensils. Cannon ball flowers are considered of special significance in Buddhist culture in Sri Lanka. In Tamil Nadu, it is called Nagalingam flower. The sivalingam shape is visible at the center of the flower and snake shaped pollen is the specialty of this flower and it has very good fragrance. This rare flower can be used for Shiva devotion of Lord. It is suitable only for large garden.

Crataeva religiosa (Capparidaceae) : Common name-Caper tree, Barna (Hindi)

Barna is native of India. It is a medium sized much branched deciduous tree with crooked branches, smooth pale grey bark and glossy foliage. The plant looks very handsome when it flowers in leafless condition in April-May. Flowers are white, pale yellow or reddish-yellow, borne in dense corymbs and having numerous prominent stamens with purple filaments. Seed coat being very hard, may take one year to germinate. It is a very hardy and drought resistant tree.

Elaeocarpus ganitrus (Elaeocarpaceae) : Common name-Indian bead tree, Blue olive berry, Rudrak (Hindi), Rudraksha (Bengali)

It is a large shrub or small tree (up-to 8m tall) and is native of tree. It is popular for its size, attractive white flowers and colourful blue berries. The seeds are used as beads and the necklace is most revered for Hindus. The tree is suitable for planting in lawns and along avenues.

Erythrina blackeii (Leguminosae) : It is a large shrub or a small tree of Indian origin. The tree produces dark scarlet colour flowers in April. It is suitable for planting in small garden.

Erythrina crista-galli (Leguminosae) : Common name-Common coral tree, Cockspur coral tree.

It is a dwarf tree of Brazil origin. The tree produces long and dense terminal raceme of scarlet flowers. This is also useful for planting in small compounds. Stem and petioles are sometime spiny.

Erythrina indica (Leguminosae) : Common name-Pangri, Pharad, Dadap (Hindi), Sunshine tree

It is a small tree. The plant is fast growing and densely branched. The erect stem has black spines. The trifoliate leaves gives the plant an ornamental look. The tree flowers in deciduous condition during February-March. The flowers are scarlet red in colour and appear in a cluster.It can be planted in groups in parks and gardens or along avenues in towns and cities. All Erythrinas can be propagated from long stem cuttings.

Gliricidia maculata (Leguminosae) : Common name-Madre Tree of South America

Gliricidia maculata is a fast-growing, tropical, leguminous tree up to 10-15 m. high. It is one of the commonest and best-known multpurpose trees in many parts of Central America, where it probably originated. Used for timber, firewood, medicinal purposes, charcoal, living fences, plantation shade and green manure, it has good potential as fodder for livestock. The tree produces pale pink flowers in deciduous condition during February-March. The tree is recommended for planting in parks, gardens and along avenues. The tree is killed by frost in north India.

Gustavia augusta (Lecythidaceae) : Common name-Heaven Lotus

It is native of Tropical America. *Gustavia* is a medium-sized tree with a straight trunk that is often unbranched, with just one cluster of leaves at the top of the trunk (like a palm). Leaves are very large. They are toothed, long, narrow at the base and broad at the apex. The plant bears beautiful, scented, white, water-lily like flowers during July-August. There is another species *Gustavia gracillima* which produces rose-red colour flowers.

Holarrhena antidysenterica (Apocyanaceae) : Common name-Easter tree, Karra, Kaura (Hindi)

It is a small tree of Indian origin. The tree flowers during March-May, flowers are creamy white and strongly scented. The bark yields an anti-dysenteric drug.

Jacaranda mimosaefolia (Bignoniaceae) : Common name-Nili Gulmohar

Jacaranda is a Brazilian vernacular name which refers its origin and *mimosaefolia* refers to its feathery mimosa like leaves. It is a graceful open branched tree of medium height with fern like bipinnate leaves. The blue-mauve flowers are borne profusely in loose pyramidal terminal panicles from end of March till about mid May. It is an excellent tree for avenues, parks and gardens cultivated for its graceful foliage and beautiful flowers.

Lagerstroemia flos-reginae (Lythraceae) : Common name-Queen's flower, Pride of India, Crape flower, Jarul (Hindi)

Lagerstroemia is named after a Swedish botanist, Magnus v. Lagerstrom and *flos-reginae* means 'Flower of the Queen'. It is native of India. The tree is deciduous, large in moist areas of Eastern India but small in dry places in Northern India. The leaves turn somewhat coppery before falling in February-March. The showy, purple or mauve flowers appear during April-May and again during July-August. It is a well known ornamental tree, cultivated for its beautiful flowers, can also be used as avenue tree.

Magnolia cambellii (Magnoliaceae) :

It is a large deciduous tree of Indian Origin, which may grow up to 50m in wild. It can be grown at high altitude. The plant bears huge (15-25cm across) lotus like reddish pink fragrant flowers in leafless condition during February and March or May. The tree is most ornamental when in bloom. However, the tree rarely flowers before 20 years of age.

Magnolia grandiflora (Magnoliaceae) : Common name- Lily tree, Bull Bay

It is a evergreen tree of pyramidal in shape. The plant is origin of Southeast U.S.A. It may grow upto 25m but in cultivation it is generally much smaller. The leaves are 15-25 cm long and tapered at both ends. The leaves are thick, glossy dark green above and rusty-felted below. The lotus shaped flowers are large (20-25 cm across) and sweet scented.

Mesua ferrea (Guttiferae) : Common name- Iron Wood Tree, Nagkesar (Hindi)

It is a medium size tree, native of India, Sri Lanka and Malaysia. It is suited to hot and moist area and needs partial shade.The leaves are very ornamental, shining, leathery and lanceolate shaped. The flowers are large, white petalled, with a yellow centre and highly scented. The flowering time is February to March.

Michelia champaka (Magnoliaceae) : Common name-Golden Champa, Champa (Hindi), Swarnachampa (Bengali)

It is native of India and Java. It is a medium sized tree (10-13m tall), having long leaves with wavy margins and slightly resembling mango leaves. The flowers are golden coloured, 5-7 cm long, highly scented and silky in appearance. The tree likes a humid atmosphere and grows up to medium altitudes. It can be planted along avenues and in parks and compounds.

Milletis ovalifolia (Leguminosae) :

It is a dwarf tree of African origin. The plant has ornamental ovatet shape leraflets. Flowers are small and lilac in colour. It flowers in deciduous condition during April. It is suitable for planting in houses, parks and in public places.

Millingtonia hortensis (Bignoniaceae) : Common name- Indian Cork Tree, Jasmine Tree, Akash Neem or Neem Chameli (Hindi)

Millingtonia is native of Mayanmar. It is a fine tall and straight evergreen tree, reaching up to 20m, with narrow crown and yellowish grey corky bark, having drooping branches and deep green very ornamental foliage. Flowers are silvery white, sweet scented at night, and appearing in terminal panicles in November and December and again from April to June. The tree does not seed in most part of India. The wood being brittle, and suffers much from storms. It thrives best under moist conditions but does well in dry climate.

Oroxylum indicum (Bignoniaceae) : Common name-Broken Bones Plant, Indian trumpet flower, midnight horror, Bhut Vriksha (Hindi)

It is a small (10-12m), upright tree of Malaysia origin which branches very rarely. The leaves are tripinnate, 90-150 cm long and elliptical in shape. The large leaf stalks wither and fall off the tree and collect near the base of the trunk, appearing to look like a pile of broken limb bones. The tree is a night-bloomer and fleshy flowers are large, funnel shaped and arranged in long peduncled racemes appears during rain. The colour is dirty brown outside and yellowish inside. The flowers have foul smell. Pollination by bats. They form enormous seed pods that hang down from bare branches. Those long fruits curve downward and resemble the wings of a large bird or dangling sickles or swords in the night.

Parkia biglandulosa (Leguminosae) : common name-Badminton Ball Tree, African Locust Tree, Chendul ka Jhar (Hindi), Sivaling mara (Kannada)

African locust tree is a tall handsome tree, native of West Africa. It is a large and fast growing evergreen upright tree with handsome feathery and bipinnate foliage. The flower heads are globular, hanging down the branches suspended by long peduncles during December-January. The farinaceous pulp which surrounds the seeds is edible and so also are the seeds themselves, which taste like garlic. Presence of two glands at the base of leaf, lends this species the name, biglandulosa. It is a good avenue and shade tree.

Parkinsonia aculeata (Leguminosae) : Common name-Jerusalem Thorn, Vilaiti kikkar (Hindi)

It is a small, thorny tree with drooping branches and is native of Tropical America. The leaves are bipinnate with numerous very small leaflets. The plant produces yellow scented flowers which covers the whole plant during February to March. It is a good avenue tree for dry regions. It can also be used as hedge. Propagated from seeds.

Peltophorum inerme (Leguminosae): Common name-Yellow gulmohar, Rusty Shield bearer.

It is a large, handsome tree of Australian origin. The leaves are bipinnate and fern like which look very ornamental. Flowers are yellow, mildly scented, borne in large panicle, terminally on the branches. Flowering occurs during February to May and again during September to November. The large copper colour pods are conspicuous and ornamental until they become black. It is a beautiful ornamental tree, suited for avenues, parks and gardens.

***Plumeria* sp.** (Apocynaceae) : Plumeria is a small genus of 7-8 species native to tropical and sub-tropical America. The genus consists of mainly deciduous trees and shrubs. Each of the separate species of *Plumeria* bears differently shaped alternate leaves and their form and growth habits are distinct.

Plumeria alba (Frngipani, Pagoda Tree): It is an evergreen tree, 6-7m tall, having pure white, yellow-eyed fragrant flowers. The leaves are lanceolate to oblong-lanceolate and do not have the conspicuous marginal vein. It flowers during March-April and again during July-September.

Plumeria obtusa : It is a small evergreen tree with large dark-green blunted leaves. The margin of the leaves tend to roll under. The flowers are pure white, much larger than other species. The broad petals are conspicuously overlapping and slightly incurved so as to give them a round shape.

Plumeria rubra (Frangipani, Pagoda tree, Temple tree, Tree of Life) : It is the most widely grown tree in our gardens. It is a low growing, 6-7m tall spreading tree of deciduous habit, shedding the leaves between winter and rainy season. The leaves are large, broadly lanceolate, tapering at both ends, with conspicuous parallel veins. The leaves are crowded in spirals at the apex of the long branches. The flowers are variable in colour, generally white with yellow throat, rose or yellow. *Plumerias* are good for planting in home garden and in parks.

Poinciana regia (Leguminosae) : Common name-Gulmohar, Peacock flower, Flamboyant

One of the most conspicuous flowering trees seen in the tropics. Bright fiery red/ orange blossoms cover its mimosa type leaves which close up and go to sleep for the night. It can be grown as a potted plant. This large tree, which naturally assumes a spreading umbrella shape, is now found in gardens, parks and planted along streets throughout the tropics. It can grow as tall as 18-20m and has smooth greyish-coloured bark and attractive feathery, fern-like leaves, which drop annually during the dry season. At the same time as the new leaves appear, the tree is covered with masses of five-petalled flowers that are usually bright red-orange but may also appear in pale apricot. Blooming is followed by long, flattened, leathery dark brown or black seed pods. Poinciana requires full sun and adequate space to take its characteristic form. It flowers best in areas that have two distinct seasons but can be impressive even in moister places.

Pterocarpus indicus (Leguminosae) : Common name- Burmese Rosewood, Gold Mohur of Singapur.

It is a tall tree (10-12m), with spreading rounded top and drooping branchlets. The golden coloured, sweet scented flowers are borne several times a year. It is suitable for large gardens. The wood is a valuable timber.

Pterospermum acerifolium (Sterculiaceae) : Common name- Kanakchampa

Kanak Champa is a tree of Indian origin, which reaches a height of 15-20 m. Leaves are simple, alternate, have stipules and are palmately ribbed. It has large fragrant nocturnal white flowers, occuring in axillary fascicles during February to May. Fruit is a capsule, angled and furfuraceous. It yields a reddish wood used for planking; often grown as an ornamental or shade tree.

Rhododendron (Ericaceae) : *Rhododendron* is a large genus with over 1000 species and most have showy flower displays. They do well in temperate regions or at high altitudes. The genus is characterized by shrubs and small to (rarely) large tree. The leaves are spirally arranged; leaf size can range from 1–2 cm to over 50 cm, exceptionally 100 cm in *Rhododendron sinogrande*. They may be either evergreen or deciduous. *Rhododendron arboreum* is an evergreen tree which grow up to 13 m. The flowers are in dense clusters and are of red colour. It flowers in the Himalayas from March to May. Flowers are acid in taste and are used for chutney and squash making by hill people.

Saraca indica (Leguminosae) : Common name- Ashok, Sita-Ashok

The tree is of Indian origin. This is a very slow growing and evergreen erect tree that has a smooth grey bark. The top of the tree is well shaped and compact. Usually, plant can produce flower throughout the year but more abundant during February to May, when plethora of rich orange, slightly fragrant flowers give the tree a view of absolute beauty. It is a sacred tree for both Hindus and Buddhists.

Sesbania grandiflora (Leguminosae) : Common name- The Sesban, or Agastya, Agasti, Gachh-munga (Hindi).

Sesbania is native of tropical Asia to North Australia. This is a quick growing small tree having ornamental value. The flowers are creamy-white in colour, very large and pea shaped and are edible. The flowering time is December to January. The plant can be used as hedge or as a shade tree. It is also used as a green manure plant. The plant attains almost full height in six months and flowers the same year.

Solanum macranthum (Solanaceae) : Common name-The Night Shade or Potato tree.

It is native to Brazil, Potato tree is a small tree widely cultivated in the tropics. This plant grows quickly into a bushy tree of 4.5 m in height. Grown for its ornamental purpose. The leaves are large, lobed and prickly. Flowers are fragrant and change their colour from white to pink to lavender. The flowers are 2.5 cm across and resemble potato flowers. The flowering season is from March to November. It requires a rich soil for good growth. It is suited for planting singly.

Spathodea campanulata (Bignoniaceae) : Common name- Flame or Tulip tree, Fountain tree, Scarlet Bell Tree, Rugtoora (Hindi)

Originated from Equatorial Africa, it is a slender tree, which can grow up to 30 m but is often kept smaller in gardens. It has dark green compound leaves and frequently produces clusters of large, tulip-shaped flowers at the ends of the branches. The most common flower colour is bright red-orange, with a yellow border on the petals. There is also a rarer, pure yellow variety. In North India flowering time is February to March but in Bangalore, the main flowering season is between October to December, though sporadic flowering is also seen in July. The blooms are followed by long, boat-shaped pods that open to release masses of winged seeds. *Spathodea* grows rapidly from seed (those of the yellow-flowering variety do not, however, breed true) and prefers full sun, though it tolerates a wide range of conditions and poor soil. The wood tends to be brittle and on taller specimens and breaks easily in strong winds.

Stereospermum suaveolens (Bignoniaceae) : Common name-Paral (Hindi), Parul (Bengali)

This is a middle sized flowering tree, a native of Bengal. The flowers are large, of a dark crimson colour and exquisitely fragrant. Steeped in water they impart their fragrance to it. Rubbed up with honey they are given to check hiccup. The flowers are used for worship. The root-bark is an ingredient of *dasamula*, and is thus largely used in native medicine. It is regarded as cooling, diuretic and tonic, and is generally used in combination with other medicines. It is propagated from seeds, cuttings and by air layering.

Tabebuia avalandi (Bignoniaceae) : This is a dwarf (5-7 m), umbrella shaped tree, native of Brazil.The plant has a good shape and looks very ornamental when bloom during November to January in Bangalore. The mauve flowers are borne terminally in round bunches. It is very suitable for planting as a specimen tree or for avenues, especially in eities or town.

Tabebuia rosea (Bignoniaceae) : It is a small to medium size tree of Mexico and Central America. The leaves are digitate, simple in young plants, leaflets 5, ovate to oblong and acuminate. The flowers are pale mauve and are borne in large terminal clusters. A good tree for avenues.

Tabebuia spectabilis (Bignoniaceae) : It is a small tree with ornamental digitate foliage. The leaflets are ovate-oblong. The plants sheds leaves March or April in Bangalore when the plant is covered by bright yellow funnel shaped flowers, 7 cm across, in dense, short terminal panicles. A good tree for parks and home garden.

Tecoma aegentea (Bignoniaceae) : Originated from South America, it is the most striking tree when in flowering. It is a small tree with thick, narrow, lanceolate leaves. The plant bears dense, terminal clusters of bright yellow, funnel shaped flowers in a leafless condition. The tree in full flowering looks most beautiful. It is good for planting along avenues and in parks and home gardens.

Tecomella undulata (Bignoniaceae) : Common name-Wavy-leaved Tecoma.

It is a large shrub or small tree of Indian origin. It has drooping branches and greyish green foliage. The leaves have wavy edges. The orange yellow flowers are borne in bunches at the apex of lateral branches. The tree looks beautiful when in full bloom from March to April. It is a drought tolerant plant and suitable for landscaping and avenue planting in dry regions.

Thespesia populnea (Malvaceae) : Common name-Portia, Indian Tulip tree, Bhendi Tree

This is a medium sized (10-13 m), quick growing, evergreen tree of Tropical Asian origin. The leaves are poplar-like and form into a head of foliage, providing enough shade. The large bell-shaped flowers are yellow in colour with reddish blotches at the base. The old flowers turn rosy-violet. The flowers resemble those of vegetable okra (bhendi). The tree flowers almost throughout the year, the peak time being the cold season. Easily propagated from seeds or large cuttings. The plant is salt resistant and hardy. It is often planted near churches and temples.

Wrightia coccinea (Apocyanaceae) :

It is a small tree (4-5 m), native of India. The leaves are 7-12 cm long and elliptic or elliptic-lanceolate in shape. The plant bears numerous red flowers in the hot season when it looks beautiful. Another species is *Wrightia tinctoria* , its wood is used in the manufacturing of toys. The tree bears star-shaped, jasmine like scented flowers, 1-2 cm across, during March to May.

Adansonia digitata (Bombaceae) : Common name-Gorakh- Chinch, Gorakh imli, Baobab, Dead-rat tree, Monkey bread tree, upside down tree.

It is native of tropical Africa and introduced in India by Arabs. Adansonia is a giant tree with smooth bottle shapes trunk. The large leaves are digitate having five leaflets radiating from a central point with hairy surface, leafless during hot weather. Flowering occurs during July. Flowers are large, pendent on a long thick peduncle with creamy white petals. Its flowers bloom at midnight and weather by next mid-day. The timber being spongy, is used for raft-making.

Adenanthera pavonia (Leguminosae) : Common name-Coral wood tree, bead tree, Red sandle wood tree

Red Sandal wood a big beautiful, medium to large-sized tree ranges from 6-20m in height, with pinnately compound leaves and dense racemes of fragrant, light-yellow blossoms. The seeds are used in necklaces and ornaments. Although the raw seeds are toxic, when cooked they are edible. The hard reddish wood is used for cabinet making. A red dye, obtained from the wood, is used by Brahmins to mark religious symbols on their foreheads. It thrives best in humid localities.

Ailanthus excelsa (Simarubaceae) : Common name- Maharuk, Mahanimb (Hindi), Indian Tree of Heaven.

They are fast-growing deciduous trees growing to 25-45 m tall, with spreading branches and large (40-100 cm) pinnate leaves with 15-41 long pointed leaflets. Flowering occurs during August. The small yellow to greenish flowers borne on branched panicles. They turn reddish later in the year and eventually brown. They stay on the tree for a long time; the male flowers have a strong odour. The odour tends to resemble the smell of strong cat urine or the spray of a male cat. Touching the leaves give an unpleasant smell on the hands. The tree grows fast in poor soil and a dry and hot climate.

Anthocephalus cadamba (Rubiaceae) : Common name-Kadamba (Hindi).

It is a sacred tree and associated with Lord Krishna. It is indigenous to hotter parts of India. It is a large graceful deciduous tree with a straight stem about 15 m high. The spreading crown bears drooping branches and yellow ball like flowers. It flowers during rainy season. Leaves are large oblong and shining. The tree grows best in humid climate and thrives best in well-drained soil.

Araucaria cookii (Pinaceae) : Common name- Araucaria, Monkey puzzle.

They are magnificent evergreen trees, with apparently whorled branches and stiff, flattened, pointed leaves, found in Brazil, Chile, Polynesia and Australia. The name of the genus is derived from Arauco, the name of the district in southern Chile where the trees were first discovered. Young plants are widdely used as potted plant. It thrives very well in mild climates as of Bangalore and in eastern India and in the hills.

Brassaia actinophylla (Araliaceae) : Common name- Umbrella tree.

It is native of Australia and New Guinea. It is a handsome medium growing (6-7m) tree which at young stage used as a beautiful pot plant. The tree is evergreen with large radially arranged leaves and has few branches. The spikes are handsome and bright scarlet or coral red in colour, borne terminally and pointing radially.

Caesalpinia coriaria (Leguminosae) : Common name- Divi-divi.

It is native of Central America. This is a medium size tree with umbrella type canopy. The light feathery foliage and scented yellow flowers borne in July are the plus points in this plant. It is grown more for its ornamental shape than for flowers. The pods are very useful for dyeing and tanning.

Calophyllum inophyllum (Guttiferae) : Common name-Alexandrian Laurel, Sultan Champa (Hindi).

Calophyllum inophyllum is a large evergreen tree. It is native from East Africa, southern coastal India to Malaysia and Australia. It is a low-branching and slow-growing tree with a broad and irregular crown. It usually reaches 8 to 20 metres in height. The tree is more attractive for its large shining leaves than for the white sweet scented flowers which appear during May-June. The timber is used for ship-building.

Casuarina equisetifolia (Casuarinaceae) : Common name- Junglisaru (Hindi), Whistling Pine, Beef wood, She-oak.

Whistling Pine has a conifer-like appearance which is increased by hanging green branchlets and cone-like fruits. The species name *equisetifolia* refers to the resemblence of the leaves to a horse's tail. The soft singing of the air through its innumerable slender twigs is a pleasant sound, which lends it the common name Whistling Pine. It is a large vase-shaped tree that grows 3.0-4.5 m in height with wispy grey green twigs reminiscent of pine needles. The weeping branchlets look a little like jointed rushes and are ringed at their nodes by tightly overlapping little scalelike leaves. The stout trunk is covered with thick pebbly textured brownish grey bark.

Dalbergia sissoo (Leguminosae) : Common name-Sissoo tree, Indian Rosewood, Shisam (Hindi).

Shisham, is an erect deciduous tree, native to the India. The plant can withstand drought as well as submerged conditions for a fairly long duration. Shisham is best known internationally as a premier timber species but is also utilised as an important fuel wood and for shade and shelter. The timber is good for making boats, railway sleepers, gun carriages and furniture.

Dillenia indica (Dilleniaceae) : Common name-Chalta (Hindi and Bengali).

It is native of India. This is an upright, evergreen, slow-growing, 10-12 m tall tree with rounded crown. The leaves are pretty long as well as broad, with serrated margins. The fragrant flowers are large and white, blooming in July. The fruits are large acidic, but edible when cooked. It prefers humid climate and is susceptible to frost. It can be grown in small garden in dry areas and in large public parks as individual tree for shade and decoration.

Diospyros embryopteris (Ebenaceae) : Common name- Persimmon, Tendook (Hindi).

It is native of India. This is an evergreen, slow-growing tree of medium height but spreading to a considerable extent. The branches are shining and blackish-brown. The new leaves are very ornamental because of the brilliant red colour. The fruits are decorative and edible. It is a good shade tree.

***Eucalyptus* sp.** (Myrtaceae):

There are more than 700 species of eucalyptus mostly native to Australia. Eucalyptus is grown for their ornamental, medicinal value as well as for fuel and timber. Some species are suitable for growing in hills, e.g. *Eucalyptus lobulus* (Blue gum)-It is

60 m or more tall and have blue-green leaves. *Eucalyptus ficifolia* (Red gum) 10 m tall; *Eucalyptus multiflora,* which is 30 m tall. *Eucalyptus citriodora* is a moderate tree with lemon scented foliage, which thrives well in the plains. All species have brittle branches and likely to be broken during strong cyclones.

Ficus bengalensis (Moraceae): Common name-Banyan, Bar or Borh (Hindi).

It is native of India. This tree is considered sacred in India and often shelters a little or larger temple underneath but is offered worship on its own. It is the National tree of India. It is a huge tree (20 m tall) with huge crown of foliage.The aerial roots originating from the branches strike into soil and gives a columner support to the large crown. The leaves are large and leathery. The tree bears crimson berries in August-September. The tree is suited for planting in large parks and along national highways.

Ficus benjamina (Moraceae) : Common name-Java fig, Golden fig, Weeping fig.

This is a moderate to large, evergreen tree with drooping branches. It is native of tropical Asia. Leaves are glossy, 6-13 cm long, oval with an acuminate tip. It is a very popular house plant, due to its elegant growth and tolerance of poor growing conditions; it does best under bright, sunny conditions but will tolerate considerable shade. When grown indoors, it can grow too large for its situation and may need drastic pruning or replacing.

Ficus elastica (Moraceae) : Common name-Indian rubber Plant.

This is quick growing, medium tree having large and leathery, smooth and shining leaves. Young leaves remain enclosed in a pinkish stipule giving the plant an ornamental look. It grows best in heavy rainfall areas. It is used more as a foliage plant than a shade tree.

Ficus infectoria (Moraceae) : Common name-Pakur, Pilkhan.

It is a spreading, evergreen, low-crown tree, providing a lot of shade and is especially suited for town and city roads. The seedling plants produce straight trunks and high spreading crown, whereas, those from cuttings produce a low crowned, ugly stemmed specimen.

Ficus krishnae (Moraceae) : Common name-Krishna bor, Makhan Katori.

Krishna Fig is a very large, fast growing, evergreen tree up to 30 m tall, with spreading branches and many aerial roots. Leaves stalked, ovate heart-shaped, 3 nerved, when young velvety on both sides. The unique feature of the tree is that the leaves have a pocket-like fold at the base. Leaf stalks with a broad smooth greasy gland at the apex, compressed, downy. The plant is also known as Krishna Butter Cup. As with most things in India, there is a mythological story of Lord Krishna related to the leaves of this tree. The story goes that Lord Krishna was very fond of butter and would even steal it. Once when he was caught by his mother, Yashoda, he tried to hide the butter by rolling it up in a leaf of this tree. Since then, the leaves of these trees have retained this shape.

Ficus religiosa (Moraceae) : Common name-Sacred Fig, Peepal (Hindi).

It is native of India. It is associated with three deities of Hindu religion i.e., Brahma, Vishnu and Shiva and also with Lord Buddha, hence, it is considered to be sacred tree and is worshipped. It is huge tree with spreading branches. Leaves are cordate in shape and shinning. Flowers are very small hidden in syconium which appear in April-May. It is commonly planted in village near ponds for shade and in big parks.

Ficus retusa (Moraceae) : Common name-Chilkhan, Cuban-laurel.

It is native of Indo-Malayan region and China. It is a rapidly-growing, rounded, broad-headed, evergreen tree can reach15m or more in height with an equal spread. The glossy, dark green, leathery leaves are densely clothed on large, somewhat weeping branches and are usually infested with thrips. New growth, produced all year long, is a light rose colour, giving the tree a lovely two-toned effect. The smooth, light grey trunk is quite striking and can grow to 90 cm or 1.2 m in diameter, and it firmly supports the massively spreading canopy. It is useful tree for shade in parks and alongside of roads.

Ficus roxburghii (Moraceae) : Common name-Eve's Apron.

It is native of India.This is a small tree, with leaves 15-45 cm long and 10-30 cm broad, giving the tree very ornamental look. It can be grown as a specimen tree in large parks.

Filicium decipiens (Sapindaceae) : Common name-Fern –leaved tree, Soapberry

Fern Tree is a medium-sized tree, native to the Western Ghats. The young plant is very ornamental and is used for decoration. Leaves are pinnate, leaflets 6-8 pair, smooth, shining, opposite or some alternate, stalkless, linear oblong, 10-15 cm long, with a prominent midrib. Leaf spine has a leafy wing on either side between the leaflets. Flowers are small and numerous but the tree is grown for its attractive foliage.

Grevillea robusta (Proteaceae) : Common name-Silver oak, Silk oak or Australian oak.

It is native of eastern Australia. It is a fast growing evergreen tree, between 18-35 m tall with dark green delicately dented bipinnatifid leaves. It is the largest plant in the *Grevillea* genus, reaching diameters in excess of one metre. These leaves are generally 15-30 cm long with greyish white or rusty undersides. Its flowers are golden-orange bottle-brush like and appear during April-May. Flowers attract honey sucking birds and bees. It can withstand drought remarkably. The plant is very ornamental and can be planted along avenues or as lawn specimen. Young plants can be used as pot plant.

Kigellia pinnata (Bignoniaceae) : Common name-Fetish tree, Sausage tree, Jhar phanoos.

It is native of Africa. The tree is medium to large size, evergreen where rainfall occurs throughout the year but deciduous where there is a long dry season. The leaves are opposite or in whorls of three, pinnate, with six to ten oval leaflets. The cup shaped, mottled, dark-purplish flowers with a foetid smell hang down from branches on long flexible, their scent is most notable at night indicating their reliance on pollination by bats which visit them for pollen and nectar. The flowering is in April-May. The fruits are big, heavy and sausage shaped. The tree is widely grown as an ornamental tree in tropical regions for its decorative flowers and unusual fruit. Planting sites should be selected carefully, as the falling fruit can cause serious injury to people and damage vehicles parked under the trees.

Madhuka indica (Sapotaceae): Common name-Mahua.

This is a large deciduous tree (20m) with spreading habit. The new emerging leaves are copper coloured and give tree a very ornamental look during spring.The fleshy, creamy-white, globular, scented flowers appear in March-April in dense fascicles near the end of branches. The flowers are stalked and drooping. The tree may be planted along highways for shade. The flowers and fruits are source of food for tribals. The oil from seeds is used in soap-making.

Melia azedarch (Meliaceae) : Common name-Persian Lilac, White Cedar, China berry, Bead Tree.

Melia is a medium sized (5-8m), fast growing deciduous tree similar in appearance to Neem. The tree got its name from Greek word *Melia*, means ash, in illusion to the appearance of leaves and Persian word *azad-darakht*, meaning an independent tree. The leaves are beautiful and fern-like, shed in winter and new leaves along with sweet scented lavender-coloured flowers appear in March-April. The round-yellow drupe fruit also look ornamental. The seeds have a central perforation and used as beads. The plant is shallow rooted and, therefore, should not be planted in windy areas as they may be easily blown off.

Mimusops elengi (Sapotaceae) : Common name-Bullet wood tree, Mulsari (Hindi).

It is a medium sized (15m), evergreen tree of Indian origin. It has a dense crown with shining dark-green foliage.The flowers are white, very fragrant, borne in clusters during April-July and September to November. The bark, flowers, fruits and seeds are astringent, cooling, anthelmintic, tonic and febrifuge. It is mainly used in dental ailments like bleeding gums, pyorrhea, dental carries and loose teeth. The tree is suitable for planting in large lawn or as avenue tree along narrow roads.

Polyaltha longifolia (Anonaceae) : Common name-The mast tree, Ashoka.

Polyalthia longifolia is a lofty evergreen tree, native to India, commonly planted due to its effectiveness in alleviating noise pollution. It exhibits symmetrical pyramidal growth with willowy weeping pendulous branches and long narrow lanceolate leaves with undulate margins. The tree is known to grow over 20m in height. Flowers are inconspicuous. The tree is highly esteemed as an avenue tree for its graceful appearance.

Pongamia glabra (Leguminosae) : Common name-Karanj.

It is a medium tal tree of Indian origin.The tree has a short bole and spreading shady crown having smooth grey bark. Trifoliate leaves are bright green and glossy. Flowers are lilac or mauve-coloured, borne in short racemes in the axils of the leaves. The plant flowers in leafless condition in the last week of April to May. When the tree is laden with flowers, it is really worth-seeing. It is mainly used as a shade tree or for ornamental purpose. Very suitable for roadside avenues. Its leaves provide green manure and it is used for the cure of skin diseases.

Putranjiva roxburghii (Euphorbiaceae) : Common name-Lucky bean tree, Indian-Amulet plant, Wild olive, Child-life tree, Jiaputa, Jalpitni (Hindi)

Putranjiva is a famous, moderate-sized, evergreen tree, growing up to 12 m in height. It has pendant branches and dark grey bark having horizontal lenticels. Leaves are simple, alternately arranged, dark green, shiny, elliptic-oblong, distantly serrated. Male flowers, with short stalks, in rounded axillary clusters, female flowers 1-3 in leaf axil. Fruits ellipsoid or rounded drupes, white velvety; seed normally one, stone pointed, rugose, very hard. Bark and leaves used as medicine; fruits used as medicine for rheumatism. It is a very good avenue tree and can be planted in public places as a shade tree.

Ravenala madagascariensis (Musaceae) : Common name-Travellers' tree, Travellers palm.

It has been given the name "traveller's palm" because the sheaths of the stems hold rainwater, which can be used as an emergency drinking supply. The enormous paddle-shaped leaves are borne on long petioles, in a distinctive fan shape aligned in a single plane. The tree has a tall trunk (up to 30m) resembling that of palm, is evergreen. The large white flowers are structurally similar to those of its relatives, the bird-of-paradise flowers *Sterlitzia reginae* but less attractive. In tropical and subtropical regions, the plant is widely cultivated for its distinctive habit and foliage.

Salix babylonica (Salicaceae) : Common name-Weeping willow, Napoleon willow

The tree is native of China. It is a large-sized to medium deciduous tree, growing up to 20-25 m tall. It grows rapidly but has a short lifespan. The shoots are yellowish-brown, with small buds. The leaves are spirally arranged, narrow, light green, 4-16 cm long and 0.5-2 cm broad, with finely serrate margins and long acuminate tips ; they turn a gold-yellow in autumn. The flowers are arranged in catkins produced early in the spring; it is dioecious, with the male and female catkins on separate trees.

Samanea saman (Leguminosae) : Common name-Rain tree.

It is native of Central America and West Indies and is common in tropical India; particularly West Bengal. It is a large, handsome tree with spreading crown. Although the plant bears pink and white silken tufts of flowers covering the whole canopy during March to May and again during September to November. This is regarded more as a shade and ornamental tree rather than flowering tree. The tree does not well in northern India due to frost. It is wind resistant and retains its symmetrical shape in spite of wind hazards, so good for avenue trees in such locations.

Schleichera trijuga (Sapindaceae) : Common name-Ceylon Oak, Kusum.

It is native of India, Sri Lanka and Mayanmar.It is a large tree but the growth is slow. The new emerging leaves are carmine-red in colour then gradually turning to green. It is well suited for large public parks and garden.

Swietenia mahagoni (Meliaceæ) : Common name-Mahogany, Abnus (Hindi).

It is native of troical North and South America. It is a medium-sized semi-evergreen tree growing to 30–35 m tall. The leaves are pinnate with four to eight leaflets. The flowers are small and produced in panicles. *Swietenia mahagoni* is the species from which the true original mahogany wood was produced. Supplies have now become very rare due to over harvesting. In USA, it is now enlisted as endangered species. In tropical and sub tropical region it can be used as a avenue tree.

Terminalia arjuna (Combretaceae) : Common name-Arjun Tree.

It is found throughout India, Mayanmar and Sri Lanka usually on the banks of rivers and streams. It is a large evergreen shade tree, commonly planted on roadside. The flowers are pale yellowish white and crowded on a long axis. It flowers from March to June when its honey attracts swarms of bees. It has medicinal properties too and widely used by Ayurvedic physician for its curative properties in organic/ functional heart problems including angina, hypertension and deposits in arteries.

Terminalia catappa (Combretaceae) : Common name-Indian Almond.

This tree thrives as an ornamental tree in many tropical cities in the world. Tropical almond is a large deciduous stately tree, originally from India, growing up to 28 m tall with horizontal whorls of branches offering clusters of foot long; obviate leaves that turn pink-red to red-yellow before falling. It can be planted on roadsides.

Trees for bio-aesthetic planning

Professor lancelot Hogben defined bioaesthetic planning "as a conscious planning of the flora and fauna with the object of beautifying the country". It includes the planting of ornamental flowering trees along with city roads, in parks, public places and compounds of houses both in towns and villages and development of national parks for the preservation of beautiful, non-carnivorous animals and the creation of bird sanctuaries. The object of a bio-aesthetic planning for India is the encouragement of the planting of selected ornamental flowering trees in our town and villages, protection of beautiful, harmless birds such as wild ducks, egrets, geese and sarus cranes by legal declaration of our lakes as bird such as black bucks, blue bulls, sambhars and spotted deer which are being ruthlessly exterminated in national parks and zoological gardens in the vicinity of our cities. Bio aesthetic planning embraces landscape gardening as well.

The entire country is susceptible to bio aesthetic planning provided a consistent policy is followed and a persistent efforts is made over a long period. A bio aesthetic planner is a master artist whose canvas is the entire country and whose pigments are the beautiful flowering plants. He paints the canvas of the countryside in rich colours, blue, orange, red, yellow, scarlet and pink. With the blue jacarandas, yellow amaltas, orange scarlet gulmohars, scarlet colvilleas, red erythrinas and pink lagerstromias, he paints the side walks of the roads, the platforms of railway stations, the canal banks and the compounds of houses and public buildings. His objective is to lay them out in a pleasing pattern so that an attractive picture results.

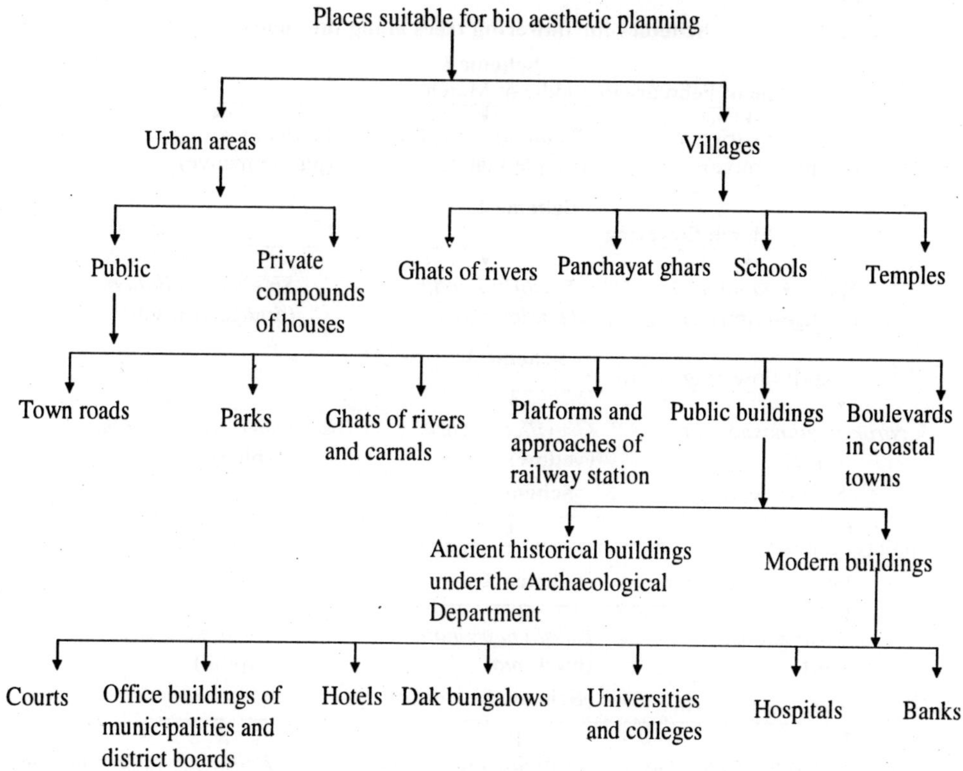

Ornamental trees suitable for town roads

Foliage trees for outer avenues	***Flowering trees for inner avenues***
Averrhoa carambola,	*Cassia fistula,*
Callistemon lanceolatus,	*Bouhinia purpurea,*
Anthocephalus cadamba,	*Bauhinia variegate,*
Eugenia operculata,	*Colvillea racemosa,*
Polyalthia longifolia,	*Peltophorum ferrugineum,*
Putranjiva roxburghii,	*Spathodea milotica,*
Sterculia alata,	*Jacaranda mimosaefolia,*
Pithecolobium saman,	*Poinciana regia,*
Melia azadirachta,	*Lagerstroemia flosreginae,*
Tamarindus indica,	*Grevillea robusta,*
	Gliricidia maculate.

Schemes for flowering trees along the roads

Scheme 1

Middle of February to middle of March

- *Bauhinia variegata* (purple-mauve)
- *Bauhinia variegata* (purple-mauve)
- *Bauhinia variegata* (purple-mauve)

Scheme 2

March flowering

- *Spathodea nilotica* (orange-crimson)
- *Erythrina indica* (scarlet red)
- *Spathodea nilotica* (orange-crimson)

Scheme 3

April flowering

- *Jacaranda mimosaefolia* (blue)
- *Grevillea robusta* (yellow)
- *Jacaranda mimosaefolia* (blue)

Scheme 4

May flowering

- Amaltas (yellow)
- Gulmohar (scarlet-orange)
- Amaltas (yellow)

Scheme 5

May and June flowering

- *Cassia nodosa* (pink)
- *Cassia marginata* (brick-red)
- *Cassia nodosa* (pink)

Scheme 6

October flowering

- *Peltophorum ferrugineum* rusty shield bearer (golden yellow)
- *Colvillea racemosa* (orange-red)
- *Peltophorum ferrugineum* (golden yellow)

Naming of Roads after trees

Bio-aesthetic planning will simplify the problem of naming roads and streets. Streets can be named after the flowering trees which are grown on the roads such as Amaltas avenue, Kachnar avenue, Gulmohar avenue and Asoka avenue. Road junction (Triangles) can be planted with trees. Trees of only one species can be planted in one triangle. Beautiful roads and well-planned parks and squares will bring the beauty of nature within the reach of a common man in our town and cities. The dwellers of slums will also appreciate the beauty and splendour of flowering trees or atleast their children will who will have the opportunity of growing up in a new environment. Those who lived in filthy surroundings for generations cannot suddenly transformed in a few years into lovers of beauty. But the attempt is certainly worth making and the results will be tangible after sometime.

Criteria for selection of trees

While shade and economic utility should be the criteria for selecting trees for national, state and district roads passing through the country, different types of trees are required for town roads. For road side avenues in towns and cities, shade and beauty are the sole criteria which one should consider while selecting the trees. The choice should be restricted to a single species for each street. Very tall trees like Eucalyptus and Milingtonia and trees with spreading crowns like banyan are unsuitable for town roads because they interfare with electric wires. Medium sized trees like *Eugenia operculata* and Pakar (*Ficus infectoria*) are ideal for shade while for beauty we have a large number of trees to choose from. Double avenues of trees are a necessity in big cities where wide roads available. The outer row should be composed of evergreen shade trees with dense foliage such as tamarind, *Polyalthia longifolia, Eugenia operculata, Putranjiva roxburghii, Mimusops elengi, Ficus retusa, Melia azadirachta* and Pakar. The function of the outer row is to provide shade only. The trees should be planted in pure avenues and not in mixtures. Growth in pure avenues provides a beautiful skyline and a pleasing effect to the uniform size and shape of the crowns of the trees of same species while mixture creates an ugly confusion with a jagged skyline. The inner row should be of ornamental flowering trees. The trees in both the rows should be planted at a distance of a metres from each other with trees in opposite rows alternating.

CHAPTER-8

BULBOUS AND FOLIAGE PLANTS

Bulbous plants constitute one of the most important groups of the floral wealth. Beauty, fragrance and colour of their bloom, the superb excellence of their flowers for interior decorations, their symbolic values and medicinal aspects have been responsible for endearing their cultivation to the garden lover. In commercial horticultural terminology, the word bulb is used for more extensively to include such underground organs as corms (Gladiolus, Crocus and Freesia), rhizomes (Canna and Calla), tubers (tuberous Begonia, Caladium and Gloxinia) and tuberous roots (Ranunculus and Dahlia).

Bulb: It is short, flattened, disc-shaped, specialized, under-ground, upright shoot bearing thick leafy bases, axillary buds and a prominent terminal bud. In bulbs the stems remains comparatively small and the food material is stored in the large, fleshy scales which invest and overlap the stem. The bulbs are of two types: (i) the scaly or imbricate bulbs, where the fleshy and scale leaves are folded around a central axis, overlapping each other at their margins, e.g., *Lilium, Fritillaria* and (ii) the tunicated, where the outer leaves, usually thin, membranous and dry are large and completely ensheath the inner portions and the central axis of the bulb like a tunic e.g., *Allium, Narcissus, Tulipa* and *Hyacinthus*.

Corm: It is a short, solid, vertical, elongated, much swollen under ground stem with one to several large buds near the top, a tuft of leaves at the upper side, ring of thick fibrous roots round the base and is covered by thin, membranous, loose scales, each more or less sheathing or completely surrounding it.

Rhizome: It is an underground or subterranean, elongated, horizontal stem growing at some depth below the surface of the soil. Like typical stems, it possesses terminal buds and produces lateral buds at the nodes in the axil of leaves, which are scale-like, thin, membranous, non green, brownish and called scale leaves. The rhizome may be thick and fleshy, serving as a storage organ as in *Dioscorea* or slender and woody as in *Iris, Polygonatum* and many members of Zingiber family.

Tuber: It is an underground, much enlarged, short fleshy, swollen stem or part of a stem, differing from rhizome in its stouter form, generally shorter internodes and the usual absence of roots and from the bulb in that the axis of a typical tuber is fleshy and swollen, serving as a reservoir of reserve material while the leaves are thin and scaly.

Bulb Culture

Most of the bulbs are easy to culture. They are planted three to four times their own depth in reasonably good and light garden soil. The depth of planting varies with the kind of species but in any one kind, the depth should be uniform. The depth should not be shallow particularly in such cases as Crocuses, Gladioli, Lilies and so on, which are subject to frost in the hills. The bulb should never come in contact with the manure.

Plant Propagation

Bulbs are easy to propagate vegetatively. Various structures concerned with vegetative propagation are as follows:

1) The offset, produced laterally towards the base, usually flat in shape.
2) The bulbet or cormlet, produced at the base of the corm and firmly attached to it, appearing as swords above ground.
3) The fragments, parts of the bulb-disc, leaves or stems. The disc is cut vertically, the leaves are removed with a bit of the adhering stem and the stem with a few leaves.
4) The bulbils, produced in the axils of leaves in lilies and occasionally in tulips.
5) The scales, these are pulled off and planted in a mixture.

Planting

The greatest advantage of growing bulbs in a natural way is that they can be left undisturbed to flower for many years. It is mostly the hardier types which can be selected for this purpose. However, bulbs look their best when planted in formal or informal beds. Sometimes they are interplanted with seasonal annuals so as to provide a splash of other colours below for contrasts or they are provided with a foliage background. Planting time of bulbs differs from place to place. In places like Delhi, dahlia tubers are planted from August to September in order to have them in bloom from January to March, while in Bangalore the planting is done in May so as to have flowers in October. The bulbs of plants like *Narcissus, Gladiolus, Oxalis, Freesia* and *Zantedeschia* are planted in autumn in Delhi to have plants in bloom during spring. *Hemerocallis, Amaryllis belladonna, Haemanthus multiflorus* and *Hippeastrum* are planted during spring for having flowers in summer and those of *Gloriosa superba, Pancratium latifolium* and *Zephyranthes carinata* are planted during summer to have splashing arrays of flowers during the rainy season in the plains of North India. In the hills, most of the bulbous plants are planted in February after the danger of frost and snow is over.

Stages in the life history

Bulbous plants pass through three stages in their life history: the blooming period, the rest period and the growing period. In nature, most of them usually go to rest after flowering and put forth beautiful flowers or vegetative growth immediately after this period is over. Some produce leaves and flowers simultaneously but in some as *Haemanthus multiflorus,* the flowers are followed by the foliage; or as in *Narcissus, Gladiolus* and *Freesia,* the foliage precedes the flowers. Nevertheless, in most of the cases, leaves start withering after flowering and soon die. At this stage, watering is stopped so that food reserves could be stored in the bulbs. After this accumulation, the plants go to rest and enter the rest period which may extend over a few weeks.

Lifting and storage

After the leaves are dead, the bulbs are dug out, the roots are cut away and so is the top. They are then stored in dry, dark, airy place until the next planting time. During storage, both dampness and too dry conditions are harmful, the former proves fatal as, generally, it creates favourable conditions for growth of the green mould *Penicillium gladioli.* Corms of *Gladiolus* are highly susceptible to this mould, which attacks and gradually destroys the stem disc. Similarly, the tubers of *Dahlia* and *Caladium* suffer badly. *Dahlia* is attacked by *Sclerotinia sclerotiorum* and *Narcissus* and *Daffodils* by *Penicillium narcissi.* To avoid fungal contamination, all mud and dirt should be washed off the bulbs at the time of division and separation. They should be dried properly in shady and airy place and when moderately dry, stored in dry sand in boxes in a cool and airy place. The sand may be changed after every two weeks till replanting. Bulbs of some species need transplanting immediately after separation. But, when the site for replanting is not ready, these may first be planted separately in small pots and later transplanted to the required sites. When bulbs are to remain in the ground after the foliage has died down, these should never be watered till growth restarts in the next season. If watering is continued, they rot and perish.

Growing in Pots

Most of the bulbous, tuberous and rhizomatous plants are grown successfully in old or new pots. The old pots should be washed thoroughly before use and the new ones placed in water for about half an hour before use. The pots should not be actually wet, when used, for the soil and eventually the roots will stick to it. The tender roots do not freely circulate around the pot, nor will plants easily slip out of a dirty pot while being repotted. New pots should be soaked in water for about two hours to make them completely moist so that the soil does not lose moisture. The pots should be dried later. The soil should be filled up to 2.5 cm of the top of the pot. After planting, the pots also should be soaked in water and later placed in the open on a garden table or a slate. This prevents worms from getting into the pot. Where possible, the pots may be clothed with wet fibre so as to do away with frequent watering. It is advisable to place the pots in dark because it encourages good root growth. After the crown makes about 2.5 cm of growth, the pot may be moved gradually to full light and liberally supplied with water. Manure, may also be added. However, water requirements and nutritional needs of individual species vary greatly. The number of bulbs to be planted per pot depends on the species and the size of the pots.

Growing in Bowls

Many bulb such as *Crocuses, Daffodils, Freesia, Fritillarias, Hyacinths, Leucojum, Muscari, Narcissus, Ornithogalum, Oxalis, Pyroliron, Scilla, Tulips* and *Zephyranthes* may be grown successfully in bowls. These bowls look highly admirable and add colour and gaiety in schemes of interior decoration. A variety of bowls are available in interesting shapes and sizes; those selected should be simple in shape and colour. The colour of the bowl should not distract attention from or clash with the beautiful blossoms produced by the bulbous plants. The bowls should be 13 – 15 cm deep, glazed and not porous. The bowls are filled with fibre to within 12 mm of the rim. In the larger ones bulbs are planted in small clumps but in smaller ones they are filled so that they nearly but not quiet touch each other. In either case, their tips should show above the level of the fibre which is pressed around firmly but gently. The bowl is watered to the extent that it remains just moist but not wet. The bowl is kept in dark in an airy corner till the crowns grow to about 25 mm. it is gradually brought out in light. Once the shoots turn a healthy green, the bowls are removed to the window and sunshine. After it is placed in light, the bowl requires an occasional turning so that the shoots do not grow only in one direction and become lop-sided.

Bulbs in Herbaceous Borders

Herbaceous borders can be planned with the help of bulbous, tuberous and rhizomatous plants in formal and informal situations where they provide a succession of bloom almost throughout the year. Due consideration, however, has to be given to the height, the colour of foliage and flowers and the ultimate spread of a particular plant. Such borders are laid along roads, water ponds, streams and lakes. An excellent use can be made of plants whose leaves do not die after the flowering is over to keep the elegance of the border after the blooming season is over. Their attractive foliage will add gaiety and charm to the borders. This sequence can be achieved effectively by planting the bulbs in irregular groups rather than in single rows around the front of the border. The kind of bulb and size of the borer should be kept in mind. The hardy bulbs which may be left in the beds after flowering should not be planted closed to or beneath the perennial elements of the border because they cannot grow well in this way. Special care should be taken of the tender species. The taller growing plants may be planted among the low growing foliage elements.

Description of some important bulbous plant

Achimens grandiflora: Family: Gesneriaceae

It is a tuberous rooted, annual flowering plant growing to a height of about 25 cm. The rhizome is filiform and produces pear shape tubers at its end. The flowers are crimson in colour, axillary, solitary or clustered, flattened a little and petunia like. They are produced from June to October.

Acidanthera bicolor: Family: Iridaceae

It flowers in winter in the plains and during summer in the hills. It attains a height of about 0.5 -0.7 m. The stem is arching and unbranched, bearing linear leaves and flowers in loose spikes. The flowers are fragrant, possessing chocolate-brown marking on the creamy petals. The corms are globose.

Agapanthus africanus: Family: Liliaceae

It grows to a height of about 1 m, the foliage is graceful, evergreen and about 60 cm long, linear and forming a rosette. The inflorescence is many flowered umbel. Flowers are produced profusely. The tufts of azure-blue flowers are borne on leafless spathes. Each spathe raises its head well above the foliage and bears about three dozen flowers.

Allium ramosum: Family: Liliaceae

It has pale-brown bulbs, attains a height of 22-45 cm and bears many white flowers. The leaves are four or more, linear or cylindrical and 30 cm long. The scape is 15 to 37 cm high.

Allium paradoxum: Family: Liliaceae

It has 22 to 30 cm high scape, bearing few white flowers.

Allium neapolitanum: Family: Liliaceae

It bears linear to lanceolate leaves and many white flowers. Each flower is about 37 mm long. The leafless scape is 22-30 cm long, carrying a luster of flowers at the apex.

Alocasia macrorrhiza: Family: Araceae

This species has green leaves but the form in cultivation has variegated leaves, blotched and mottled white. Propagation is by division of rhizome.

Alocasia sanderiana: Family: Araceae

The under surface of the leaves is purplish and the upper surface has white nerves and white margin.

Alpinia sanderae: Family: Zingiberaceae

It is an evergreen plant and grows to about 2 m. the leaves are variegated, each being lanceolate with a sheating base. It is mostly planted for its handsome foliage.

Amaryllis belladonna: Family: Amaryllidaceae

It is a bulbous plant, 45 to 60 cm in height, bearing strap-shaped and acute leaves. The inflorescence is an umbel having a few flowers. The latter are large, fragrant and rose coloured. They are borne on scape which attains a height of 60-120 cm.

Anemone japonica: Family: Ranunculaceae

It grows to a height of about 60-90 cm, bearing rosy, purple or carmine flowers.

Anemone quinquefolia: Family: Ranunculaceae

In the hills, it flowers from April to May. It is 10-15 cm tall with a horizontal rootstock and bearing white flowers and deeply lobed leaves.

Anemone rivularis: Family: Ranunculaceae

It flowers in April. It is rhizomatous, having a fleshy rootstock resembling turnip in shape, it is 30 to 60 cm tall and has white and blue flowers with purple anthers.

Arisaema flavum: family: Araceae

This species has two leaves per plant and a globose rootstock. It is a Himalayan species, has a greenish yellow spathe, coloured purple on inside and a conical spadix unlike other species where it is tubular.

Arisaema nepenthoides: family: Araceae

It is in the prime of its beauty during spring in Sikkim. It has a very large globose tuber and two leaves. The spathe is whitish within and yellow without. The spadix is whitish.

Arisaema speciosum: family: Araceae

It is commoly called as Snake Lily, blooms in March in the temperate Himalayas. It has a solitary leaf with a green, often brown or purple specked petiole.

Arisaema tortuosum: family: Araceae

It flowers during May and June in the hills. It has long petiole (30-90 cm) which is green and often mottled with purple. The leaves are 2 to 3 per plant. The spathe is pale green or purplish. The tubers are large, spheroidal and about 12.5 cm in diameter.

Asparagus sprengeri: Family: Liliaceae

The plants are perennial, rhizomatous or tuberous, bearing dry scale leaves and green, needle like, linear and appearing highly decorative. The flowers are small, greenish white and borne in racemes or umbels. The fruit is berry. It turns red on ripening.

***Begonia* spp.:** Family: Begoniaceae

Begonia is divided into two groups: the bulbous including the tuberous rooted species and the rhizomatous types also consisting of fibrous rooted species.

1. Tuberous rooted Begonias: The plants are usually 45 cm tall. There is a diverse variety of colour and form available in the flowers of tuberous rooted begonias. They may be fringed, fimbriated and crested, single or double in attractive colours of vermillion white and pink. It includes species like *Begonia* davissi, *Begonia froebelii, Begonia bicolor* and *Begonia evansiana.*
2. Rhizomatous Begonias: This group also flourishes in the hills. Plants may be erect, creeping, trailing or climbing and free flowering. It includes species like *Begonia rex* and *Begonia convolvulacea.*

***Belamcanda chinensis*:** Family Iridaceae

It is a tuberous rooted herbaceous perennial, attaining a height of 1-1.3 m. The leaves closely resemble those of iris. The flowers are borne in loosely arranged clusters. It is actually the perianth which is colourful.

***Caladium* spp.:** Family: Araceae

The plants are in their prime during rainy season. The leaves are thin, usually peltate and variously coloured. The petioles are normally green but the blade is a riot of colours. The spathe has aboat shaped limb enclosing an erect spadix.

Canna indica: Family: Cannaceae

The stems attain a height of 1 -1.7 m. The leaves are 30-45 cm long. The staminodes are three in number and about 50 mm long. These may be red or rosy or the upper portion of the petaloid stamens is bright red and the lip is red yellow possessing red dots. The rhizomes are tuberous.

***Chlorophytum* spp.:** Family: Liliaceae

The rhizome is horizontal or more or less ascending, usually with thick roots. The leaves are evergreen, slender, green or variegated. The flowers are not conspicuous, being small and white. They are borne on a loose, 45-75 cm long spike.

Colocasia affinis: Family: Araceae

The leaves and scapes are usually radical, the former about a metre long and black violet in colour. The tubers are round, rich in starch and edible and thus are of great economic value.

Convallaria majalis: Family: Liliaceae

It is a rhizomatous, herbaceous, perennial plant which attains a height of about 23 cm. Rhizome is creeping and has slender branches. Each plant bears a couple of attractive, oblong to lanceolate and radical leaves. The flowers are drooping, delicate, white and sweetly scented.

Cooperanthes: Family: Amaryllidaceae

The flower appears in hot weather on leafless scapes which vary in height from 15 – 30 cm. They are upright, having a soft rose colour with white ground on the inside, the perianth being deep pink on outside. The glory of the individual flower is short lived as it lasts only for a day or so and then fades.

Cooperia pedunculata: Family: Amaryllidaceae

It is commonly known as Giant Prairie Lily. It has about 30 cm long leaves. The flowers are white and larger.

Cooperia drummondii: Family: Amaryllidaceae

Commonly known as Evening Star. It produces white flowers with a red tinge on the outside. The leaves are about 30 cm long and the bulb is roundish.

Cooperia oberwettii: Family: Amaryllidaceae

The leaves are glaucous but flowers are similar to those of ***Cooperia drummondii***

Costus speciosus: Family: Zingiberaceae

It is a rhizomatous plant which resembles ginger in habit. It grows to a height of 1.33-3 m. The stem is woody and covered with spirally arranged fleshy foliage. The leaves are 15-23 cm long, oblong or oblanceolate and dark green in colour, with underside velvety to touch. The flowers are showy, more commonly being red, white, yellow and orange.

Crinum asiaticum: Family: Amaryllidaceae

It has bulb up to 15 cm thick with 10-15 cm long or even longer necks. The leaves form a rosette, each being smooth, about a metre long, 10-15 cm wide and of deep green colour. The flowers are white and borne in an umbel.

Crinum yuccaeflorum: Family: Amaryllidaceae

It is a charming species bearing zygomorphic, white flowers with red bands at the back of each perianth. The scape is slender and about 30 cm high. It generally bears one to two flowers.

Crinum defixum: Family: Amaryllidaceae

The leaves are linear, about 25 mm wide and 30 cm to 1 m long. The flowers are borne in an umbel of a dozen large sized flowers. They are highly fragrant, especially at night. The bulbs are about 10 cm thick.

Crinum distichum: Family: Amaryllidaceae

It is an evergreen plant. It never sheds its leaves, and bloom throughout the rainy season in the plains. The flowers are white, tinged red on the outside of each segment.

Crinum americanum: Family: Amaryllidaceae

It is ideal for growing in swampy and marshy situations. It has creamy white and highly fragrant flowers.

Crocus sativus: Family: Iridaceae

The leaves are grass like, arising from the corm and 0.33 to 0.5 m long. Each plant has six to eight leaves. The flowers are borne on scapes enclosed in a tubular sheath.

***Cyclamen* spp.:** Family: Primulaceae

The leaves are radical, cordate or reniform and stalked. The flowers are solitary and borne on scapes rising well above the foliage. They are nodding or declined and white, purple or rose coloured, pretty, single, delicate and shuttle like. Prominent colours are white, pink, crimson and purple.

Cyrtanthus mackenii: Family: Amaryllidaceae

The plants grows to a height of about 30 cm. The leaves are two to six in number, linear, 20 to 30 cm long, slender and about 0.63 cm wide. The inflorescence is an umbel which is nodding or pendulous and the scalp is hollow. The number of flowers in an umbel varies from four to ten. The leaves and flowers appear simultaneously during spring.

Dahlia coccinea: Family: Asteraceae

It grows to a height of about a metre. The popular colours are scarlet, orange and yellow. The leaves are bi-pinnate. The flower heads are single, possessing sterile ray-florets in wild form but fertile ones in the garden forms.

Dahlia rosea: Family: Asteraceae

It attains a height of 1-1.5 m. The leaves are one-pinnate. The ray florets are fertile. The species are variable and a huge variety of colour is available. There are single and double forms.

Dahlia pinnata: Family: Asteraceae

It is 0.75-1 m tall, bearing 5 foliate leaves and large flower heads. The rays have bluish-red margins and are in several rows appearing as semi double flower heads.

Dahlia imperialis: Family: Asteraceae

It is a very tall species, about 2-6 m high, with a four to six angled stem, bearing two to three pinnate leaves and 10-18 cm across flower heads. The flower heads are long stalked, nodding and normally white with the ray tinged red.

Dahlia excelsa: Family: Asteraceae

It is erect and grows to a height of 7 m or more. The leaves are two-pinnate, about a metre long and 0.75 m wide. The flowers heads are purple, the disc being crimson pink.

Dahlia juarezii: Family: Asteraceae

It is commonly known as Cactus Dahlia. It bears bright-scarlet flower heads, possessing florets at irregular lengths.

Dianella tasmanica: Family: Liliaceae

The plants are 60 cm – 1.5 m high. The leaves are grass like broadly ensiform, rigid in appearance, 90-120 cm long. The flowers are bluish in colour, borne in panicles on dropping pedicels. They bloom during spring and summer.

Dierama pulcherrimum: Family: Iridaceae

The stem is about 2 m high, bearing narrow and sword like leaves and deep blood-red or bright purple coloured flowers on a scape which is 0.75-2 m long.

Dierama pendulum: Family: Iridaceae

It blooms in June-July is about a metre tall, bearing very stiff, about 50 cm long leaves and white or pink to purple flowers.

Eichhornia speciosa: Family: Pontederiaceae

It is a thick, rhizomatous plant which grows to a height of 15-30 cm. The leaves are large, fleshy, orbicular and borne in tufts. The flowers are funnel shaped and about 37 mm long. The inflorescence is about eight flowered spike and the scape is about 30 cm long.

Eucharis grandiflora: Family: Amaryllidaceae

It grows to a height of 15-22 cm. The leaves are green, 25-30 cm long and lanceolate. The inflorescence is an umbel. The scape attains a height of 30-45 cm, bearing about half a dozen, drooping, white and sweet scented flowers.

Freesia refracta: Family: Iridaceae

It grows to a height of half a metre. The leaves are about 15 cm long. The flowers are borne in loose spikes and the perianth is greenish yellow or bright yellow with a few violet veins and its segments are two lipped.

Fritillaria imperialis: Family: Liliaceae

The bulbs are large, round and scaly. The stem is 60-90 cm long. The leaves are 12.5-15 cm long, alternate, lanceolate, often whorled in the upper region.

Gladiolus **spp.:** Family: Iridaceae

It is popularly known as the Corn Flag or Sword Lily, because its leaves resemble the sword. It is a beautiful bulbous plants which blooms during spring in the plains and from July to September in the hills. *Gladiolus* has a wide range of attractive shades: White, crimson, pink, orange, salmon-red, scarlet, purple, cream, apricot, cherry red and rose.

Gloriosa superba: Family: Liliaceae

It is a ornamental bulbous plant. The flowers, very showy and looking like frozen flames are produced on long axillary peduncles. On opening, the flowers have their tips red and the lower portion yellow, the whole changing to a deep orange red or red on attaining maturity.

Haemanthus multiflorus: Family: Amaryllidaceae

The leaves are broad, obtuse, fleshy, sheating and 15 – 30 cm long. The inflorescence is a dense, many flowered umbel, producing football-like globular heads. The flowers are blood red and borne on a 0.33 - 1m high scape.

Hedychium **spp.:** Family: Zingiberaceae

It is a success both at low and high elevations in India, blooming freely during rains. It is valued both for its foliage and fragrant flowers. The leaves are sheating and lanceolate. The inflorescence is a many flowered spike.

Hemerocallis **spp.:** Family: Liliaceae

It is a hardy perennial plant. The roots are tuberous and fleshy. The leaves are radical, linear, acute, grass-like and yellowish green. The flowers are borne on tall scapes. The flowers are large lily-like, yellow, orange or reddish.

Hippeastrum **spp.:** Family: Amaryllidaceae

They are hardy tunicated bulbous plants which grow to a height of 0.5-0.75 m. The leaves are linear or strap-shaped. The flowers have segments of four different sizes. The inflorescence is usually an umbel bearing flowers on a scape about 30-45 cm long.

Hosta plantaginea: Family: Liliaceae

The leaves are large, with long stalks, cordate-ovate, up to 30 cm long and 10-20 cm broad. The plants bloom during summer and autumn. The flowers are white, fragrant, trumpet-shaped with the lobes up to 12.5 cm long.

Hyacinthus orientalis: Family: Liliaceae

It has a large, whitish or purple, globular bulb with a pleasing metallic lusture and upto 45 cm long, hollow scape. The leaves are thick and strap shaped. The flowers are fragrant in many colours, prominently purple, white and blue.

Hymenocallis calathina: family: Amaryllidaceae

The plant is about 60 cm tall. The leaves are as long as the plant or less, six to eight in number and two ranked. The inflorescence is an umbel. The flowers are greenish white, fragrant, funnel or cup shaped with a fringed crown, borne on the spathe which is 0.33-0.75 m long.

***Iris* spp.:** Family: Iridaceae

The stem is simple or branched and the leaves sword like and radical. The flowers are showy and interesting and the perianth with six segments in two whorls of three each. The outer segments are called falls and the inner ones which are smaller, called standards. The falls are reflexed and usually possess a beard at the base.

***Ixia* spp.:** Family: Iridaceae

It is a dwarf cormous plant, possessing a single tunic. It is closely related to sparaxis. The foliage is grass-like. The inflorescence is a simple or branched spike, bearing star-shaped and Narcissus like flowers with a perianth tube.

Kaempferia rotunda: Family: Zingiberaceae

It is a very dwarf tuberous plant, short stemmed or stemless, bearing four or five ornamental, oblong leaves. Each leaf is dark green above, purple on the lower surface and about 15-20 cm long. The flowers are white tubed and violet lipped, the lip consists of two petals borne on the leafy four to six flowered spike.

Kniphofia uvaria: Family: Liliaceae

It is commonly known as Torch flower. It has rhizome with long roots and is 1.33-1.75 m tall. The leaves are radical, several, narrow, 0.6 – 1 m long, 25 mm wide and acuminate. The scape is many flowered. The flowers are drooping in dense racemes, those towards apex are coral-red and those towards are base yellowish.

Leucojum aestivum: Family: Amaryllidaceae

It is an hardy bulbous plant growing to height of 30-45 cm. The bulbs are ovoid, bearing slender and linear or loriforum leaves, pendulous, one to many and white tinged with red or green flowers arranged in an umbel.

***Lilium* spp.:** Family: Liliaceae

The lilies have been divided into two categories, according to the mode of their root bearing: (i) those developing roots from the base of the bulb e.g., *Lilium bulbiferum, Lilium candidum, Lilium croceum, Lilium martagon, Lilium pardalinum, Lilium parryi, Lilium superbum* and *Lilium washingtonianum;* and (ii) those in which the roots at first develop from the base of the bulb but later from the stem as well e.g., *Lilium auratum, Lilium davidii, Lilium longiflorum, Lilium regale, Lilium rubellum, Lilium speciosum, Lilium tigrinum* and *Lilium wallichianum.* There is a huge variety of colours and many peculiar shapes and forms are met. The stem is erect and generally covered with leaves which are either scattered or borne in whorls or sometimes present with the bulbils in the axils. The flowers are showy and colourful, borne in an erect, horizontal, drooping, pendulous or a solitary manner in a raceme or an umbel.

Mirabilis jalapa: Family: Nyctaginaceae

It is popularly known as Four-o' clock plant because the flowers open at about 4 O'clock in the afternoon and close the next morning. It is a tuberous rooted bushy herb, growing to a height of 30-45 cm. The leaves are opposite, smooth and ovate-lanceolate. They are stalked in the lower and sessile in the upper region. The inflorescence is cyme. The flowers are fragrant, possessing expanded mouths and long perianth tubes which are constricted above the ovaries.

Moraea iridioides: Family: Iridaceae

It is a metre or slightly more in height. The foliage is handsome, basal, fan-like, each with a distinct midrib and 45 – 50 cm long. The flowers are about 10 cm wide, sweet scented, attractive and without the perianth tube.

Muscari botryoides: Family: Liliaceae

It flowers during February and March in the plains and April to May in the hills. The leaves are radical, a few, linear and erect. The inflorescence is short raceme bearing flowers like a bunch of grapes. The flowers are sky-blue, as long as wide and resemble in size with black currants.

***Narcissus* spp.:** Family: Amaryllidaceae

The leaves are linear, rush like or strap shaped. The flowers are small, white or yellow, borne in solitary, umbellate or drooping manner or in clusters. The spathe is membranous. The corona of the true narcissus is of a dark brown, orange colour with white perianth segments.

Nelumbo lutea: Family: Nymphaeaceae

It is commonly called as American Lotus or Water Chinkapin. Leaves are 30-60 cm across, raised 60-180 cm out of water. Flowers are yellow and fragrant, 10-25 cm across.

Nelumbo nucifera: Family: Nymphaeaceae

It is commonly called as lotus or Padma or Kamal. Flowers are white, tipped rose or pink but with many variants, 30 cm across and overtopping leaves. Flowering is during the summer.

***Nymphaea* spp.:** Family: Nymphaeaceae

These are commonly called as water-lilies. There are types which can be grown in very shallow waters (*Nymphaea pygmaea* and *Nymphaea tetragona*), in medium depth of water (*Nymphaea alba* and *Nymphaea odorata*) and still others requiring deep water. Nymphaeas are propagated by division of clumps, tubers or by cuttings from the rhizomatous stems of a few species. Seeds germinate easily but the seedlings come to flowering only after about 2-3 years.

Ornithogalum arabicum: Family: Liliaceae

It has nearly globular bulbs and is up to 60 cm tall. The scape is as long as the long strap-shaped leaves. The flowers are many, showy, sweet scented, white with a black centre. The plants bloom during spring.

***Oxalis* spp.:** Family: Oxalidaceae

Oxalis is commonly grown in gardens. They are usually dwarfs with trifoliate and weed like leaves and small but impressive flowers of a variety of colours, e.g., white, yellow, purple, pink and red.

Phaedranassa schizantha: Family: Amaryllidaceae

It is a half hardy bulbous plant, about a metre high, bearing broad, oblong and stalked leaves and a drooping umbel on hollow scapes that rise well above the foliage and bear showy brick red flowers. The perianth tube is funnel shaped with the lobes spreading at the tips.

Polianthes tuberosa: Family: Amaryllidaceae

It grows to 60 cm or slightly more than a metre high. The leaves are long, light green, radical, crowded and 15-23 cm long. The flowers have a funnel shaped perianth, are fragrant, waxy, white, about 25 mm long, single or double and borne in spike.

Ranunculus asiaticus: Family: Ranunculaceae

It is about 22 – 45 cm high, has erect stems, radical, toothed and deeply cut leaves and flowers of various colours with large petals and sepals. The wild form bears single red flowers. Honey is present in a partially concealed manner and the flowers thus attract hordes of insects.

Scilla hispanica: Family: Liliaceae

It is commonly Known as Spanish Bluebell, attains a height of 30-60 cm. Flowers are blue to rose-purple, about 12 in number and borne on erect spikes. The main flowering season is May.

Sparaxis tricolour: Family: Iridaceae

It is 45-60 cm tall, bearing fan like leaves, large, solitary and showy flowers in various colours, the popular being red, mauve, white, orange, yellow, purple and crimson. Each flower has a bright yellow throat and each segment a dark blotch at the base.

Sprekelia formosissima: Family: Amaryllidaceae

The stem is a tunicated bulb, globose and 25 mm in diameter, bearing Amaryllis like, 30-45 cm long leaves, dark velvety crimson, solitary, irregular flowers. The later are large, showy and two-lipped.

Tulbaghia violacea: Family: Liliaceae

It is a bulbous perennial herb. The plant is 30-60 cm tall, bearing grass like, more than half a dozen, 20-30 cm long and radical leaves and 8 to 20, purple violet flowers in an umbel. The scape is 30-45 cm in height.

Tulipa clusiana: Family: Liliaceae

Flowers blooms during April and May. It bears about 15-22 cm long leaves and delicate, solitary, bicoloured flowers, cherry-red on outside and white on inside, on about 30 cm long stems.

Tulipa fosteriana: Family: Liliaceae

It produces solitary, very large, 15-22 cm wide and brilliantly coloured scarlet flowers borne on 45 cm long stems in April. The bulbs are globose and about 5 cm thick.

Tulipa gesneriana: Family: Liliaceae

It grows up to 15-60 cm high. It has a erect stem with four or more leaves. The perianth is red or variously coloured.

Vallota purpurea: Family: Amaryllidaceae

It has large hardy bulbs and flowers during April to May in the hills and spring in semi-shady locations in the plains. The leaves are 30-45 cm long, the flowers are lovely bright scarlet, borne in umbels on 30-60 cm tall stalks. The stamens are shorter than the almost regular perianth.

***Watsonia* spp.:** Family: Iridaceae

It is a half hardy, tunicated bulbous plant, with tall stems, long and sword like leaves and numerous, scarlet, white or rosy, six-lobed flowers borne on spikes. Each flower is sheathed by one bract and two bracteoles at the base and is slightly tilted to the side, this feature lends grater grace.

Zantedeschia aethiopica: Family: Araceae

It is a thick rhizomatous plant, about 60-75 cm or 1.33 m in height, bearing arrow shaped, dark green and twice as long as broad leaves and a dense flowered spadix with handsome and conspicuous spathe, white with a creamy base and fragrant.

***Zephyranthes* spp.:** Family: Amaryllidaceae

Zephyranthes is a half hardy tunicated bulbous plant, bearing linear, hollow, strap-shaped or grass like leaves and solitary, white, pink, red, yellow, rose coloured flowers on hollow scapes. The perianth consists of six segments, which are united at the base to form a tube.

Description of some important foliage plant

***Aechmea* spp.:** Family: Bromeliaceae

This species have attractively marked leaves arranged in a rosette and are grown for indoor gardening as table or small floor plants. Although the foliage is attractive, they are usually sold after inflorescence formation has been induced. Flowers are short lived but the bracts remain colourful for a month or so, followed by colourful berries. Plants are epiphytes, therefore, well-aerated soil mixtures should be used.

***Aeschynanthus* spp.:** Family: Gesneriaceae

Aeschynanthus have opposite or whorled, usually simple leaves and often attractive flowers. They are used in hanging baskets or as pedestal plants.

***Agave* spp.:** Family: Agavaceae

They are monocarpic, flowering once and dying and are often called century plants because they take a decade or longer to flower. They produce fleshy leaves arrange in rosettes. The leaves of many species are harvested for fibre content or fermented for alcoholic beverages. Small specimens are used indoors as table plants and larger ones are used as floor plants.

***Aglaonema* spp.:** Family: Araceae

Aglaonemas have deep green foliage highlighted with silver or white markings, and their ability to grow in low light indoors makes them popular foliage plants.

***Alocasia* spp.:** Family: Araceae

Alocasias have short internodes, long petioles, and usually large peltate to sagittate soft leathery leaves which may be solid green or highly coloured. Most hybrids have unusual leaf patterns and many are grown as landscape ornamentals in subtropical and tropical regions. A few are occasionally used in building interiors for their distinctive forms. A high relative humidity is required to keep plants looking attractive.

***Aloe* spp.:** Family: Liliaceae

Aloe is a genus of succulent herbs, shrubs and trees containing about 255 species native to arid regions of Africa and Asia. Many species are grown as landscape plants in frost free regions and several small species are grown indoors. Thick, succulent leaves are arranged in rosettes and many plants are acaulescent.

***Ananas* spp.:** Family: Bromeliaceae

All nine species in the *Ananas* genus are terrestrial bromeliads with relatively stiff armed leaves arranged in a rosette. The pineapple species are native to tropical America and is grown throughout the tropics. Most species grown for interior use are used as novelty.

***Anthurium* spp.:** Family: Araceae

Anthuriums are epiphytes or terrestrials and the widest grown types produce a spathe subtending the spadix. Most have a plain inflorescence and are grown for their large leathery, arrow-shaped, green or attractively marked leaves. Some

Anthuriums look similar to large leaved philodendrons but can be identified by a swelling on the petiole base. Large leaved *Anthuriums* are used in large plantings in airports and hotels and those with showy foliage or inflorescence are grown as specimen plants. *Anthuriums* are propagated from cuttings, divisions and by tissue culture.

***Aphelandra* spp.:** Family: Acanthaceae

The *Aphelandra* genus contains over eighty species native to tropical America Where most grow as semiwoody plants with attractive opposite leaves. Both terminal and axillary inflorescence usually have short-lived flowers but persistent colourful bracts. Most aphelandras are used indoors as small container plants. The most common grown commercial species is *Aphelandra squarrosa*. It is grown in 95% shade to keep plants vegetative.

***Araucaria* spp.:** Family: Araucariaceae

Araucaria is a small genus with about fifteen species of coniferous trees occurring in wide areas over the southern hemisphere. Whorled branches and stiff needle like leaves are typical of this genus. Most species grow to heights over 30 meters, but their symmetrical evergreen foliage and slow growth in containers makes them popular as indoor trees.

***Ardisia* spp.:** Family: Myrsinaceae

Ardisia comprises about 250 species of woody shrubs and trees native to warm temperate, subtropical and tropical countries. Cultivated species are grown primarily as landscape subjects but *Ardisia crenulata* or coralberry, is commonly grown as a foliage plant for used as a specimen pot plant with fruit or as a small filler plant in dish gardens or terrariums.

***Asparagus* spp.:** Family: Liliaceae

Genus *Asparagus* contain herbs, woody vines and shrub forms. Excluding the edible asparagus, *Asparagus officinalis*, cultivated members are grown as ornamentals, cut foliage, landscape plants or as interior plants. None has true leaves and what appear to be their leaves are modified branches called cladodes. Depending upon growth habit, asparagus species are used in hanging baskets, indoor vines and tables and floor plants in well lighted interiors.

Aspidistra: Family: Liliaceae

Aspidistra is a genus of about eight species native to Asia. Of these, ***Aspidistra elatior*** or cast iron plant is widely used as a landscape and an indoor plant. Aspidistra is propagated by division of thick underground stems. *Aspidistra* is sensitive to fluoride injury. Water quality should be checked and soil amendments adjusted to increase soil pH to eliminate fluoride damage.

***Asplenium* spp.:** Family: Polypodiaceae

The genus *Asplenium* include approximately 700 species of fern, most of which have evergreen foliage that may be entire, deeply cut, or compound. Most types are propagated from spores or vegetative bulblets or plantlets that form on fronds of parent plants. Species that have spreading crowns are divided.

***Beaucarnea* spp.:** Family: Agavaceae

Beaucarnea genus contain six species, all eventually attain a tree height in their natural habitat of Central America. *Beaucarnea recurvata* or ponytail is widely grown as a foliage plant since it is extremely slow growing. Seedling make unusual container plant that stay small enough for desk or table tops for years before becoming large enough for use as a floor plant.

***Begonia* spp.:** Family: Begoniaceae

The *Begonia* genus contains over 1,000 species native to tropical and subtropical regions. Plants vary from 5 cm to 1.8 m and are herbs and semi-woody shrubs with rootstock that may be fibrous, bulbous, rhizomatous or tuberous. The asymmetrical leaves are petioled and alternate. Begonias are extensively cultivated and over 10,000 hybrids have been developed. Most plants are used as bedding plants, flowering pot plants or foliage plants. They are usually divided into three groups: fibrous-rooted, rhizomatous and tuberous forms. Only fibrous-rooted and rhizomatous forms are commonly used indoors.

***Brassaia* spp.:** Family: Araliaceae

Brassia is a genus of about forty species of trees and shrubs native to tropical and subtropical areas of Asia and South Sea Islands. Mature leaves are palmately compound with long petioles. Small plants are used as low floor plants while seedlings of *Brassia actinophylla* are used in dish gardens.

***Calathea* spp.:** Family: Marantaceae

Calathea is a genus with about 100 species of herbaceous plants native to tropical America. Most have short underground stems with attractively marked leathery leaves arranged compactly near the soil surface. Most cultivated species are produced for interior use as container specimens in terrariums and dish gardens or occasionally are grown as landscape ground covers. *Calatheas* are usually propagated by division, although cuttings from mature plants with aboveground shoots are sometimes used.

***Carissa* spp.:** Family: Apocyanaceae

About 30 species of *Carrisa* are native to tropical regions of Asia and Africa, consisting primarily of small shrubs and trees. Many are used for landscape plantings, and some cultivars of *Carissa grandifloras* are sold as interior plants.

***Ceropegia* spp.:** Family: Asclepiadaceae

Ceropegia is genus of about 150 species of succulents twining herbs or subshrubs. Almost all have xerophytic adaptations, thick leafless, swollen stems or enlarge water soaking leaves. Most commercially grown species are vine like and are grown as hanging baskets.

***Chlorophytum* spp.:** Family: Liliaceae

Chlorophytum is a genus composed of 200 or more species of acaulescant, herbaceous plants native to subtropical and tropical areas. Sessile leaves are arranged in basal rosettes that grow from fleshy rootstocks. *Chlorophytum* develops a long pedicel. And, after flowering, plantlets develop on the pedicels. This makes plants especially useful as hanging basket.

***Clusia* spp.:** Family: Guttiferae

The genus *Clusia* contains about 145 species of trees and shrubs native to tropical and subtropical regions of America but only one, *Clusia rosea* or autograph tree is commonly grown as a foliage plant. It is used as a floor plant or indoor tree where coarse texture foliage is required.

***Codiaeum* spp.:** Family: Euphorbiaceae

Codiaeum is a small genus of six species of woody shrubs and trees native to the South Sea Islands and the Malay Peninsula. One variegated species, *Codiaeum variegatum*, is cultivated as a landscape shrub in tropical countries and selected cultivars are grown as interior foliage plants. Leaves are thick, leathery and glabrous. Shape of leaves vary from ovate to linear, entire or lobed, flat or twisted. Young and emerging leaves are green to yellow and later on colour changes according to varietal characteristics.

Coleus: Family: Labiatae

Coleus is a perennial foliage plant grown for its colourful foliage. Most of the garden cultivars of *Coleus* are developed from *Coleus blumei*. The plants grow to a height of 30-50 cm. It can be used as pot plants, in window boxes and some dwarf types can be grown as carpet bedding. It is generally observed that pot-bound plants develop better leaf colour. Flower should be removed constantly.

***Cordyline* spp.:** Family: Liliaceae

Cordylines are evergreen shrub or trees and are valued for their colourful foliage. They are excellent pot plants and at young stage they are widely used for table decoration. They are also suitable for growing in beds and shrubberies, for shade gardens and greenhouses. *Cordyline* is closely related to *Dracaena* and differs to the latter only in the structure of the ovary. Several species of Cordyline are commonly known as Dracaena.

Dieffenbachia x Bausei: Family: Araceae

A hybrid between *Dieffenbachia picta* and *Dieffenbachia weirii.* The pointed leaves are beautifully coloured with yellowish green and dark green with white and dark green spots at the edges.

Dieffenbachia bowmannii: Family: Araceae

The leaves are very large, up to 75 cm long and 30 cm broad, the colour of the leaf is deep rich green, with lighter lateral parallel markings.

Dieffenbachia exotica: Family: Araceae

A mutant possibly from *Dieffenbachia hoffmanii.* Very attractive. The leaves are ovate, matt-green and highly variegated creamy white.

Dieffenbachia hoffmanii: Family: Araceae

The leaves are deep satiny green, much marbled and spotted white including the petioles, mid rib white.

Doryanthes excelsa: Family: Amaryllidaceae

Commonly called as Globe Spear Lily. Inflorescence 4.5 m long with heavy heads 10 cm in diameter, funnel-shaped with paler inside flowers, bracts green.

Doryanthes palmeri: Family: Amaryllidaceae

Commonly known as Spear Lily. Inflorescence 3 - 4.5 m long, spike pyramidal with 6 cm diameter, funnel shaped scarlet red flowers, bracts coloured.

***Episcia* spp.:** Family: Gesneriaceae

Herbaceous perennial plants from Tropical America having fleshy showy foliage and often bearing showy flowers. They are good for hanging baskets.

Fatsia japonica: Family: Araliaceae

An attractive foliage plant from Japan. The leaves are leathery, palmately lobed, shining green in colour, the broad lobes terminate in points and are toothed.

Ficus elastica: Family: Moraceae

A good house plant but grows into a tree up to 30 m tall. The leaves are showy, large, leathery, oblong in shape and deep green in colour. The young leaves are enclosed in a rosy sheath.

Fittonia argyroneura: Family: Acanthaceae

A dwarf, creeping herbaceous plant with bright green oval shaped leaves netted with white veins.

Gynura aurantiaca: Family: Asteraceae

Commonly known as Velvet Plant. It is a herbaceous perennial plant which grows to a height of 60-90 cm, has velvety fleshy leaves covered with violet or purple hairs and have purple veins. The flower heads are brilliant orange.

***Heliconia* spp.:** Family: Musaceae

The plants are grown for their colourful foliage and in some species these have beautiful markings. Some species bear boat shaped flowering bracts which are useful for indoor decoration. The plants do not tolerate direct sun.

Hoffmannia ghiesbreghtii: Family: Rubiaceae

The leaves are lanceolate, soft velvety quilted, bronzy to moss green, rosy red on the reverse.

Homalomena picturata: Family: Araceae

The heart shaped large leaves are variegated silvery white on either side of the mid rib. The leaves are borne on long slender petioles.

Manihot utilissima: Family: Euphorbiaceae

Commonly known as Tapioca. It is a shrub but is often grown as a greenhouse and indoor plant for its ornamental foliage.

Miconia magnifica: Family: Melstomaceae

The plants are useful for potting and for planting in beds in the shade garden. The thin ovate leaves may be upto 75 cm long, velvety green, the sunken veins are ivory-white, with a reddish purple underside.

Monstera deliciosa: Family: Araceae

A heavy root climber, forms long hanging cord like aerial roots. Stem 6m long or more. The leaves are large, 90 cm across, leathery, perforated with oblong holes and pinnatifid at margin.

Musa x paradisiaca vittata: Family: Musaceae

A strikingly beautiful plant. Leaves light green with variegation of milky green and white, the mid rib is also white and the margins are red.

Musa sumatrana: Family: Musaceae

Deep grayish green leaves are blotched with wine red having a red dish undersurface but only in young leaves.

***Neoregelia* spp.:** Family: Bromeliaceae

Grown mainly for the ornamental foliage but the lowering bracts are also very ornamental.

Nepenthes Khasiana: Family: Nepenthaceae

Commonly known as Pitcher Plant. It has tubular, green to reddish-green pitcher with a lid at the end of the mid rib of the leaf. Grows in a boggy shaded position and is carnivorous in nature, trapping insects through the pitcher.

***Ophiopogon* spp.:** Family: Liliaceae

A lovely plant with tufted, linear and grass like leathery leaves. It needs a sandy soil. Some important species are *Ophiopogon intermedius argenteo-marginatus, Ophiopogon jaburan variegatus* and *Ophiopogon japonicus.*

Oxalis: Family: Oxalidaceae

Oxalis is grown as a greenhouse and indoor plant, mainly for its foliage but it bears pretty flowers.

Pandanus baptistii: Family: Pandanaceae

The leaves are spirally arranged, arching beautifully and tapering to a long point. The leaves are blue green in colour with 1-4 longitudinal yellowish white stripes and have no spines.

Pandanus sanderi: Family: Pandanaceae

The leaves are sword like, 120 cm long, shining green with length wise stripes and bands of light and golden yellow. The young foliage is golden orange in colour. Leaves are armed with fine spines.

Pandanus utilis: Family: Pandanaceae

Leaves are strap like, leathery, long, spirally arranged and spiny at the margins. The plant becomes a tree about 18 m tall with age and bears highly scented flowers.

Pandanus veitchii: Family: Pandanaceae

A beautiful houseplant. The leaves are 60 cm long, thin leathery, somewhat recurving, spiny toothed, narrowing to a long point, deep green in colour and broadly margined with creamy white.

Pedilanthus tithymaloides cucullatus: Family: Euphorbiaceae

A herbaceous succulent plant with erect, fleshy, black-green stems. Leaves lanceolate, pale green tinged red and dark green near the mid rib. A hardy plant which is propagated from cuttings.

Pellionia daveauana: Family: Urticaceae

A succulent creeper, stem pinkish, leaves 2 ranked, flattened, oval when young and lanceolate with age and upto 6.5 cm long. The colour of the leaves is dark bronzy olive-green with a slight violet tinge, the central area is pale green or grey.

***Peperomia* spp.:** Family: Piperaceae

Small, succulent, herbaceous, mostly perennial plants with very ornamental foliage, often prettily marked. *Peperomias* are usually fleshy and creeping in habit. The flowers appearing like slender catkins are very attractive.

***Philodendron* spp.:** Family: Araceae

Mostly shrubby creeping plants, or stemless herbs of great ornamental value for their graceful foliage which are leathery, heart-shaped, egg shaped, arrow-shaped or oblong or ovate, either entire or lobed. In some species, the foliage is perforated and pinnatifid.

Pilea cadierei: Family: Urticaceae

It is a rapid growing succulent, suitable as an edge plant in the shade, as a rock plant in shaded portion and as ground cover in a shade garden or in a shrubbery. The obovate, quilted leaves are about 7-8 cm long, vivid green or bluish green in colour and painted shining silver aluminium on the surface.

Pilea muscosa: Family: Urticaceae

It is commonly known as Pistol Plant. The pollens are ejected with force which can be observed if the plants are kept in the sun just after the foliage has been watered. This is a small trailing densely branched plant with handsome minute fern-like foliage.

Polyscias fruticosa: Family: Araliaceae

An erect shrub having a height of 1.8 – 2.5 m tall. Leaves leathery, irregularly 3-pinnate, margins of leaflets cut into segment and often edged white. The rachis and stalk spotted.

Polyscias paniculata variegata: Family: Araliaceae

A handsomely variegated species. Leaflets pinnate, leathery, serrated, green splashed with creamy white and greenish white.

Pseudopanax crassifolius: Family: Araliaceae

While young, the leaves are ovate-lanceolate, finely toothed, dark green with yellow blotches above and purple beneath. Older leaves 3-5 foliate.

Rhoeo spathacea: Family: Commelinaceae

Leaves are lanceolate, stiff and waxy in rosettes. The colour of the yellow leaves are dark green above and purple below. The minute white flowers peep through the boat shaped bracts.

Ruscus hypoglossum: Family: Liliaceae

An interesting tufted, compact, dwarf (45 cm tall) shrub. The tiny greenish flowers are to be found in the mid rib of the cladodes. Berries very rare and red in colour.

***Schismatoglottis* spp.:** Family: Araceae

The plants are somewhat similar to *Aglaonema* and *Alocasia*. The foliage is very ornamental, oblong or ovate-cordate and often marbled or spotted

Scindapsus aureus: Family: Araceae

A fleshy root climbing vine with thick long aerial roots. The leaves at young state are broadly ovate, waxy, green, having yellow variegation. The mature leaves become 60 cm long and the blades become lobed or slashed.

Setcreasea purpurea: Family: Commelinaceae

The plant is purple coloured in bright light. The plants are trailing, leaves clasping, lance shaped, purple, surface of leaves covered with pale hairs and the blue flowers resemble orchid blooms.

Strelitzia reginae: Family: Musaceae

A stemless, comact plant, about 1.5 m tall. The stiff leathery banana like bluish grey leaves are borne in long peduncles. The flowers are exceedingly beautiful which are bordered red. The numerous petals are pointed and brilliant orange in colour and there is an arrow shaped tongue of contrasting vivid blue. The fully opened flower looks like a flying bird.

***Syngonium* spp.:** Family: Araceae

Quick growing, ornamental foliage climber suitable for small pots and trellises. The plants are quite hardy and not fastidious about soil.

Tacca chantrieri: Family: Taccaceae

The bat like inflorescence in both shape and colour. There are two broad wing like maroon black bracts from which trailing filaments or whiskers come out.

Tradescantia albiflora: Family: Commelinaceae

A freely branching plant having comparatively large and lanceolate fleshy leaves which are bluish-green, striped and bordered white.

Tradescantia blossfeldiana: Family: Commelinaceae

Crepping or trailing plant branching profusely. Stem purple, leaves olive green above with purplish underside and covered with silvery hairs.

Tradescantia fuscata: Family: Commelinaceae

A clustering rosette, leaves broad and oblong, olive green in colour with a central silvery band and covered with brown hairs, the reverse is purple. The large blue flowers appear at the base.

***Xanthosoma* spp.:** Family: Araceae

A group of ornamental foliage plants with arrow-shaped leaves which are often variegated. The compost for growing should mainly consist of leaf mould. They need a shaded moist atmosphere and good drainage.

Yucca aloifolia: Family: Liliaceae

Leaves dagger like, sharply pointed, arranged in crowded rosette and galucous green in colour. Flowers cup shaped, creamy white tinged purple at base. In variety *marginata* the margins of the leaves are creamy yellow. In variety *tricolor* the pungent dagger-like leaves have ivory margin with partly yellow centre and young leaves are tinged red.

Yucca gloriosa: Family: Liliaceae

The most commonly cultivated species are variously called Spanish Dagger or Adam's Needle for the needle pointed leaves. The leaves are sword shaped, long, flat, grey-green with reddish margins. Flowers are bell shaped, white and striped purple on the outer side.

Zebrina pendula: Family: Commelinaceae

A trailing and popular plant for hanging baskets, rockeries, edging and carpet bedding. The ovate leaves are succulent, deep green or purple with two silver bands and purple beneath. Flowers are rosy purple.

Zebrina purpusii: Family: Commelinaceae

A rampant creeper. The foliage is purplish brown with light stripes and purple beneath. Flowers are lavender coloured.

CHAPTER-9

CACTI, SUCCULENTS AND FERNS

Cacti

The group of plants belonging to the family cactaceae and many other plants belonging to the genera Agave, Aloe, Cotyledon, Echeveria, Euphorbia, Haworthia, Kalanchoe, Sansevieria, Sedum, Sempervinum and Stapelia are all succulent plants. Botanically each plant in the family cactaceae must has all the following five characteristics in common:

1. Areoles or spine-cushions are present in all the members.
2. All are perennial plants.
3. Fruit are called berry.
4. All belong to dicotyledons group.
5. The flower petals arise from the top of the ovary.

No other group in the whole plant kingdom has such strange variation in plant shape and form, size and colour of areoles and thorns. The beauty of the flowers with a remarkable metallic sheen as the cactus group of plants. The range of colour of flowers may vary from white to pink, purple, yellow, crimson, dark, crimson red, violet and combinations of various colours with spots and streaks. The flowers are short lived. The size of flowers varies from 1cm in some Mammillarias to about 35 cm across in a few of the night flowering types. In the natural habitat, most of the cacti grow in adverse climatic conditions. The fleshy green stems are used as reservoirs for storage of water to be used during drought and they serve as manufacture of food. There are species which grow in a good loamy soil while others inhabit rocks and mountain slopes. Beautiful flowering cacti grow as epiphytes on trees.

Housing of cacti

All cacti like plenty of sunshine but it is the morning sun which should be preferred. In places where the sun becomes very hot during the summer it is advisable to exclude midday and afternoon sun. Cacti grown in shade become lanky and do not flower or flower sparsely. Excess of water is harmful for most of the species and hence all cacti should be housed under glass or polythene roof, although a few hardy species can be grown in the open. For the production of plenty of flowers and for development of good texture of plants, abundant circulation of fresh air is essential. Hence, a cactus house should have only the roof made of glass, fibre glass or polythene, supported on pillars while the sides remain open. Such houses should run in the north south direction facing the east, the west may be blocked with a brick wall in extremely hot places.

Compost

Compost consisting of one part of loamy or sandy loam soil, one part of well rotten cow dung manure, two parts of leaf mould of medium coarseness, one part of sharp sand and small quantities of broken pieces of bone meal is quite suitable for growing most of the species. To this compost, 0.1% nuvan or chloropyriphos should be added to keep away the ants and to some extent root mealy bugs. Freshly prepared compost should not be used for planting but a time gap of 15 days should be allowed between mixing and planting cacti especially the very thorny types do not require heavy feeding with fertilizers if they are repotted every alternate year. Generous feeding with fertilizers makes the plants lush green and these become liable to rotting.

Pots

Earthen pots should always be preferred. The pots should be cleaned and dried before potting. The correct size of the pot should be used which is just large enough to hold the plant. Plants grown in small pots become pot bound and stunted in growth.

Time and method of planting and potting

Cacti should be planted or potted when growth starts slowly in March or April. One third of the pot at the bottom is filled with bold pieces of crocks with the concave face down to facilitate drainage. Then the compost is filled, leaving a gap of about 2 cm on the top to facilitate watering. Before planting all dead roots, roots attacked by disease and affected by nematodes should be removed. The cut end of the roots should be treated with sulphur dust or blitox paste. At the bottom layer of the compost a few crystals of paradichlorobenzene may be put to drive away the mealy bugs. The roots of the treated plants should be dried before planting. While repotting the same procedure is followed as in case of potting. It is not necessary to repot every year. The large specimens should be repotted every alternate year or once in three years. Unless the compost is really in a dry state the newly planted cacti, especially those with injured roots, should not be watered for a few days after planting as these might rot easily because of presence of an abundance of moisture. While planting the spines should not be damaged because once damaged they will never grow again. Since moat of the cacti are spiny it is difficult to handle the plants during these operations. Rubber gloves can be used while for filling the compost a table spoon can be used. The compost around the plant may be firmed with an old table knife handle.

Irrigation

Correct irrigation is the most important single factor in the success of growing these plants. Overwatering is more dangerous than under watering as the farmer practice may kill the plant. The frequency of irrigation and the amount of water needed depend upon the time of the year, the type of compost, potted or a ground plant and upon the type of the cactus. The water used should be neutral plant in a small pot will need more frequent irrigation than a plant in the ground. Hit the side of the pot gently with a wooden hammer and if the resultant sound is a ringing one, the compost is dry while a dull sound will indicate that it is still wet. For a plant planted in the ground, the top soil may be forked up a little to inspect the moisture content in the inner layers. Cacti should not be watered during winter. To prevent any drying up of roots, the plants may be watered a little, once in a month during the winter, watering should be commenced again from March to April. Where the winter is not very severe irrigation may not be delayed.

Staking

Most do not need any staking but some of the tall columnar types may need some kind of staking.

Plant Propagation

Seeds

The best time of sowing in the plains is between March and September. The optimum temperature is 21° C. Seeds are best sown in shallow seed pans. Good seed compost consists of equal parts of well decomposed sifted leaf mould and sand.

Offshoots and Cuttings

Many cacti produce offshoots from the base of the mother plants which may root while still attached to the plant. Such rooted offshoots can be separated and planted immediately while unrooted offshoots are used as cuttings. The plants from which the cuttings are to be taken should not be watered for a few days. The cut end should immediately be smeared with either fine sterilized sand or charcoal powder and kept in a shady place for 4 to 5 days. The compost of raising the cuttings consists of equal parts of sharp sand and leaf mould. The base of the cutting should just penetrate the compost and staked. Deep planting should always be avoided. During the process of rooting, the cuttings are watered sparingly even during the hot weather. It will be better if the cuttings are raised under glass or polythene cover. Fifteen days to 1 month is required for rooting. This is useful method for rapid multiplication of the rootstock.

Grafting

Cleft graft is performed in certain species. Stock has to be headed back at the desired height and a desired V-shaped notch is given on the top of the stock just long enough to accommodate the scion and never longer than that. Two slanting cuts are given on both sides at the bottom of the scion to form a wedge. To obtain a perfect union all the cuts should be even. The wedge shaped cutoff the scion is inserted in the cleft of the stock and held in position by pinning two long cactus spines through the stock and scion. Tie a string around the graft to prevent the notch from spreading. Once the union is complete spines and string should be removed carefully. Splice grafting can be done. Grafting is generally done in summer. In and around Delhi, September is found to be a good period. As soon as grafting operation is over, the newly grafted plants are removed to a warm shady place so that the freshly cut surface does not dry up rapidly. Normal watering of the stock has to be done, taking care that water does not enter the graft joint. Rootstock-scion incompatibility may lead to various problems such as stunted growth of the scion, the scion sending roots into the stock, bulging of the stock below the joint and hence it is imperative to select the right stock for each scion.

Name of rootstock	Name of scion
1. *Cephalocereus albispinus*	*Cephalocereus senilis*
	Cephalocereus senilis 'cristatus'
	Cleistocactus strausii 'Cristate'
	Espostoa plumosa
	Espostoa plumosa 'Cristate'

	Haageocereus bicolor
	Mammillaria angularis 'Cristate'
	Notocactus leninghausii
	Opuntia tunicate
2. *Cephalocereus* spp.	*Cleistocactus strausii 'Cristate'*
	Haageocereus bicolor
3. *Cleistocactus baumannii*	*Aporocactus flagelliformis*
	Chamaecereus silvestrii
	Mammillaria elongate
	Mammillaria gracilis
4. *Myrtillocactus geometrizans*	*Cephalocereus senilis 'cristatus'*
	Gymnocalycium mihan ovichii
5. *Opuntia tomentosa*	*Opuntia microdasys*

Classification of Family Cactaceae

Cactaceae

↓

Tribes

↓

Cereeae ↓ Subtribe

1. Cereanae
2. Hylocereanae
3. Echinocereanae
4. Echinocactaneae
5. Cactanae
6. Coryphanthanae
7. Epiphyllanae
8. Rhipsalidanae

Opuntieae ↓ Genus

1. Pereskiopsis
2. Pterocactus
3. Nopalea
4. Opuntia
5. Grusonia

Pereskieae ↓ Genus

1. Pereskia

Detail Description of Subtribes

1. Cereanae: Plants of this subtribe are terrestrial, erect, bushy, occasionally diffuse, slender, stout, the stems and the branches are with few joints or many jointed and generally very spiny. Flowers are borne singly, rarely many, on the upper part of matured aeroles. Flowers may either be day blooming or night blooming. A few important genera of this subtribe are: *Cephalocereus, Cereus, Cleistocactus, Espostoa, Haageocereus, Myrtillocactus, Oreocereus, Pachycereus, Pseudoespostoa* and *Trichocereus.*

2. Hylocereanae: Some important genera are, *Aporocactus, Hylocereus* and *Selenicereus*. The plants of this subtribe are mostly epiphytic, elongated, vine like climbing, pendent or trailing. The stems and branches are ribbed or angled, rarely flat. These plants are mostly night-blooming with large flowers.
3. Echinocereanae: Low growing terrestrial cacti, solitary or occasionally forming clumps, stems ribbed and spiny. Flowers are borne from lateral old areoles and not on the top of the plant. Some important genera are: *Chamaecereus, Echinocereus, Echinopsis, Lobivia* and *Rebutia*. The cacti of this subtribe are commonly known as Hedgehogs.
4. Echinocactaneae: Terrestrial plants, usually low and small, but occasionally several metres tall, solitary, sometimes in clumps, stems are ribbed, spherical or short cylindrical. Flowers are solitary, borne from young areoles on the apex of the plant and are among the showiest of all. The important genera are: *Ariocarpus, Astrophytum, Echinocactus, Ferocactus, Gymnocalycium, Hamatocactus, Lophora, Notocactus* and *Parodia*.
5. Cactanae: the characteristic of this terrestrial subtribe is the curious wooly or bristle like structure formed through the crowding of aeroles on the top of the plant. The genera included are *Cactus* and *Discocactus*. The plants are commonly known as Melon Cactus.
6. Coryphanthanae: Low growing terrestrial plants, mostly globose, occasionally cylindrical and rarely elongated, solitary but frequent forming clusters. Stem tuberculate and the tubercles are usually arranged spirally. Flowers are borne solitary at lateral or apical areoles but never at spine areoles. Some important genera are: *Coryphantha, Mammillaria* and *Thelocactus*.
7. Epiphyllanae: Mostly tropical epiphytic plants, generally growing on trees, but also in ground which is rich in humus. The stems are flattened leaf like, many branched and usually spineless. Flowers are large and showy, usually night blooming. Some important genera are: *Epiphyllanthus, Epiphyllum* and *Zygocactus*.
8. Rhipsalidanae: These are epiphytic plants, generally growing on trees, occasionally on rocks and are commonly called Chain Cacti. Stems are much branched, slender, cylindric or flat and spineless. Some important genera are: *Erythrorhipsalis, Pseudorhipsalis, Rhipsalidopsis* and *Rhipsalis*.

Description of some important cacti

Aporocactus flagelliformis: It is known as Rat-Tail-Cactus. Stems are slender, creeping or long pendent, closely ribbed having brownish spines. Flowers are 7-8 cm long and crimson in colour.

Ariocarpus fissuratus: A star shaped rosette, the surface horny and irregularly fissured. The flowers are lovely pink.

Astrophytum asterias: The plants are low, circular, rather dome shaped, with a star shaped depression, green but tinged coppery with white scales and areoles are woolly and spineless. The flowers are yellow with red markings in throat.

Astrophytum capricorne: Sub globose, up to 25 cm high, ribs 7-8, spines curved and flowers are lemon-yellow with red throat, large and widely spreading.

Astrophytum myriostigma: Commonly called Bishop's Cap. Generally 5 ribbed, which are very broad, acute, covered with small white spots and areoles spineless. Flowers are yellow, with brown tips on the outer petal.

Cephalocereus senilis: Commonly called Old Man Cactus. A beautiful cactus of slender column, growing up to 12 m in natural habitat, loosely ribbed, covered with long gray hairs. Flowers are rose in colour.

Cephalocereus senilis cristatus: A curious cristate form of the above, fan shaped, thickly covered with snow white hairs.

Cereus peruvianus monstrosus: A garden form commonly called Curiosity Plant. The monstrose branches grow continuously in an irregular fashion, bluish-green and spiny.

Chamaecereus silvestrii: The short cylindric green stems come in clusters, which are covered with soft white spines. The flowers are orange-scarlet and borne very freely, especially when grafted.

Cleistocactus baumannii: The columnar stems are thin, ribbed and branching at base, covered with whitish spines, sometimes yellow or brown. Flowers are tubular and orange scarlet.

Cleistocactus strausii: The slender columnar stem is green, clustering in habit and covered with bristle like white spines with yellow tinge. Flowers are tubular and carmine in colour.

Coryphantha echinus: A small, ball like globular plant up to 5 cm diameter, solitary, numerous radial white spines pressed against the plant. The flowers are yellow.

Echinocactus grusonii: This develops into a giant globe of about one metre diameter, numerously ribbed which are thin and high, light green but covered with numerous golden yellow spines which fade with age. Flowers are yellow and are borne on the apex during day time.

Echinocereus dasyacanthus: Commonly known as Rainbow Cactus. The plants are small, cylindric, spines are radial, spreading, pinkish when young but changing to gray. Spines of intermediate ages are variously coloured, hence the popular name. Flowers are yellow and tinged red.

***Echinopsis* spp.:** Plants are generally low, globular or short cylindric. The flowers are large and often fragrant.

***Epiphyllum* spp.:** The plants of this genus were previously known as *Phyllocactus.* Plants are generally epiphytic, branches are flat, leaf-like, sometimes 3 angled, spines numerous when young but at adult stage wanting. Flowers are very large.

Espostoa lanata: The plants are columnar, 2-4 m high. Stem sometimes branching, 4-10 cm in diameter, covered with cotton like white hairs through which the numerous spines protrude out. Flowers are pinkish.

Espostoa plumosa: Another beautiful species similar to the above but more hairy, with smaller thorns. There is a cristate variety which is very ornamental, fan shaped, covered with white hairs, the hair colour changing when grafted, depending upon rootstock.

Ferocactus horridus: Globular large plant, broadly ribbed, numbering 8-13, spreading radial spines 8-12, all central spines are straight, reddish except one which is long, flattened and hooked.

Ferocactus latispinus: The plant are large, globular, somewhat depressed, ribs 15-23, radial spines 8-10 in number, white to pink, central spines are 4 or more, stouter and highly coloured compared to radials, straight except one which is flat and hooked. Flowers are rose to purple.

Gymnocalycium mihanovichii: The plants are hemispherical, greyish green, banded red, ribs 8 in number, prominent, acute, spines spreading, radial and straw coloured. The flowers are yellowish green tinge with red and free flowering.

Gymnocalycium multiflorum: Small globular or sometimes short columnar, 10-15 ribbed, spines radial and flat. The flowers are light pink.

Haageocereus bicolor: A columnar cactus of light green colour, ribs dense and 14 in number, aeroles thickly covered with creamy, woolly tufts. Spines are radial, fine and tipped brown.

Hamatocactus setispinus: The plants are globose, 15 cm tall, ribs thick, 13 in number, spines radial, grey brown and the central spines with fish hook. The flowers are yellow with red in throat.

Hylocereus lemairei: A climber with 3 angled dark green stems and rooting on one side, flowers are very large (25 cm long), linear outer segments yellowish green, tipped bronze, rather broad inner segments are white and tinged pink. Stamens are numerous and night blooming.

Lobivia famatimensis: The plants are small, cluster forming, stems short cylindric, spines many, short, yellowish and very free flowering. Flowers borne at the top of the plants and colour varying from pale yellow to red.

Mammillaria bocasana: It is commonly called the Powder Puff, because of its appearance like a cotton ball as the small round plant is covered with silky white hairs, the fish hook spines are brown in colour. The flower buds are rose coloured but the flowers are white.

Mammillaria Bravoae: A small (5-7 cm high) globose plant almost covered with spines and wools, radial spines are white and the central one is stiff. The flowers are pink.

Mammillaria candida: It is popularly called Snowball. Plant globose, grow in tufts, almost hidden by white spines, flowers are 2 cm long and rose coloured.

Mammillaria elongata: The plants are small, cylindrical in shape, densely clustering, erect, ascending or prostrate. The interlacing radial yellow spines are arranged in a most artistic manner almost covering the plant and flowers are white.

Mammillaria geminispina: The plants are club shaped becoming cylindric, clustering, radial spines many, white, central few (2 to 4), stouter, longer and black tipped. The flowers are red.

Melocactus melocactoides: The characteristic feature of this genus is the formation of a wolly cap or cephalium on the apex when plants attain flowering size. It contains wool and bristles but no spines. At this stage the main stem stops growing but the cephalium grows annually. This species is small (8 cm high, 15 cm broad), conical, light green, with 10 broad ribs, radial spines white, cephalium white with brown bristles and flowers are pink.

Notocactus haselbergii: A beautiful, small, globular species having 30 low ribs. The silvery white spines with yellowish tip are soft. Flowers are orange red in colour.

Notocactus scopa: Globular when young but becoming cylindric with age. Almost covered with white radial and long brownish central needle like spines. Flowers are satiny and carny yellow in colour.

Nyctocereus serpentinus: Stems are cylindric, many ribbed, growing in clumps, initially erect, then clambering against bushes or walls or if no support available creeping or hanging up to 3m long. Areoles wooly, spines white to brownish, funnel shaped flowers are large and white and a night bloomer.

Opuntia microdasys: It is commonly called as Bunny Ears, because of the young pad like growths coming on the older ones and appearing like ears. Joints are flat, oblong or roundish, velvety, areoles close and conspicuous because of neat arrangement and light brown tufts of bristles which stick easily if touched and painful. Flowers are yellow.

Opuntia tetracantha: A low, branched bush (1.5 m tall), slender joints cylindrical in shape, spines needle like and flowers are greenish purple.

Opuntia tomentosa: It is grown to a tree (3.5 m tall), joints very fleshy and thick, green spines few, flowers are yellow and the carmine red fruits at the apex looks ornamental.

Opuntia tunicata: A species with whorled branches, growing to 60 cm, joints globular or short cylindrical. The plant is covered thickly with vicious white sheathed and barbed spines. Flowers are yellow.

Opuntia vulgaris: It is joints flattened, fleshy, green, practically spineless, flowers are yellow and the unriped fruits root and form little ears.

Oreocereus celsianus: It is grown in clumps to about 1 m high, the new branches are either prostrate or ascending at basal portion, erect above, 8 cm thick, ribs 10, areoles have long hairs and reddish spines. Flowers are dark red.

Oreocereus maximus: Stout columnar, spines colourful and body entirely covered with white hairs.

Oreocereus trollii: Columnar, branching at base, body covered with long and silky creamy hairs. Flowers are rose in colour.

Parodia aureispina: It is commonly called as Tom Thumb. A small bluish–green round plant, ribs spiral, spines white and central bright yellow. The flowers at early stage are golden yellow in colour.

Parodia maassii: A small round plant, yellowish-green in colour, ribs spiral and prominent, 13 in number, spines radial on knobs, white in colour and central spine hooked.

Pereskia aculeata: A shrubby, leafy plant with woody stems, branches clambering behaving as vines. Spines brown and needle like. Flowers are creamy and lemon scented.

Pseudoespostoa melanostele: Similar to *Espostoa lanata,* having rows of brown-tipped needle like spines, densely covered with hair and the density increasing with age.

Rebutia fiebrigii: A small plant, globose to cylindrical, clustering, tubercles spiraled, spines white and flowers are vermilion.

Rebutia haagei: A green to reddish clustering cactus, tubercles spiraled, spines white and flowers are vermilion.

Rebutia kupperiana: A globe with depressed top, tubercles in 20 rows covered with light spines, very free flowering even when about 2.5 cm high. Flowers are scarlet and attractive.

***Rhipsalis* spp.:** These are epiphytes, the stems are much-branched, either cylindrical, angled or flattened. The areoles are hairy, woolly or with bristles and are found irregularly scattered on the cylindrical forms or on the margins of the flattened forms. The small flowers are borne singly at an areole during day or night. Fruits are round, white or coloured and juicy.

Selenicereus grandiflorus: The stems are clambering, 2.5 cm in diameter, night bloomer, flowers about 30 cm long, white inside, salmon outside with a powerful vanilla smell. It is an epiphyte.

Selenicereus urbanianus: An epiphyte possessing aerial roots, clambering, 4-5 angled joints, stems usually light-green but occasionally turn purple throughout. Spines about 1 cm long and brownish. A night bloomer, flowers are large (20-30 cm long), white within and tan without.

Trichocereus candicans: Flowers are very large and highly sweet-scented.

Trichocereus schickendantzii: Flowers are white and lasts for several days. It is a night bloomer.

Trichocereus spachianus: Flowers are 30 cm long and 15 cm in diameter and white in colour.

***Zygocactus* spp.:** An epiphyte, stems are flattened, jointed, dichotomously branched and margins serrated. There are two prominent teeth or claws at the apex. The flowers are 6-7 cm long and last for several days. Flowers are irregular from scarlet to white.

Succulents

Succulents have very fleshy foliage or stem or both. These plants inhabit mostly dry desert localities in open situations and are capable of withstanding long hot spells of drought as they store sufficient moisture in their succulent body parts. Succulents show a great diversity in form, many having very ornamental appearance while others bear beautiful flowers. Cacti come under the cultural group of succulents. The cacti are different from the succulents in that they have areoles which are minute vertical pores occurring as incomplete canals and not perforating the wall completely. Besides, the plants of the cacti group are usually almost leafless, with only vestiges of leaves present which are not visible to the naked eyes except for the genus *Pereskia*.

Climatic and Soil requirements

Succulents inhabiting the arid regions will do well in most of the places. The succulents do very well in the mild climatic conditions of Bangalore, Kalimpong and other places with a similar climate. The climatic and other requirements of most of the succulents with a few exceptions, are most similar and hence these can be grown together under one greenhouse. The succulents are not at all fastidious about the soil as long as it is porous. Although a few can grow well even in pure sand and others in a comparatively rich compost like 1 part by volume of leaf mould + 2 part by volume of coarse sand + 1/3 part by volume of well rotted cowdung + 1/3 part by volume of garden loam + 1/3 part by volume of crushed brick and charcoal. For Agaves, Aloes and Euphorbias, the compost can be made a little richer by increasing the quantities of leaf mould and cowdung manure.

Plant Propagation

Seed: For a majority of the succulents, propagation from seeds is possible. The ideal climatic conditions required for proper germination are a temperature of 30-35°C and a relative humidity of 90 per cent. After germination, the seedlings should be shifted to a drier place.

Hardwood Stem Cutting: The cutting are taken from a mature and woody growth. The cutting is taken with a sharp knife and the cut end is placed in powdered charcoal and allowed to dry thoroughly. The cutting is then rooted in sterilized coarse sand. *Adenium, Euphorbias, Pedilanthus* and others, can be propagated by this method. The succulents such as *Cotyledons, Echeveria* and *Sedum* can be multiplied from leafy cuttings. Well-developed and matured leaves are detached and treated the same way as stem cuttings and are just laid over coarse sand for rooting.

Irrigation

Watering is the most important. A perfect drainage is absolutely necessary. One fourth of the pot is filled with broken bricks and charcoal and then the compost is filled. The best time to irrigate a succulent is when the soil is sufficiently dry but not completely dry. Succulents have very small and limited root system and hence over watering is harmful.

Repotting

It is an important cultural practice in succulents. The time for repotting depends upon the type of succulents. Those having rest period are reported at the commencement of growth during the spring while others having no rest period can be repotted any time but preferably during the spring. The general belief is that all succulents benefit from repotting every alternate year. But the vigorous growing ones whose growth over the whole pot surface within one year should be repotted every year. At the time of repotting the old compost including the crocks should be replaced completely. The compost should be filled in a crumbly moist condition. When this method is followed the repotted plant need not be watered for about 4 to 7 days, depending upon how long the compost takes to dry.

Description of some important succulents

***Aeonium* spp.:** Succulent herbaceous plants with woody and more or less branched stems. The leaves are borne in rosettes at the end of the branches. Plants require plenty of water in the summer and a rich sandy soil.

***Agave* spp.:** The plants are sometimes commonly known as 'Century Plants' because of the popular belief that they flower once in 100 years but actually different species flower between 10 and 40 years. Agaves are very common succulent plants with typical xerophytic looks. The leaves are borne in rosettes which are thick, leathery and sword like. The margins of the leaves are usually teethed, the apex ending in a stout spine. Sometimes, the margins may be smooth but the tip will have a spine. The flowers are borne in a large column like flower stalk containing innumerable florets.

***Aloe* spp.:** A group of hardy succulent plants mostly stemless or with short stems but some species are tree-like. Leaves are in rosettes, fleshy, margins entire or toothed. In some species, the surface is variegated or spotted or striped. Many species bear attractive tubular flowers in long stalks. Aloes should not be exposed to rains as water will collect between the leaves and the plant may rot.

***Apicra* spp.:** It is closely related to *Aloe* but resemblance is much closer to *Haworthia* being differentiated from the latter by the regular form of the flowers. These are ornamental small plants useful for indoor decoration.

Bowiea volubilis: It is commonly known as climbing Onion. The light green bulb 20 cm, sometimes 45 cm in diameter, remains about the ground from which a twining branched stem of green colour with a few fleshy basal leaves, climb upward if supported by a trellis.

***Bryophyllum* spp.:** A small group of succulents similar to Kalanchoes and often included in it but being distinguished from the latter by the drooping and not erect flowers, the sepals jointed. Not free and the stamens inserted at the base of the corolla tube, not above.

***Caralluma* spp.:** The plants resemble *Stapelias* and require similar cultural treatments. The stem is usually 4-angled and branching is generally at ground level.

***Ceropegia* spp.:** Succulent plants which are often without leaves but mostly twining with opposite fleshy leaves. The roots are generally tuberous or corm like. Flowers are borne in small clusters which are beautiful and somewhat resemble *Stapelias*.

Cissus cactiformis: The species is more or less similar to *Cissus quadrangularis* but the internodes are much thicker about 4 cm across.

Cissus quadrangularis: A very thick fleshy 4-angled succulent which is much contracted at nodes. It is a quick growing climber and is generally leafless. A sandy loam soil and a moist situation suit the plant well.

***Cotyledon* spp.:** Ornamental succulent herbs, shrubs or sub-shrubs. They like a rich sandy soil. Some grow compactly and form clumps.

***Crassula* spp.:** This genus represents a large number of succulent shrubs and herbs. Excepting a few, all *Crassulas* are easy to cultivate but they perform better on hills. Most of the plants have attractive and handsome forms.

***Duvalia* spp.:** These succulents are allied to *Stapelias*. *Duvalia elegans* and *Duvalia pillansii* are two important species.

***Dyckia* spp.:** They somewhat resemble *Agaves* but the spines are smaller and they flower regularly. A perfect drained sol is essential.

***Echeveria* spp.:** A much branched succulent plant which forms clumps or small bushes with short stems. The leaves are ornamental, in various shapes and sizes, very fleshy and spirally arranged into rosettes. Most of the species are beautiful and suitable for growing indoors.

***Euphorbia* spp.:** This genus represents a large group of plants. The succulent *Euphorbias* are of varied habit. The form in *Euphorbias* may vary from thorny fleshy shrubs to plants having slender branches with the thickness of a pencil, some even with columnar stems while others having spherical stems. Besides these, various intermediate forms are also available. In most of the species the leaves are very much reduced or are small and soon drop off. In few species the leaves are conspicuous. Through the majority of *Euphorbias* have sturdy thorns from the leaf base, some are thornless as well. Some resemble the cacti in form and are often mistaken as such. *Euphorbias* exude a milky latex when injured.

***Furcraea* spp.:** A group of succulent desert plants from Tropical America resembling *Agave.* Some of the species are very suitable for planting as specimens in the lawn, especially the variegated ones. They are also useful for rockeries, greenhouses and for growing in pots and tubs for display.

***Gasteria* spp.:** A group of showy plants with fleshy thick leaves somewhat resembling Aloes. The leaves are usually arranged in 2 ranks and sometimes in rosettes. The tounge shaped leaves are spotted with purple or white. They are popular plants for growing in rooms.

Graptopetalum paraguayense: A succulent with a rosette of thick fleshy leaves resembling *Echeveria.*

***Greenovia* spp.:** The plants are closely related to *Sempervivum* and resemble *Aeonium* without the tall stem. The plants produce offsets.

***Haworthia* spp.:** These were formely included in Aloe but are now grouped separately because of the 2-lipped flower. The plant may or may not have a short stem. The leaves are fleshy, arranged in rosettes or closely overlapping, often covered with pearly tubercles.

Kalanchoe daigremontiana: Leaves are arched, fleshy, tricoloured and brownish green in colour. Plantlets are produced at the margins of leaves. Flowers a grey violet in colour.

Kalanchoe tomentosa: A most beautiful succulent known as the Panda Plant. Stem is erect and branching. The leaves are spoon shaped, soft, fleshy and entirely covered with a dense white felt. The teethed margins of the leaves are tinged brown. The flowers are white marked with brown stripes.

***Mosembryanthemum* spp.:** This genus includes the most interesting plants among the succulents, some are strikingly beautiful in plant form. Most of them bear beautiful flowers. In many species, the plants are in the form of tufts, the shape of bodies are obconical and the upper surface or the apex is truncated as if cut across by a knife.

Nolina recurvata: The plant attains a height of 9 m, the stem is slender, swollen at the base and branching only at the top. The leaves are green, slender, recurving, smooth-edged, 2 cm wide and 90-180 cm long.

***Pedilanthus* spp.:** It is commonly known as Red Bird Cactus. These are cactus like shrubby succulents. The plants are hardy and suitable for greenhouse collection, indoor display and rock garden planting.

Pelargonium carnosum: A weird-looking succulent with a thick stem. Leaves are pinnately lobed and pinnatifidly cut. Flowers are in 6 to 8 flowered umbels and are creamy rose in colour.

Pelargonium gibbosum: It is commonly called Knotted Geranium. A climbing, intricately branched shrub and the branches being thin. Leaves are pinnately lobed and ruffled while the greenish yellow flowers emit scent in the evening.

Pelargonium juttae: A curious looking low-growing succulent with short, tuberously thickened stem. There are a limited number of short branches on which the long stalked, bisected leaves are borne.

Portulacaria afra: It is commonly called Elephant Bush. A succulent shrub which may attain a height of 3 metres, with thick, fleshy and browny stems. Leaves are obovate to roundish, thick and juicy. Flowers are inconspicuous and pink in colour.

***Sansevieria* spp.:** Herbaceous perennials which are succulent in growth and are usually grown for the elegant, erect, stiff and sword like leaves which are usually variegated. These are quite hardy plants and are frequently used for indoor decorations as they need very little sunlight. These are suitable for growing in rock gardens.

***Sedum* spp.:** These are perennial herbs, rarely sub-shrubs which are succulent in nature. Most of the species are very showy and popular with the garden lovers. A few species are useful for carpeting poor and waste places (e.g., *Sedum acre*) such as cemeteries. Some species are very popular for carpet bedding. Sedums are also useful as rock plants especially in a mild climate or in the shady portion of a tropical rock garden. Sedums are excellent for decorating greenhouses and the best species is *Sedum spectabile*, which is possibly the showiest among the sedums.

***Sempervivum* spp.:** They are commonly known as House Leek. These are low plants forming clumps or cushions and are generally stemless. Leaves are alternate and arranged in spiral rosettes in a crowded fashion, sessile, lanceolate, obovate or acute, thickly fleshy and green, reddish or bluish in colour. The flowers are borne in terminal many flowered inflorescence and are greenish, white, yellow, purple or pink in colour. The rosettes bearing flowers perish after flowering and fruiting.

***Stapelia* spp.:** These are fleshy cactus like succulents, grown for their odd shapes and for the singular and often large beautiful flowers. The stems are fleshy, sometimes decumbent at the base but the numerous branches are erect. The branches are leafless, coarsely 4-angled but at young stage rudimentary leaves may be found in the teeth of the branches. The flowers are often large, deeply lobed, generally star shaped and mostly reddish brown or purplish in colour often marked with yellow.

Tradescantia navicularis: It is commonly known as Chain Plant. It is a half creeping, tufted plant with short-jointed stems rooting at the nodes. The imbricated leaves are arranged in two rows which are shaped, fleshy and grey green in colour.

Ferns

Ferns are extremely handsome because of the elegance of their foliage and hence are widely useful for different purposes in the garden. Ferns are very suitable for a shade garden, pots and pans for indoor decoration, wire or hanging baskets and drywalls. Ferns can be used in decorating roof and terrace gardens, leaves are highly prized for their use in vase and table decoration, in preparing bouquets, button holes and wreath. The dried leaves of maiden- hair ferns are very popular for pasting greeting cards. Ferns are grown in bottle garden, wardian case or terrarium and window gardens.

Plant Propagation

Spores

Ferns are propagated by spores. Spores are sown in shallow pots or pans. Various pot mixtures may be used. A 10 cm deep pot should first be filled with coarse sphagnum moss to a depth of about 6cm. Then compost consisting of equal parts of humus, top soil, building sand and very finely chopped sphagnum moss is prepared by mixing the constituents thoroughly which is screened. The pots should be sterilized along with the compost by heat. The clay pots are then submerged in a pan of water upto the neck and then left long enough to make the contents as well as the pots saturated with water. The coarse sphagnum at the bottom serves as a reservoir of water in between the two watering. Sowing the microscopic spores on a board paper and topping this over the sowing pan. After sowing, the pans should be covered with a glass pan and removed to a warm, shady place. The subsequent watering is done by placing the pots erect on a saucer containing water with the drainage hole submerged. The germination time varies with the species (5-15 days) when the small plants are sufficiently large to handle these are pricked 2-3 cm apart in seed pans containing a mixture of equal parts of sifted leaf mould and sand. Till the fronds are well developed these should not be watered from above. Propagation from spores can be done any time in the year but preferably during a warm and moist period.

Division of clump or creeping rhizome

The easiest and the most common method of propagation is, of course, propagation by division of the clump or by division of the creeping rhizome. Any part of the rhizome can be used for this purpose. The best time for propagation by division is the spring when repotting is done. In most parts of the plains this can conveniently be done during the monsoon season. The staghorn ferns produce suckers from adventitious buds on their roots as they grow older and these are easily separated. Some ferns produce a number of bulbils or plantlets on the surface of their fronds while some produces a solitary bud at the apex of the fronds. In such species, the fronds should be pegged down flatly in sandy leaf mould or the tip should be pegged to encourage the plantlets to form roots. Once rooted, there are separated and planted individually. The tip cuttings from the trunks of certain tree ferns root in a moist porous soil or when kept in a container having coarse gravel in shallow water.

Culture

Ferns dislike bright sunshine except in a few cases. The temperature requirements of ferns depend upon the origin of the species. Ferns of the tropics like a warm humid temperature and those from the high hills or temperate regions grow better under a cool climate. Ferns growing in the temperate regions prefer to send their head in the sun and the roots in the shade. In the tropics, ferns are always grown in shade or semi shade. The natural choice of the site for ferns will be under the shade of trees. When ferns are grown under trees, it is essential to mulch them with leaf mould twice in a year. Once during the spring and again during or after the rains. This will give the ferns the much needed additional nutrients, replenishing the loss due to competition from the adjoining trees.

The soil where ferns are to be grown should be light, porous, well drained and should contain enough lime. The moisture loving ferns should be planted in the marsh garden or around a lily pool. For growing ferns in pots and pans the same compost as suggested for germination of spores can be used but with little addition of bone meal. The compost should be sterilized by heat. The same compost should be used in the pockets when grown in the ground. In the above compost, one half part of broken pieces of charcoal may be added. The bottom of the pan or pot should be filled with broken crocks. Oversized pots should never be used and the size of the pot should be just enough to hold the roots of the ferns. Ferns are generally repotted. If the fern has covered the whole pot, it is time to repot. In case of repotting, only the next size pot (2-3 cm more in diameter) should be used. Top dressing of leaf mould can be done once or twice in a year.

Irrigation

The success of growing ferns depends much on watering. More ferns die of overwatering and bad drainage than due to under watering. The requirement of water differs from one kind to another kind of ferns, although all of them like moisture. Supply enough water to penetrate the soil thoroughly and to permit the excess water to drain off. Over watering accentuated by poor drainage may result in the death of the plants. When grown indoors, ferns will like to have moist, cool air, around their foliage. Rooms heated with steam are not often suitable for growing the ferns. In the north Indian plains, it is very difficult to grow most of the ferns because of excessive dry heat during the summer and frost during the winter. With a little effort, it is possible to grow many ferns under such conditions. It is better to grow fern under conservatory. Conservatory is a semi shaded place which is suitable for growing ferns. The inside humidity can be increased by providing a shallow pool and a stream running around the fernery. During hot and dry weather, the fern should be protected against draughts of hot winds and provided with humidity by occasional syringing. It is possible to acclimatize ferns of the Himalayas in the hot climate of north India.

Description of some important ferns

***Adiantum* spp.:** Family- Polypodiaceae. Ferns of this group are most popular in the Indian gardens and are commonly known as Maiden Hair Ferns. The beautiful foliage is usually borne at the end of a relatively long, slender polished black or purplish stalks. *Adiantums* are good as potted plants and are widely used for veranda or indoor decoration and for hanging baskets. The fresh leaves are used in preparing bouquets and buttonholes along with flowers and the dried leaves are very handsome in preparing greeting cards.

***Alsophila* spp.:** Family- Cyatheaceae. It is variously known as Grove Fern and Norfolk Island Fern. These are moisture loving ferns. The plants like shade and plenty of moisture. The plants of tree fern groups have a straight, tall stem or trunk similar to that of a palm. The large leaves are borne at the apex of the trunk giving the plants a palm like appearance. The ferns are suitable for cultivation at medium to high altitudes.

Aneimia rotundifolia: Family- Schizaeaceae. It is also known as Flowering Ferns. In this fern, the portion of the leaf which bears spores does not have any expanded leaf lamina and hence looks like an inflorescence. The sterile fronds consist of pairs of oval leaflets along the rachis and have the normal look of leaves. The ferns are suitable for pot culture and hanging baskets.

Angiopteris evecta: Family- Marattiaceae. A swamp dwelling fern. The plants develop a stout stem. The bipinnate leaves are borne in a stalk as long as 4.5 m. the pinnae are linear-oblong in shape, succulent, dark green in colour and finely toothed.

***Asplenium* spp.:** Family- Polypodiaceae. This species consists of some attractive species of ornamental ferns, either with entire leaves or with finely divided fronds. Many species produce plantlets on the surface and the edge of pinnae and are multiplied from these.

***Blechnum* spp.:** Family- Polypodiaceae. Many species of this genus are good for indoor decoration. The genus resembles *Lomaria* and the plants have short stems and many have palm like leaves. The leaves turn black and brown if watered from overhead. Some ornamental species are *Blechnum auriculatum, Blechnum brasiliense* and *Blechnum occidentale.*

***Davallia* spp.:** Family- Polypodiaceae. This genus consists of some of the most handsome ferns, with scaly creeping rhizomes which in some species resemble a hare's or a squirrel's feet. There are species which form excellent potted plants while others are suitable for hanging baskets. *Davallia bullata* is a suitable species for hanging baskets and for training on frames resembling birds and animals.

Drynaria quercifolia: Family- Polypodiaceae. This is suitable for outdoor decoration. It has fronds which are large and have some similarity to oak leaves.

***Dryopteris* spp.:** Family- Polypodiaceae. A large genus of ferns with handsome dissected foliage. Most of the species are easy to cultivate.

***Lygodium* spp.:** Family- Schizaeaceae. A group of twining or climbing ferns belong to this genus. Lygodiums are suitable for growing in pots over ballon like trellis made of Galvanized Iron wire fitted to the pots.

***Nephrolepsis* spp.:** Family- Polypodiaceae. These ferns are popularly known as Sword Ferns. Most of the species are ideally suited for growing in hanging baskets because of their drooping nature while others are good for conservatories. Most of the species produce slender runners and are easily propagated from these.

Onychium japonicum: Family- Polypodiaceae. A small fern whose waxy green fronds are lacily sub divided into small segments. It is suitable for indoor decoration.

Osmunda regalis: Family- Osmundaceae. The best species in this genus and commonly called as Royal Fern. The fronds are feather like, plain or sometimes crested and the fertile portions are contracted. The fern may grow as tall as 150-180 cm.

***Pellaea* spp.:** Family- Polypodiaceae. These are small ferns suitable for growing in limestone rocks and hanging baskets. The compost for them should be light and porous with minimum soil. The roots should never go dry and at the same time the foliage should not be syringed.

***Platycerium* spp.:** Family- Polypodiaceae. These ferns are very handsome and epiphytic in nature. The fronds are divided at the margin like the horns of stags and hence the ferns are popularly known as Stag Horn Ferns. These can be grown like orchids in logs, preferably supported by fibres such as coconut and sphagnum moss. These ferns can be attached to free fern blocks. These are suitable for hanging baskets.

***Polypodium* spp.:** Family- Polypodiaceae. A large genus of ferns, many species of which are handsome. The rhizome should not be buried deep only the roots should be covered. Only well established plants produce handsome fronds and hence these should not be disturbed for a long time, once planted.

***Polystichum* spp.:** Family- Polypodiaceae. These are moisture loving hardy ferns which grow better in semi shade or shade, though tolerate enough sunlight. These ferns dislike poor drainage. The fronds are very useful in flower arrangements.

***Pteris* spp.:** Family- Polypodiaceae. A large genus which consists of several handsome species, many of which possess beautifully variegated fronds. The ferns in this genus are excellent for pot culture and dish gardening for table decoration.

CHAPTER-10

ORCHIDS

Orchids from 9% of our flora and are the largest botanical family of higher plants. It is estimated that about 1,300 species (140 genera) of orchids are found in our country with Himalayas as their main home and others scattered in Eastern and Western Ghats. Orchids belong to a group of flowering plants under the family Orchidaceae. India has a very large variety of orchids and hilly regions have one or the other orchid flowering almost throughout the year. The diversity is so large that there are large-flowered, terrestrial, epiphytic and saprophytic orchids. In general terrestrial orchids are more common in North-Western India, epiphytic orchids in North-Eastern India and small flowered orchids in Western Ghats. The largest terrestrial genus is *Habenaria* and the largest epiphytic genus is *Dendrobium.* Most of the Paphiopedilum species are restricted to north eastern Himalayas except for *Paphiopedilum druryi* which has been reported from kerala but now is almost extinct from its original habitat. Some orchids are endemic are so ornamental and in demand that their natural populations have been over exploited. Some species in the genera like *Arundina, Cymbidium, Coelogyne, Dendrobium, Paphiopedilum, Renanthera and Vanda* are almost extinct. Orchids are perennial plants of varying growth habits. A majority of them which grow on trees are epiphytes, some being terrestrial, growing on the forest floor or open ground. A few grow in water as semi-aquatics and two rare genera of Australian origin are subterranean, at the most the tiny flower head reaching the soil surface.

Types

Orchids can be divided into two groups i.e., *monopodial* or *sympodial based* upon their habit of growth. Monopodials grow from a single vegetative apex. They do not have rhizome and pseudobulbs. Sympodials are characterized by the presence of rhizome or a modified stem. They grow from a number of vegetative species. In addition to the epiphytic orchids, terrestrial orchids which grow like ordinary plants with their roots in soil. Most of the temperate zone orchids are terrestrial and tropical orchids are epiphytes. There are more species of orchid than any other flower in the world. Some of the most common and popular orchids include *Brassavola, Cattleya, Cymbidiums, Epidendrum, Dendrobium, Paphiopedilums, Phalaenopsis Oncidium* and *Vandas*. *Brassavola* flourish in warm to temperate climates and blossom often. *Cattleya*, is one of the most familiar types of orchids. It is a beautiful flower with a wonderful fragrance. *Cattleya* blooms once or twice per year and is easy to grow. *Cymbidiums* produce beautiful fragrant flowers. They can tolerate cool temperatures. There are about 1500 species of *Denrobium*. They grow throughout the summer and rest in the winter. *Epidendrum* has a variety of both large and small flowers. There are a variety of beautiful and fragrant hybrids as well. *Paphiopedilums* come in various sizes, shapes and colours. They make popular houseplants since they are easily grown indoors. *Phalaenopsis* is known as the Moth Orchid. It is a popular and adaptable variety that flowers in shades of pink, yellow and read. The moth orchid is a good choice for a houseplant. Most species of *Oncidium* bloom once per year. Some species prefer warm temperatures whereas others do fine in cooler climate but overall they can withstand diverse habitat. *Vandas* have large, vibrant flowers that love light, warmth and humidity.

Cultivation

Orchids in nature grow protected from the tropical sun by the shades of trees. Under controlled condition the orchids can be grown in specially designed orchidaria or orchid houses, running North and South and made from materials like split bamboo, glass and shade nets. A central tank filled with water or by using artificial fogging nozzles helps in increasing humidity. However, it must be clear that all types of orchids cannot be grown under one roof. While tropical orchid enjoy humid, warm atmosphere and burst into activity during rainy season, temperate orchid should be growing in cool houses. Orchids dislike sudden change in temperature, however, a difference of 10°C – 20°C between day and night temperature is beneficial. The best suitable range is 18°C to 30°C, proper ventilation is must to provide fresh air and also helps in reducing the temperature. There are also orchids which can be grown in open sun. At present the most important centres of orchid cultivation are Darjeeling district of West Bengal and Shillong. They can be cultivated in other areas like Bangalore, Ooty and Shevaroy Hills. The genera which are suitable for commercial exploitation in Darjeeling and Shillong are *Paphiopedilum, Cymbidium, Vanda* and *Dendrobium*. *Dendrobium* species do well in Bangalore. In warmer places like Calcutta, *Aerides, Dendrobium* and *Rhynchostylis* can be grown in an orchid house. With good arrangement for humidity and temperature control in glasshouse, orchids can be grown in many places in the humid tropical and sub-tropical areas of the country. The general principles of cultivation are more or less the same but each genus and often each species in a genus has its special requirements for artificial cultivation.

Air

As most of the commonly cultivated orchids are epiphytic, they require freely moving air at all times. Hence the glasshouses where orchids are grown should have proper arrangements for circulation of air. Many tropical orchids like *Vanda, Phalaenopsis* and *Aerides* which develop aerial roots prominently do best when grown in baskets kept hanging from the beams of the greenhouse or lathhouse.

Light

Indirect sunlight is ideal for orchids. Seedlings requires less than adult plants. Very poor light tends to produce weak plants and retards flowering. A plant which has been grown in shades should be gradually be shifted to sunlight conditions. The optimum requirement of light varies between species to species. *Cypripedium* and *Phalaenopsis* require only 200-300 foot candles. Whereas genera like *Vanda* and *Aranda* thrive best under 800 foot-candles. Majority of orchids are day neutral and are not influenced by day length. *Cattleya* both short-day and long-day plants are met with.

Temperature

Orchids require proper temperature for good growth and flowering under artifical conditions. It is very much correlated with light as sunshine provides the natural warmth to the plants. Orchids may be divided into three major groups in relation to their night temperature requirements. (a) Cool orchids: The night temperature requirement of this group is 7.2 to 10°C. (b) Intermediate orchids: The night temperature requirement of this group is 12.8 to 18.3°C. (c) Warm orchids: The night temperature requirement of this group is 18.3°C and above.

Moisture

Humid warm atmosphere is most essential for the growth of most of the tropical orchids which do not have well established root system. It is a good idea to have a water tank or pool in the center of the orchidaria to maintain humidity which should not be less than 30% at night and 80% during day time. The plants should be watered 2-3 times a day and should not be allowed to dry up during hot climate. Plants in active growth require more water. Similarly, plants in baskets require more water than those in pots. Care should be taken to water the plants with a fine spray by using standard nozzles and not to hit the plants with powerful jets of water. Plants which are freshly potted should be watered very sparingly till the new roots appear and watering should be gradually increased.

Container

Orchids should be potted in small containers according to the size of the plants. As a thumb rule, orchids should be under potted to get more flowers. Container which can hold medium and provide aeration is suitable. Most of the people prefer plastic pots which retain moisture longer than mud pots. *Vandaceous* and *Sarcenthene* orchids can be grown in teak-wood baskets. The drainage hole at the bottom of the pot should be enlarged to assure adequate drainage as good drainage is essential for successful growth of any orchid. Orchid plants should not be disturbed frequently and repotting done only when absolutely necessary. Orchids like *Cymbidium*, react favourably when repotted after 2-3 years whereas *Vandeceous* orchids and *Paphiopedilum* should not be disturbed unless very necessary. Terrestrial orchids like *Spathoglottis, Phaius* and *Calanthe* should be grown in 20-25 cm pots with 1:1:1 mixture of leaf mould, FYM and sand. For *Paphiopedilum* a mixture of 2 parts leaf mould, 2 parts loam soil and 1 part each of brick pieces and charcoal is recommended.

Manuring

In nature, orchids obtain their supply of inorganic nutrients like calcium, magnesium, iron, potassium, nitrogen and traces of manganese, boron, copper and zinc. from the tree on which they are growing and also from atmosphere and decaying vegetables and dropping of birds. However, under controlled conditions they have to be supplied with all these major and minor nutrients. Taking into consideration, the special need of different orchids, a large number of fertilizer mixtures, both solid and liquid, are available in market. Liquid fertilizers are much more quickly absorbed and can be applied more frequently. As the orchids are slow growing, slow release fertilizers like osmocote can be used to get very good result. Usage of fertilizers should also depend on stage of growth. During vegetative growth, large quantities of nitrogen are required while during flowering, nitrogen should be reduced and amount of phosphate increased.

Outdoor cultivation of orchids

In tropical and subtropical countries, the weather is favourable for growing orchids outside the greenhouse on trees and on ground. Growing orchids on trees is not difficult but certain problems are encountered. The tree should preferably be a rough barked, such as an oak or mango. Before placing on the tree, the potting medium and dead roots should be trimmed off and the plants be fixed on the tree by galvanized staples or tied by coconut fibre or nylon string. The plants should be tightly fixed against the tree so that they become immovable. Orchids are slow growing and take from few months to one year to get them established. Till then they should be given more water than in greenhouse, since evaporation is higher. They require copious light. Liberal applications of weak manure-water are beneficial for such orchids especially during the period of their establishment. The manure may be applied by a fine sprayer on the roots and foliage. Many tree ferns and plants with porous trunk like some of the palms and screw pines are admirably suited as host plants for outdoor orchid culture as the porous trunks retain moisture over a long period. Some orchids grow on rocks under natural conditions such as some of the *Cattleya, Laelia, Pleurothallis, Epidendrum* and *Oncidium* species. They can be grown in rock gardens in temperate areas. Bare root orchids can be placed in any depression in the rock and carefully held down with small stones without injuring the young parts. A thin layer of *Osmunda,* tree fern fibre or sphagnum moss should be put below the plant until new roots are produced and grow through this moisture retaining material before they are attached to the stone. The most suitable rocks are the pumice stones which are of volcanic origin and extremely porous and soft. Pieces of granite can be used but they are harder. Alkaline limestone should be avoided.

Plant Propagation

Orchids like other Horticultural crops, may be propagated either sexually or Asexually. Since most of the commercial orchids are highly heterozygous they are not raised through seed and are propagated through vegetative means to get true-to-type plants. Conventional methods like cuttings, division of shoots or Keikis, are followed along with mericloning through tissue-culture techniques.

Sexual Propagation

Seeds: Raising of orchids from seeds is not a simple process. It requires good amount of experience and knowledge. The seeds are very minute and produced in a large number in a fruit (capsule). They do not possess any stored food material or endosperm, as most of the other plant seeds contain. For successful germination of these seeds it is necessary to protect them from pests and fungal infection and to supply food to the developing proembryos, so that they may continue to grow. In nature, the food is supplied by a fungus growing inside the seed, the minute branches of which supply both carbohydrate for food and some acidity to help in germinations of seeds. These seeds are grown in special beds. Flat pans about 10 cm in diameter are suitable. They should be thoroughly cleaned and half-filled with broken bricks to facilate drainage. Then fill with compost consisting of equal parts of finely cut *Osmunda* fibre and fresh sphagnum moss slightly below the rim and make the surface smooth. Seeds are then sown. The pans are then covered with a sheet of glass to retain moisture and warmth. The glass should be lightly painted or covered with tissue paper to avoid burning of the young plants by sunlight. Watering should be carefully done with a fine nozzle spray. If the beds dry out they may be kept moist by partly dipping in water. Extreme wetness or dryness should be avoided. After eight weeks or so, the tiny green globules will appear. When the first little leaves appear they should be transplanted in other pots and treated in the same manner as juvenile plants. The seed beds should be retained undisturbed, as more seedlings may appear during subsequent months.

The fruits after harvesting from the plants should be kept in a desiccators with calcium chloride. The period for storing them in the desiccators for drying depends on the variety which may vary for a few days to even a month. After the capsule is dried, it should be stored in a Frigidaire. Before storing, the fruits of some types, which are prone to infection, should be fully sterilized against fungal attack by treatment with calcium hypochlorite solution for 15 minutes. If calcium hypochlorite is not available, 3% hydrogen peroxide may be used. Seeds after this treatment are put in a filter paper in petridish and put in a shaker so that they become thoroughly dried. Sowing of the seeds in the sterilized tubes of agar medium (contain calcium 10,000 ppm, urea 250 ppm, potassium and phosphorus 200ppm and sugar 2%) should be done with a sterilized needle by inserting the needle in the tube of agar medium inside a box under ultraviolet light. These tubes are kept air-tight. It takes about 2-3 months for the seeds to germinate but there are some species which can germinate even within a week. After they germinate and become swollen, they are transferred to another set of tubes by the same method and kept for about a year in artificial light with 18 hours daylight and at a temperature of 23.9 to 29.4°C. When these plants become big enough in the agar tubes, they are transferred to the pots filled with potting mixture of broken peat 1: sphagnum 1: sand 1 (sterilised). These pots are then retained in the greenhouse at 29.4°C.

Vegetative Propagation

Cuttings: Orchids like *Aerides, Arachnis, Epidendrum, Renanthera, Phalaenopsis, Vanda* and *Dendrobium* can be propagated by cutting. Orchids cutting are usually bigger and should posseses one or more roots. Cutting are usually potted in propagation beds or directly in pots after treating the cut ends with fungicides to prevent rotting. Cutting of genera like *Aerides, Arachnis* and *Vanda*, are very hardy and can be directly potted in pots, whereas, those of *Dendrobium* and *Phalaenopsis* need special care to root and should be potted in propagation beds. The propagation of orchids through cuttings is getting popular again and some of the nursery men like to propagate their orchids through cuttings to get uniform plants. The percentage of variation through this method is almost nill as compared to in vitro propagation through tissue culture. Further some orchids like *Anaectochilus* respond more to vegetative propagation through cutting than any other method. Most of the sympodial orchids like *Coelogyne, Cattleya, Dendrobium* and *Cymbidium* are propogated through this method. The method involved consists of dividing large clumps into smaller units. However, care should be taken not to divide the plants unless there are 8-10 pseudo-bulbs. *Dendrobiums* which are very fast growing can be divide every year.

***Off-shoots and Keikis*:** In some monopodial orchids like *Ascocenda* and *Phalaenopsis*, keikis or off-shoots emerge frequently on the main stem. This usually happens when the apex has lost its effectiveness in suppressing axillary buds. In most of the commercial orchid nurseries topping of the stem is commonly practised to induce Keikis formation. Induction of Keikis can also be induced through the use of cytokinins which force the dormant bud to develop into keikis.

Aerial shoots: Most of the *Dendrobiums* produce aerial shoots or bulbs on old back bulbs devoid of leaves. They usually arise on the upper part of the back bulbs and grow out slowly. These aerial shoots take 90-120 days to develop roots. At this stage, they are detached along with the portion of back bulb and potted as independent plant. In genera like *Goodyera,* rhizomes gives off special lateral branches which turn up and produce aerial shoots. When they are properly rooted they get detached from the mother plant and establish separately.

Micropropagation: Vegetative multiplication by shoot-tip culture has revolutionized orchid propagation, particularly for *Cymbidium, Cattleya* and some other genera. In this method the apical portion (about 0.2-0.5 mm) of the shoot and young leaves below it are removed. It is better to sterilize the shoot by dipping it into alcohol and soaking it in hypochlorite solution for 10 minutes, so that no fungal or bacterial spores are carried with the shoot, which may cause infection. The scalpel used to cut the shoot and needles and all the other equipments should be sterilized with alcohol and heating over a flame. The shoot tip should be placed in sterile Knudson's medium or any other suitable medium. After a few days, a small round protocorm develops in the medium and produces a root and a shoot as in the case of plants growing from seeds. Before the new shoots develop, the protocorm should be cut into small pieces and transplanted in separate flasks with new media at monthly intervals. By continuous cutting of the protocorm sections and transferring to separate flasks, a large stock of any one clone can be produced. After the seedlings attain about half the height of the flask, these should be taken out carefully with a sterile forceps and planted separately in small pots with sterile medium and kept in glasshouse. Care taken should be same as in the case of young plants.

Description of some important orchids:

Acanthophippium bicolor: It grows in India, Ceylon and Southern China. The plants are terrestrial with oblong pseudobulbs and prominently ribbed leaves. The spikes erect with several fairly large and spurred flowers which are yellow flushed with red-purple. It produces flowers in spring.

Aerides crispum: It grows in Western Ghats from Mahabaleshwar south and Himalayas. It is tall, robust, handsome plant, usually with dark violet purple leafy portion. Inflorescence drooping, twice or thrice longer than the leaves. Flowers 5 cm across, very attractive, fragrant and rosy purple. Flowering in May-June and lasts for a long time.

Aerides fieldingii: It grows on trees in Khasi and Jaintia Hills in Assam and the Himalayas. It is commonly known as Fox Brush Orchid. Stem densely covered with dark green leaves. Inflorescence 50 cm or more in length, pendant and sometimes branched. Flowers 3.75 cm across. Sepals and petals are amethyst purple with white or purple spots.

Aerides maculosum: A common epiphytic orchid in less open deciduous forests of Chota Nagpur, Deccan and Western Ghats. An epiphyte with leaves green and mottled with purple. Inflorescence about 24 cm long. Flowers about 2.5 cm across, faintly scented. Sepals and petals white flushed with pink mauve.

Aerides odoratum: It grows in Nepal, Sikkim and Assam. One of the most beautiful among *Aerides species.* Inflorescence a raceme, axillary, 15-25 cm long, pendulous, laxly many flowered, 1-3 in each plant. It produces in May-July. Flowers sweet scented white with numerous pink spots about 2.5 cm across.

Aerides vandarum: It grows in subtropical eastern Himalayas, Manipur and Assam. It resembles *Vanda teres* in appearance. Stem thick, 90-120 cm long. Flowers white, sweetly scented, borne on 2-3 flowered racemes, about 3 cm across. Sepals and petals twisted which make the flowers attractive. It flowers in February-April.

Anoectochilus roxburghii: It grows in the Himalayas from Shimla to Bhutan, Assam and Manipur. Leaves few, forming a loose rosette, about 5 cm long and very velvety with golden veins. In the middle part of the leaf has a distinct golden zone and margins reddish. Inflorescence erect, about 2.5 cm long and few flowered. It produces flowers in November. Flowers are pinkish white about 1.5 cm long.

Anoectochilus sikkimensis: It grows in Skkim and Assam at 900-1500m. Leaves elliptic, the upper surface very dark red with golden yellow veins, lower surface uniformly dark red and 5-10 cm long. Inflorescence a raceme and many flowered. Flowers brown with white lip about 2 cm long. Flowering in November.

Arachnanthe clarkii: It grows wild in eastern Himalayas at 1800-2100 m. Stem stout about 40 cm long with leaves having undulate margin. Inflorescence, 2-3 flowered about 7-15 cm long. Flowers about 7.5 cm across, blooms during November-January and lasts for 2 months. Sepals and petals bright chestnut brown with yellow lines.

Arachnanthe cathcartii: It grows wild in eastern Himalayas at 900-1350 m. This is a magnificent orchid. Stem 60-90 cm long. Inflorescence 4-6 flowered. Flowers attractive about 8-9 cm across and blooms in March-April. Sepals and petals yellow with horizontal red-brown bands.

Ascocentrum ampulaceum: It grows wild in tropical valley of Himalayas from 300-900 m. It is allied to *Vanda* but popularly confused with *Saccolabium* which belongs to a separate distinct group of orchids. It is an attractive plant with stout stem and leaves mottled with red-brown. Inflorescence many flowered. Flowers about 20 cm across, beautiful pink coloured and blooms during May-October.

Bulbophyllum cylindricum: It grows wild in Sikkim and Khasi Hills at 1800-2100 m. It has no pseudobulb and the leaf arises directly from rhizome. Inflorescence long and blackish purple. Flowers densely crowded, blackish purple, about 4 cm long and blooms in December-January.

Bulbophyllum leopardinum: It grows in Sikkim and Khasi Hills in Meghalaya. It is very handsome species. Pseudobulbs crowded. Flowers about 3 cm across and blooms in October-November. Sepals and petals yellowish with crimson spots.

Calanthe biloba: It grows in Sikkim at 1200-1800 m. It is a beautiful species with stout pseudobulbs and 30 cm long elliptic leaves. Inflorescence 1 or 3 about 30 cm long and many flowered. Flowers 3.75 cm across and blooms in September and October. Sepals and petals yellow and attractively mottled with purplish brown.

Calanthe herbacea: It grows in shady areas in Sikkim Himalayas at 1200-1800 m. very handsome species with 2.5 cm long fusiform pseudobulbs. Inflorescene about 30-60 cm long with a dozen or more flowers. Flowers blooms during June-July. Sepals are brownish green.

Calanthe masuca: It grows in Sikkim and in Western Ghats at 450-1200 m. Very attractive, beautiful evergreen orchid with pseudobulbs about 5 cm long and dark green leaves. Inflorescence lateral about 45 cm long and many flowered. Flowers about 5 cm across, distinctively violet and blooms in July-September.

Calanthe puberula: It grows in Himalayan ranges from Shimla in H.P. to Bhutan and also in Kasi Hills of Meghalaya. Very charming when well-grown in pots. Leaves borne on a small pseudobulb. Flowers lax about 2.5 cm across of very beautiful uniform pale lavender colour and blooms in August.

Cirrhopetalum cornutum: It grows in Sikkim and Assam from 900-1500 m. Pseudobulbs are narrowly ovoid and compressed. Inflorescence 10-20 cm long with a lax umbel of 6 or more reddish brown flowers with lip of darker tint. Flowering in August.

Cirrhopetalum guttulatum: It grows in Sikkim and Assam at 600-1500 m. Pseudobulbs are crowded, ovoid and tapering at apex. Inflorescence 8-15 cm long with 6-9 flowers. Flower about 2 cm across, pale yellow; beautifully spotted with purple and blooms in July-October.

Cirrhopetalum ornatissimum: It grows in warm valleys of Sikkim. It is a beautiful orchid with large long tailed, light yellow striped and shaded with purple flowers in a few flowered umbel. The dorsal sepal is prolonged into a long drooping filiform appendage and deeply rose coloured. It produces flowers in October-November.

Cirrhopetalum refractum: It grows in Sikkim at 1200-1800 m. Pseudobulbs dwarf and wrinkled with two leaves. Inflorescence drooping, 7.5 cm long with 6 or more flowers which are about 5 cm across. Petals yellow spotted with purple. It blooms in October-November.

Coelogyne barbata: It grows in Bhutan, Manipur, Khasi Hills in Meghalaya and Nagaland at about 1200-1500 m. An attractive plant which is winter flowering. Pseudobulbs ovoid, 2-leaved. Inflorescence arising on top of pseudobulbs, 15-35 cm long, bears about 8 flowers and 6-7 cm across. Sepals and petals are white, fimbricate with shaggy blackish brown hairs at the margin which make the flower attractive.

Coelogyne corymbosa: It grows in eastern Himalayas and Assam at 1500-2100 m on thickly moss covered branches of trees under shade. Pseudobulbs obscurely 4-sided, crowded on a stout rhizome. Inflorescence from the base of pseudobulb with 3-4 flowers. Flower about 5-7 cm across. Sepals and petals white, lip white with 4 yellow eyes bordered with orange. Flowering in March-May and lasts for three weeks.

Coelogyne cristata: It grows in Kumaon, Sikkim and Assam at 1200-2100 m. It is one of the finest Indian orchids which has great decorative value. Pseudobulbs are stout, obscurely angled with sessile leaves. Inflorescence about 20 cm long with usually 6 flowers about 10 cm across. Sepals and petals are snowy white. Flowering in March-April.

Coelogyne flaccida: It grows in Nepal, Sikkim and Assam at 900-1500 m. Pseudobulbs ovoid-cylindric with a pair of leaves. Inflorescence 8-10 flowered about 12 cm long. Flowers about 3.75 cm across and blooms in March-May. Sepals and petals creamy white and lip dark brown.

Coelogyne nitida: It grows in eastern Himalayas, Bhutan and Khasi Hills at 900-1800 m. A beautiful winter flowering orchid with crowded subglobose pseudobulbs. Inflorescence arising on the top of pseudobulbs, 3-6 flowered and slightly drooping. Sepals and petals are white and lip with yellow eyes.

Coelogyne punctulata: It grows in eastern Himalayas, Bhutan, Assam and in Cherrapunji area of Khasi Hills in Meghalaya. Inflorescence on the top of pseudobulbs. Flowers white, about 5 cm across and blooms in April-May.

Cryptochilus sanguineus: It grows in Nepal, Sikkim, Bhutan, Assam and Nagaland at 1500-2100 m. An epiphytic orchid with small crowded pseudobulbs with a pair of leaves. Inflorescence erect and 12-20 cm long. Flowers blood red, blooms in July-August and lasts for a long time.

Cymbidium affine: It grows wild in north India at 1200-1800 m. Plants with woody pseudostem. Inflorescence axillary bearing 4-6 flowers, about 6.5 cm across, pure white orange coloured disc of the lip and sweet scented.

Cymbidium devonianum: It grows wild on the Himalayas at 2100-3000 m. The plants are very attractive even when not in flowers. Pseudobulbs are very short with 2 or 3 dark green, strap-shaped narrow leaves about 22-30 cm long. Inflorescence lateral, inclined or drooping and as long as or larger than leaves. Flowers about 2.5 cm across, variable in colour but usually buff or olive green with purplish markings and blooms in May-July.

Cymbidium giganteum: It grows wild on the Himalayas from Kumaon in Uttarakhand to Sikkim and on the Khasi Hills in Meghalaya at 1200-1500. The prominent pseudobulbs are compressed, about 10-12 cm long with sword like leaves about 40-60 cm long. Inflorescence robust, arched, laxly many flowered and as long as the leaves. Flowers large about 8-10 cm across and blooms in October-December. Sepals and petals are yellowish green with dark purple nerves.

Cymbidium longifolium: It grows wild on the Himalayas from Garhwal in Uttarakhand to Sikkim at 1500-2100 m. Pseudobulbs short, sheathed, with many linear leaves about 40-60 cm long and 1 cm broad. Inflorescence arising from the base, sub-erect but decurved above, shorter than the leaves with about 15 flowers about 6-8 cm across. Flowering occurs in September to December.

Cymbidium mastersii: It is found on the branches of trees high above the ground in Assam, Sikkim and Bhutan at about 1500 m. Pseudobulbs more or less compressed with linear leaves 30-50 cm long infolded at base. Inflorescence axillary from among the leaves, 10-15 cm long, decurved with 4-6 flowers which are white, flushed with pink towards the apex, sweet scented, about 3 cm across and blooms in October to November.

Cypripedium hirsutissimum: It grows wild in Khasi and Patkoi Hills of Meghalaya at about 900 m. the flowering stalk is distinct as being clothed with dark purple hairs and it bears a single flower about 12.5 cm across. Flowering in April-May and lasting for about six weeks.

Cypripedium spicerianum: It grows among ferns on lofty rocks by the side of rivulets on tropical hills of eastern Assam. A very pretty and useful species with linear oblong leaves, undulate margin and purple spotted underside near the base. The scape is long, pubescent, purple, 1 or 2 flowered about 7.5 cm across and blooms in November-December.

Dendrobium aggregatum: It is found growing on trees along the base of Patkoi and Arakan ranges in Meghalaya. A pretty, dwarf, evergreen plant with single-leaved, clustered pseudobulbs, longitudinally wrinkled and 10 cm long. Inflorescence slender, drooping with 6-12 flowers about 5 cm across. Flowers yellow sometimes almost orange-yellow with a deep orange-yellow lip lasting for about 10 days. Flowering occurs in March-April.

Dendrobium amoenum: It is found in eastern Himalayas below 1300 m, extending to Assam and Myanmar. A very charming orchid with slender, pendulous stem, slightly thickened at nodes about 60 cm long. Leaves linear lanceolate. Inflorescence with 1-3 flowers which vary in size and colour and have delightful fragrance. Flowering occurs profusely in June.

Dendrobium amplum: It is a native of northern India, found growing on tree trunks or on rocks at about 1500 m. Pseudobulbs short, four sided, arising from a creeping rhizome at intervals, bearing 2 elliptic oblong leaves about 12 cm long. Flowers are large, about 8 cm across, solitary, borne on the apex of pseudobulbs and blooms during October.

Dendrobium crepidalum: It is found in the tropical valleys of the Himalayas upto 900m, extending to Assam and Myanmar. It has a drooping, thick stem, strongly jointed and thickened upwards about 30-45 cm long. Flowers are small, about 2.5 cm, borne in pairs in short clusters, produced freely from the nodes and blooms in April-May. Sepals and petals are white tipped with pink.

Dendrobium clavatum: It is found in valleys of Sikkim Himalayas, Khasi Hills in Meghalaya and upper Myanmar at about 900 m. It is very handsome with thick stem, about 45 cm long. Inflorescence about 5-8 cm long, horizontal or decurved, bearing 4-5 flowers about 7.5 cm across, yellow with lines of darker shade. Flowering occurs in May-June.

Dendrobium devonianum: It is found in Khasi Hills, at about 900-1200 m, hanging from branches of trees. It is one of the most beautiful *Dendrobium species* producing numerous flowers. Stem pendulous, slender about 90 cm long. Flowers long-lived, fragrant, borne in clusters of 2 or 3 from the upper nodes over a greater part of the stem, about 7 cm across, white tipped with amethyst purple. Flowering in May-June.

Dendrobium draconis: It is found in Assam and in the Patkoi Ranges in Meghalaya at about 1200 m. Stem with black hairs about 30-45 cm long. Flowers borne in small clusters, waxy ivory-white in colour about 5 cm across and comes in flowering in spring-summer.

Dendrobium farmeri: It is found growing on tall Sal trees along the tropical base of Sikkim Himalayan Ranges at 300-600 m. Plant is dwarf having quadrangular stem and laxly flowered inflorescence. Stem about 30 cm tall and 4 angled with slender base and elliptic lanceolate leaves about 15 cm in length. Inflorescence pendulous, rather loose, bearing numerous flowers, about 5 cm across, pale mauve when they first open gradually changing to pure white. Flowering in April-May and lasting for two weeks.

Dendrobium Hookerianum: It grows wild in Sikkim, Bhutan and Khasi Hills in Meghalaya at about 1500 m. It is one of the most charming among the yellow flowered *Dendrobium* spp., 180 cm long stem, bearing oblong lanceolate, 7-12 cm long leaves. Inflorescence pendulous, about 13 cm long bearing 8-12 flowers. Flower about 10 cm across, golden yellow in colour and blooms in April-May.

Dendrobium gibsoni: It grows wild in eastern Himalayas and Khasi hills in Meghalaya upto 1300 m. A showy, evergreen orchid, stem 60-90 cm tall and vertically ribbed. Inflorescence pendulous, 15-20 cm long, lax, bearing about 10 flowers. Flower about 5 cm across, orange yellow in colour and blooms in May-August.

Dendrobium moschatum: It is found in Sikkim Himalayas, Bhutan, Khasi Hills in Meghalaya and Myanmar at 600-900 m. It is a very robust, sturdy plant, with minutely notched stem, about 130-180 cm long, narrowed at base. Inflorescence arises from the apex of stem, 10-20 cm long, laxly flowered with a dozen or more flowers. Flowers about 10 cm across with a musky scent and blooms in June-July.

Dendrobium ochreatum: It grows wild in Assam on trees or rocks at 1200-1500 m. It is another showy yellow flowered orchid. Stem cylindrical, curved, stout with swollen joints about 25 cm long, having leaves about the same length. Flowers borne in pairs on young stem. Flower rich golden yellow, 5-7.5 cm across and blooms in April-May.

Dendrobium pierardii: It grows wild in tropical valleys of eastern Himalayas, Assam and Southern India. A pretty orchid which becomes attractive and magnificent when bloom because it becomes decorative on account of innumerable flowers in season. Stem about 90 cm long, slender, pendulous with sessile, lanceolate and 5-10 cm long leaves. Spikes crowded with numerous pairs of 5 cm wide, semi-transparent flowers, beautifully rose coloured. Flowering occurs in March-April.

Dendrobium primulinum: It grows wild in tropical Himalayas from Kumaon in Uttarakhand to Manipur. It is a lovely, deciduous orchid, which is greatly admired. It has the fragrance of primrose flowers for which it is named as primulinum. Stem slightly pendulous, about 30 cm long. Flowers solitary or in pairs from the nodes, 5-6.5 cm across and blooms in April-May. Sepals and petals are pale primrose-yellow with basal purple veins.

Dendrobium regium: It grows wild in Chota Nagpur, Bihar on trees where the summer is very warm and there is a long dry period from October-June. Sepals and petals are magenta coloured with darker transverse markings. Lip cream coloured with magenta throat and markings like sepals and petals.

Gastrochilus acutifolius: It is found in eastern Himalayas and in Khasi Hills at 900-1200 m. Stem 25-30 cm long with rather long leaves about 12.5 cm. inflorescence shorter than the leaves with six or more flowers about 1.2 cm wide crowded together in a corymb. Sepals and petals are light yellow spotted with red-brown colour. Flowering occurs in November-December.

Gastrochilus dasypogon: It grows wild in the tropical valleys of the Himalayas from Nepal to Assam at about 300 m. It is a beautiful orchid with flowers borne in corymbose raceme. Sepals and petal are bright yellow with brownish purple spots. Flowering in November-December and lasts for a long time.

Habenaria susannae: It is found in western and eastern Himalayas at 900-1500 m extending to Khasi hills in Meghalaya. It is an exceedingly handsome and showy orchid. Stem erect, 30-60 cm tall with sessile leaves sheathing at base. Inflorescence terminal, 5-10 cm long and 2-5 flowered. Flowers are white flushed with greenish yellow, sweet scented, 7-10 cm wide and blooms during August-September.

Ipsea speciosa: It grows in southern India. This is popularly known as Daffodil Orchid. A graceful, slender, terrestrial orchid with grasslike leaves arising from an underground tuber. Spike about 45 cm tall, carrying 2-6 bright yellow, fragrant flowers about 7.5 cm wide.

Phaius flavus: It is found in tropical valleys upto 1200 m, extending from Nepal to Khasi Hills in Meghalaya. Pseudobulbs clustered, ovoid and 12 cm long. Leaves 4-6, plaited about 45 cm long. A distinct feature is yellow spots on the leaves. Spike erect, upto 90 cm tall, carrying several flowers, 5-7.5 cm wide. Sepals and petals are buff-yellow. Flowering in March-April.

Phaius mishmensis: It is found in hot valleys of Sikkim Himalayas, extending to Assam, Mizoram and Myanmar at 900-1500 m. stem cylindric, 90-120 cm tall. Inflorescence axillary and few flowered. Flowers are very pretty, rose-coloured, about 4 cm across and blooms in October-November.

Phalaenopsis mannii: It is found in lower Himalayas and tropical valleys of Assam. A pretty orchid with leaves about 30 cm long. Inflorescence pendulous and many flowered. Flowers about 3.5 cm wide and blooms during May-June. Sepals and petals yellow with dark brown markings.

Pleione praecox: It is found in Sikkim Himalayas at 2200 to 2700 m and in Meghalaya at 1500 m. it is a beautiful orchid with egg-shaped pseudobulbs, bearing

2 plaited leaves about 30 cm long. Flowers usually solitary, 7-10 cm wide, fragrant, long lasting, rose-purple in colour and blooms in late winter to early winter.

Rhynchostylis retusa: In India, it is found at the base of Himalayas from Garhwal in Uttarakhand to Bhutan and Khasi Hills in Meghalaya up to 1000 m. Stem robust about 25 cm long. Leaves strap shaped about 25 cm long. Inflorescence pendulous, about 60 cm long densely flowered. Flowers fragrant, waxy, variable in colour, about 1.5 cm across and blooms during summer to autumn. Sepals and petals are white with copious amethyst-purple spots.

Saccolabium calceolare: It is found in Himalayas and Khasi Hills in Meghalaya at 1200-1800 m. a pretty orchid with short and stout stem. Flowers are borne in umbellate raceme. Sepals and petals are yellow. Flowering in March-April.

Thunia alba: It is found in Garhwal in Uttarakhand to Sikkim Himalayas and Assam. It is a handsome orchid, with stout, erect stem about 60 cm tall. Flowers 4-5, in short, drooping racemes, about 6.6 cm wide, white and blooms during July-August. Sepals and petals are pure white.

Vanda bensoni: It grows in Myanmar and in eastern Assam at 900-1200 m, usually on trees. Stems about 45 cm tall with leaves about 25 cm long. Spike suberect, about 30 cm long, bearing 12 or more flowers about 5 cm wide. Sepals and petals are yellowish green, with reddish brown veins. Lip rose or purple. Flowering in various seasons but mainly in spring.

Vanda coerulea: It is found in Myanmar and Khasi Hills in Meghalaya at 900-1300m. Stem 25-30 cm tall with stiff, erect leaves and 15-27 cm long. Inflorescence erect or gracefully arching, upto 60 cm long and mostly 5-15 flowered. Flowers highly variable in shape, size and colour, 7.5-10 cm wide and blooms during autumn to winter. Sepals and petals almost equal, usually pale-blue with darker reticulations, varying to pure white and pink in certain forms.

Vanda cristata: It grows from Kumaon in Uttarakhand to Bhutan, Nepal, Sikkim and Assam and Meghalaya at 600-1800 m. the forms growing at higher altitudes have two large flowers and those at lower altitudes with 4-5 flowers. Stems 10-12 cm long, with leaves 8-12 cm long. Inflorescence shorter than leaves and 2-5 flowered. Flowers 4-5 cm across, greenish yellow to purple, blooms in April and remain for long in beauty.

Vanda roxburghii: It is very common on mango trees in the plains of West Bengal and also found in adjoining states. Plants 25-50 cm high with leaves in two rows growing on trees. Spikes about 25 cm long, slightly pendant and 5-12 flowered.

Flowers about 5 cm wide, strongly scented and blooms in April-May. Sepals and petals undulated, white outside, pale yellowish green inside tasseled beautifully with olive brown.

Vanda stangeana: It grows in eastern Assam at 1200-1500 m. Spikes axillary and 4-5 flowered. Flowers about 6.5 cm wide, ochre yellow tasseled with brown or red brown and blooms during summer. Lip yellowish white with blue blotches and apex bi-lobed with darker colour.

Vanda teres: It is widely distributed over the hot valleys of Sikkim and Assam. It is regarded for its great ornamental values and greatly appreciated by the horticulturists. Stem roundish, often profusely branching from base and above, forming a dense tangled mass, 60-210 cm long, with round and 12 cm long leaves. Spikes appear opposite the leaves with 3-6 flowers of graceful form and delightful colouring and 15-30 cm long. Flowers 7.5-10 cm wide, long lasting, variable in colour and fragrance. Sepals roundish, slightly wavy and white with rose shade. Petals larger, rose or rosy magenta. Lip longer than sepals, funnel shaped, yellow boldly lined with purplish brown and red specks in the throat. Flowering almost throughout the year in the tropics but mainly in May-July. It has great demand as a cut flower, as beautiful flowers have great decorative and commercial value.

CHAPTER-11

PALMS AND CYCADS

Palms

Palms are admired for their ornamental, economical and ecological importance. This group of plants contain about 212 genera and 2779 species and belonging to family Palmae or Arecaceae. Almost all species except one genus which is native of Europe are tropical and sub-tropical in origin. The Palm tree has been termed the princes of the vegetable kingdom. Neither the anatomy of the Palm tree stems nor the conformation of their flowers, however, entitles them to any such high position in the vegetable hierarchy. Palms exhibit an enormous diversity in physical characteristics. Palms inhibit nearly every type of habitat within their range from, rainforest to deserts. Most species have an unbranched, erect tall, cylindrical and columnar stem, which is called the trunk. The trunk of the palm aids considerably in the identification of the palm. It is also the focal point and main ornamental feature of many palms. Based on the trunk character, palms are divided into five groups-solitary, clumping, branching, abnormal branching and trunkless. Solitary palms (single trunk) and clumping palms (multiple trunk) represent majority of species. Trunkless palms have very much reduced trunk and are referred to as acaulescent. These are small palms. Sometimes some damage to the single growing point proliferates into two, three or four in different directions, which eventually grow out to become branches. This type of palm is known as abnormally branched palm. The rare in famous examples in our country are the three branched *Brassus flabellifer* near Tirunelveli in Tamilnadu.

Palm leaves, often called 'fronds' also vary much in form and size. Palms are generally grouped under two heads, the fan leaved and pinnate or feather-leaved kinds. The inflorescence of palms consists generally of a fleshy spike, either simple or much branched, studded with numerous, sometimes extremely numerous, flowers, and enveloped by one or more sheathing bracts called ' spathes'. It should be remembered that in almost all palms, the beauty lies in their attractive trunk, leaf colour, shapes, plant structure and growth habits rather than the flower or inflorescence. The Palm tree fruit is various in form, size and character; sometimes, as in the common date it is a berry; sometimes it is a kind of drupe as in the coconut.

Importance of palms

Palms are of great ornamental value. There are several species suitable for decoration of conservatories, verandahs, for avenue planting, for indoors and for decoration of shade garden. Though a majority of palms attain great heights when planted out, they may be kept in pots remaining in beauty for many years, due to their very slow growth. The predictable nature and growth of palms make them an ideal planting material in landscaping. Palms in general create a feeling of tropics in any landscaping plantings. Palms are well suited to planting as specimens, or in clumps and spaced at convenient spacing. In such planting, the palms impart an interesting appearance. Palms of various statures can be planted below the canopy of large spreading trees and their stately grace and sculptural elegance can be enhanced by complimentary planting around them with ferns, other shade loving foliage plants and ground covers. Certain palms are of great economic value. Some of them affording shelter, food, clothing, fibre, timber, oil, sugar, starch, wax, wine, resin, tannin-dye-stuffs and many other products of great utility. The importance of Date and Coconut is well known. Stems of rattans, *Phoenix dicksonii* and leaves of a variety of palms are extensively utilized as construction materials of hut by forest dwellers. Leaf shingles and mats are typical of tribal homes. Leaf axis, leaf sheath fibres and stem fibres are used as cordage and for preparation of brooms, baskets, brushes, hats and many other house hold material. Fishtail palm fibres were once famous as 'Kitul' fibres. Foliage of *Wallichia densiflora* and several other palms of the north-eastern region are commonly employed as staple fodder for ponies. The central soft part of the stem of *Corypha umbraculifera*, *Corypha urens*, *Corypha obtusa*, *Phoenix rupicola*, *Phoenix acaulis*, and *Phoenix humilis* are a rich source of starch. Palms are felled to extract this central 'pith' which is dried, powdered, stored and used for preparation of bread by natives. Tribals of Khasia hills cultivate *Phoenix acaulis* and *Phoenix humilis* for this purpose. Stem apices of *Corypha urens*, *Corypha obtusa*, *Wallichia disticha* and *Borassus condapanna* are chewed raw or cooked as a delicacy by the natives. Such uses have endangered the populations of these palms in their native habitat. *Borassus flabellifer*, *Corypha urens*, *Arenga saccharifera* and *Arenga wightii* (Dudsal) exude a sugary sap from their cut flowering axis that yields country liquor on fermentation. The mature nuts of *Areca triandra*, *Areca nagensis* and *Pinanga* species are employed as substitutes for betel nuts, specially in the north estern region where they are called 'Tambols' or 'Ram tambols'.

Cultivation and maintenance of palms

Palms are easy to cultivate. They are tropical in nature and thriving in a warm humid atmosphere in light loamy soil containing a large quantity of humus. They grow both in shade and sun and rapidly recover if they have suffered from heat or cold. At medium elevations they are not so rapid in growth as in coastal regions where a salty and warm humid atmosphere prevails. They can be grown under glass in higher elevations. Palms are propagated from seeds. Some kind of palm e.g., Rhapis palm, which produce a number of suckers from the base, are increased by dividing the clumps into several pieces, each having some roots. Propagation of palm from seed is very slow. Palm seeds have to be harvested as they are ripen and are to be sown immediately for obtaining best quality seedlings and also a high percentage of germination. Delay in sowing results in very low germination and extended germination even up to 2 years from the same lot. Seeds vary in size from the size of pea to the size of coconut or larger in several species. They are covered with a thick coat which makes germination very slow. They should be sown in well drained fine soil and covered to the thickness of their diameter. Seeds may be sown at any time of the year but it is best during spring and summer. The seedlings should be lifted as soon as the first pair of leaves appear and potted off singly in small pots which is just sufficient to accommodate the roots and the seeds with some little soil. As the plants grow and fill the small pot, they should be shifted to pots of the next larger size. A few important points need particular attention in the cultivation of palms in pots. They prefer to pot bound and thrive in under-sized pots. They are best allowed to remain in the same pots till the roots increase and fill them, almost to the point of breaking or forcing the pots open. At the time of repotting, the fleshy large roots are best not injured. Planting should not be too deep. The collar, that is, the point where the roots emerge from the trunk should just rest on the soil surface. Palms should be regularly and liberally supplied with water. Those which suffer by neglect in watering seldom recover. Top dressing once or twice a year is necessary. For the foliage to be maintained fresh and green, the plants need feeding with liquid manure. Oil cake water may be alternated with weak Ammonium sulphate solution (15 g per litre of water) once in fifteen days. Regular supply of water, overhead watering once in two or three days by spraying, good drainage and periodic supply of weak liquid manure conduce to healthy specimen.

There are very few diseases and pest to which palms are subjected to, scales and mealy bugs are often noticed on the veins of leaves and are often hidden under the base of leaves clasping the stem. The stem should be kept clean and old leaves and leaf-stalks should be removed carefully without injuring the stem. Parts of the stem infested may be sponged and sprayed with fish oil soap or methylated spirits. Rhinoceros beetle attacks young shoots, boring holes and making way for weevils which may kill the plant in course of time. The beetles are best killed by harpooning them with a thick wire thrust into holes.

Examples of different types and utility of palms

Solitary palms: Coconut, *Phoenix*, *Elaeis*, *Roystonias*, *Hyophrobe* and *Aiphanes*.

Clumping palms: *Areca lutescens*, *Ptycosperma macarthurii*, *Crtostachy renda*, *Chamadorea seifrizii* and *Raphis humilis*.

Branched palms: *Hyphaene indica* (above ground branching type) and *Nypa fruiticans* (below ground branching type).

Trunkless palms: *Phoenix acualis*, *Phoenix pusilla*, *Chamadorea radicalis* and *Syagrus liliputiana*.

Feather-leaved palms: *Areca lutescans*, *Caryota mitis*, *Cocos nucifera*, *Royatonea regia* and *Roystonea oleracea*.

Fan-leaved palms: *Borassus flabellifer*, *Chamaerops excelsa*, *Hyphaene thebaica* and *Licuala grandis*.

Palms which can tolerate deep shade: *Areca catechu*, *Caryota mitis*, *Chamadorea elegans*, *Licuala grandis*, *Livistonia rotundifolia and Raphis excelsa*.

Palms suitable for avenue planting: *Arenga saccharifera*, *Royatonea regia*, *Roystonea oleracea*, *Hyophorbe verschaffeltii*, *Livistonia rotundifolia*, *Phoenix dactylifera*, *Washingtonia filifera* and *Washingtonia robusta*.

Palms for coastal areas: *Chamaerops humilis*, *Cocos nucifera*, *Hyophorbe verschaffeltii*, *Livistonia rotundifolia*, *Phoenix dactylifera*, *Royatonea regia* and *Washingtonia filifera*.

Palms for tropical climates: *Borassus flabellifer*, *Caryota urens*, *Hyophorbe* species, *Lantana* species and Roystoneas.

Palms for moist boggy wet soils: *Cyrtostachys renda*, *Licuala spinosa*, *Livistona decipiens* and *Nypa fruticans*.

Palms for indoors: *Caryota uren*, *Chamadorea elegans*, *Hyophorbe verschaffeltii*, *Licuala grandis*, *Livistonia rotundifolia*, *Rhapis excelsa* and *Washingtonia filifera*.

Description of some important palms

Feather leaved palms: The chief veins run out of the sides of a long midrib, the leaf being very often divided into long and narrow segments.

Acanthophoenix crinata : It is 18 m tall. The brown crown shaft trunk is covered with black spines. The leaves are 3-4 cm long, pinnate and carry black spines on blackish petiole. Propagation is from seeds which may take up to two years to germinate.

Archontophoenix cunninghamii : This is native of Australia, popularly known as Bungalow palm or Piccabeen Palm. The palm is solitary, tall and slender with a prominent crown-shaft, leaflets with long, thread like tips and green beneath. Inflorescence is very attractive with lilac colour flowers. It is propagated from seeds.

Areca lutescans : It is native of Bourbone and up to 8 m tall. The plant forms an attractive clump and has a beautiful yellowish stem. The arching leaves are yellowish green in colour and very attractive. The species is very ornamental and suitable for planting in lawns and in shade garden. It is propagated from seeds or suckers.

Areca triandra: It is native of Assam and Mayanmar and is similar to *Areca catechu* but more ornamental.

Arenga saccharifera: It is commonly called as sugar palm or sago palm. It is a beautiful, magnificent tall species, with enormous shining. Leaves are dark green, 50-60 cm long with a graceful curve towards the summit, thrown up erect from the sides of trunk. It forms a good avenue tree. Looks very impressive if planted at the entrance of garden or a building. The pith of the trunk is used as sago and from its juice an excellent sugar is made.

Bentinckia nicobarica: It is 20-30 m tall, graceful palm from Nicobar islands and commonly known as Nicobar palm. The leaves are 1.5-2.5 m long and leaflets are 25-60 cm long. It is now a endangered species due to its habitat loss. It can be used as a specimen tree.

Arecastrum romanzoffianum : It is native of Brazil and popularly called as Queen Palm. It is a solitary palm. The grey trunk is fairly slender and grows up to 15 m in height and is crowned by spreading and feathery looking fronds. This palm is fast growing and fertilizer responsive. It is suitable for planting in parks, streets as well as in home gardens.

Calamus lindeni : It is native of Malaysia and Indonesia, commonly called as Rattan Palm or Cane Palm. It is thorny and rambling in habit. When young it can be grown in pots. Another species *Calamus ciliaris* is native of India and excellent for table decoration when young. Its stem and leafstalk are spiny.

Calyptrocalyx spicatus : It is native of Moluccas. It is commonly cultivated for its colourful foliage and is good for pot culture. It requires protection from cold and dry winds which kills it.

Caryota mitis : It is native of Mayanmar, Malaysia and Indonesia and is commonly known as 'Clustered Fishtail palm', because the leaflets are delta or fish tail-shaped. The palm is quick growing and attains a height up to 7 m. It has spineless, stout and ringed stem. The leaves are 1-3 m long and wedge shaped leaflets are 10-20 cm long. It is propagated from suckers.

Caryota urens : It is native of Sri Lanka, Mayanmar and India, commonly known as 'Solitary fish-tail palm' toddy palm, wine palm or jaggery palm. Fishtail palm is a fast growing feather palm that makes a beautiful addition to the landscape. It has a gray trunk that is covered by regularly spaced leaf scar rings. Toddy palm has a leaf shape that resembles the lower fin of a fish. When these palms grow to reach 60m, they start producing flowers at the top of the trunk with subsequent flowers produced lower and lower on the trunk. When the lowest flower blooms, the tree dies. Flowers are long plait like bunches hanging down.

Cocos nucifera :It is coconut palm more commonly grown as commercial purpose than ornamental purpose. For ornamental purpose king coconut with yellow-green or red fruits are useful.

Cyrtostachys lakka : It is native of Malaysia, Indonesia and Borneo and commonly called as Lipstick palm or Sealing wax palm. Sealing Wax Palm is probably the most beautiful of all palms. Adorned with pretty looking leaves, it develops a brilliantly red trunk. Leaves are feather-like, pinnate with very narrow and long leaflets. The leaf-stalks are of a bright scarlet red, the colour of red sealing wax which is where the palm gets its common name. Sealing Wax Palm has a clustering habit. It is propagated from seeds which are very slow to germinate and takes up to one year.

Dictyosperma album : *Dictyosperma alba* is widely cultivated in tropics but reached near extinction in their natural habitat. It is commonly called as Princess palm or

Hurricane palm due to its ability to withstand strong winds by easily shedding leaves. The ringed trunks are solitary at 15 cm in diameter with a slight bulge at the base, occasionally reaching up to 12 m in height. The crownshaft is over a meter tall, swollen at the base, and covered in white wax— which has given the palm its epithet *album*— and small, matted brown hairs, producing a rounded leaf crown 4.5 m wide and 3 m tall. The 2.5 to 3 m leaves are borne on short 30 cm petioles; the arching leaflets are pointed at the apice, from 60 – 90 cm, dark green in color, and emerge from the rachis in a single plane.

Dypsis madagascariensis : It is a rare clump forming, slender-trunked, feather leaved palm from Madagascar. It is threatened by habitat loss.

Elaeis guineensis : It is native of West Africa. It is commercialy cultivated to produce palm oil. Mature tree is single stem and reached up to a height of 20 m with stout deeply ringed stems which are not spiny. Leaves are pinnate and 3-5 m long. The leaflets are 3-5 m long, ark green in colour, and the stalk is spiny-toothed; leaflets are 50-60, linear lanceolate, and acute. Young plant can be grown in pots.

Geonoma gracilis : It is a dwarf palm (2-3m tall) native of Brazil. It is useful for table decoration.The flowers are very showy and in long drooping spadices in yellow colour. Propagation is from seeds or suckers.

Hyophorbe amaricaulis : It is native of Mauritius. It is a gravely threatened species and now only a single specimen is present. The palm is about 20 m in height with relatively thin grey trunk with a waxy crown. The leaves are pinnate, spreading 1.2-1.8 m. The pinnae are stout and in a pairs of 40-60.The stalk is deep maroon in colour, glaucous, with an orange line along outer edges of midrib.

Hyophorbe verschaffeltii : It is commonly called as Palmiste Marron or Spindle palm. It is 8-10 m tall. The trunk is swollen at about half-way mark. The leaves are 1.2 to 1.8 m long, gracefully arching at the top; pinnae in pairs of 30-50, about 60 cm long and 3 cm wide. The leafstalk is about 7 cm long with a yellow band from the upper part of the leaf sheath to the end of blade. The flowers are orange yellow in colour. Spindle Palms are elegant looking palms that are prized for landscape palms in the tropical and semi-tropical areas of the world. They are fairly short palms with 8-10 leaves that are held somewhat erect. Spindle palms have a crownshaft that becomes a light gray-green as the palm ages. Horn-like flower spikes emerge from below the crownshaft on mature specimens.

Martinezia caryotaefolia : *Martinezia caryotaefolia* may be described in a general way as bearing some resemblance to *Caryota urens*, except that the latter is without spines. It is 10-15 m tall and native of Columbia, Eucador and Venezuela. The general colour of the leaves is deep green and the habit of the plant very graceful.

Phoenix : It is a genus of ornamental and economic palms including the date palm and the toddy or sugar palm.The following species are very useful in pots for decorative purposes.

Phoenix reclinata : It is 7-9 m tall. The leaves are 1.8-2.5 m long, and leaflets 30-60 cm, linear and bright green.

Phoenix roebelenii : It is commonly called as 'Pygmy Date Palm'. It is highly ornamental species, with graceful light feathery arching pinnate leaves, almost hiding the base from view. It is most commonly grown in this genus and popular for its fine delicate graceful plumose pinnate fronds.

Phoenix rupicola : It is native of India and Nepal. It is considered to be the most handsome species in this genus. It grows to a height of 5-6 m. The trunk is about 20 cm thick. The leaves are 3 m long, bright green and flaccid, leaflets 45 cm long.

Phoenix sylvestris : A wild date or toddy palm is quite ornamental when young.

Phoenix canariensis : It is Canary Island Date palm and widely cultivated throughout the world. The stout, woody trunk grows up to 20 m height and is crowned by long, pinnate, light green fronds which are spiny at the base. It is very good for avenues and for large open areas.

Pinanga kuhlii : It is a dwarf, slender clustering feather palm. They look like *Arecas* and forms several slender yellowish-green stems up to 10 m in height. When young, it is very well suited for table decoration.

Ptychoraphis augusta : It is a native of Nicobar Islands. It is quite ornamental like the cocos weddeliana or Geonoma gracilis. The other species, *Ptychoraphis singaporensis,* is a multi-stemmed palm. The stems are slender, case-like, ringed, black in colour and feather leaved.

Roystonea: It is a small genus of elegant Tropical American palms, with slender rigid swollen stems bearing large terminal pinnate leaves, with long sheath-like stalks forming a cylinder around the summit. They should be sheltered from winds to maintain them in a beautiful state. They are fit for ground culture and are unsurpassed for majesty and grace.

Roystonea oleracea : It is commonly called as 'cabbage palm'. The stem is slender and swollen at the base. Leaves are 1 to 1.5 m long with gracefully arching leaflets. It is generally planted along avenues.

Roystonea regia : It is commonly called as 'Cuban Royal palm, Bottle palm, or Royal palm'. The plant grows to a height of up to 20 m or more with spindle shaped trunk. The plant is uneqalled among the palms in its beauty, majesty, and grace. The palm is very slow growing. It is planted along avenues.

Wallichia : It is a small genus of six palms restricted to the Himalayan region of Northern India, Bangadesh and Southern China. In the clumping species the leaflets are generally broad with ragged margins and somewhat resemblance to *Caryota* species.

Wallichia disticha : It is a dwarf (3-5 m) tall palm with 2-3 m long graceful leaves. The leaflets are 30-60 cm long and 3 cm wide. It is propagated from seeds or by separating the suckers. Other two Indian species *Wallichia densiflora* and *Wallichia caryotoides,* are also ornamental.

Fan-leaved palms: The chief veins of the leaf blade appear to arise from the top of the leaf blade.

Borassus flabellifer : It is commonly called as 'Palmyra palm'. It is one of the hardy palms but have not much ornamental value in the garden.

Chamaerops : It is a genus of slow growing palms of medium height. It is very easily grown and highly ornamental. It is propagated from seeds and sometimes by suckers. It is better suited for medium elevations.

Chamaerops excelsa : It is native of China and Japan. It is commonly known as 'Windmill Palm' or 'Fortunes Palm'. The stem is covered with a mat of long, dark-brown fibres. The leaves are 1.2 to 1.5 cm across.

Chamaerops humilis : It is European Fan Palm. It is only palm native to Europe. It produces suckers at the base and could attain a height of 1.8 to 3 m. The leafstalk is about 1.2 m long, armed with stiff straight or hooked spines.

Corypha umbraculifera: It is native of South India and Sri Lanka and commonly called as 'Talipot Palm'. In their native home it can attain height of 30 m. They are very slow growing. The leaves are fan shaped, plaited, forming a complete circle of 3.5 m and bright green in colour. The stalks are spiny. Its dried leaves are used for making crude umbrellas in Kerala. The large broad leaves are used for thatching.

Hyphaene thebaica : It is native of Europe and commonly called as 'Doum palm'. This may be called as botanical wonder due to its repeatedly branching habit. The branches are smooth. The leaves are 60-75 cm long, and the petiole is spiny. The orange-yellow fruits are edible. Another species *Hyphaene indica* is native of India.

It is very hardy and slow growing. It makes excellent specimen planting due to its unique branching habit.

Latania : It is a genus of three species of solitary, large fan palms. They are handsome palm with large striking leaves. They are very hardy and slow growing. It can be used as a pot plant in young stage.

Latania commersonii : It is commonly called as 'Bourbon Palm or Red Latan Palm'. It is native of Mauritius and Reunion. This species is also known as *Latania lontaroides* and *Latania barbonica*. It is striking, very handsome, distinct species with a smooth and slender red stem and rich shining, brown-green, red-veined, deeply incised, gracefully recurved leaves. Leafstalks are long and smooth and are coloured bright crimson. It is rare and costly.

Latania verschaffeltii : It is commonly called as 'Yellow Latan Palm'. It is similar to above species except that leafstalks are orange-yellow in colour. Leaves are light green in colour with golden coloured ribs.

Licuala grandis : It is native of New Guinea. It is most sought after plant for indoor gardening. It has very beautiful symmetrical glossy dark green leaves and neat habit of growth. The circular, pleated leaves are up to 1 m across and have notched margins. They are generally slow growing and therefore excellent for pot culture.

Licuala peltata : It is of Indian origin. The palm is 4-5 m tall. The leaves are peltate and the lobes of the leaves droop gracefully. It is highly ornamental and very rare in cultivation.

Livistonia : This genus contained about 28 species that are found from India to Australia. They are solitary, fan-leayed palm with stout thorns on their petioles.

Livistonia decipiens : It is commonly called as 'Weeping Cabbage Palm' and native of Australia. The leaves are fan shaped with long trailing ends, grey-green in colour and create a very soft weeping crown atop the long slender trunk. It requires ample moisture, good drainage and prefers part shade.

Pritchardia pacifica : It is native of Fuji and known as 'Fuji Fan Palm'. This fan-leaved palm has a smooth, attractive trunk, 9 m tall and 25-30 cm thick. The leaves are many, short-stalked, 1.2 m long and 1 m in breadth, bright olive-green in colour and leathery. Most ornamental species for pot culture.

Rhapis: This genus contain dwarf, rattan-like palms with slender stem and fan-shaped leaves, deeply cut into segments. They are excellent for bushy clumps in shade gardens or for pot culture. They produce large number of suckers and propagated by suckers.

Rhapis excelsa : It is commonly known as ' Ground Rattan palm' or ' Large lady palm' and native of China and Japan. The stem is bamboo like, 45 to 120 cm tall and forms clumps from underground suckers. The stem is persistently covered with leaves. The leaves are 5-7, glossy green, deeply cut into several segments, stalks obscurely toothed in margins. It is propagated from suckers. It is very useful for planting in shade gardens and growing in tubs.

Rhapis humilis : It is similar to above species except that, it is less vigorous. The leaves are larger than above and stalks are smooth. It is commonly called as 'Slender lady palm'.

Sabal adansonii : It is native of United states and commonly known as ' Dwarf Palmetto' and 'Blue Palm'. Its stem is too short and appears stemless. The leaves are orbicular, fan-shaped, 60-90 cm long, the segments 20-30, slightly cleft at the apex. The stalk is smooth and shorter than leaf. It is noble looking and most ornamental palm.

Thrinax: It is a genus of dwarf fan-leaved palms and commonly called as 'Thatch Palm'. This genus contains four species and native to West Indies and Florida. The plant is solitary with very slender trunk.

Thrinax argentea : The stems are 3.5 to 4.5 m tall and foliage is very ornamental. The leaves are deeply divided and star shaped, glossy green above and silvery below. The leaf segments are united at the base.

Verschaffeltia splendida : It is native of Seychelles. It is a very handsome palm with aerial silt roots. The top of the stem and petioles are spiny at first. The leaves are 90-150 cm wide, bright green veined and shaded with yellow. It is a very rare species.

Washingtonia : It is a small genus of two species, native to USA and Maxico. They are solitary, large with persistent fan leaved palm.

Washingtonia filifera : It is commonly known as American Cotton Palm or Petticoat Palm. It is a tall, distinctive palm with a fat, grey trunk and a spreading crown of grey-green, fan-shaped leaves. The old leaves persist as a petticoat covering the trunk. Once established the plants are very drought resistant. The mature leaves have the cottony threads in between the leaf segments.

Washingtonia robusta : It is commonly known as Washington Palm or Skyduster. It is similar to above species but grows taller and with a much thinner trunk. Also the leaf segments lacks the cottony thread. It makes an excellent palm for avenues, driveways and in parks.

Cycads

Cycads are an ancient group of seed plants with a crown of large compound leaves and a stout trunk. They are often referred to as 'living fossils'. They are a minor component of the flora in tropical and subtropical regions today but during the Jurassic Period, they were a common sight in many parts of the world. For this reason, the Jurassic is often referred to as the "Age of Cycads". Today only a handful of cycads still exist and many are facing possible extinction in the wild (such as *Microcycas* in Western Cuba). However, because of their large attractive leaves, many cycads have found a home in public and private gardens around the world.

The term 'Cycad' is the common name for members of the order Cycadales. Along with conifers, ginkgos and gnetales, Cycads belong to the taxon Gymnospermae with one common characteristic; they all bear naked seeds. Cycads are woody stemmed plants, some with thick columnar caudices or trunks and others with caudex completely subterranean. The trunk consists of a central core of rather fleshy conducting tissue on the outside of which is a thick layer of row upon row of persistent leaf bases rising from base to crown. They are mostly unbranched but multiple heads on mature Cycads and Lepiodzamia are quite common. The Cycad crowns may have one of several different forms, although the general shape is palm like. Leaves are feather-shaped, pinnately compound and spirally-arranged and in most plants are replaced approximately every two years. The leaves are as in the palms are called fronds and in a few species even rise circinately (uncoiling) from the crown as in the true ferns. The beautiful crown of leaves is the primary attraction of these plants. Cycads are dioecious, that is to say they consists of separate male and female plants. Cycads grow very slowly, at rates of between 0.5 and 2.5 cm per year. Cycads are also very long lived. A few documented live Cycads are thought to be 500 to 1000 years old and their rootstocks could be a great deal older.

Propagation of Cycads is chiefly by seeds. Vegetative propagation is by means of large bulb-like buds which appear at intervals on the stem and as off shoot from subterranean trunks. These bulbous buds grow freely when taken off the plants and planted in well-drained soil in a moist shady situation. Cycad seeds should be collected on ripening and sown within a month to obtain higher rate of germination. Most of the Cycads prefer partial shade during their young stages of growth.

Description of some important cycads

Cycus: It is a genus of hardy palm-like plants of great beauty. The stem is short and cylindrical and is usually unbranched and terminated at the top by a fine crown by deeply pinnate leaves varying in length from 0.5 to 1.5 m. It is propagated from suckers or seeds.

Cycus cercinalis: It is native of India and commonly called as 'Queen Sago'. It performs better under shady condition and produce lusterous crown of leaves, which emerge in tufts of bright parrot-green and maturing to dark green fronds. The seeds as well as pith contain considerable starch and are used as tribal food. It can be used as a specimen plants.

Cycus revoluta: This is the hardiest and most widely used stately Cycads. It is commonly called as 'Fern Sago' or 'Japanese Sago'. It is originated in Japan and frequently grown as bonsai subject.

Dioon: *Dioon edule* and *Dioon spinulosum* are both from Mexico. These are larger than Cycads and have more leaf segments as well. Very slow growing.

Encephalartos caffer: It is native of South Africa and commonly called as 'Kaffir Bread'. The plants are handsome, palm-like with a stout stem which may grow up to 5.5 m. A crown may consists of 14 leaves, each about 60 to 120 cm long.

Encephalartos hildebrandtii: It is a beautiful species from tropical East Africa, grow up to 6 m. The leaves are up to 2.7 m long and the main stalk is woolly when young.

Macrozamia: This genus is endemic to Australia comprising of 14 species commonly referred to as 'Burrawang'. All the species make attractive rockery feature plants. The very dark green fronds which have a bluish hue when young are very finely pinnate. These plants are well suited for pot culture and make excellent indoor plants. Most of the Macrozamias do not have a well defined trunk the exception, however, being *Macrozamia moorei*, which can produce a stout trunk.

Zamia: Zamias are mostly native of the Florida, Caribbean Islands and tropical America.They are commonly known as 'Coontie or Cardboard Palm'. Zamias are mostly low growing plants with a very short stout bulbous trunk. The plants are tropical and subtropical and resemble palms and to some extent ferns. They can be propagated by division, seeds and offsets. However, in Indian condition, they seldom produce seeds or suckers. Hence the propagating materials or plants are to be imported. Some of the important species are *Zamia furfuracea* and *Zamia integrifolia*.

CHAPTER-12

BONSAI

The word bonsai comes from Japanese language, *bon*- tray or a shallow container and *sai*- a plant, so literally it means "tray planting". It is the art of aesthetic miniaturisation of woody and semi woody trees and shrubs in a shallow pan. It is different from shallow potted plant in that here the unique look of miniature form of plant is main appeal rather than its foliage or flowers. By growing the trees in shallow container only the growth is checked or dwarfed but the plant is not starved. It is the certain cultural technique which tend them to grow in limited space and produce artistic appeal. Though seem mysterious but a bonsai creation needs only an artistic eye and some garden principles like pruning, training and knowledge of growing plants in containers. Bonsai is now being adorned by all section of people, particularly those living in cities, where growing tree in a home would be a wild fantasy. It could find its place anywhere in your home be it bedroom, living room, window-sill, veranda and other smaller places. With the rising of 'going green' slogan now it could also be seen in offices, hotels, malls and so on.

Bonsai through Ages

This aesthetic branch of horticulture was developed by Chinese over 2000 years ago and later redefined by the Japanese who are credited for its introduction in the western world. Chinese bonsai were of two forms- 'penjai' and 'penjing'. Word 'penjai' was used to denote a tree planted in a container without any landscape while, the word 'penjing' on the other hand, represented a tree planted in a container or on a tray with a landscape. However, the word 'penjing' is widely used in China to mean both forms of bonsai. It is not clear which form appear first. If we consider 'penjing' as an early bonsai, the legend and literature reveals that this art is far dated back to the early period of Han Dynasty during 206 BC to 220 AD. One legendary tale states that Fei' Jiang Feng of the Han Dynasty, was blessed with a magic power of miniaturizing mountains, trees, rivers, houses, people and animals which he used to put inside a tiny disc. It is believed that Feng was the first man to bring landscape indoors. Pictorials and paintings of pine, cypresses, palm trees, bamboos and so on, growing in tiny dishes, of Jin Dynasty (265-420 AD) are believed to be the earliest pictorial record on 'penjing' bonsai. On the other hand the first reference of 'penjai' is found in literature of Qin Dynasty during, 221-207 BC. While bonsai is believed to be originated from China, it gained popularity in present form in Japan. It is estimated that the art reached Japan almost 1000 years ago by Buddhist monks during 10th and 11th century. Bonsai was treated then as religious object- stairway leading to Heaven—to create a bridge between God and mankind. At the beginning of 13th century this art become highly disciplined and restricted to sophisticated people. The art, in the beginning remained within the Japanese aristocracy and only by the end of the 18th century became popular with all sections of the people. At the beginning of Meiji period in 1869, the name bonsai was officially proclaimed by the sponsors and was adopted throughout the Japan.

It was Japanese who first presented the Bonsai to the world, first in Paris at the world fair 1878 and subsequently in London in 1909. After the exhibition in 1934 at the Ueno Park Art Gallery, bonsai first received official recognition as a work of art and was given competitive status with other known arts. It is still not clear that when bonsai introduced in India. It is believed that bonsai reached India sometimes in the early of 19th century. It is from Bengali literary writing of Abanindra Nath Tagore (1871-1951), some reference is found that Japanese miniature trees were displayed during that period but it does not reveal that whether bonsai culture actually started at that time. Late Mr. V.P. Agnihotri of New Delhi has developed the Indian version of bonsai and popularised it in India during nineteen sixties.

Traditional style of bonsai is based on shape, size and grouping of trees. Diversity of tree characteristics gives bonsai artists' enormous opportunities to create new style. Broadly it can be divided into two categories- first depending on size of bonsai and second according to the shape of bonsai.

A. ***Size of bonsai*** : There are four groups of size in traditional Japanese classification.

1. Miniature bonsai: It is also called as 'mame' or 'finger tip' bonsai. It maintains a height of 5 to 15 cm. Such bonsai may be held on the tip of the finger. These extra small bonsai is difficult to develop and hard to get true effect.
2. Small bonsai: It reaches a height of 30 cm. Both shrubs and trees can be selected for this group.

CLASSIFICATION OF BONSAI

BONSAI STYLES

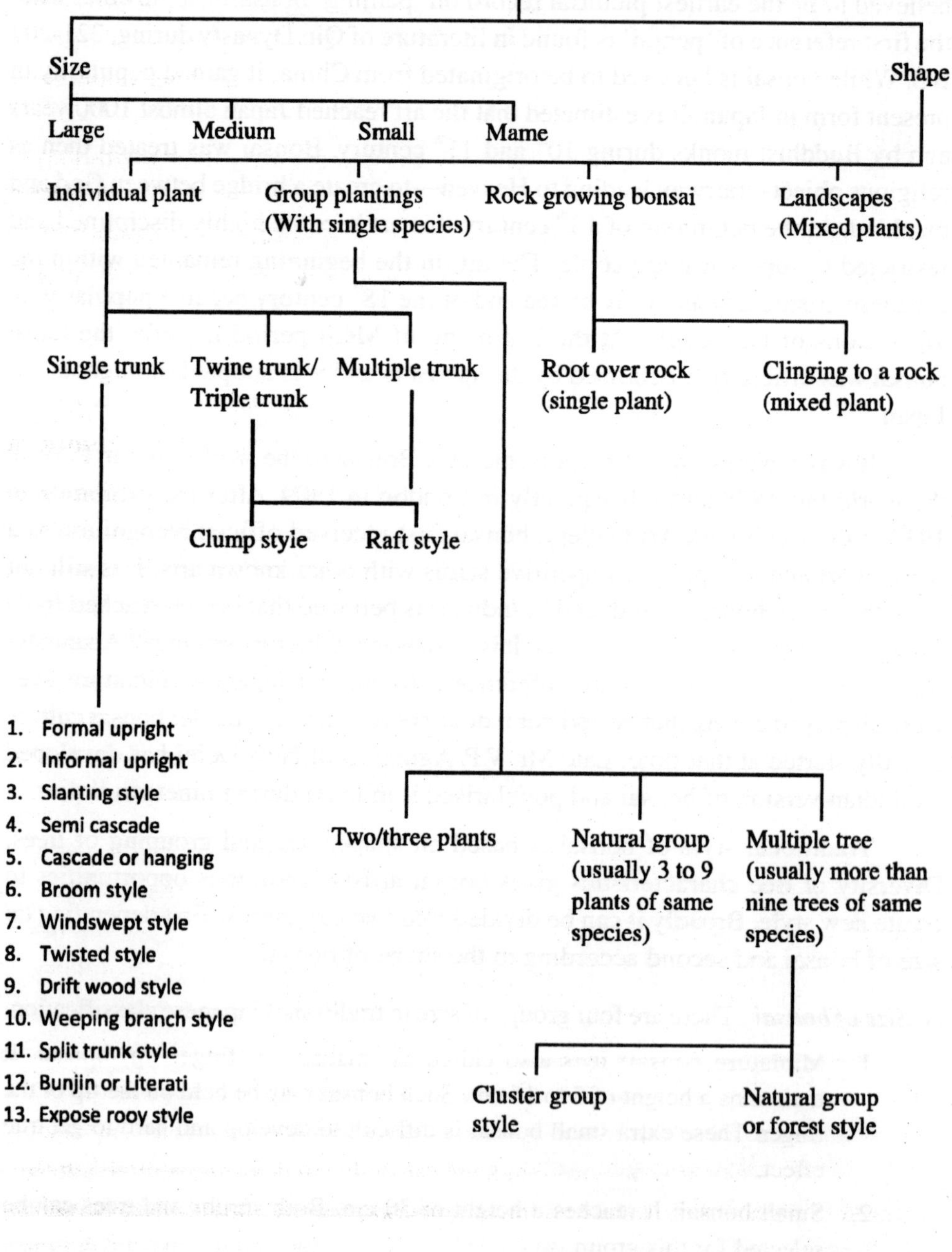

3. Medium bonsai: It attains a height of 30-60 cm and perhaps the most popular size. This group of bonsai can be conveniently developed to a beautifully proportioned tree and it is very convenient to handle, lift and shift.
4. Large bonsai: Bonsai beyond the height of 60 cm are considered large. Maximum height is described as 100cm but bonsai beyond 100 cm are also brought under this group. Here training of large plants and handling of the plants with large container and volume of soil is possible.

Shape of Bonsai: Bonsai style is described with the shape of the trunk at maturity. Many shapes could be possible depending on the artists' imagination, but broadly five types are more common.

1. Formal upright style: In this bonsai the trunk is trained straight, tapering towards the apex, erect apex, clear trunk with alternately arranged branches, trained into a pyramidal or spherical shape.
2. Informal upright: Growing upward but irregular in movement, trunk may have well-balanced curves, apex slightly tilted towards the front and the branches are alternately arranged. The branches should carry symmetrical irregularity with the trunk.
3. Slanting style: In this style trunk grow slantly on the right or left of the roots, trunk line may be straight or curved. The tip of the tree is always kept upward and arrangement of branches is somewhat different from the upright style as more branches are encouraged towards the apex. Conifers are suitable for this type of style Rectangular or oval pot is the best for this purpose.
4. Semicascade style: Here the trunk grows horizontally, trunk line may be straight or curved, branches arise from the upper side of the trunk in a very unusual pattern, the branches are so trained that it produces a tree like shape on the upper side of the trunk. This style of bonsai usually grown in tall pots, with round, square or hexagonal shapes.
5. Cascade style: Here the trunk hangs over the edge of the container as if it was hanging over the ledge of a mountain. Tall pots are good for this purpose. Plants, like bougainvillea having natural weeping habit or horizontal growth together with semi climber in nature, are suitable for this style.

Culture and Management

Selection of Plant

The selection of planting material depends upon the personal liking of individuals. Before selecting a plant certain prerequisites should be considered like plant character and its climatic requirements, adaptability in container and feasibility in growing in artificial condition. Sizes of leaves, flowers, fruits, trunk with branch arrangements are the subsequent consideration in selecting a particular plant. Trees incapable of resisting the shock of pruning are not suitable. Therefore, palms, papaya, travellers tree and so on, should not be selected for bonsai making. A plant for bonsai may be raised by seeds, seedlings, cuttings, layering or plant collected from wild. Plant raised from seeds or seedlings will take some time to train as bonsai. Hence layering, cutting or grafting may be used for bonsai preparation. Some wild old plants, if selected, will need very little training. Large seedling plants can also be obtained from nurseries.

Containers and Soil

Bonsai literally means, "planting in shallow container" so a container for bonsai must be shallow. The shape may be round, oval or rectangular. For a single upright stem an oval or a round container will suit better while for cascade style a rectangular container look more artistic. An unglazed container is preferred to a glazed one as the former allows aeration of the soil. A container should also have one or two drainage holes, depending on size. The colour of the container should be as natural as possible and is generally black, green, or brown. For a flowering tree having red or pink flowers and a brown colour pots should be avoided. No ornaments should be used in the containers which will detract attention from the bonsai. Any ornaments, if to be used at all, it should be small and antique. Soil or potting mixture for bonsai should have good water holding capacity, good drainage and a balanced nutritional status. Since bonsai plants undergo severe training and pruning, therefore, plants should be healthy and nutritionally balanced to endure the shock. One of the balanced mixtures can be prepared by mixing 3 parts loam, three part farm yard manure and two parts of sand. However, the proportion of various ingredients may vary according to the specific requirements of some plants. As for example, conifers require soil mixture with less retention capacity and early drainage of excess water. Hence, more sand or brick pieces are to be added to the potting soil.

Training and Pruning

Pruning and training are probably the most vital techniques for imparting dwarfism and desirable shape of the bonsai. They give plant a graceful appearance. Pruning is mainly done to check the height of plant. It encourages new branches at young stage and to thin the dense growth. Pruning is also carried out to encourage branches in a desired direction. The younger plant needs more pruning than an old plant.

Mature plants need light pruning to control size and to maintain shape. Pruning of outer tips is continued in some plants where dense leaf canopy is desired.

Root pruning is a routine work in bonsai and is to be continued till the plant survives. Root pruning encourages new roots and it should be done at regular intervals. Pruning of roots is carried out to train the root system to fit in a shallow container and also to control the root system of a matured plant. In bonsai, elongated taproot may be cut up to two-thirds safely, encouraging fibrous root system. Fibrous roots are most functional and desirable in bonsai plants. At the younger stage, root pruning is conducted at an interval of one or two years, whereas, in case of matured old trees it is five to ten years. Generally root pruning is done at the time of repotting.

Training: Training is mainly done through wiring to achieve the best shape with graceful curve of the trunk and neat arrangement of the branches. The method consists of tying wire around the trunk or branches and curving them in direction or angle desired. The technique should be adopted at the younger stage of growth when the trunk and branches are flexible. Copper wire of difference thickness is used for the purpose. Thickness of wire to be used depends on the thickness of stem which shall hold the trunk or branches in position as desired. For standard work, 1.65 mm to 2.76 mm wire is sufficient. In order to avoid damage by wiring, paper tape may be wrapped before the use of copper wire. While wiring the trunk, one end of the wire should be anchor in soil firmly and then coil around the trunk efficiently keeping 45° angle. Coiling should be firm but not too tight and care should be taken to prevent any breakage. After wiring, the plant must be put under shed to overcome the shock at least for a week or so. The effect of wiring is obtained within two or three months and even may be left for a year depending upon the nature of curving.

Potting and Repotting

Potting is the transferring plants in pots. Planting material for bonsai may be planted in pot or ground for attaining certain height and to receive preliminary training. Seedling should be first planted in small pots, whereas, the other should be planted in pots of suitable sizes. Repotting is the beginning of presenting a plant in a special form. Repotting in bonsai is removal of plant either from the ordinary pot or ground or from bonsai pot and replacing the plant either first time in the bonsai pot or in the same ornamental bonsai pot. It is always done in association with root pruning and complete or partial modification of soil mixture. The plant should be placed in a pot suitable for its style and size of bonsai. In round or square shaped pot, the plant is positioned in the centre. In oval or rectangular pot, placement should be at one-third of length of the pot from any end. The plant may be placed at the right or left end of the pot depending upon individual likings. Best time for repotting is early spring or monsoon. Even though it can be done at any time avoiding the hot summer days. Frequency of repotting depends on the plant and its root growth. Evergreens, like pines and junipers require repotting only after three to five years while flowering and fruiting trees may need repotting every year.

General guideline for repotting:

1. Clean the pot and place fine plastic or wire mesh preferably copper wire mesh on the drainage hole. Spread some soil over mesh and levelled.
2. Insert two ends of a piece of copper wire through the outer sides of the bottom holes.
3. The tree is taken out from the ordinary pot or ground. Remove upper and side layers of soil from the root ball.
4. Root pruning: Tap root may be cut up to two-third of its length along with some fibrous roots. When the plant is taken out from bonsai pot, all exposed roots are cut.
5. The plant is then placed in position in container, tied with wire, keeping its base visible above the level of the pot.
6. Now, fill the pot with soil mixture. In order to achieve an attractive profile, the soil is shaped and lightly compressed. The upper surface of soil is slightly raised so that plant appears to grow in a mound of soil. Moss may be used as ground cover. This enhances look, check evaporation and at the same time helps to prevent soil being washed out at the time of watering.
7. The first watering should be done either through misting or by placing tray in the tray of water allowing water to enter through bottom hole which slowly rises to the top.

Watering

Bonsai, since have a limited amount of soil it needs frequent watering. Watering should be done according to the condition of soil and weather. As a general rule, bonsai should be watered before surface soil become dry. A lightening of the colour of surface soil is good visual indication that watering is needed. Watering should be continued until there is leakage from the drain hole. Amount of water necessary for bonsai varies with the season. In the spring, when the tree become active and start budding, water will be required often. In the summer, potted soil dries out even more quickly, so water must be given in abundance frequently. Spraying of water onto the leaves also washes dust from the leaves and prevents burning by the sun. It is a good practice to spray the leaves both in morning and in evening, except in winter. During winter, since the bonsai are kept generally kept indoors, the soil will dry up quickly and require large amount of water even though some species are dormant.

Feeding

Main objective of bonsai is miniaturisation so vigorous growth with excessive new shoots is undesirable. Therefore the quantity of fertilizers used should be sufficient enough to perform its normal function without any extra growth. Feeding through organic manure is safe. Bonemeal, bloodmeal and oil cake are good. Liquid manure can be prepared by allowing decomposition of oil cake and cowdung in equal proportion for some days and can be applied to the plant in diluted form. It can be applied once in two weeks during the growing season for the second or third year or till the next repotting takes place. Inorganic fertilizers are hardly used in bonsai culture. If are to be used, should be used in liquid form judiciously.

Defoliation

In general this method is practiced in broad leaf-trees to reduce their leaf sizes in long run. The best time to practice is July to August to February to March, but it largely depends on the plant species. It encourages new leaves of smaller size and gives a fresh look to the plant. This method is practised by cutting all leaves but without damaging buds at the leaf-axil. Defoliated plant should be kept under shed and should be watered carefully. Just before defoliation or immediately after defoliation, no extra food should be applied. This method is much used in deciduous trees or when the leaves are damaged.

Pinching

Leaf pinching or shoot tip pinching with scissors or with fingers are very necessary for bonsai. Shoot pinching is generally done in plants which are grown for flowering beauty. It is very often used in chrysanthemum where many flowers are wanted. In plants with needle leaves, like pines, junipers and many such plants, new shoots should be carefully pinched out to produce close smooth balls of foliage.

Plant Protection

Like all the other plants, bonsai plants are susceptible to pest and diseases. So, a number of preventive and corrective measures should be taken depending upon the type of insects, diseases and trees. First of all, it is imperative to keep bonsai plant in good health since insects and diseases tend to attack weak trees. A bonsai should be kept under constant vigil and application of proper insecticides and pesticides should be done regularly to keep off pests and diseases.

Some important plants for Bonsai:

Trees:

Callistemon lanceolatus, Cordia sebestena, Cinnamomum camphora, Casuarina equistifolia, Diospyros peregrine, Ficus bengalensis, Ficus benjamina, Ficus infectoria, Ficus religiosa, Ficus diversifolia, Ficus nitida, Fortunella japonica, Junipers chinensis, Malpighia glabra, Punica granatum, Pinus roxburghii, Salix babylonica, Cynadon oblangifolia, Malus baccata, Rhododendron spp., *Camellia* and *Prunus* spp.

Shrubs:

Adenium obesum, Azalea, Brya ebenus, Berberis asiatica, Cotoneaster horizontalis, Fortunella japonica, Hamelia patens, Jatropha podagrica, Murraya exotica and *Bougainvillea.*

Wooden climber:

Combretum, Derris scandens, Hiptage madablota, Roupellia grata and *Wisteria sinensis.*

CHAPTER-13

PRINCIPLES AND FEATURES OF GARDEN DESIGNS

A garden is an outdoor living room and has to be considered an extension of the house. It should be attractive and comfortable as any of the rooms in which we live. Without some previous thought and early planning, it will be difficult to achieve this objective. To create a pleasant garden, we have to create a mental picture of our requirements. We have to seek inspiration from various sources including nature. Our past experiences with materials, with plants, with things beautiful in nature such as moving streams, large sheets of water, hills, mountains, waterfalls, the evening sky full of wonderful colours, sunlight and moon beams and many more will help us project a series of pictures from which we can pick and choose the ideas.

Principles of Garden Designs

There are eight basic gardening principles that a gardener should follow to achieve a garden that is pleasing to the senses and provides a pleasant outdoor living space. These include balance, repetition, proportion, transition, simplicity, unity, rhythm, and focalization. Elements of art to keep in mind also are color, line, form, texture and scale. These elements are used as tools to adjust the design principles.

Balance: There are two types of balance used in garden design. These are known as formal or symmetrical arrangements and informal or asymmetrical arrangements. With symmetrical arrangements, imagine a dividing line going through the center of the garden and the plantings and arrangements on each side are identical. With the asymmetrical or informal arrangements, the plantings or arrangements are not alike on either side.

Repetition: Repetition is when plants with similar shapes, colour, scent, and/or texture are repeated throughout the arrangement to achieve unity in the design.

The repetition should not be overdone which could cause the arrangement to appear busy or crowded.

Proportion: It refers to using elements in the garden that agree in size. No oversized fountains or trees in a small garden or tiny trees next to a large building.

Transition: It is the gradual change of elements in the garden with no sudden changes in the height, colour, texture, or theme.

Simplicity: It refers to keeping the design simple. Having a simple theme that does not have too many elements or colours will help to achieve a landscape design that is pleasing to the eye without being overdone or busy.

Unity: Using a consistent style to express a main idea is called unity. Mass planting and repetition can help to achieve unity in a landscape design. Repeating a particular colour or theme throughout the landscape will help to achieve unity.

Rhythm: It is a sense of motion created by the elements in a landscape design which lead the viewer's eye through the garden area and beyond the design. This is achieved through the use of colour schemes, line, and form which can be repeated to attain rhythm in the design.

Focalization: This refers to the placement of an object at a position, preferably at the centre of the garden, to attract attention. The object might be a fountain, a sculpture, spruce and herbaceous perennials.

The other elements used in landscape designs are briefly discussed below:

Axis: This is an imaginary line in any garden around which the garden is created striking a balance. In a formal garden, the central line is the axis. At the end of an axis, generally there will be a focal point, although another architectural features such as bird-bath or sundial can also be erected at about the midpoint.

Focal Point: A focal point is essential in good garden design. It directs the eye to a highlight in the garden and it will be the first thing the eye will notice in any garden. The purpose of the focal point is to bring attention to it, after which one will be able to appreciate it and then scan the rest of the garden appreciating the various plants one by one.

Line: In garden design, the form of a line creates a sense of direction as well as a sense of movement. The eye automatically follows a garden line, whether it be the edge of a walkway, the curve of a flower bed or the outline of plant materials. The character of a line yields specific responses. Gentle, slow curves and horizontal lines tend to be experienced as restful while jagged diagonals or vertical lines create more excitement and tension.

Mass effect: The use of one general form of plant material in large number in one place is done to have mass effect. To see that such mass arrangements do not become monotonous, the sizes of masses should be varied.

Proportion and Scale: Proportion is the relationship that exists among the components of a landscape. It describes the relationship between the components of the landscape and the landscape as a whole. Proportion involves the size relationships between and among the components making up the landscape. Proportion describes the mathematical relationships among the dimensions of space and site components making up an area. These mathematical relationships are totally separate from human perception dimensions. In a sense, proportion is similar to a ratio. For example, corner plantings next to a house that are two-thirds the distance from the ground to the eave are proportional to the house. The height of the corner plantings is proportional to the height of the eave. Scale is the human perception of the size of space and form related to the human dimension. Scale is relative to the perception of the viewer. For a large two-story house, corner plantings that are proportional to the house may appear out of scale to the viewer. Because scale is relative to perception, a designer can manipulate scale psychologically within the site. Although the components of the site may remain proportional, a change in the placing of the components will dramatically affect the scale. Plan for trees in settings relative to the size of the matured trees. Plant tall trees near a tall, narrow house or building. A small house surrounded by large trees appears smaller than it actually is. A large house surrounded by small trees appears larger than it actually is.

Space: The aim of every garden design should be such that the garden should appear larger than its actual size. One way to achieving this is to keep vast open spaces preferably under lawn and restrict the plantings in the periphery normally avoiding any planting in the centre. But if any planting has to be done in the centre the choice should be a tree which branches at a higher level on the trunk and not a bushy shrub.

Texture: Texture in the garden creates sensual and visual excitement. It is generally read as the mass and void of foliage, bark, or flowers and changes with the light during the day and with the seasons. Up close, the size and shape of the leaves and twigs become the predominant textural elements of a plant. From a distance, it is the quality of light and shadow on the entire form, the patterns of light and dark that translates as texture. Rough, coarse textures tend to create an informal mood and are visually dominant while fine, smooth textures are associated with formal, elegant, subdued moods and are visually more passive. Fine-textured plants are visually translated as being farther away, so fine textures can be a tool for providing a sense of perspective in a small garden and making the space appear larger. On the other hand, the predominance of coarse-textured plants make a garden space appear smaller. Strong textural contrasts add drama and interest to a garden. Bark and foliage are two ways of adding textural interest to any space.

Time and light: In a garden, the time factor is very important. There are three different categories of time garden. First comes the daily time which provides different quantities and qualities of light during the course of the day. As the morning sun is vital for all flowers, the designer has to take into account while planning. In most of the parts of India, the garden design should be planned in such a way that in the afternoon it is possible to sit in a shaded place from where the best part of the garden can be viewed. The second type of time is the seasonal changes in the year. A good planner must roughly take into account the seasonal movement of the sun and where the shade and light are likely to fall during the different parts of the season. A lawn which receives shade during the early parts of the day in winter will not grow or remain patchy. A good and knowledgeable gardener can visualize such eventualities. The third time, which most people overlook and cannot visualize, is the fact as to what shape and proportion the shrub and trees will attain height in the years to come. Often we can see sick and lanky shrubs growing near the trunk of a large tree because of lack of light and nutrients. The right type of tree should be planted at the proper place so that shade is obtained during the hot days. A cleverly planted tree can protect a window from strong afternoon sun or an unplanned tree can ruin the view of the garden from inside a window. The pattern of shade cast by a fine leaved tree on lawn looks very artistic. Similarly, straight trunked trees like the Royal palm (*Greodoxa regia*) or Eucalyptus, when planted in a row along a path, will throw oblique bars of shade in the mornings and afternoon and will cheer up a dull walk.

Tone and Colour: Artists and designers use the colour wheel to study colours and their relationships. A position for all colours exists on the colour wheel. Red, blue, and yellow are referred to as the primary colours. These colours cannot be made from any other colour. Combining any two of the primary colours produces a secondary colour. The secondary colours are violet, green, and orange. Mixing red with blue makes violet. Combining equal parts of a primary colour and an adjacent secondary colour produces a tertiary colour. Using colour in a landscape is the same as with any other form of art. Knowing the effects of colour is important to the designer when contemplating the landscape design. Designers use colour in the landscape as a background or basic "gentle wash" to harmonize the view onto the landscape. Colours used in this manner are pleasing and smooth. Another use of colour in the landscape is for accent. Colour is an "emphasizing factor" for the composition. Colour combinations incorporated in a design influence the moods of those who interact with the design. Bright colours excite or stimulate emotional responses. Cool colours slow down emotional responses and express a sense of restfulness. Yellows, reds, and oranges are warm and advancing colours. These colours are associated with warmth because they are the colours of the sun, fire, and heat. Warm colours add a dramatic and excited feeling to an environment. These colours appear to advance and move toward the viewer. The cool colours of blue and green express restfulness and coolness. These colours are associated with ice, sky, and water. Cool colours have a receding visual effect. These colours provide the viewer with a sense of depth. Cool colours make the object of interest appear to be receding into the background.

Style: Lastly, one has to decided about the style to be adopted for one's garden. Every garden lover has to invent his own styles of gardening commensurate with his budget, taste and the nature of site. But a man can develop his own design only when he studies carefully all the great garden styles and grasps the underlying principles in them.

Styles of Gardens

The different styles of gardens are:

Formal Gardens:

A formal garden is laid out in a symmetrical or a geometrical pattern. In this garden, the design is stiff as everything is done in a straight and narrow way. In such gardens everything is planted in straight lines. If there is plant on left hand side of a straight road, a similar plant must be planted at the opposite place on the right hand side. The flower beds, borders and shrubbery are arranged in geometrically designed beds. Trimmed formal hedges, *Cypress*, Ashoka trees and topiary are typical features of a formal garden.

Informal Gardens:

Informal gardens are characterized by flowing curves, non-symmetrical arrangements of features and spaces and plants that are allowed to grow into their natural shapes. In the informal garden, the underlying framework is almost entirely disguised by planting and the garden should look as though it has grown up naturally. Informal gardens are harder to design than formal ones as they are ruled by irregularity and natural looking planting. A site that isn't a geometric shape can be a good basis for an informal garden. Some structure needs to exist or everything will relapse into uncontrolled wilderness. Diagonal or curved paths work well and boundaries between the various areas of your garden are often formed using native mixed hedging. In general, planting in informal gardens will include tall shrubs and taller trees to add to the vertical dimension and these will often hide the edges of the plot to create a feeling. The garden should revel in colour and should look as natural as possible. If you would like to introduce water, natural looking ponds and pools are ideal features. Planting should include water plants as well as marginal and bog plants.

Wild Gardens:

A comparatively recent style of gardening, namely, Wild Garden was expounded by William Robinson in the last decade of the nineteenth century. The concept of wild garden is not only against all formalism but it also breaks the rule of landscape styles. His main idea was to naturalize plants in shrubberies. He preached that grass should remain unmowed, as in nature and few bulbous plants should be grown scattered in the grass to imitate a wild scenery. He suggested that passages should be opened in the woodland and tress, shrubs and bulbous plants should be planted among the forest flora to fulfill his idea of a wild garden. His other idea was to allow the creepers to grow the trees naturally imitating those of the forest.

Different Features of a Garden

Garden Walls

A walled garden is specifically a *garden* enclosed by high *walls* for horticultural rather than security purposes, though traditionally all *gardens* have been *hedged* about or walled for protection from animal or human intruders. Garden walls may also serve a decorative purpose, but their essential function in the *north temperate zone* has been to shelter the garden from *wind* and *frost*. The shelter of walling can raise the *ambient temperature* within the garden by several degrees, creating a *microclimate* that permits *plants* to be grown that would not survive in the unmodified local *climate*. Most walls were constructed from *stone* but lining walls with *brick*, which absorbs and retains solar heat, raised the temperature against that wall. The walls may be covered by creepers such as *Ficus repens*. Low brickwall with some grills is preferred so that the garden can be seen from outside.

Fencing

Fencing is used for marking the boundary and for protection. Sometimes, fences are put to separate one part of garden from other. Several materials such as wood, bamboo, wire, wire nettings and chain link fences may be used for this purpose. The sight of an expanse of fencing does not suit to the artistic design of a nicely laid out garden and hence people would like to obscure it from view as quickly as possible by growing quick growing and elegant creepers such as *Bignonia venusta, Lonicera periclymenum* and *Vernonia elaegnifolia.*

Steps

Sometimes it becomes necessary to have steps in a garden as for example, when a path goes from one level to the other or one has to climb or get down from the terrace garden. Steps can be made of various materials used are concrete, stone, wood or gravel. The gravel can be held in position with a stone retaining wall. Grass should not be used in the steps as it becomes slippery when watered.

Garden Drives

A garden must have a carriage drive leading to the house and the garage besides several other paths or walks leading to different parts of garden. The main criterion of a good garden drive is to provide a flat, dry and pleasant passage for the persons or vehicles and it should harmonize with the other garden features. Materials used for the construction of drives are either gravel, asphalt or concrete, whereas, for garden paths much more attention should be paid for the appearance and as such concrete or asphalt is seldom used. The width of the garden roads should be about 3-5 m, it should be little higher (2.5 cm) than the surrounding ground and should have the slope of 1:100.

Paths

The path of the garden is its backbone, as its position is determined by various garden features such as the flower-beds, lawns, fountains and arches. The path connects the different parts of the garden as well as to the main road. Paths are skeleton frame work of a garden and a means of circulating around the place. The paths are of two types. They may be 90-120 cm wide and formed of earth or soil where soil is of medium texture. The main path is often paved. Hard paths are essential in those places which take a great deal of wear and tear e.g., the vegetable plot, green houses and around frames. The paths can be made up of a variety of materials - grass, bricks, cobbles, stones and crazy paving. Paths which are necessary for proper working should be approximately leveled and wherever a fall occurs it should be connected by steps. Sloping paths on a terrace should be avoided. Brick paths are made up of stones, sand and hard brick. The bricks are often cemented. The brick paths are used when old, establishment effects are to be given. Paths of gravel or stepping stones through flower beds give an informal look. Delightful edging to garden paths may be made by planting lawn grass. The lawn grass requires careful maintenance.

Side Drains

The central portion of the garden path should not become a storm-water drain during the rainy season. Open or closed side drains should be made when building the path or road. In fact, the centre of the path should be raised slightly so that rain water may roll away easily. Whatever the surface of a path, it should have a solid foundation. Garden paths constructed in a hurry on soft ground will shrink during rains.

Lovely patterns

Paths can be turned into interesting garden walks with a little imagination and ingenuity in selecting and arranging the various materials. Concrete paths are perhaps the easiest to lay, but they are expensive and may not blend well in a colourful garden unless mixed with a suitable colouring matter. With bricks, many patterns can be arranged. A simple pattern can be had even on a metal or sand foundation. The bricks can be fixed with cement joints. If grass is to be grown, the bricks joints may be set wide and in wet earth to be planted subsequently with clumps of grass or tiny flowering plants such as the yellow daisy, *Portulaca, Zinnia, Verbena* or a few dwarf nasturtiums. For this type of path, only well-baked bricks should be chosen. The best informal and harmonious way of lying out a garden path is the crazy pavement walk. Broken pieces of thick Shahbad stone are used for this purpose.

Wooden Blocks

Mature and seasoned wooden blocks cut to a height of 23 to 30 cm from the trunk and arranged as a path pavement give a very good effect. Hardy trees such as the Babul, mango, shisham and kher can be used for this purpose.

Flower Bed frames

A flower bed is an element of many *gardens*. A flowerbed is a garden area especially prepared for growing *flowers*. The area is typically marked off, often by low-lying structures of brick or similar materials, designed to highlight the flowers and reduce the spread of *weeds*. These structures can often be elaborate, as in the formal gardens of *Shalimar* and *Nishat* or the *Taj Mahal*. There are different types of flowerbeds which include different types of plants such as seasonal bedding schemes containing *annuals* and *biennials* such as marigolds, alyssum and lobelia and *herbaceous perennials* containing plants such as delphiniums, lupins and foxgloves. Flower beds should be simple in design as it is easier to maintain them. Flowers beds are the most important part of a formal garden and these are marked out most ornamentally in pairs. But in a landscape style garden the number of flower beds are less compared to a formal garden as the flowers are mostly grown in the borders or in front of the shrubbery, for livening up the landscape design. The beds should always be placed in full sun except when these are meant for growing shade loving plants.

Garden adornments

There are several garden adornments and accessories such as fountains, statues, garden seats, ornamental posts and pillars, arches and pergolas, trellises, hanging baskets, tubs, vases and urns with plants which make the garden more enjoyable. Playing of a fountain is an interesting feature in a garden and the water in the cistern should be kept clean. Garden seats made up of stones, concrete or metal are placed under the tree. Handsome tubs, vessels and urns are utilized to display plants in conspicuous places. Arbours, arches, pergolas and trellises serve as support to several beautiful plants and to dispel monotony in garden. Arbours are usually open in all sides. Very often a long wall or the end of a pergola leads to an arbour. Arches are generally erected over walks, usually at the entrance and are usually two meters in height. Pergolas are series of arches connected over a walk.

Birdbath

A Birdbath is an artificial "*puddle*" or small shallow pond, created with a water-filled basin for birds to bathe and 'cool off' in and drink from. A Birdbath can be a *garden ornament*, small *reflecting pool*, *outdoor sculpture* and part of creating a vital *wildlife garden*. A birdbath is an attraction for many different species of birds to visit *gardens*, especially during the *summer* and *drought* periods. The traditional birdbath is made of molded *concrete* or glazed *terra cotta* formed in two pieces, the bowl and the pedestal. The bowl has an indentation or socket in the base which allows it to fit over the pedestal. The pedestal is typically about one meter tall. Both bowl and pedestal can be clean or decorated with *bas-relief*. Bowls can be pure curved geometry, or have motifs of a shell or pseudo-rocky *spring*. The pedestal can be a simple *silhouette* or incorporate decorations. However, birds seem unconcerned with the aesthetics with even a shallow plate, pie-tin, or *puddle* below a slowly dripping water outlet used. Birdbaths can be made with other types of materials including glass, metals (i.e., *copper*), plastics, mosaic tiles, *marble* or any other material that can be outdoors and hold water. In *natural landscape* gardens rocks and boulders with natural or *stonemason* carved basins can fit in unobtrusively. Some birdbaths use a recirculating pump as part of a *fountain* or *water feature* and can include filters, a *float valve*-water connection for automatic refilling or a *drip irrigation* emitter aimed into the bowl. Some use a *solar powered* pump, floating or submerged to recirculate the water. Birds are attracted to the sight and sound of running water with integrated or nearby fountains an important element to bring birds to the garden.

Floral Clocks

A floral clock or flower clock is a large decorative *clock* set into a *flower* bed in a *park* or other public recreation area. The floral clock was a form of *carpet bedding* set onto an operational clock-face, invented in 1903 by John McHattie of Edinburgh Parks in *Princes Street Gardens*, Edinburgh and first seen in spring of 1904. These are generally operated by electricity, having huge hands for showing the seconds, minutes and hours. The machinery of the clock is concealed in an underground chamber with only hands showing above the ground against a dial of carpet bedding plants or flower beds. A carpet bedding of green plants, e.g., *Pilea muscosa* and *Sedum* with figures made of red plants e.g., *Alternanthera* and *Iris* spp. or vice versa looks quite ornamental.

Fountains

A fountain is a piece of architecture which pours *water* into a basin or jets it into the air either to supply drinking water or for decorative or dramatic effect. Fountains were originally purely functional, connected to springs or *aqueducts* and used to provide drinking water and water for bathing and washing to the residents of cities, towns and villages. Until the late 19th century most fountains operated by gravity and needed a source of water higher than the fountain such as a reservoir or aqueduct to make the water flow or jet into the air. In addition to providing drinking water, fountains were used for decoration and to celebrate their builders. Roman fountains were decorated with bronze or stone masks of animals. Fountains are used today to decorate city parks and squares; to honor individuals or events; for recreation and for entertainment. A *Splash pad* or *spray pool* allows city residents to enter, get wet and cool off in summer. The *musical fountain* combines moving jets of water, colored lights and recorded music, controlled by a computer for dramatic effects. *Drinking fountains* provide clean drinking water in public buildings, parks and public spaces.

Garden Seats

Garden seats are a necessity in any garden. What types of seats have to be provided in a garden should be decided judiciously. The seats should be comfortable, durable, artistic looking and should not look out of place. Wooden and fabric seats are comfortable to seat compared to those built in stone or iron. When wooden seats are selected they should be made of good timber like teak to withstand the vagaries of weather especially moisture as the furniture has to remain outdoors. The wood is treated with preservative and painted with moisture proof chemicals.

Japanese Lanterns

These are highly sought-after garden ornaments. The lanterns should preferably be carved in stone and should be low and decorative as the Japanese would prefer. The coloumn may be cylindrical or square faced with ornamental carvings. Similarly, the fire box should also be carved in an ornamental manner. The roof may be broad-roofed, commonly called Snow View, because it gives a charming effect to the landscape when it is snow bound. Obviously these types of lanterns are made of white stone or white marble and are suitable for areas having a snowfall. The lanterns should be positioned in suitable places near the house or near a stream or pool.

Ornamental Tubs, Urns and Vases

These add beauty to the garden. Plants displayed in ornamental tubs or urns at suitable places look beautiful. The tub or the vase can be made of timber or preferably of brick, concrete or carved out of stone. These can be built permanently in position or may be kept just like that and moved whenever needed. When fixed permanently, these should generally be positioned over an ornamental pillar keeping in view the proportion between the two. If there is a paved path an ornamental vase or tub can be placed at the end of it or one each on both sides. Similarly, these can be placed near the gate or near the staircase of the main entrance. Ornamental urns preferably of metal with carvings outside look beautiful in the terrace, near the staircase or even inside the house.

Ornamental Stones

Ornamental stone pillars or pieces of rounded form or other abstract designs, if properly placed, improve the look of any garden to a great extent. The stones can be placed near lily pools, along or in the midst of streams and waterfalls. Large ornamental pieces can be placed at the corner of the doorway and other suitable places. The Japanese create most artistic stone gardens with pieces of stones. First a large bed of crushed stone is made which is raked artistically to create ripples to simulate sea, over which single large piece of stone or a group of stones are placed artistically at intervals.

Plant Stands

The plant stands are very useful structures for decorating the gardens. Plant stands are generally made of mild steel rods moulded in different fashions with various sized rings attached to hold the pots growing the plants. These can be displayed in the terrace garden at the entrance of the house, in the roof garden or in any other advantageous position in the garden where these will add to the beauty of the garden. Some plant strands are specially made for fixing in the walls of the house where indoor plants can be displayed.

Statues

Statues of animate or inanimate objects are used in the garden to improve the looks. The statues can be carved out of stone or made of bronze. The concrete statues can be placed in the midst of a running stream or a pool, at the inter-section of two roads or at the end of a road or near the doorway of the house. The statues should be of good taste and artistic value.

Sundials

Sundial is a device that measures time by the position of the Sun. In common designs such as the horizontal sundial, the sun casts a shadow from its style onto a flat surface marked with lines indicating the hours of the day. The style is the time telling edge of the gnomon. As the sun moves across the sky, the shadow-edge progressively aligns with different hour-lines on the plate. Such designs rely on the style being aligned with the axis of the Earth's rotation. Hence, if such a sundial is to tell the correct time, the style must point towards the true north and the style's angle with horizontal must equal the sundial's geographical latitude.

CHAPTER-14

INDOOR GARDENING

Indoor gardening is the art of growing plants indoor for their aesthetic purpose. For todays world it is more than just gardening. Men besides with animals have an innate association with nature. The rapid development encloses men in concrete jungle and gifts him with anxiety and depression. Indoor plants give coolness to the eyes and tranquility to the soul, besides a sense of satisfaction. It is also the primitive way to cultivate the ornamentals. For ardent garden lover, who lives in cities, it is the only means of exercising garden adventures. For elderly and sick people, it is a good time pass and a source of recreation. Indoor gardening is never out of season. Besides, their exception value in interior decoration their role in abating indoor pollutants cannot be overlooked. The other facets of economic growth are addition of harmful substances into our environment, leading to global warming. **The air within homes can be more polluted than the outdoor air.** Indeed, the U.S. EPA has found in some buildings. Indoor air can be up to 100 times more polluted than outdoor air leading to "SICK BUILDING SYNDROME". The symptoms of which include, burning and watering eyes and nose, burning in trachea, cancer, chronic fatigue, debilitating fibromyalgia, dizziness, dry, itchy skin, exhaustion after normal activity, headaches, heart palpitations, hoarseness, cough and sore. Research conducted by NASA corroborates the presence of harmful volatile organic compounds such as formaldehyde, benzene and trichloroethylene in the indoor air. The U.S. Environmental protection agency estimates that indoor air pollution costs $ 1.5 billion a year in medical expenses and $ 60 billion in productivity losses. The NASA in 1973 has made an experiment to find a solution to maintain air quality inside confined spaces and the results show that plants clean indoor air. Scientists funded by NASA and other vigorous advocates say that using plants is the most reasonable method for indoor air pollution control. Since different plants absorb different pollutants, it will be a good idea to mix a minimum of two plants per 30 square metre of floor space.

Histrocial Overview

The origin of indoor gardening is about 3500 years old as revealed by stone carving of Babylon. The most prominent example of growing plants in stone vessels is the Hanging gardens of Babylon constructed by Nebuchandnezzar II in 605 B.C. and one of the seven wonders of world. Records from China, Greece, and Roam indicate an interest in ornamental horticulture by people in those civilizations. The ruins of Pompeii show definite proof that plants were grown in decorative containers, some of which were works of art. The Greeks has originated the idea of using potted plants to decorate their surroundings. Most Greeks celebrated the spring arrival of Adonis, mythological god of the growing world by decorating his statue with seeded pots of fast growing plants such as lettuce and barley. Thus Adonis Garden thoroughly established pot gardening as an ornamental technique. The practice of pot culture continued intermittently through succeeding centuries. The Romans, who enjoyed the cultivation of unusual plants and fruits, cultivated those using stone containers in the inner courtyard of their homes. After the fall, of the Roman Empire in 476 AD, the growth of horticultural knowledge stagnated, kept alive primarily in the monasteries. The monks continued the use of earthenware pots for the cultivation of medicinal and culinary herbs. The decorative use of pots was practiced during the medieval times in southern Spain by the Moors. They also developed a patio style of gardening that featured water for its cooling effect and abundant potted plants to decorate steps and other architectural features. Columbus' discovery of America in 1492 was important in that his expedition introduced the cactus, agave and pineapple to Europe. Exploration in early fifteen century helps in the introduction of plants from East into Europe. Dealers in Holland and Belgium have imported plants from Asia Minor and East Indies. A desire for exotic flowering plants and trees developed among the aristocracy of France and England by the middle of the sixteenth century. During the Renaissance, in Germany it was custom to decorate windows with decorative plants growing in clay pottery. It is the most direct historical link to our current practice of indoor gardening. The Renaissance movement brought the garden pot into focus as a major garden element particularly in Italy, France and England.

Many wealthy persons in Europe constructed orangeries which lead to the development of conservatories in the seventeenth century. About 5,000 species of exotic plants had been introduced in Europe by 18th century. House plants became very popular in Europe as a result of these. At the end of eighteenth century and continuing through the Victorian Era (1841-1903), English interest in exotic plants reached its peak. By 1820, the now famous Kew Botanical Garden in England had 8000 species. The early nineteenth century was characterized by a flood of horticultural and botanical periodicals, most of which were graced by large plates of exotic plants recently introduced into the country by the increasingly large number of explorers. Although plants continued to stream into Europe during the early eighteenth century, it was not until around the middle of the century that explorer was able to overcome the plant losses that occurred during the long ocean voyages. Dr. Nathaniel Ward, a London surgeon has accidently observed the growth of plant in sealed containers and achieved a significant feat of sending plants around the world in large glass containers. These glass containers were then called as Wardian cases and now more commonly known as "Terrariums", made it possible to export rare and tender plants to Europe with great success. These terrariums are now used for indoor gardening. In 20th and early 21st century with rapid economical and technological development indoor gardening has gained a rapid impetus and become an essential component of modern architectural design.

Selection of house plants

The house plants are fall in two categories, first include, "the flowering plants" which are adorned for their splendid appearance by the virtue of their magnificent flowers. Once the flowering is over, these plants have very little use inside a room and hence their usefulness as house plants is only for a limited period. The other category include plants which are prized for their graceful foliage and sometimes with their architectural or unusual form (e.g., Bonsai). An ideal house plant should be compact in growth habit, evergreen in nature and should robust in nature so that it can tolerate varying degree of shade, temperature and drought. Before procuring a house plants one has to consider many points. The first consideration is that under what conditions a plant has to grow i.e., whether there is sufficient light or the humidity is adequate or the temperature is favorable. Second due thought has to be given as for what purpose the plant is needed. It is for decoration of a small table, the plant should be compact and bushy in nature. Another important point is the experience of the grower in handling a house plant. A beginner must try his hand with hardy plants. A busy men having less time for plants should choose plants which are easy to grow. Lastly, plants should be purchased from a reputed nursery.

Culture of House Plants

Pots and potting media

Earthenware pots are most commonly used for growing house plants. Glazed clay and China (porcelain) pots, dishes, shallow bowls and troughs are available. A variety of pottery containers in contemporary designs are also available in the shops. Earthenware pots are cheaper and being porous provides better aeration of soil. Metal receptacles of brass and copper are used. However, these become hot quickly during the summer and therefore are not very useful for growing plants, especially in a warm climate. Plastic pots, dishes and bowls are used, particularly for growing cacti and succulents which need dry conditions. These are not suitable for growing moisture-loving plants i.e., bromeliads, orchids and ferns. Large plants can be grown in cement or wooden barrels. The wooden planters should preferably have castors to facilitate their movement whenever required. Large rectangular planters made of seasoned wood are best for placing pots inside them. The wooden planters must be painted from inside as well as outside with waterproof paint. Earthenware pots and pans should be frequently cleaned and painted outside with burnt sienna, if these are not painted with waterproof oil-paints. Similarly, the metal receptacles and wall brackets may be kept clean and polished with brasso or any other similar metal polish. The pots can be plain or ornamental in design, depending upon the interior furnishings of the room with which these should harmonized in colour and in texture. The shape of pots, bowls, dishes and troughs may be round, oval, elliptical, cone-shaped, rectangular, square, oblong, heart shaped or of any other shape. The pots and other receptacles must have 2-4 drainage holes at the bottom. Bewildering ranges of potting mixtures are available to foliage plant producers. Factors which influence the selection of potting mixture components are economic, physical and chemical characteristics of components. The economic factors include, cost, availability, reproducibility, ease of mixing and appearance of the components. Selection of components will be affected by container size. Coarser material should be used for smaller containers and finer-textured materials for large containers. Larger pores in coarse potting soils permit better drainage in the small soil volumes while the continuity of water in small pores permits good drainage in large containers.

Physical properties of soil and potting mixtures

The important physical properties vary with intended use. A soil that is excellent in a field may be entirely unsatisfactory in a pot. Physical properties of soils and other potting components which are mainly considered includes, bulk density, pore space, water holding capacity, texture and soil types. Bulk density expresses soil weight (grams per cubic centimetre) and takes into consideration solid and pore spaces between particles within a volume. Bulk density between 0.5 to 0.75 g/ml is best for container grown plant. Pore space of a field soil or potting mixture is an important measure of its suitability for foliage plant production. Foliage plant growth is often reduced and sometimes plants are killed because of poor aeration caused by compaction, excessive rainfall or over watering of soils and potting mixtures with inadequate pore spaces. The total pore space should be 5-30 per cent while the non-capillary pore space should be 5-10 per cent or more in potting mixtures. This is especially true with organic potting mixtures since they decompose with time, resulting in decreased non-capillary pore space. Container walls and bottoms also act to reduce non-capillary pore space by creating an interface of high surface tension to hold water. Excessive total pore space is not desirable, since it indicates a low water holding capacity and causes more rapid dying of soil or potting mixtures. Water holding capacity is the ability of soil or potting mixture to hold water against the pull of gravity and is measured as per cent of dry weight or per cent of volume of water held after gravitational drainage. Water holding capacities should be in the range of 20 to 60 per cent by volume, provided 5 to 30 per cent pore space is present after drainage. Texture of the potting media is determined by the particle sizes of components i.e., clay, sand and silt and it should be moderate.

Chemical Properties of Soils and Potting Mixtures

Chemical properties of soils and potting mixtures have direct effects on production costs and quality in foliage plant industry. The important chemical properties which are taken into consideration are C/N ratio, cation exchange capacity, pH and soluble salts. The carbon: nitrogen ratio (C:N ratio) indicates the amount of carbon present in a soil or amendment relative to nitrogen. When the C:N ratio is high, most of the nitrogen will be required by soil micro-organisms during decomposition of the organic components, and the higher the ratio, the more nitrogen required. Competition for available nitrogen between micro-organisms and plants can cause nitrogen deficiency. A C:N ratio of 1:50 to 1:200 is good for potting media. If saw dust or any other organic components with a high C:N ratio are to be used, it should be as coarse as possible. Material with a high C:N ratio can be composted 2 to 3 months with 8 kg of nitrogen per cubic meter of material to produce an acceptable medium component. Cation exchange capacity (CEC) refers to the ability of soils or potting mixtures to retain fertilizer ions against the leaching effects of water and to release them for plant growth. Organic materials are usually high in CEC and provide buffering action against rapid changes in nutrient availability and pH. Materials with high CEC have high nutrient reservoirs, whereas those with low CEC retain small amount of nutrients and require more frequent application of fertilizer. A cation exchange capacity range between 10 to 100 milliequivalents per 100 cubic centimeters is satisfactory for container grown plants. Most foliage plants should be grown in media having a pH range of 5.5 to 6.5 and soluble salts should be less than 500 ppm.

Environmental Factors

Growth and quality of foliage plants depend on interactions between environmental factors and the genetic constitution of a particular plant. Each plant has inherent characteristics such as colour, leaf shape, size and growth that determine its potential for consumer satisfaction. Environmental factors determine profitability of foliage plants because they influence quality, size, and turnover time which determines unit cost of production. Economic considerations are necessary before making environmental changes, since the cost of changes may be greater than potential increase in yield.

Light: Light energy received by plants is used to produce carbohydrates and oxygen evolved in this process. The amount of light plants receive within a broad range determines amounts of carbohydrates synthesized and resultant growth and quality potential. Growth of foliage plants under specific light intensities is an important aspect of production, since many plant genera included in the foliage plant groups evolved under widely divergent environmental conditions of light intensity, temperature, humidity and soil type. These conditions range from tropical forest under stories, where light intensity may be no more than 60 metres to open savannas where 3000 metres are reached. To acclimatized into varying light intensities plant species change their some anatomical and physiological features. Sun leaves of *Ficus benjamina* for example, are smaller, thicker and light green in colour than shade leaves and often folded at the midrib. Yield, foliage colour, foliage size and/ or shape, density of foliage, amount of stored carbohydrates, and susceptibilty to diseases or insects influence determinations of proper light intensities. Colour intensity of colourful plants such as *Cordyline terminalis* and *Codiaeum variegatum* are severly reduced as light intensity is decreased below 900 metres. Foliage plants with variegated leaves, *Epipremnum aureum*, have less yellow varigation when light levels are less than 1200 metres. *Aglaonema* and *Diffenbachia* leaves assume a nearly vertical position when grown under excessive light which reduces plant quality since surfaces of leaves cannot be viewed from the side. *Aphelandra* develops sunken and uneven leaf surfaces which detract from its appearance. Minimum light intensities are necessary for adequate flower production in many potted plants sold as flowering foliage plants. *Aphelandra*, *Saintpaulia* and others grown for flower production must accumulate carbohydrates before flower initiation can occur. Therefore, relatively high light intensities are necessary for flowering. Incidence of fluoride toxicity increases as light intensity increases due to increased transpiration increasing the movement of free fluoride in soil solutions. Increased levels of mite infestations on susceptible plants occur more frequently on stock plants grown under fiberglass or glass due to lack of rainfall or overhead application of water.

High Light Loving Plants	Medium Light Loving Plants	Low Light Loving Plants
Codiaeum	*Calathea*	*Maranta*
Dracaena (some cultivars)	*Cordyline*	*Pilea*
Ficus	*Diffenbachia*	*Peperomia*
Sansevieria	*Dracaena (some cultivars)*	
Yucca	*Monstera*	
Philodendron		

Temperature: Temperature affects growth rate of foliage plants by influencing rates of photosynthesis and respiration. Temperature needs of each foliage plant species should be determined since some are tropical, others subtropical and others temperate in their requirements. A difference of 2-5°C between day and night temperatures is ideal for indoor plants. Night temperatures below 18°C can seriously reduce growth of many tropical and subtropical foliage plants especially *Aglaonema*, *Diffenbachia* and *Epipremnum*, but *Hedera*, *Ardisia*, *Podocarpus*, *Pittosporum* and other temperate foliage plant genera can tolerate lower temperatures without serious loss in growth and quality. The best general day and night temperatures for foliage plant production appear to be 21°C night and 32°C day. Commercial foliage stock plants producers often recognize benefits of increasing soil temperatures through the use of bottom heat and practice this technique by using steam or hot water pipes beneath benches and skirting the benches to retain heat by using forced hot air through convection tubes or by placing heating cables in benches. Use of cold irrigation water lowers soil temperatures during winter months and can injure foliage of several species by foliage contact. Water of 7°C can injure *Aglaonema*, *Diffenbachia*, *Philodendron*, *Siantpaulia* and *Sansevieria* foliage when air temperature is 16°C or higher.

Relative humidity: Relative humidity is the percentage of moisture in the air relative to the amount of moisture the air could hold if saturated at any given temperature. Relative humidity affects transpiration rate and hence water usage. Relative humidity is to some extent related to temperature. During summer it is very low while in the rainy season it is very high. The humidity can be increased by occasionally spraying fine mist of tepid water on the foliage, sponging the leaves with water and placing the pots on moist sand, gravel or pebbles kept in platters or trays. In kitchen and bathrooms the relative humidity is higher than in living rooms. Low humidity may cause tip-burn in leaves of foliage plants i.e., *Diffenbachia* and *Dracaena*.

Ventilation: Along with men and animals, plants also require fresh air for their survival though not to that extent. Droughts should be avoided and therefore a location between doors and windows where there are cross currents of air is not suitable. Natural gas from stoves or furnaces is harmful to house-plants. The affected plants become yellow, drop their foliage and appear pale.

Watering: Successful growth or failure of a house plants depend largely on watering. One of the main causes for the injury or death of house plants is improper watering, particularly inadequate or over watering. The requirement of water varies with different house plants. Cacti and succulents need less frequent watering than *Cypress* (Umbrella plant) and *Calla* which can grow even under wet conditions. Besides this, the frequency of watering will depend on the stage of plant growth, size of the plant in relation to its pot, soil, light, temperature and humidity. Plants in bloom need more water than those in young stages of growth or those which are newly potted. In summer months, when temperature is high, plants require more frequent watering than during winter when the temperature is low and plant growth is slow. Wilting should not always confuse with insufficient soil moisture. It may also be due to constantly saturated soil or due to poor lighting. Pots can be watered both from top and bottom. Watering from the bottom is better than from the top, as it avoids over watering and is preferable for cacti and succulents. It is always a good practice to saturate thoroughly the soil while watering and then again water it when it is on the verge of drying but before it is completely dry. On holidays, when plants are left on their own, it is better to group them. In such cases watering through a wick is useful. The pot is kept in a saucer or dish and moistened wick is placed in a saucer. One end of which is kept immersed in a bucket or any other large container filled with water. The water slowly passes from the bucket to the dish and rise up in pot and is replenished through the wick whenever the soil is dry. Now self watering flower pots having a fibre-glass wick are available. Covering of pots with polythene is for conserving moisture for long time.

Nutrition: Generally the nutrients present in the pot soil and organic matter are adequate for the growth of house plants. The plants do not need extra feeding unless they become pot bound. Pot bound plants can be fertilized by applying half to one teaspoon of any complete fertilizer containing all the three essential nutrients viz., nitrogen, phosphorus and potassium. The fertilizer should be raked in the soil a little away from the base of the plant and the soil watered heavily immediately. It should be given only once every two months or so. Do not apply fertilizers on a dry soil or when the plants are resting or dormant during the winter. Fertilizers should be applied when the plant is actively growing. One must remember that rapid growth of house plant is often undesirable and therefore fertilizers must be applied with care. Soot water and liquid cow dung manure are beneficial, especially to foliage plants. Application of 1 teaspoonful of carbonate of ammonium dissolved in 1 litre of water to foliage plants brightens their leaves.

Potting: Before potting, a pot appropriate to the size of plant may be selected. Potting in very large pots is harmful to plants as it tends to deplete the soil of its nutrients by leaching before new roots develop and occupy the soil. The plants should be thoroughly cleaned and then crocks put over the drainage hole. The plants should be set in the centre of the pot and the soil filled gently around the roots. When the pot is full, the soil may be made firm by pressing with fingers leaving about 1 to 2 cm at the top, below the pot rim, to allow for water. The potted plant should then be watered thoroughly and placed in partial shade until it established itself. If there is no drainage hole in the pot, a 2.5 or 4 cm thick layer of coarse sand or gravel should be spread at the bottom to ensure good drainage. For transplanting young seedlings into pots, a hole with a dibbler or a finger may be made in centre of prepared pot and then firm the soil with fingers leaving 1 cm space below the rim of the pot for watering. The seedlings should be watered thoroughly and the pot should be kept in partial shade for a few days before shifting it to its location inside the room.

Repotting: When a plant becomes pot bound it needs repotting. House-plants require repotting occasionally depending upon their growth. A few plants such as cacti, succulents and *Aspidistra* are slow growing and do not need frequent repotting while others like *Geranium* and *Begonia* are fast-growing and require shifting to a larger pot at least once a year. The repotting should preferably be done during rainy season when it is easier for them to become established and form new roots. A day prior to repotting, the pot should be watered lightly to facilitate removal of the earth-ball intact from the pot. The presence of matted roots indicates the need for repotting. The plant should be set in a larger pot in the centre after removing a little of soil from its earth-ball. Then the soil should be put in the pot to set the plant to a right height and the new soil mixture filled around the roots. The same soil mixture used for potting may be utilized in repotting and firmed with fingers. Below the pot rim 1 cm space may be left to allow for water. The plant should then be thoroughly watered and placed out of direct sun until it is well established.

Pinching and pruning: In pinching, the apical shoots or tips are removed to encourage side growth. This is commonly practiced in *Coleus*, *Geranium*,

Pelargonium, *Fuchsia* and *Chrysanthemum*. It makes the plant busy. Pruning is done to control the shape of the plant or to stimulate new growth. Roses are pruned once a year to encourage new growth and for production of better flowers. *Bougainvillea*, *Pelargonium*, *Geranium* and *Fuchsia* are generally pruned after flowering to maintain their shape while *Chrysanthemum* is headed back about 10 to 15 cm above the ground after flowering to stimulate the production of suckers. Sometimes a trailing plant like the Wandering Jew (*Zebrina pendula*) or *Scindapsus* may need light pruning of old and dry shoots or thinning out to check its heavy growth. Faded flowers should be removed from all flowering plants and should not be allowed to seed. It will help in the growth of plants. In *Coleus*, the inflorescence should be pinched off as soon as this emerges to encourage good vegetative growth.

Training: Climbing house plants need support to climb and for this purpose moss-sticks are ideal. The moss sticks are placed in the centre of the pot. The moss sticks are placed in the centre of pot. A 25 cm strip of 1 cm wire-net or chicken wire-net about 75-90 cm wide, rolled in the form of a cylinder and fastened to the edges with thin wires at intervals of 15 cm make a good moss stick. At the bottom of cylinder two small sticks are pushed through the holes to keep the cylinder straight and erect in the pot. The cylinder is put vertically straight in the centre of the pot and the potting mixture filled. It is useful to push a small pot at the top of the cylinder in which water may be filled occasionally to keep the moss moist, as it will help the vines to established and twine around the cylinder. About 3 to 4 young vines be planted around the cylinder according to the size of pot and the vines fastened to the cylinder with hair pins. A simpler moss stick by fastening thick layer of moss stick around a stout stick or bamboo can be made. Vines can be trained on trellies, bamboo sticks or strings fixed in the pot. They may be trailed on a trellis or strings to form a screen for dividing space in a large room.

Cleaning: The foliage of house-plants must be cleaned regularly by sponging with water preferably with lukewarm water to remove dirt, dust and grease. A small amount of milk or a few drops of vinegar may be added to the washing water to improve the appearance of leaves. Syringing the foliage with a fine spray of water is very useful, particularly during summer months. The hairy and silver-grey leaves should be gently cleaned with a soft brush. The hairy leaves of African Violet and Rex Begonia may be gently brushed with soft-bristled paint-brush.

Growth Regulators

Plant bio-regulators include auxins, gibberellins, cytokinins, ethylene, growth inhibitors, and growth retardants, and are used commercially to modify plant growth.

Auxin: Auxins are defined as chemicals that produced cell elongation in oat coleoptile. Research since the 1920 has shown auxins to be involved with a multitude of plant responses. Auxins are mainly used as root promoting compounds. Application of auxins to plants has induced flowering in bromeliads and others, shifted sex expression in flowers and insured fruit set.

Gibberellins: Gibberellins are not of great commrcial importance in foliage plant production. They could, however, be used to increase seed germination, to stimulate elongation of axillary buds and to influence flowering. Gibberellin spray induced flowering in many plants that normally require vernalization or long days to develop flowers. Floral sex expression may be modified by GA_3 treatment with staminate or male flowers normally induced but some plants produced an increased number of pistillate or female flowers.

Cytokinins: Cytokinins influence a variety of plant physiological responses, including regulation of cell division and differentiation, cell enlargement, flower bud dormancy, vegetative bud break, seed germination, fruit set and delay of senescence. Plant responses to cytokinins depend on amount and kind of cytokinin present and the active level of other growth regulators particularly auxins. Cytokinin treatment, substituted for light requirement in germination of lettuce seeds, increased germination at supraoptimal soil temperature and delayed chlorophyll breakdown in detached and attached leaves.

Ethylene: Symptoms of ethylene injury include thickening of stems, shortening of internodes, leaf distortion and leaf abscission. Ethylene has been used to induce flowering in bromeliads, retard growth in poinsettias, chemically pinch azaleas and defoliate deciduous trees and shrubs.

Growth inhibitors: Growth inhibitors are compounds that supress apical dominance by inhibiting cell division in the apical meristem. Morphactins and maleic hydrazide supress or inhibit growth by disrupting the function of apical meristem, preventing normal leaf and flower initiation. Distorted growth produced by most growth inhibitors has discouraged their use by foliage plant growers.

Growth retardants: Growth retardants have been defined as substances that slow cell division and elongation in the sub-apical meristem but do not completely inhibit these processes. The result on responsive plant species is a compact plant with shorter internodes but approximately same number of nodes as an untreated plant. Other effects may include darker green leaves, accelerated or delayed flowering, increased drought tolerance, increased resistance to air pollutants, diseases, and delayed senescence. Growth retardents have become widely used in the ornamental industry since treated plants usually do not show growth malformations or reduced vigor, and plants respond over a wide range of concentrations. Shortened internodes usually results in more aesthetically pleasing plants especially potted ones and provide better support for leaves and flowers. Their use often permits commercial plant growers to better program production and assure crop uniformity. The most commonly used growth retardents are ancymidol (A-Rest), chormquat (cycocel), phosphon and SADH (Alar, B-9).

Modes of Indoor Gardening

The simplest method is to grow individual plants in pots and keeping them in appropriate places in the house. In western countries some affluent people may even have an elaborate indoor roof gardening. The other popular methods of growing indoor plants in hanging baskets, China baskets, troughs made of cane wood concrete, bowls, dishes, bottle gardening, miniature gardens, window gardens and vertical gardens.

Gardening in tubs and urns: Tubs or urns are very useful for display in the terrace, roof garden, backyard, veranda and on the doorsteps. Tubs and urns are portable and hence can be used for temporary decoration indoors or elsewhere. Wooden tubs are best suited for hot sunny position. Rot resistance woods i.e., teak, oak and poplar are best suited for this purpose. In addition to this, wooden tubs should be treated with rot resistant chemicals i.e., cuprinol. A variety of materials are available which can be used as tubs or urns. Tubs and urns of different shapes and designs can be made from fine grade concrete. In western countries, fibre glass urns are also available. All tubs should stand on their leg or should be placed over bricks for easy drainage. Each tub or urn should have one or more drainage holes. Wooden or cement tubs are painted to match with the colour of house. The main criterion in selecting a tub is to insure that it holds sufficient amount of soil and have provision for proper drainage; though a container without drainage hole is useful if sufficient drainage material such as gravel is put at the bottom and over watering is avoided. At the same time, the tub should be quite aesthetic in look.

Culture

The potting mixtures generally used for pots can be used for tubs or urns. The tub plants need frequent manuring and it is advisable to feed them with liquid manure every fortnight or so depending upon the type of plant. Besides this, each tub has to be top dressed with fresh compost every six months or once a year. This is done by scrapping out 7-15 cm of the used top soil and replacing this with new compost.

All plants in tubs or urns need to be replanted every two or three years to replenish plant food. In India, under tropical climate, repotting should be done during rainy season. But in milder climate as that of Bangalore and Pune this can be extended till December or January. In temperate regions, repotting is done during the spring. Repotting should be avoided in the summer. Frequency of watering depends on the weather, type of plant and size of tub. Bougainvillea and jasmine need dry conditions at the time of flowering.

Planting Material

Wide variety of planting materials are available for planting in tubs or urns:

Annuals: African marigold, chrysanthemum, sunflower, hollyhock and so on.

Bulbous plant: Canna, bird of pardise and datura.

Foliage plants: *Fatsia*, *Aralia*, *Dracaena*, *Yucca* and so on.

Shrubs: Hibiscus, oleander, lantana, camellia, azalea and bougainvillea.

Ferns: Bird's nest and so on.

Palms: Most of the ornamental palms.

Trees: *Arucaria cookii*, *Brassia actinophyllaand* so on.

Topiary: Tubs offer a good opporunity for exhibiting topiary and espaliering work.

Gardening in Hanging Basket

Gardening in hanging baskets has become very popular after the Second World War in Europe, especially in England. In recent time, this is a popular hobby of city dwellers. Hanging baskets with trailing or cascading plants are suited for indoors and outdoors. Hanging basket can be placed in the hall or the drawing room besides a well lit window or the bathroom above a fluorescent light. A plain wall in a sunny room or a passage can be artistically decorated with hanging baskets. Out of door hanging basket can be suspended from trees, electric poles and fences. In conservatory shade loving trailing plants are suspended from the poles and roof, grown in hanging baskets.

Culture

Container: The container used as hanging baskets should be attractive, light, easy to hang and preferably with a drainage hole. Selection of containers should be done according to climatic conditions, place to be display, type of plants and cost. Wire baskets with three hooks, for hanging is a good container as they provide good aeration but should not be used in hot climate. Wooden pattern baskets are good for dry places and are better looking. Earthen pots of various sizes and shapes are available for use as hanging baskets. Dried gourd and coconut shells are used as hanging baskets. For indoor purposes basket of brass, copper and glazed pottery may be used. A wire or wooden pattern basket is to be lined properly to prevent soil being washed out. First a inner lining of a gunny cloth is put over which about 2-3 cm thick sphagnum or sheet moss is spread. Over this, the soil is filled up to the rim leaving a gap of 2-3 cm for watering. A compost made of equal parts of peat moss, leaf mould, garden loam, sand and cowdung is best for hanging baskets. For larger basket two or three types of plants can be used. In such cases, one vertical plant such as Dracaena or geranium is put at the centre and at the periphery trailing plants such as Zebrina pendula, petunias and verbena (perennial) are planted. For single planting trailing plants should be preferred.

Watering: Hanging baskets should be watered with care especially those which are kept indoor or in the case of pots having no drainage holes. The moss packed wire or wooden baskets are dipped in a tub of water and hanged outdoors to allow the excess water to drain off before putting them back indoors. Such baskets can be watered at the place where it hung provided water is poured slowly from the top allowing enough time between two applications for the water to soak. Such baskets can be placed over a plastic bowl cover.

Planting Materials

Asparagus sprengeri,	*Tradescantia flumiensis,*
Begonia pendula,	*Zebrina pendula,*
Chlorophytum,	*Cissus,*
Hoya carnosa	*Ficus pumila*
Hedera,	*Scindapsus,*

Window Garden

Window gardening or window–box gardening refers to the kind of gardening where plants are grown within the room just opposite or close to the window or on the window- sill outside. This is a most satisfying way of gardening for flat-dwellers of cities, where, there is space crunch. The plants can be placed on the windowsill and shelves or on plant stand, tiered tables or plant trolley or planters. Now-a-days window ledge is a part of the architecture for keeping the plants. These permanent planters should have proper drainage. While placing plant in window, due care must be taken to choose the right type of plants. The plants requiring plenty of sunshine should be placed on the south side as well as on the east and west sides, while the shade loving plants can be placed on window facing north and those needing medium light may be grown successfully on east and west sides. The climbing plants can be used effectively for framing the window when grown on the sides or for dropping effects in the front edge of the planters.

Culture and Management

There are different type of window boxes which can be used for gardening:

1. Fibre glass box: This type of box is mostly used in Europe. This is light, decorative and durable but most expensive.
2. Pottery boxes: Terracotta boxes of different sizes and designs are available in some parts of India. These are generally smaller in size.
3. Iron boxes: Iron boxes can be made by order. These are heavy but durable.
4. Cast cement and Asbestos Boxes: These are long lasting and can be decorated with engraving of different figures.
5. Plastic boxes: Plastic boxes of different size can be used. These are light in weight and cheap but not very durable.
6. Wooden boxes: Wooden boxes of various sizes are most suitable for window gardening. Teak and oak timbers are suitable for this purpose. The timber of *Arjun* tree is moisture resistant and may be used for making window boxes.

The size of the box should be comparatively small as these may be hanging outside the house in most of the cases. Even small boxes containing soil especially wet soil become heavy. A manageable size is 20 cm deep, 25 cm wide, and the length vary according to situation but never longer than 180 cm.

Drainage: All these type of boxes should have atleast one drainage hole at the bottom. For large boxes two or more holes can be provided. For wooden boxes drainage hole is made with red-hot poker as charred wood is more resistant to water and rot. Water will drip from the boxes and to catch this metal or tile tray should be placed below the boxes keeping a gap of 1-2 cm from the box. Constant contact with water can cause rotting in wooden boxes and to prevent this, the inside is charred by burning. Cuprinol, a wood preservative can be used. For metal can cement boxes, moisture and corrosion-proof coaltar or moisture proof paint may be used.

Compost and potting mixture: In the window garden, the density of planting is more and the nutrients are drained off more quickly, so rich compost should be used. Now in market readymade window box compost are available which cater the need of different plants. Compost can be prepared at home: 3 parts good fibrous loam, 1 part well-decayed coarse leaf-mould, ½ part well-rotten cow manure, and a handful of bone-meal serve as good compost for window gardening. An alternative is to grow the plants in individual pots each having the right type of compost and then place these pots in the box. The pots may be camouflaged with moss. In cities having the problem of severe air pollution, the compost is likely to be replaced every year. But in cleaner cities and towns the replacement may be carried out every third year provided the plants are well fed. Fertilizers, if applied, should be given in liquid form. Watering should be done according to the type of the plants grown and necessity, depending on weather. Both over and under watering are undesirable. The first cause water-logging and the second leads to wilting. Syringing during the hot summer is helpful. Plants varying widely in their water requirement should not be grown in the same window box. A cactus cannot be grown along with a flowering annual such as phlox which will need more frequent watering than the former. This problem can be overcome to some extent by growing plants in individual pots and placing them in box.

Planting Materials

Plants for window garden should be dwarf in nature, otherwise they will obscure the view and the container will appear top heavy. Trailing plants are generally preferred to upright plants.

For North window

Aglaonema,
Araucaria,
Begonia rex,
Bromeliads,
Chlorophytum,
Dieffenbachia,
Ferns,
Hedera,
Zebrina pendula
Impatiens sultanii,
Mostera deliciosa,
Pepromia,
Philodendron scandens,
Sansevieria,
Scindapsus,
Selaginella,
Tradescantia fluminensis,

For South window

Acalypha,
Amaryllis,
Beloperone guttata,
Bromeliads,
Cacti,
Chrysanthemum,
Lantana sellowiana,
Lilium longiflorum,
Muscari (Grape hyacinth),
Narcissi and daffodils,
Geranium,
Poinsettia,

Cissus,
Coleus,
Miniature rose,
Succulents

For East or West window

Anthurium,
Araucaria,
Begonia,
Beloperone guttata,
Bromeliads,
Caladium,
Cissus,
Dieffenbachia,
Dracaena,
Eucharis,
Fuchsia,
Fern,
Gloxinia,
Hedera,
Palms,
Pandanus,
Tradescantia flumiensis,
Zebrina pendula,
Zygocactus truncates,
Zantedeschia

Gardening in Troughs, Dishes, Bowls and Trays

This type of gardening is most rewarding for city dwellers but anyone can take interest in it. Gardening in troughs and dishes is generally done with indoor plants only. Though the principle is the same, trough garden differs a little from the dish and bowl gardening. A trough is larger in size which may contain more number of plants and can be displayed in the window-sill, on the floor or at the entrance of the house under the cover of varanda. Bowls and dishes are meant for decorating dining tables, television sets, radio sets and tea table. A trough generally has a drainage hole while bowls and dishes have generally none. Hence watering has to be done more carefully for dish and bowl gardens. Dishes and bowls can be kept on any shining surfaces without the fear of spoiling them from seepage water. Troughs can be of many kinds. The difference between miniature and trough gardens is that in the former many miniature garden features are created, whereas, in a trough garden indoor plants are just displayed in an artistic manner.

Culture and Management

Fruit bowls, conical baskets, wooden dishes or bread trays, pottery, china and low plastic bowls and pedestal vases used for flower arrangements are very suitable for starting a dish bowl garden. When a large trough is used, the bottom 2-3 cm is spread with gravel for drainage. Over this compost, consisting of equal parts of good garden loam, peat, leaf mould and soil is filled upto the rim leaving a gap of 2-3 cm for watering. For bowl and dishes, the potting mixture consists of an initial thin layer of gravel and few charcoal chips followed by compost. The compost in the dish or the bowl should preferably slope from the centre towards the periphery. Water is added just enough to moisten the compost. Over watering will create drainage problems. The selection of plants for troughs and dishes are to be done with extreme care. Plants liking same growing conditions are to be planted in each container. A cactus needs sunny and dry growing conditions and, therefore, should not be grouped with shade and moisture loving plants such as *Fittonia* or *Peperomia*. The second point to remember is that the plants are to be arranged in an aesthetic manner. To achieve this plants of various heights should be used with tallest one being used in the centre or in the corner depending on the display area. The shy grower should be grouped in a separate container. Even though only indoor plants are grown in dish gardens, they need some diffuse light. Sometimes, after planting, the dish garden should be fertilized with weak liquid manure every fortnight or third week in small quantities with a view not to starving the plants and at the same time not to allowing fast growth. Occasionally pruning of plants should be done to check the growth of plants. Plants in the bowls and dishes are spent very quickly and replanting should have to be done yearly or even every six months. Glass or metallic florists tubes can be inserted into dishes or bowls for the display of cut flowers which will enhance the beauty of garden.

Planting Materials

Group A: Cacti and succulents; *Agave* (Dwarf type), Aloes, Cacti (*Opuntia, Echinocactus* and *Chamaecereus*), *Crassula argentea, Echeveria coccinea, Gasterias, Haworthias, Sedum sieboldii* and *Sempervivum tectorum*.

Group B: For large size arrangements, the following cominations are suggested.

Combination I: *Aralia elegantissima, Dracaena sanderiana, Hedera helix, Peperomia obtusifolia* and *Syngonium podophyllum*.

Combination II: *Aphelandra squarrosa, Dracaena sanderiana, Ficus benjamina, Fittonia verschaffeltii, Peperomia argyreia, Pilea muscosa* and *Zebrina pendula*.

Group C: For small size arrangements, *Chlorophytum comosum* 'Vittatum', *Begonia rex, Peperomia rotundifolia* and African violets.

Vertical Garden

The idea of vertical gardening was conceived by Patrick Blac, a botanist. Vertical garden is known as living wall. This is an important feature for those short of planting spaces in condos or apartment with small balconies. It is perfect for blooming flowers, herbs, cactus, strawberries and bulbs. It makes a great gift for the advanced or beginner gardeners. This consists of a wooden frame of thickness varying from 15 cm to 30 cm depending upon the convenience. The height and breadth of the frame varies depending upon the available space. The broader faces are inclosed with wire netting whereas two vertical sides and the bottom are covered with wooden flates. The top is kept open. Sphagnum moss or coarse peat is pressed within the wire frame which serve as growing medium. It is possible to grow many dwarf flowering and foliage plants in such frames provided the medium is supplied with nutrient and water regularly.

A vertical garden can be shifted from place to place and even used as ornamental partition in the drawing room. The vertical garden should be planted with either sun loving dwarf and trailing flowering plants such as *Semperflorens, Begonia rex* or ornamental leaved begonias, *African violets, Fittonia, Peperomia, Oxalis* and *Zebrina pendula* on the broader sides which are expected to grow horizontally with the tendency to go vertical. A single vertical garden should not have mixed planting i.e., a combination of shade-loving plants. The vertical garden is provided with legs on the sides to enable it to stand on its own. A rot resistant wood such as teak and oak should be used for the frame in addition should also be treated with rot resistant chemical such as cuprinol.

Jar and Bottle Gardening

Bottle gardens may be called as miniature greenhouse in which liliputian landscapes are planted. Any size of bottle, a jar, a wide mouthed wine glass or a jug is suitable for gardening provided these are made of clear glass. Bottle gardening is a novel way of growing certain moisture loving indoor plants which may be otherwise impossible to grow in dry house. This type of gardening offer good display on a table, a stand or a well lit window. A jar made of glass having tall sides with or without lid is good for bottle gardening as this conserved moisture. The jar has wider mouth than a bottle. A bottle should be wide at the bottom with taller sides and a narrow but wide enough (2-3 cm diameter opening) mouth for enabling the plant to be inserted. A bottle can be placed either vertically or horizontally on a stand. Horizontal space provides more space for landscaping.

Culture and Management

Plants, chiefly ferns are grown in large bottles. A bottle should be thoroughly cleaned with soap and water and made to sparkle by rubbing it with a clean cloth. A mixture of coarse sand and crushed charcoal may be poured into it to form 3 cm thick layer at bottom and later a mixture of equal parts of soil, sand and leaf mould is put in through a paper funnel. While introducing the soil care should be taken that it does not cling to the sides of the bottle. Small plants can be introduced with a fork or dessert spoon tied to thin bamboo canes with wire or tape. The plants should be watered lightly with a tube after planting. The bottle is then corked tightly. If desired, one can get the cork fitted with lamp holder to use the bottle garden as an attractive and novel table lamp. The bottle garden needs very little watering. Watering is done normally once in two months. Bottle garden should be displayed in semi-shade.

Terrariums

Dr. Nathanial Ward, a London physician conceived the idea of terrarium gardening in serendipity. Terrarium is a sophisticated technique of growing plants indoor inside transparent glass container in a manner to make it a complete ecosystem. The principle of terrarium gardening is more or less same as of bottle gardening.

Culture and Management

The size of terrarium can vary according to the need. The convenient size is 1m (Length) × 0.5 m (breadth) × 0.5 m (height). Aquarium cases can be used for this purpose. The terrarium case is covered with glass lid which is removed occasionally to provide ventilation. A terrarium may or may not have a hole. If there are no holes at the bottom, a layer of coarse sand and small 65 mm charcoal pieces about 3 to 6 cm thick may be spread at the bottom before filling in the soil mixture consisting of 1 part each of soil, sand and leaf mould. The level of soil on a particular sides can be raised by placing small pieces of rocks and filling soil around them. Since the terrarium is closed, the plants do not need frequent watering. The arrangement of plants in the terrarium should be planned before planting. The young and small plants should be firmly planted and watered carefully. Thereafter the top of the terrarium should be covered to conserved moisture and it helped the plants to get established. Overcrowding of plants should be avoided. Very fast growing plants should not be avoided. Very fast growing plants should not be included for planting as they may outgrow quickly than other plants. Only healthy, disease and insect free plants should be planted. With a proper choice of plants and careful watering the plants in a terrarium may live for several years without replacement.

Planting materials

For terrarium and Bottle gardening

Aglaonema commutatum, *Nephrolepis,*

Asparagus plumosus, *Ficus pumila,*

Begonia rex,
Billbergia nutans,
Calathea illustris,
Cryptanthus bivittatus roseo-pictus,
Dracaena godseffiana,
Adiantum cuneatum,
Asplenium nidus,
Davallia bullta,
Fittonia verschaffeltii,
Maranta leuconeura var. kerchoveana,
Peperomia obtusifolia,
Philodendron scandens,
Pilea microphylla,
Saintpaulia ionantha,
Tradescantia fluminensis,
Zebrine pendula

CHAPTER-15

ROCK AND WATER GARDENING

Rock Gardening

In a rock garden, the rocks and soil are arranged in such a fashion that conditions are created for the growth of different plants. A rock garden is artificial in the sense that is man made but a well prepared and well managed rock garden should become one of the most attractive and interesting features of the garden. A real rock or alpine garden can not be created at elevations less than 2000-2500 m because most of the true rock or alpine plants do not grow below this altitude. The rock garden should be situated in an open part of the garden and should be away from large trees and nearby hedges. In the hills, south facing slopes or terraces are ideal for sun loving plants whereas the shade loving ones can be accommodated on the northern slopes. Rocks should be of local origin, porous and have a weathered look. Weathered lime stone is ideal while granite is unsuitable. Rock plants do not grow exclusively on rocks and hence a good soil is needed for every rock garden. A rock garden should be situated in an open part of the garden. It is often advised that a shaded corner of the garden should be devoted for making the rock garden. Rock gardens are created round the trunk of a large shady tree with a mound of earth and a few stones placed here and there planting in between a few hardy plants. The rock garden should get all sun possible or atleast for half of the day, preferably in the forenoon. It should be away from large trees and nearby hedges as their roots may interfere with the rock plants. If an undulated land is available the rock garden should be situated there, if possible. A miniature rock garden may be all right if it is situated near a wall or a house. A large rock garden should be situated in a place where this will fit with other garden features. A large rock garden will look out of place in a too formal garden. The site should be well drained and if natural drainage is not there, some artificial means should be provided.

Construction

Although limestone or hard sandstone is the best choice for rockeries and other garden stonework, it is sometimes very costly. If the gardner resides within a few kilometers of a quarry where natural stone can be acquired, he may be able to afford some good rockery materials. By all means obtain some good stone wherever possible, and be sure to get different sizes of stone when ordering some large rocks must be included but not too many for a small gardens. It is very important, though, to keep to one type of stone. If no limestone or sandstone is available, some rough, porous concrete blocks of various size can be used. Uneven slabs of stone and broken paving stones can be utilized. If some are covered with moss they will be even more suitable. The site for a rockery should be open and away from trees. Any shade which is needed for some alpine plants is provided by the special placing of the rocks. The important point about the soil on the chosen site for the rock garden is that it must be well drained. All the soil should be excavated to a depth of about 60 cm and a layer of clinker is spread over the bottom followed by a layer of inverted turves. A lime-free soil is to be preferred as many rock plants are lime-intolerant.

A rock garden is a permanent feature of the garden and it should be laid out after careful planning. Before placing and setting the rocks the mound should be allowed to settle for some time and firmed by beating, if needed. The placement of stones will be such that it gives protection to the roots. The stones are placed in a slightly slanting position gently leaning backward, not forwards, so the rain water flows towards the plant roots. No rock should slope in the same direction with the best faces visible, so that they represent a natural stone strata. Pockets are created in between stones varying in size from 15-60 cm across. These pockets, where plants are to be grown, should be irregular in shape and constructed in such a manner that the compost inside is not washed out. All stones should be bedded firmly and there should not be any air-pocket or loose soils round the stones. While placing stones the use of concrete should be restricted to the minimum. The mounds and slopes in the rockery are to be arranged naturally, but artistically and the peak should not be very steep. A broad path, about 45-60 cm, should wind through the rockery between the gorges and the valleys and make all parts of the rockery accessible. The path may be made of gravel or stepping stones. The rockery should be planted with grown-up and well established plants. The first thing that is to be kept in mind is that dense planting should be avoided. It will be wise to plant thinly as in course of time the plant will fill up the space as they grow. The best planting season is during the rains in the plains of India. In high hills, planting is done during the spring or the early summer. Potted plants can, of course, be planted any time in the year but in places having a severe winter this should be completed by the early autumn.

Management

In places having a severe winter delicate plants will need protection. When plants are small a glass sheet resting on the rocks may be placed over the plants. For larger plants four strong galvanized wires may be inserted in the ground and the glass placed over this. If the weather is very cold the sides should be covered with glass or polythene sheets. The rock garden should be weeded periodically and all dying or dead leaves and the branches are removed. The rockery should be watered by sprinkling water over the rocks as the rains would have watered. Rock plants need replanting every 4 or 5 years as the soil becomes stale or sour. This is a laborious operation. Instead the plants may be top dressed every year with a compost consisting of good sterilized garden soil, fine sand and leaf mould in equal proportions. The top few centimeters of soil is scraped out and in its place the new compost is filled in long with a little quantity of bonemeal about 25-50 g depending upon the plant. Periodically the rock plants should be fed with liquid manure but, if the soil in any pocket turns sour, replanting with fresh soil will be a necessity.

Plants suitable for Rock Garden

Cacti and Succulents

Some hardy species of *Opuntia, Cereus, Mammillaria* and so on. Among the succulents, many species of *Agave, Aloe, Euphorbia splendens, Furcraea, Gasteria, Haworthia, Kalanchoe, Sansevieria, Sedum, Sempervivum, Stapelia* and *Yucca* can be planted in the rock garden.

Ferns

Some hardy ferns belonging to the genus *Drynaria, Nephrodium, Nephrolepsis* and *Polypodium* can be grown in the shady portion of the tropical rock garden.

Shrubs

Many shrubs are suitable for planting in the rock garden, especially for large rock gardens. Shrubs will provide greenery for the rock garden and produce flowers all the year round e.g., *Adeneum obesum, Asclepias curassavica, Asystasia coromandeliana, Azalea* spp., *Calliandra inaequilatera, Callsitemon lanceolatus, Cassia alata, Cassia biflora, Catesbaea spinosa, Crossandra* spp., *Cuphea* spp.,

Duranta plumieri, Juniperus chinensis, Lantana sellowiana, Rullia spp., *Russelia juncea, Thuja spp.* and *Vaccinium spp.*

Herbaceous Plants, Bulbs and others

Angelonia grandiflora, Aster amellus, Crocus, Dracaena sanderiana, Fittonia argyroneura, Impatiens holstii, Oxalis rubra, Portulaca, Sansevieria cylindrica, Tradescantia zebrine, Verbena erinoides, Vinca rosea and *Zephyranthes spp.*

Flowering Annuals

Alyssum, Antirrhinum, Bellis perennis, Brachycome iberidifolia, Browallia elata, Dianthus chinensis, Hymenatherum tenuifolium, Phlox, Salvia splendens, Verbena hybrida, Viola tricolor hortensis and *Zinnia linearis.*

Some Rock Plants for the Hills

Adonis vernalis, Androsace lanuginosa, Anemone spp., *Campanula* spp., *Draba* spp., *Iris* spp., *Lilium longiflorum, Narcissus, Potentilla* spp., *Primula* spp., *Selaginella spp.* and *Tulip spp.*

Water Gardening

Water garden is one of the oldest arts of gardening in India. Lotus and water lilies are the important plants of water gardens. The muslim and British rulers neglected water gardening. The first point to the success of any water garden is to ensure adequate supply of water as no aquatic plant will survive any length of time in a dried pool. Water lilies and most of the other water plants do best in still waters but a gentle current of water will not much upset the growth of certain varieties.

Informal Pool

The base of such pool is made impervious to water by the puddling. This can be achieved easily if the sub soil itself is clayey or by importing clay and laying it to a depth of about 30-40 cm at the bottom. After puddling, the pond is filled with water. Water lilies do best in still waters. There are certain varieties of water lilies which can be grown in running water depending upon the velocity of the current. A gentle current of water will not much upset the growth of certain varieties.

The Formal Pool

A formal pool should never be constructed below a tree as this robs the pool of its prominence over the tree. Moreover the shade of the tree interferes with much needed sunshine required for water lilies and falling leaves of the tree foul the water and roots may cause cracks and crevices in the walls of the pool. The shape and size of a pool depend upon the size of a garden and on personal liking and disliking. A pool may be formal and informal in shape. Constructing the pool at ground level is the usual practice but this runs the risk of children getting drowned. The shape may be simple, rectangle or square, round or oval, kidney shaped or any artistic design. A formal pool is made of concrete. The first step in constructing the pool is to mark out the design on the ground and then digging out the soil of the marked area to a depth of 30-90 cm in proportion to the size of the pool and the thickness of the concrete base. All loose soil is removed and the base is made firm as this will support the tremendous weight of the concrete and water. If the base is not clayey or hard, it should be made hard by ramming in rubbish, morrum or cinder and then the concrete base is laid. Before any concrete work is started pipes for inlet of water and draining the pool must be placed in position and an overflow pipe should be provided. The drainage and overflow pipe should be situated at convenient points and the pool should slope towards these outlets. The most ideal solution will be to connect the drainage pipe to the nearest sewer. Alternatively this pipe may be laid to a large pit 120-150 cm deep, filled upto 30 cm from the surface with small pieces of rocks and broken bricks. The drained water may be utilized for irrigation in the garden. It may not be needed at all to have any elaborate drainage system as well as constructed pool may need draining once in a year. Draining of water can be done with the help of a fractional horse power water pump. The overflow pipe will maintain the water level. A 15-22.5 cm thick concrete layer is laid at the bottom of the excavated area. The concrete should be firmed with a shovel or a vibrator to ensure that no air-pockets are left. The bottom is leveled but not smoothed too much. To avoid any joint, the side vertical walls should be constructed, simultaneously with the floor when it is still wet. The concrete used should consist of 3 parts aggregates (<2 m) 2 parts sand and 1 part cement. The concrete should be cured by placing wet gunny bags for a few days from the construction date, when the concrete has set, the pool is to be made completely water tight, by putting a lining of cement mortar consisting of 1 part cement and 3 parts fine sand and a proportionate amount of a water-proofing material. The mortar should be 1.5-2.5 cm deep and should be put in two coats. The coatings are kept wet by covering with wet gunny cloth for a few days to prevent cracking. Special care should be taken to ensure that the corners are completely water tight. The inner walls should be constructed at a distance of 45-75 cm from the edge of the pool and the height should be 20-25 cm lower than the sides. The surrounding may run all along the periphery of the pool or it may be confined only on two sides.

Drainage apertures are provided at the bottom of the walls to allow water to pass at the time of emptying the lily pool. The space between the outer and the inner walls is filled with good compost consisting of a good loam and peat or loam and leaf mould. The soil is banked up to cover the tops of the outer wall. The edge of the outer walls should slope outwards to prevent surface run off water entering the pool. The usual depth of the pool is 60 cm but in the plains of the tropics many species of water lilies thrive and flower even in 180-250 cm of water. In places having a severe winter such depth will force the lilies to go dormant. Before filling up the pool finally it is desirable to fill water and rain it several times to wash out excess alkali and outer chemicals harmful for plants. Potassium permanganate crystals may be added to the water just sufficient to make it light pink in colour for remaining toxicity. At this time pool should be tested against leakage.

Planting

The more common method of planting is to fill the entire tank to a depth of 30-40 cm with heavy loam or clay mixed with sufficient quantities of FYM. About 50-75 g of bonemeal may be mixed with every square metre area. The lilies are planted directly in the soil and then water is filled in just to cover the crown of the plants. More water is filled in stages as the plants make new growth. In no case the plants be submerged. The other method is to use large sized consent boxes or tubs filled with a good compost i.e., heavy loam and F.Y.M. (2:1) mixed with liberal quantities bonemeal. The size of the boxes will vary according to the kind of species. The largest size will be about 75 cubic cm for large sized varieties. The lilies are then planted in these boxes and water is filled gradually in the same manner as above. For shallow pools while constructing the floor, water proof concrete boxes are prepared at desired intervals, 45 cm deep from the floor level. The dimensions of such boxes are 45 square cm with 45 cm depth. These boxes are then filled with required compost and the water plants planted in them. In the already filled up pool the planting procedure is first to plant the water plant in a basket, tub or plot filled with compost and then lowering the basket in water keeping in view that the crown remains above the water. This can be ensured by keeping the basket on bricks for a week or two and when new growth takes place, it is gradually lowered to the floor of the pool. If the pool is quite deep and lilies need shallow water, the basket or the pot can be kept over bricks or an inverted tub to give the desired depth of water. The soil surface in each basket or ant other container is covered with 2 cm of washed gravel or pebbles to avoid disturbance of soil while immersing. In an empty pool with a layer of soil while filling it with water the water should not fall directly in the soil but the inlet pipe or hose should run into a bucket or basin.

The pool is filled in several stages. While filling some plants may get displaced and float up which are pushed back and kept in position with stones.

Care

Lilies are generally very hardy and grow quite well if left undisturbed. These plants are lifted and replanted only when they appear unhealthy. Some of the water lilies make too much of leaf growth and deprive the pool of essential sunlight. Such plants are lifted, divided and replanted. Often a slimy green growth of blanket weed covers the surface and the side walls of the pool. This can be controlled by adding 30 g of potassium permanganate to each 100,000 to 125,000 litres of water or 115 g of copper sulphate for the same volume of water. A second application after a week may be necessary if the first fails.

Other Types of Pools

Fibreglass Pools: Ready made fiberglass pools of various shapes and sizes are available. For installing these pools a hole little larger all round than the size of pool is dug, all stones are removed and the bottom is leveled. The pool is placed in position and soil is rammed from all sides. Fibre glass pools are very durable but cost is very high compared to plastic or PVC.

Vacuum-formed Mouldings: There are certain other prefabricated pools available, made from such plastics as PVC and polythene. These are inexpensive but often the depth are not sufficient to grow most of the aquatics.

Pool Liners: The simplest method is to line an excavation with a sheet of flexible plastic commonly called pool liner. The common material used is 500 gauge polythene in black or blue colour; the former is preferred. The pool is dug in the required shape and the dug-up pool is cleared of all stones and the surface is smoothened with a layer of sand. The polythene sheet is then placed in position with 15-20 cm polythene overlapping the edges of pool. Two sheets are placed one above the other or one sheet folded double is used as a safety against leakage. The edges are covered with soil or paved with stone or growing dwarf plants over the soil. Though this is the cheapest and the quickest method to make a pool, the major disadvantage is that it may develop leaks at any time and polythene becomes brittle with sunrays above the water line. Polythene does not stretch, so this must be tucked right down along the excavation. Once punctured, a polythene cannot be repaired and has to be replaced. The best liner is possibly PVC which is superior to polythene. Moreover, PVC is stretchable and can be stretch-fitted.

Plants for Water Garden

Plants for water garden can be divided into several groups such as (a) surface flowering aquatics, (b) oxygenators, (c) floaters and (d) marginals.

1. *Surface Flowering Aquatics*

Aponogeton distachyus: Family: Aponogetonaceae

It is commonly known as Cape pond-Weed or Water hawthorn because of its hawthorn like scent. The oval leaves are floating and the flowers project just above the foliage. Flowers are snow-white, while the anthers are black.

Euryale ferox: Family: Nymphaeaceae

A large annual aquatic herb, next in size to *Victoria regia*. Leaves are circular about 60 cm across.

Limnanthemum indica: Family: Gentianaceae

It is commonly known as Water Snowflake. Leaves are *Nymphaea* like and floating. Flowers are white, numerous, short lived and it flowers most of the season.

Monochoria hastifolia: Family: Pontederiaceae

Flowers are blue in crowded umbels. It is propagated by division.

Nelumbo lutea: Family: Nymphaeaceae

It is commonly called as American Lotus or Water Chinkapin. Leaves are 30-60 cm across, raised 60-180 cm out of water. Flowers are yellow and fragrant, 10-25 cm across.

Nelumbo nucifera: Family: Nymphaeaceae

It is commonly called as lotus or Padma or Kamal. Flowers are white, tipped rose or pink but with many variants, 30 cm across and overtopping leaves. Flowering is during the summer.

Nymphaea: Family: Nymphaeaceae

These are commonly called as water-lilies. There are types which can be grown in very shallow waters (*Nymphaea pygmaea* and *Nymphaea tetragona)*, in medium depth of water (*Nymphaea alba* and *Nymphaea odorata*) and still others requiring deep water. Nymphaeas are propagated by division of clumps, tubers or by cuttings from the rhizomatous stems of a few species. Seeds germinate easily but the seedlings come to flowering only after about 2-3 years.

Orontium aquaticum: Family: Araceae

It is commonly known as Golden Club, deriving the name from the densely-crowded, tiny yellow flowers in the white-stemmed flower spikes. The leaves are velvety, silvered blue-green which grow either 30 cm above water surface or float, depending on the situation.

Victoria regia: Family: Nymphaeaceae

This lily can only be cultivated in large ponds. The leaves are floating, up to 1.5 m in diameter, the margins are upturned and 5-12 cm broad. The leaves have projecting air-filled ribs beneath which give the leaves great buoyancy to support great weights. This is an annual and needs 1.2 m of water. The flowers are large and cream coloured.

2. *Oxygenators*

Callitriche autumnalis: Family: Callitrichaceae

It is the best oxygenator in the family. This is entirely submerged and grows in running water. It is a suitable plant for sheltering fish and providing food to them.

Ceratophyllum: Family: Ceratophyllaceae

The two species planted are *Ceratophyllum demersum* and *Ceratophyllum submersum*. These slender branching, fragile and submerged plants do not need formal planting, instead are just dropped in the pool and grow in wide situation like deep, shaded or cold pools. This water weed should be removed periodically or they cover the whole tank.

Elodea canadensis: Family: Hydrocharitaceae

It is of vigorous growth but is probably the tidiest and shortest among the good oxygenators. Thick growth provides shelter for the fish.

Ranunculus aquatilis: Family: Ranunculaceae

It is commonly known as water Crowfoot or Water butter cup. This has fine submerged foliage and in running water the foliage comes in long waving tresses. This bears in May numerous, small, white flowers on the surface.

Vallisneria spiralis: Family: Hydrocharitaceae

It is commonly known as Eel or Tape grass. Leaves are long in deep and short in shallow waters and about 1 cm broad. The female flowers are borne in coiled-stalks under the water which uncoil to bring the female flowers to the surface where it is pollinated by a detached floating male flower. It serves as a food for aquatic wild-life as well as a good oxygenator.

3. *Floating Plants*

Azolla caroliniana: Family: Salviniaceae

It forms a crinkled surface carpet of mossy green and in temperate regions during the autumn it gets beautifully tinted with lilac and red.

Eichhornia speciosa: Family: Pontederiaceae

It is commonly called as Water Hyacinth. It is a floating plant which if not kept in control will fill the pond by itself. Blue flowers are borne in erect panicles.

Lemna gibba and ***Lemna minor***: Family: Lemnaceae

These are commonly called as Duckweeds and good as fish food. It should be collected by pond nets occasionally to check rampant growth.

Trapa natans: Family: Onagraceae

It is commonly known as Water Chestnut. The overlapping triangular bronzy-green leaves are attractive. It is an annual regenerated by the production of nut like seeds. The four angled spiny fleshy fruits are edible and known in vernacular as Singara.

4. *Marginal Plants*

Acorus calamus variegatus: Family: Araceae

It is a form of the commonly known as Sweet Flag having leaves stripped with green and creamy white. Both *Acorus calamus* and *Acorus calamus* variegatus are water loving herbaceous perennials bearing greenish white flowers on a 5-7 cm long spadix.

Calla palustris: Family: Araceae

It is called Bog Arum and has shiny rounded leaves projecting 15 cm above water. It blooms arum-like white spathes which if fertilized by water snails develop red fruits.

Cyperus alternifolius: Family: Cyperaceae

The numerous leaves are arranged in an umbrella like fashion over an angular stem. Leaves are quite attractive and are used for table decoration. In the variety *variegatus* the stems and leaves are moftled white or sometimes completely albino.

Iris laevigata: Family: Iridaceae

It is the best among the marginal plants with clear violet blue flowers.

Iris pseudacorus: Family: Iridaceae

It is commonly called as Yellow Flag or Water Flag and is vigorous-grower having yellow flowers.

Iris kaempferi: Family: Iridaceae

It performs well only when the soil is just covered with water. Flowers are of various colours, from reddish purple to shades of yellow to white.

Sagittaria sagittifolia: Family: Alismataceae

It is also known as Common Arrow-head with large sagittate leaves. Flowers are white but turns pale blue. A good oxygenator. In var. *florepleno* the flowers are double.

Typha angustifolia: Family: Typhaceae

The brown cylindrical flower heads are borne in long stalks. This should be kept in check by occasional thinning. The flower heads with long stalks are good for indoor decoration.

Fish in Pools

Ornamental fish can be introduced in a pool. No fish should be introduced into the pool at the time of planting as the fish have the habit of nibbling at the oxygenator plants. The fish are introduced after about three weeks when such plants have made sufficient growth and withstand the damage. The colour gold fish are the best for a pool. The usual rate of fish population initially is 2.5 cm long (excluding tail) fish for every 4.5 to 5 l of water. Fish need some hiding place especially in shallow pools from birds such as crow, egret and crane. This is provided by the densely growing water plants. Fish, apart from adding beauty to the water garden, eat up the larvae of mosquitoes.

Marsh Gardening

This is also called as Bog garden. The bog garden is actually a marsh where the soil is not sour or acid and a shallow stream or trickle runs through it. A pond is not an essential feature of any bog garden. The main criteria of a marsh garden is to keep it moist and in a swampy state all throughout. A site of marsh garden should be low lying where the surface drainage water will collect naturally. The whole area intended to be developed into a marsh garden is dug up to a depth of 60 cm and a thin layer of clay, 10-12 cm deep, is placed at the bottom to form the base of the marsh garden. Then a 12 cm layer of rubble or large stones are placed over this to ensure that the water in the marsh does not become stagnant. The rest of the hollow is filled with a compost of garden loam and leaf mould in the proportion 1:1 and the level made up with the surrounding land. All parts of the marsh garden is made accessible by laying paths of rough stones or bricks, winding round the marsh and putting stepping stones over them. It must be noted that all marsh plants need water but in varying degrees. Accordingly, marsh plants can be categorized into three broad groups. In the first group belong plants which love 5-10 cm of standing water and termed as "swamp dwellers". In the second category are placed, the plants which live on or a little above the waterline, with their roots standing in water logged soil. In the third group are placed those plants which grow above the saturated soil but near enough to send their roots in search of water. A marsh garden can accommodate any moisture loving plant, those which are found commonly growing on the banks of streams or ponds. Some of the plants which can stand in 12-15 cm of water are also included in a marsh garden. In some pockets of the marsh even plants growing in shallow water can be accommodated. While planting, the main point one should bear in mind is not to overcrowd the bog. It is better to plant one type of plant in a group of 3 to 6 allowing sufficient space in between before another group of different colour, size and height is planted. The actual plants selected for a marsh will, however, depend upon the size of the garden and the undulation of the marsh. If the marsh is in one plane it will not be possible to grow the plants of all the groups mentioned earlier. In a small area it will be advisable to create a greater variety by growing the dwarf marsh plants. But in a vast area the vigorous growing ones should be used more freely, especially to create background effects.

Plants for Marsh Garden

Alocasia **spp.:** The plants are having beautiful broad leaves of sagittate-cordate shape. It flowers in June-August.

Arundinaria **spp.:** The plant height is 30 cm – 2.5 m. Leaves are bamboo like and produces flower all the year round.

Arundo Donax: The plant height is up to 3.5m. Leaves 30-60 cm long, 3.5 cm broad. Flowering season is autumn.

Asplenium: Plant height is 10-60 cm. Fronds are of evergreen nature.

Calla palustris: Commonly called as Bog Arum. Leaves shiny, flowering spathe white, arum like.

Caltha palustris var. ***plena:*** It is commonly called as Double Marsh Marigold. The showiest Caltha with bright yellow double flowers. Flowering season is March-May.

Cypripedium spectabile: The plant height is 45-90 cm. Flowers white or flushed rose.

***Eriophorum* spp.:** Commonly known as Cotton Grass. Plant height is 45-60 cm. Plumes silky white. Flowering season is summer.

Filipendula palmata: Flowers pale pink turning white. Flowering season is summer.

Filipendula ulmaria* var. *aurea: Leaves gold-splashed, flowers cream and flowering season is summer.

***Hemerocallis* spp.:** Leaves narrow, grass like. Flowers funnel shaped in many shades. Flowering season is summer to autumn.

***Hosta* spp.:** It is commonly known as Plaintain Lily. Bold foliage plants for group planting. *Hosta glauca* have blue-green leaves. *Hosta undulata variegata* have dark green leaves splashed with pale-green and cream.

Lysimachia nummularia: It is commonly known as Creeping Jenny. Stem spreading studded with yellow flowers. Flowering season is June-August.

Lysimachia punctata: It is a less branched perennial herb, flowers yellow. Flowering season is June-July.

Osmunda regalis: It is commonly known as Royal Fern. Plant height is 90-180 cm. A good plant for making clumps at borders of water.

Pandanas odoratissimus: It bears scented flowers. Need pruning to keep dwarf. Flowering season is summer.

Primula aurantiaca: Plant height is 30-60 cm. Flowers orange red. It is suitable for mild and flowers in temperate climates. Flowering season is May-July.

Primula florindae: It is commonly known as Giant Cowslip. One of the best primulas for a wet place. It is suitable for mild and temperate climate. Flower sulphur-yellow. Flowering season is July-August.

Sunken Gardening

In this garden is laid below the ground level. A sunken garden can be laid out in an already existing depression of land or a portion of the garden may be especially dug to lay out such a garden. The cost of laying will be much cheaper in the former than in the latter case. Since a sunken ground is likely to collect water, adequate drainage arrangement should be made. The simplest method will be to have one or two drainage outlets and connect them to the sewerage system. Some drainage materials such as stones and rubbles may be placed below the surface of the sunken garden at a depth of about 1 m from the surface. The thickness of these materials may be about 60 cm. There is no hard and fast rule as to what is to be planted in a sunken garden. This will depend mainly on the area available and the choice of the grower. If the area is small only some annuals and herbaceous perennials are grown in formal beds. In a large sunken garden an elaborate formal or informal garden can be laid with paths, lawns, flower beds, shrubbery, trees, rose garden and greenhouse. The ideal depth of sunken garden is about 120 cm. In case sufficient depth is available one or all the walls of the sunken garden can be developed into dry wall. This will help to support the raised sides of the sunken garden in addition to beauty. In dry localities, fountains and streams may be provided to increase the humidity. It is always advisable to have an attractive central feature such as sundial or bird bath or stone figure. This helps tie the composition of the garden together. A sunken garden is likely to be more humid, especially in high rainfall areas, than the portion above the ground. Hence, it is likely that moisture-loving plants such as ferns, Ixora, Gardenia and so on, will do better in such a garden. The approach to a sunken garden is generally by a staircase, preferably made of stones. The surface of sunken garden can be decorated with crazy paving, gravel and steps in addition to neatly arranged beds and borders. It is also possible to have a sunken rock garden. When the paths in a rock garden are dug deep to create the mounds and hillocks, it takes the appearance of a sunken rock garden.

Gardening in Shade

The home gardens, a portion of which may be shaded, is a blessing in disguise if one can take full advantage of it. But many people consider shade in the garden as a nuisance as no plants are likely to flower properly under it. This is a hasty conclusion, as some people might have grown few sun loving plants such as sunflower, marigold or zinnia, which naturally might not have done well under shade. The garden has three types of shade. One in the category of dense shadow in north or north-west corner under a high wall or below low spreading trees such as *Ficus benghalensis, Brownea ariza* and so on, where the ground is semi dark. There are other places where though there is shade, but the sun penetrates to a considerable extent. Finally, there are places which are in half shade like on the east or west sides of the building.

Problems under shade

The first thing to be investigated from a shaded portion is the nature of the soil. An indication will be available from the health of the natural undergrowth. If these are lanky or weak the plants may either be suffering from lack of water or plant food or both. While gardening under shade of trees, the tree roots will pose a problem. They compete with the plants grown under it for water and food. Therefore, the soil under the trees is to be dug deeply to cut the surface feeding roots. This operation should be repeated every year by digging deep along the borders of the beds. The beds are to be fertilized more liberally as some of these fertilizers will be utilized by the tree itself. One general notion is that shade gardens need less watering. This is true as far as a shade from an inert object such as a wall is concerned. But if the shade is from a living tree, it may be necessary to water the shade garden more frequently as a major part of this water will be utilized by the tree itself. For this rationing of water and plant food, shade garden plants under trees are spaced much wider than in open.

Plants for shade

Aphelandra cristata, Azaleas spp., *Caladiums* spp., *Coleus* spp., *Ficus repens, Hedera helix baltica, Geranium, Impatiens sultanii, Pothos aureus, Sanchezia nobilis variegata* and *Strobilanthes* spp.

CHAPTER-16

ROOF GARDENING

A garden always provides a space to relax but the limitation of space in big cities and towns has already set the door for enjoying the beauty at home. Along with the rapid growth in population on a global basis, many cities in the world are fast becoming highly urbanized with the construction of buildings and structures in close proximity to each other. Cities represent dense development with more and more people living on less and less land. The scarcity of urban land demands an increasingly creative use of roofs and terraces to replace the land that is lost. The reduction of ground level urban land for open space demands the fullest utilization of green roofs. As most modern buildings are constructed of reinforced concrete, this high concentration of thermal mass, together with the resultant loss of green areas, has created a host of environmental issues such as the Urban Heat Island effect. This in turn causes a substantial increase in air temperature within the urbanized areas and results in higher energy consumption for cooling loads. Plants and vegetation are known to help in trapping dirt and dust in the air as well as to generate oxygen in the day through photosynthesis and with their destruction in urbanized zones, the air quality is also adversely affected. In a highly urbanized and build-up area, rainwater tends to flow quickly from the roofs of buildings into the storm sewer and when such sewer system could not cope with the increased flow, flooding generally occurs. Building green roofs, storm water management and green spaces in the city have become major topics in the planning process. Roof gardens or "green roofs" and "eco-roofs" have been used extensively in Europe, North America, South Korea, Japan and Singapore to mitigate such adverse effects of urbanizations. Rooftops traditionally are considered as remnant spaces and abandoned to housing elevator shafts and mechanical systems, should now be used for accessible social and recreational purposes. Well researched green living landscapes including roofs, balconies, terraces and walls provide a linkage to the street and open spaces beyond. Greening rooftops provide many benefits to users, developers and those who enjoy the view from adjoining buildings. Green rooftops are an undervalued economic asset and are often not appreciated as an environmental resource. A fully developed green roof as a source of urban recreation is a welcome developmental asset for the building occupants and the immediate neighborhood. The evident benefits of green rooftops may potentially outweigh the cost of installation and add to the enjoyment of a city. Vegetation on roofs increases the bio-mass of the city, reduce pollutants, improve the micro-climate, reduce heat island effects and delay storm water runoff.

What is 'Green Roof' ?

A 'Green Roof' is a vegetated space that is structurally integrated on top of a man made structure. The word 'roof' in this context refers to any continuous surface designed for the protection of inhabitants from the elements, whether open or closed on the sides. The vegetated space may be below, at, or above grade; located on a podium deck, a 'sky garden' on an intermediate floor level or at the very top level of the building but in all cases the plants are not planted in the ground. It is often used to describe many other landscape and architectural terms: Roof top garden, Green roof, Turf roof, Living roof, Sod roof, Eco roof and Garden roof.

History of Roof Gardening

From time immemorial man has dreamt of the Garden of Eden and built gardens on the ground and on roofs. They have grown plants atop structures since antiquity. Ornamental roof gardens have their origin back to the ancient roman times of the 7th Century B.C. Roof gardens are existed in ancient times. Records tell us of ziggurats of ancient Mesopotamia (4th millennium BC – 600 BC) had plantings of trees and shrubs on above ground terraces. The best known gardens are the hanging gardens of Babylon built by King Sennacherib of Assyria in the City of Ur about 700 B.C.E. They tell us of a most intricate system of mechanical irrigation, loading over columns and exotic plants for the enjoyment of all. The art of roof gardens flourished in ancient Rome example was the Villa of the Mysteries in Pompeii which had an elevated terrace where plants were grown and the tradition continued in the Renaissance as evidenced by the terraced roof gardens designed by the of Count Borromeo III at Isola Bella in Lake Maggiore. This roof garden features plants on various terraces with fruit trees, flowers and clipped box hedges and it is still in existence today. A roof garden has also been discovered around an audience hall in Roman-Byzantine Caesarea. The medieval Egyptian city of Fustat had a number of high-rise buildings that Nasir Khusraw in the early 11th century described as rising upto 14 stories, with roof gardens on the top story complete with ox-drawn water wheels for irrigating them. Primitive dwellings used locally available prairie turf over birch bark sheathing or thin a clay skim coat over pine planks. Scandinavia, Turkey and Iran are countries that widely used turf as a simple and inexpensive roof material. The use of concrete as a roof material around 1840 saw the design of sloped 'nature roofs' in western Europe. Architects Frank Lloyd Wright and Le Corbusier experimented with green roofs on their building designs in the early 1900's. Generally, this treatment was highly ornamental and structurally expensive. The high maintenance and roof leakage issues of turf roofs gave way to the readily-available, inexpensive shingles and hot tar roofing in the 1920's. Not until the early 1980's were advances in root barriers and superior waterproofing materials made main-stream. The creation of world's First Botanical Roof Garden was started in Augustenbog (1999) in Malmo, Sweden.

Types of Green Roofs

Generally there are two types of roof gardens and they are classified as:

1. Intensive Roof Gardens

These gardens are developed to be accessible and may involve elaborate landscaping requirements such as water features and hardscapes including paving stones and seating. They are usually heavy in loading and the roof must be specially designed to accommodate such requirement. Soil is the common medium for planting and the average thickness of the soil layer can varies between 40 cm for turfing and shrubs to as much as 150 cm for bushes and trees. Intensive roof gardens require regular maintenance such as mowing, fertilizing, watering and weeding.

2. Extensive Roof Gardens

Extensive green roofs are lightweight in design and developed mainly for aesthetic and environmental/ ecological benefits. The planting medium consists mainly of volcanic stones and pumice and the average thickness is about 10-15 cm. Plants are carefully selected to be dry-resistant types and usually a rainwater storage reservoir is incorporated in the system to minimize maintenance. Extensive roof gardens are lightweight in nature and generally not accessible.

Currently most of the roof gardens in this region tend to be intensive types and were developed mainly for aesthetic purposes. However, with the growing awareness of the needs to protect our environment against the Urban Heat Island effects, extensive roof gardens are expected to provide the ideal solution to the problem.

Benefits of Green Roofs

The benefits of Green Roofs are numerous and well-researched overseas. These benefits are grouped as Amenity and Aesthetic benefits, Environmental benefits and Economic benefits.

1. Amenity and Aesthetic Benefits

(1) ***Leisure and Functional Open Space*** - With the inevitable increase in the density of urban construction, sustainable recreation opportunities need to been encouraged and with limited areas of ground level open space flat roofs present enormous potential in providing urban dwellers with the amenity and recreational space essential for healthy living. A visit to a clean, safe park or garden situated locally should not be a luxury. It should be the right of all citizens. An extensive Green Roofs can be designed to support play equipment, ponds, and shade structure. These green ideas can be incorporated at the residential unit level right through to large offices and apartment complexes.

(2) ***Visual Amenity Value*** - An obvious and significant benefit of a green roof is the potentially attractive view offered to overlooking buildings. This is of great importance in a dense urban environment such as Hong Kong, where, it is considered to have a high significance if a large number of green roofs are established.

(3) ***Health and Therapeutic Value*** - Psychological studies have demonstrated that the restorative effect of natural scenery holds the viewer's attention, diverts their awareness away from themselves and worrisome thoughts and elicits a meditation-like state. Garden are pleasant place to be and can provide significant health benefits. Studies have shown that just passively looking at trees and plants reduces stress, lowers blood pressure, relieves tension in muscles and increases positive feelings. In fact, the belief that contact with trees, shrubs, grasses and flowers is beneficial for human wellbeing dates back to the designs found in many ancient cities. A 1984 study in Pennsylvania researched the effects of natural views on the post – operative recovery time of surgical patients. Two groups of patients in the same hospital, undergoing the same operation (gall bladder) were placed in two types of rooms. One room looked onto a brick wall while the other looked out over a landscaped count yard. Not, surprisingly, the study showed that patients overlooking the courtyard had shorter post – operative stays, fewer negative evaluation comments from the nurse and took less pain medication (Ulrich, 1984). Horticulture Therapy is a branch of both the Alternative Medicine and Occupational Therapy fields. Active participation in outdoor and gardening activities are a relatively new

approach to healing for programs in therapy and rehabilitation (Michael and Thomas, 2003).The studies show exiting Green Roofs on hospital building and suggest that more thought and research should go into the sitting of the patient's room in relation to views of natural space. Further research may show the ability for Green Roofs to save public and insurance companies spending. These savings would ultimately justify the added capital and maintenance costs of gardens and green roofs. With many of the hospitals in the country desperate for more beds, a sustainable solution is to improve the recovery conditions for patients, thereby, shorten their stay and freeing up beds. The studies conducted in prisons reported that prisoners with cells looking over farmlands or forests were less likely to report for sick call than those whose cells looked out onto wall, buildings or other inmates. High density developments in America are notorious for the image of concrete jungles. Studies have shown that people living in these developments that have a garden either on a terrace or balcony are less susceptible to illness. The environmental and aesthetic benefits of green space are complimented by the therapeutic benefits derived from caring for plants.

2. Environmental Benefits

(1) ***Alleviating Urban Heat Island Effect***: The Urban Heat Island effect is caused by the absorption and retention of solar heat in buildings and hard structures in highly urbanized cities resulting in the air temperature in such areas becoming significantly warmer than in the rural areas. A typical profile showing the Urban Heat Island effect on increasing air temperature in the city by as much as 4°C compared to the rural area. This higher temperature means that the buildings in the city will need to increase the air-conditioning load and, therefore, uses more energy than otherwise would. This in turns discharges warm exhaust air from the air-conditioners into the outdoor air thus aggravating the Urban Heat Island phenomenon.

A similar study in Toronto by Environment Canada and the National Research Council indicated that Toronto's summer temperature are 4°C to 10°C higher than those of the surrounding countryside. The resulting increase in energy consumption to cool buildings is not only an economic burden but also leads to more air pollution in the form of smog and sulphur dioxide and greenhouse gases (GHG). The study concluded that a reduction in summer temperatures in Toronto of 1° to 2°C could be achieved by installing green infrastructure on just 6% of the total available roof space. Environment Canada states that: as little as 1°C reduction in urban island will result in a 5 per cent decrease in Electricity demand for cooling and refrigeration, resulting in lower GHG emissions. Combined with direct energy costs per year and reduce GHG emissions by an estimated 2.18 mega tones and remove 30 metric tones of pollutants from the air.

A study in 1993 at Berkley concluded "The nationwide electricity costs due to summer heats Islands are approximately US $1,000,000 an hour. In Singapore National Parks authority is involved in providing sky rise greening". A publication called "Handbook on Sky Rise Greening in Singapore" states, "We must look beyond the greening concept where even buildings become complementary components of the garden." In regards to UHIE, the handbook cites, "In Singapore roof surface temperature can be heated to a high of 58°C during the day. At night time, this heat is reradiated into the surroundings. Rooftop greenery reduces the roof surface temperature by upto 31°C. Ambient temperature can be reduced by as much as 4°C. On a macro level, the increase in energy consumption means that more fossilized fuel will be used to generate the extra electricity and this increases the emission of greenhouse gases and other pollutants which directly impact the issue of global warming and higher pollution level. The research report a definite increase in temperature as a direct result of urban infrastructure with difference upto 8°C being observed between urban temperature and surrounding rural areas. The use of roof gardens has been proven to lower the surface temperature by as much as 30°C and air temperature by about 4°C in tropical conditions through a field test conducted in Singapore by a research team supported by National University of Singapore, National Parks Board and the Building and Construction Authority, Singapore. These reductions in temperature are due mainly to the shading of the heat absorbing roof surfaces and the evapo-transpirational cooling effects of the plants in the roof gardens.

The average daily energy demand due to the heat flow through the Green Roof was significantly less than that of the Reference Roof in spring and summer. The field test further confirmed that a roof garden can have significant reduction on both solar radiation absorbed by the roof and the resultant heat gain. This finding is important as it gives evidence that a planted roof could effectively mitigate the Urban Heat Island effect. Comparison of measured surface temperature of hard surfaces, soil surface without vegetation cover and soil surface covered with different kinds of plants.

(2) ***Improving Air Quality***: Roof vegetation can improve the air quality by acting as a filter to trap airborne dust particles. A study has shown that 1 sq.m. of grass can remove 0.2 kg of airborne particles per year. In a study carried out in Frankfurt, Germany, streets without trees were noted to have an air pollutant count of 10,000 to 20,000 dirt particles per litre of air compared to one with trees in the same neighborhood where only 3,000 particles per litre of air were noted. A higher

temperature at roof level tends to create a thermal draft drawing up dust particles from street level. Studies on the air quality gained from vegetation in urban area have shown that trees lined street has only 10 to 15 % of the total dust particle found on similar street without trees. It follows that a green roof vegetated with only grass or similar low profile shrubs, could remove at a minimum, 200 g of particles per square meter of roof per year. Roof greening has been found to be effective in moderating the thermal draft by reducing the temperature differences between rooftop and street level. As the formation of smog is highly sensitive to air temperatures and the higher the temperature, the greater the concentration of smog. In a field test conducted in Los Angeles, it was noted that the concentration of smog measured as low atmospheric ozone is below national standard at temperatures below 21°C. However, at temperatures of about 35°C, all days are smoggy. Cooling the city by about 5°C would have a dramatic impact on smog concentration. Plants through the photosynthesis process can absorb carbon dioxide and release oxygen into the atmosphere, thus improving the air quality. About $155m^2$ of planted surface area will produce enough oxygen for one person for 24 hours. Power generation and air-conditioning collectively can contribute to the emission of about 20 tones of carbon dioxide per person per year in a highly urbanized city state like Singapore. With roof gardens reducing the surface and air temperature thereby lowering the air-conditioning load, the emission of carbon dioxide can be cut back by as much as 2%.

(3) ***Improving Water Quality***: Depending on the thickness of the various layers of the roof garden, a green roof is able to filter out heavy metals and nutrients present in rainwater. This advantage would be beneficial in urban areas where precipitation is collected for domestic usage in addition to treated potable water supply from the utility provider.

(4) ***Improving Storm water Management***: Roof gardens retain rainwater on the roof through the various layers and significantly reduce the peak discharge flow rate into the storm water drainage system. A German study has shown that in Berlin, Green Roofs absorbs 75% of the precipitation that falls on them. During intense short duration storms, the runoff is stretched out over several hours thus reducing the risk of flash flooding. The ability to absorb and retain up to 75% of rainfall thereby reducing the immediate discharge to 25% which effectively ensures that the risks of flash flooding is reduced. A grass covered green roofs with 20-40 cm thick layer of substance can hold between 10-15 cm of water. In Portland, Oregon, USA, green roofs were implemented successfully to prevent storm water from overwhelming the city's sewer system which tends to flood over during heavy storms and allowing untreated sewage to flow into the Willamette River.

(5) ***Higher Energy Savings***: In Tokyo, Japan, it was noted that a reduction of air temperature of between 0.11 to 0.84°C could be achieved if 50% of its rooftops were planted with roof gardens. Translated into real dollar value, the energy saving is estimated to be about $1.6 million per day in electricity bill. In Singapore, a DOE-2 energy simulation program was conducted on a hypothetical 5-story commercial building with a roof garden and the results showed significant savings on energy in terms of:

- ❑ About 15% of net annual energy savings can be achieved with roof garden.
- ❑ Up to 80% reduction in the peak cooling load can be achieved, resulting in the possible downsizing of air-conditioning systems and thereby savings in capital investment.
- ❑ A reduction of peak Roof Thermal Transfer Value (RTTV) of up to 80% making roof gardens as a viable substitute for roof thermal insulation.

(6) ***Preservation of habitat and wildlife***: Habitat loss, fragmentation and isolation, pollution and urban island effects have caused many species to become extinct or at the least threatened in urban areas. Green roofs can create healthy, functioning habitats in the midst of an urban landscape. It can not replace the ecological value of natural environments like rainforests or wetlands but statistics show that biodiversity has been recorded on Green Roofs worldwide. Urban regions have increasingly squeezed the variety or biodiversity, out of life. Green Roofs can be part of a larger plan to increase urban biodiversity. They can be used in two ways: as stepping stones for linking at grade habitats that are isolated or as an island habitat that remains remote and different from the at grade habitat Migratory birds and butterflies take especially benefit from green roofs because their habitat in urban areas is limited and fragmented. In Switzerland, birds have been seen using Green Roofs to forage for insects and seeds, for grooming, to search for nest material, for roosting and for singing. Studies have shown that for access to green space at Potts Point, Sydney, a warehouse with a retrofitted green roof simulating a wetland, provides a stepping stone habitat for migrating birds. In urban environments, roof space comprises up to 35% of the landscape, providing an excellent opportunity to encourage biodiversity whether in wildlife corridors, Brownfield sites or as migratory habitat. Even in densely populated areas, butterfly, beneficial insects, birds, bees can be attracted to green roofs. Studies in U.S. indicate that butterflies will fly high as 20 stories and birds up to 19.

(7) ***Sound Insulation***: Similar to heat waves, sound waves can be absorbed, reflected and deflected by vegetation on building. An Australia example, the Sydney Conservatory of Music, has covered music teaching spaces with a landscaped terrace

garden. Test have shown that a 12 cm layer of substrate can reduce sounds by 40 DB and 20 cm layer can reduce up to 50 DB. The substrate is capable of blocking lower frequencies while plants tend to block the higher frequencies.

3. Economic Benefits

(1) ***Building Insulation and Energy Efficiency***: Vegetation and soil provide a high level of temperature regulation for the occupants of the building through a complex interaction of methods. These include

- Trapping an air layer within the plants mass, cooling the building in summer and warming it in winter.
- The vegetation "shades" the actual skin of the building in summer. While in winter, the internal heat is either prevented from escaping, reflected or is absorbed.
- The vegetation acts as a buffer against wind movement along the surface of a building that can decrease the efficiency of a building by upto 50 per cent.

One of the most important tangible benefits that green roofs offer the private sector is reduced maintenance and cooling costs due to increased building insulation and energy efficiency. Research in Shanghai shows that room temperature reductions of 2°C can be expected with the addition of a green roof, at least on the top floor of any building. This also states that other studies have found room temperature reductions to be as much as 4-5°C. Similar supporting data in Singapore translates this into a net annual energy savings of around 15% (results applicable to a five-storey commercial building – the closest available model and climate equivalent to Hong Kong). Local studies have confirmed the findings, showing that roof surface temperatures in Hong Kong can be dramatically reduced by about 18° to 26°C during August 5 and by 10° to 15°C during sunny days in November and December 6.

(2) ***Green Building Assessment and Public Relations***: Green building assessment schemes exist in several countries (under the HK-BEAM system). Their purpose is to encourage environmentally sound building practice. There is considerable public relations value in projecting an environmentally conscious image for a building development or organization. Green roofs can contribute to the credit rating of developments assessed under such schemes and can be a highly visible way in which a development can draw attention to its environmental 'credentials', which may contribute to increase property value.

(3) ***Increased Roof Life***: Studies have demonstrated that green roofs, when properly constructed, can extend the life of a roof. Green roofs do this by reducing the total

run-off and by spreading the residual run-off over a longer period which can dramatically influence a city's infrastructure and maintenance cost.

(4) ***Urban Horticulture***: Several projects in Canada and USA have shown the viability of small-scale roof top garden projects. Annex Organics in Toronto grow certified organic produce on top of a downtown building. From roof garden measuring 100 square meters they grew approximately 250 kg of saleable tomatoes in 1997, grossing a profit of approximately $ 10.00 per square meter. Another outstanding example of sustainable produce is on third floor terrace of the Fairmont Waterfront Hotel in Vancour, B.C., and Canada. These gardens provide herbs and produce for the hotel's kitchen and saves approximately $ 25,000 to $ 30,000 CDN each year. The garden is functional and attractive with shaped garden beds, rivers rocks and quaint garden pathways providing a beautiful view to surrounding office buildings. Luke Garn ham of the Canadian Organization Green Roofs for Healthy Cities, writes, " Urban Horticulture provides a variety of benefits to a city, a reduction in the distance produce needs to be transported, increased food security, new employment, training and recreational opportunities, personal reconnection with ecological cycles and marketing of organic high value foods direct to consumers". Green Roofs for urban horticulture face the same issues as many other "Intensive" application, including weight and structural support constraints. Another issue facing the grower is the protection of valuable produce from the harsh environment found on top of taller buildings. Geoff Wilson of the Urban Agriculture Network, based in Queensland, cites that in their experience rooftop garden, strategically placed above commercial or shopping centers can play an important role in building a local economy and providing fresh produce. A 750 square meter Green Roof can produce fresh food worth up to $ 500,000 a year and employ about seven or eight people.

Technical Guidelines

Roof Conditions and Suitability for Greening

1. Function / Use

The primary functions a specific green roof is required to perform, will have a profound effect on its overall design. Each individual green roof project would differ according to its use, whether it was created for ecological, recreational, economic or aesthetic purposes.

2. Location

Location of the green roof plays an important role in the design process. The height of the roof, its orientation, its exposure to wind, sun and shading by surrounding buildings will have an impact. Views to and from the roof may also determine where certain elements are located for maximum effect.

3. Accessibility

Access to the green roof site is vital for the installation, ongoing maintenance and bringing up materials. If the green roof is designed for public use, then access and exiting of the roof should comply with relevant safety and security requirements through adequate elevators and staircases.

4. Climate

The general climate of place as hot, humid and under direct sun should be considered in the selection of plants that flourish in these conditions.

5. Wind, Wind Pressure and Uplift

Green Roofs and Green Walls are often exposed to high wind levels. Wind can generate positive and negative pressure forces which act on structures. Uplift forces vary with wind strength and direction, shape and height of the building and overall exposure. The factor of safety for vertical loads due to positive and negative wind pressure is considered 1.5 and the wind speed at which the force is measured to be considered as 45 m/s. Wind loads can damage anything built on top of the roof, either during construction or after work has been completed. The following areas on the roof are the most affected by the wind pressure uplift and require appropriate protection: Corners, where stress levels are very high, Edges, where stress levels are high and the central area, where stress levels are low. The depth of green roof layers at the corners and edges need to be increased or replaced by heavier materials such as gravel in order to secure borders and corner areas which are particularly at risk.

Structural and Bedding Stability

1. Structure and Design Loads

Introducing a green roof system to a building will place additional loading on the structure. If a green roof is part of the initial design of the building, additional loading can be accommodated easily for minor cost. However, if a green roof is installed on an existing building, the design will be limited to the carrying capacity of the existing roof, hence, the critical factor in deciding what type of greening to use and how to cultivate the site are the design loads of the system. Loads can be classified into two groups: Dead and Live Loads. Dead loads in a green roof or constant loads consist of super structural components such as; membranes, nonabsorptive plastic sheet component, metallic layers, fabrics, geo-composite drain layers, growth media, granular drainage media and plant materials. Live Loads in a green roof system excluding that of construction activities is defined as the weight of transient water that can be held temporarily in granular drainage materials layer and composite drainage layer i.e., the transient water held due to a continuous rainfall or irrigation until the drainage layer reaches saturation point. Architectural elements such as walkways, pavements, walls, water pools, play areas, pergolas, large scale bushes and trees, in addition to live loads of construction activities and wind loads are calculated separately. The Depth of media layers for extensive, simple intensive and intensive greening range between 2.5cm – 200cm. The weight of every layer in a green roof system is determined at the point of maximum water capacity including materials and stored water. Design Loads should not be less than Actual Loads which might be recommended by the manufacturer / supplier of the green roof system.

2. Roof Slope

Intensive green roofs are executed on slopes of up to 5 degrees while extensive green roofs on slopes of up to 30 degrees. The maximum slope for extensive green roofs which is commonly used is 45 degrees. As the steepness of the slope increases, the structure requires more protection against shear and slide forces where as controlled drainage and soil depth should be considered. Green roofs should not be applied to roofs with slopes greater than 45 degrees due to the extreme difficulty in managing soil moisture on a roof of such steepness. In such slopes the water will tend to run out of the system resulting in dry areas at the top and moist areas at the bottom. For Slopes of angles less than or equal to 20 degrees (36% gradient), anti-shear protection is not required while slopes at angles greater than 20 (36% gradient), anti-shear protection is needed. In cases where angles are greater than 30 degrees (58% gradient), separate static calculations are required to ensure that the action taken to prevent shearing doesn't create tension at the contact point with the waterproof membrane and the root barrier. To protect plants from erosion or sliding, the support coarse of the plants should be cultivated in a way which ensures that the structural soundness is not affected by water. It can be achieved through using fine to medium sized chipped gravel or through minimizing the amount of material which could get washed out. Whether a roof is green or not, a slope of 1% -2% should be applied on it to allow water to move smoothly towards the drain holes. This slope is usually maintained using a lightweight concrete (screed) layer between 50 – 70mm thicknesses.

3. Water Proofing

One of the most important components of the green roof system is the waterproofing roof membrane. For an existing building, the membrane should be carefully inspected to determine if it needs to be repaired or replaced before the installation.

4. Parapet Design and Protection against falls

Low rise buildings present fewer challenges in regard to positive or negative wind forces. A lower parapet design in low rise building may avoid potential air turbulence and help minimize uplift forces. High rise buildings are exposed to increase wind pressure resulting in higher positive and negative uplift forces. Increasing the parapet height can be an effective tool in moderating uplift forces. Strict safety standards and requirements for protection against falls have to be taken into account during planning, execution and utilization of the roof. Roof access staircases must be non slippery and equipped with handrails,

5. Fire Resistance

There is evidence suggesting that green roofs can help slow the spread of fire to and from the building through the roof, particularly where the growing medium is saturated. However, plants themselves, if dry, can present a fire hazard. The integration of "fire breaks" at regular intervals across the roof, at the roof perimeter and around all roof penetrations is recommended. Certain plants should be avoided from use on rooftops for fire safety reasons, plants that are highly flammable or that develop large root systems and thus high biomass or that are excessively thirsty.

Components of Green Roofs

Essentially roof gardens are build-up through the installation of a few key components to form the finished system. The components generally include the following layers: Waterproofing / root barrier layer, Protection Layer, Lightweight Fills and Thermal Insulating Layers, Drainage / water storage layer, Filter layer, Growing Medium / Substrate / Soils, Vegetation, Irrigation and Maintenance considerations.

1. Waterproofing / Root Barrier Layer

The primary function of a roof is to keep a building dry and, therefore, this layer serves as a crucial defense against the penetration of rainwater into the building, so waterproofing is arguably the most important pre-requisite of a green roof. Numerous waterproofing systems exist which include 1) bitumen/asphalt roofing felt or bituminized fabrics, 2) SBS modified bituminous membrane sheets set in

SEBS polymer modified bitumen and coal tar pitch/polyester built-up systems, 3) Fluid Applied Membranes, 4) Single-ply roof membranes and 5) Concrete admixture

For roof gardens, an additional requirement for the waterproofing membrane is that it should be root and rot resistance. The basic tenet of a successful roof garden should be that the installation must not compromise the waterproofing integrity of the roof itself. A common type of waterproofing membrane tested successfully for root and rot resistance by the German-based FLL and used widely in conjunction with roof gardens is the thermoplastic PVC membrane. In lightweight extensive green roofs root-barrier protection is often part of the waterproofing. A separate root protection barrier is needed if the waterproofing layer contains bitumen, asphalt or any other organic material because any penetration by roots also provides access for micro-organisms which can attack these organic oil-based materials. A root-barrier layer consisting mainly of chemically treated PE-based sheeting which incorporates a "root repellant" but it should be noted that they are not a waterproofing course and should not be used to replace the waterproofing layer. Intensive green roofs may need a far more robust root protection system capable of withstanding the penetration of tree roots. These are often thick hard plastic sheets or even metal sheets (usually copper) for exceptionally vigorous roots.

2. Protection Layer

Protection layers are usually a non-woven geo-textile that protects the waterproofing from mechanical damage. The application of protection layers is more critical if the drainage layer uses a more primitive granular mix.

3. Lightweight Fills and Thermal Insulating Layers

Lightweight fills are used primarily on Intensive Green Roofs to create differences in level. Another use may be to create sculptural contours to hide utilities or to liven up the flat surfaces commonly associated with extensive green roofs. Lightweight fills are usually made of some expanded material which has air in it. As such they are often very good thermal and acoustic insulators. In extensive green roofs they are sometimes used only for these reasons - as a thermal insulating layer. Lightweight fills include: 1) Extruded Polystyrene Sheets, 2) Polystyrene Cement 3) Autoclaved Aerated Concrete 4) Foamed Concrete and 5) Other Cements (perlite, vermiculite, and LECA).

4. Drainage / Water Storage Layer

The main purpose of the drainage layer is to drain excess water or underflow as rapidly as possible to prevent prolonged saturation Intensive roof garden that uses soil as a growing medium generally will require a drainage layer to drain off the rainwater as it percolates through it. This is because soil consolidates over time and rainwater takes longer to filter through and to prevent flooding, a drainage layer is essential. The drainage layer also helps to aerate the substrate providing internal airflow, below and through the substrate, the drainage layer also helps to reduce the vacuum which occurs due to wind uplift along the edges of an extensive green roof that has no parapet edge. There are three main types of drainage materials: 1) Granular Materials (gravel, stone chips, broken clay tiles, clinker, scoria (lava rock), pumice, expanded shale or LECA), 2) Porous mats (made from numerous materials including recycled materials such as clothing and car seats and behaving much like sponges) and 3) Lightweight plastic or polystyrene drainage modules (made of High Density Polyethylene or High Impact Polystyrene, some designs store reserve water allowing plants to derive additional moisture). There are many methods of installing a drainage layer such as the incorporation of a layer of gravel or sand. A proprietary drainage system consisting of perforated cells made from polypropylene is also commonly used in conjunction with intensive roof gardens. Example of a typical polypropylene-based cellular drainage system used for intensive roof gardens. Extensive roof garden uses a lightweight non-soil based growing medium which generally has a high percolation rate and thus requires a water-storage component to retain the rainwater for the irrigation of the plants in between rainfalls. A common type of proprietary water storage reservoir is made from molded expanded polystyrene and can store up to a maximum of 32 litres of water per square metres.

5. Filter Layer

To prevent clogging of the drainage or water storage layer, a geo-fleece is used to filter out the silt from the planting medium above. For the extensive roof garden system, the filter also acts as a vehicle for the transportation of the stored rainwater to the plants through capillary action. The filter layer prevents fine material being washed down into the drainage layer. Non-woven filter layers are ideal for most circumstances (having superior filtration) though woven versions may be considered for heavy duty applications.

6. Growing Medium / Substrate / Soils

The general requirements of all growing media are the same, namely: 1) efficient moisture retention 2) excess water easily drained, 3) well aerated 4) able to absorb and supply nutrients, 5) retains its volume over time 6) provides adequate anchorage for plants. Additional requirements important for green roofs include: 1) being light weight 2) having adequate water retention capacity 3) being inert in a subtropical climate and 4) having fire resistant properties. Lightweight growing media may be created using natural, artificial or waste minerals. Lava (scoria) and pumice, perlite, vermiculite, light expanded clay aggregate (LECA), rockwool and numerous other materials are typically used. As intensive roof garden needs to sustain a larger variety of plant growths including ornamental shrubs and trees, a heavy layer of soil is used as the planting medium. The recommended minimum thickness of soil for turfing is about 40 cm while for shrubs and trees ranges between 1 to 1.5 m. Extensive roof garden because of their light-weight nature uses a mixture of volcanic stones and pumice and generally is able to sustain selected plant growth with a thickness of between 8 to 12 cm. Lightweight growing medium used for extensive roof gardens consisting mainly of volcanic stones and pumice.

7. Vegetation

While intensive roof garden generally uses plants and vegetation associated with landscaping works, extensive garden on the other hand uses very selective types of plants which are dry-resistant or succulent types.

8. Irrigation

There are three principal ways of irrigating green roofs:

1) **Manual Hose Irrigation** – Typically a 20m hose pipe connected to water points every 40 meters.

2) **Fully Automatic Irrigation Systems** - A programmed system that irrigates at set times, running continuously with minimal supervision.

3) **Semi-Automatic Irrigation Systems** - A programmed system with various manual override options that are activated as needs require. Manual watering (with hose) is reliable, robust and tried-and-tested. Its main draw-back is its high lab our costs. Automatic irrigation systems are controlled (usually electrically) to irrigate areas of planting without human intervention. They are able to deliver precise water quantities at very specific times. For automated irrigation systems there are two major dispersal categories:

Sprinkler Head Systems which are more robust but not as accurate as other dispersal systems with water being lost due to wind and evaporation (a constraint on many green roofs).

Drip Irrigation Systems deliver a more efficient use of water but are more expensive and are prone to deterioration under UV light (a constraint often associated with many green roofs).

9. Maintenance considerations

Extensive green roofs have been developed specifically to be low-maintenance. Intensive green roofs, on the other hand are built for human usage and have maintenance considerations directly comparable to the maintenance of amenity planting at ground level locations. Maintenance requirements of green roofs are determined by many factors – height, micro-climate, soil types, soil depth, irrigation, species used and access. Access is most often the most crucial factor influencing maintenance costs. Maintenance operations include: Waterproof Inspections, Drainage Inspections, Removal of Litter, Electricity and Lighting, Plant Health Inspections, Replacement planting, Irrigation, Pruning, Mowing and Grass Cutting, Fertilizing , Diseases and Pests Control and Weeding.

Barriers against development of roof garden

1. Economic

- Strengthening of structure may be required.
- Additional costs can include the new roof components and the cost of a crane to install.
- Accessible roofs must have an additional elevator stop and second stair. This is a code requirement.
- Additional maintenance may be required, though this will vary greatly depending on the design. A planted roof requires more maintenance than a gravel roof.

2. Safety Issues

- Accessible roofs must have full perimeter protection.
- Adequate protection must be provided for maintenance staff (meet health and safety requirements).

3. Maintenance Issues

- If leaks do occur, they are more difficult to trace.
- When roofing components need replacement, a more complicated process is likely: plant material and growing medium need to be removed and replaced.
- Accessible roofs need on-going care. The more complex the planting scheme, the more care is required, e.g., pruning.

4. Education

- Training of users may be required e.g., a natural garden is more sustainable than lawn; methods of organic food production.
- Training of maintenance staff may be required e.g., re-composting and mulching; promoting urban wildlife.

5. Permits

- Fire protection of dry plant material may need negotiating with local officials.
- Access and egress on existing roofs may mean adding a stair or getting a variance.
- Accessibility for disabled persons on existing roofs may be difficult to achieve.

Plants used in roof gardening

- **Foliage plants**: Asparagus, coleus, croton, dieffenbachia,
- **Flowering plants:** Seasonal flowers like antirrhinum, phlox, verbena, zinnia and perennial flowers like carnation, chrysanthemum, dahlia, rose and tuberose.
- **Shrubs**: Acalypha, bougainvillea, camellia, china rose, geranium, jasmine and lantana.
- **Trees**: Ashoka tree, bottle brush, chrismis tree and silk cotton tree.
- **Climbers**: Antigonon, begnonia, gloriosa, ipomea and passiflora.
- **Cactii and succulents**: *Sedum* spp., Agaves and aloe.
- **Fruits**: Gooseberry, strawberry, peach, pear, pineapple and pomegranate.
- **Vegetables**: Brinjal, broccoli, chillies, lettuce and tomato.

LATHYRUS ODORATUS

A LAWN WITH WINTER ANNUALS

CACTUS

MARIGOLD IN FLOWERING

LOTUS IN FLOWERING

WINTER ANNUALS IN FLOWERI

Centaurea cyanus (Sweet Corn)

Malva sylvestris (Malva)

Papaver rhoes (Corn poppy)

Antirrhinum majus (Dog flower)

Viola cornuta (Pansy)

Salvia officinalis (Salvia)

Dianthus chinensis (Chinese pink)

Dimorphothica sinuata (Cape daisy)

Dahlia hybrida

Mesembryanthemum crinifolium (Ice plant)

Petunia nana compacta (Petunia)

Different varieties of Crysanthemum

Different type of Crysanthemum

Different varieties of *Coleus*

BOUGAINVILLEA

BOUGAINVILLEA

TUBEROSE DOUBLE IN FLOWERING

BOUGAINVILLEA

REFERENCES CITED

Akbari H., Rosenfeld A. and Taha H. (1990). Summer Heat Islands, Urban Trees, and White Surfaces. *ASHRE* Trans. American Society of Heating, Refrigeration and Air Conditioning Engineers, 96(1). Atlanta, Georgia.

Bailey, L. H. 1947. The Nursery Manual. The Macmillan Company, New York.

Bailey, L. H. 1951. Manual of Cultivated Plants. The Macmillan Company, New York.

Bailey, L. H. 1963. The Standard Cyclopaedia of Horticulture. The Macmillan Company, New York.

Balfour, A. P. 1959. Annual and Biennial F.lowers. Penguin Books, England.

Basu, R. N., Bose, T. K., Roy, B. N. and Mukhopadhyay, A. 1969. Auxin synergists in rooting of cuttings. *Physiologia Plantarum*, 22: 649-652.

Benjamin, L. 1973. The love of indoor plants. Octopus Books limited, London.

Bhadri, B., Singh, B. and Desai, B. L. 1962. Water plants. Indian council of Agricultural Research, New Delhi.

Bose, T. K. and Mukherjee, D. 1972. Gardening in India. Oxford and IBH Publishing Co., Calcutta, India.

Britton, N. L. and Rose, J. N. 1963. The Cactaceae. Dover Publications Inc., New York.

Chittenden, F. J. and Synge, P. M. 1956. The Royal Horticultural Society Dictionary of Gardening. Oxford, Great Britain.

Conder, J. 1964. Landscape Gardening in Japan. Dover Publications Incorporations, New York.

Cooke, T. 1905. The Flora of Presidency of Bombay, Volume 2. Taylor and Francis, London.

Cowen, D. V. 1965. Flowering Trees and Shrubs in India. Thacker and Company Limited, Bombay.

Desai, B. L. Planning and planting designs of home gardens. Indian Council of Agricultural Research, New Delhi. 116p.

Field, X. 1965. Window Box Gardening. Pan Books Limited, London.

Foster, G. F. 1964. The Gardener's Fern Book. D. Van Nostrand Company Incorporation, Princeton, New Jersey.

Futehally, L. 1978. Gardens. National Book Trust, India, New Delhi.

Gopalaswamiengar, K. S. 1970. Complete Gardening in India. G. Kasturi Rangan, Bangalore, India.

Grindal, E. W. 1963. Everyday Gardening in India. D. B. Taraporevala Sons and Corporation Private Limited, Bombay.

Hadfield, Miles. 1962. Gardens. Weidenfeld and Nicolson, London.

Harris, C. C. 1973. House Plant and Indoor Gardening. Octopus Books Ltd., London.

Hawkes, A. D. 1961. Orchids: Their Botany and Culture. Peter owen Ltd., London.

Hawkes, A. D. 1965. Encyclopaedia of Cultivated Orchids. Faber and Faber Ltd., London.

Heritage, B. 1973. The Lotus Book of Water Gardening. The Hamlyn Publishing Group Ltd., London, New York, Sydney, Toronto.

Jacobsen, H. 1959. Succulent Plants. Ernest Benn Ltd., London.

Jindal, S. L. 1968. Ornamental Bulbous Plants. Indian Council of Agriculture Research, New Delhi.

Johnsonn, C.2002. I See Green; NSW Government Architect Magazine Article; October 26, 18.

Johnston, J. and Newton, J. 1996. Building Green: A Guide for Using Plants on Roofs, Walls and Pavements. London .The London Ecology Unit.

Kachroo, P. 1968. Handbook of Rock Gardening on the Hills. Indian Council of Agriculture Research, New Delhi.

Kachroo, P. 1975. Introduction to Gardening. Indian Council of Agriculture Research, New Delhi.

Leeburn, M. E. 1963. Garden Lilies. W. H. and L. Collingridge Ltd., London.

Liu, K. and Baskaran, B. 2003. Thermal Performance of ROOF through Field Evaluation, Proceedings of *Greening Rooftops for Sustainable Communities*, Chicago.

Liu, K., 2009. Energy Efficiency and Environmental Benefits of Rooftop Gardens. National Research Council Canada.

McCann, C. 1966. 100 Beautiful Trees of India. D. B. Taraporevala Sons and Co. Pvt. Ltd., Bombay.

McQuown, F. R. 1963. Plant Breeding for Gardeners. W. H. and L. Collingridge Ltd., London.

Michael and Thomas R. 2003. Green Roofs for sustainable cities. Civil Engneering and design.

Minke, G. and Witter, G. 1982, Haeruser mit Gruenem Pelz, Ein Handbuch zur Hausbegruenung, Verlag Dieter Fricke GmbH, Frankfurt.

Mukherjee, S. K. 2002. Orchids. Indian Council of Agricultural Research, New Delhi, India. 32p.

Murashige, T. 1974. Plant Propagation through tissue cultures. *Annual Review of Plant Physiology*, 25: 135-166.

NParks, NUS. 2002. Handbook on Skyrise Greening in Singapore (1st edition). Singapore.

Osmundson T. 1999. "Roof gardens through history", Roof gardens: history, design, and construction, W. W. Norton & Company, pp 112–115.

Pal, B. P. 1960. Beautiful Climbers of India. Indian Council of Agricultural Research, New Delhi, India.

Randhawa, G. S. 1973. Ornamental Horticulture in India. Today and Tomorrows Printers and Publishers, New Delhi.

Randhawa, G. S. and Mukhopadhyay, A. 1986. Floriculture in India. Allied Publishers Private Limited, New Delhi. 631p.

Randhawa, M. S. 1965. Flowering Trees. National Book Trust of India, New Delhi.

Randhawa, M. S. 1976. Gardens Through Ages. The macmillan Co. of India Ltd.

Santapau, H. 1966. Common Trees. Natioal Book Trust of India, New Delhi.

Scott, S. H. 1958. The Observers Book of Cacti and Other Succulents. Fredrick Warne and Co. Ltd., London.

Severn Gillian, E. 1967. Miniature Trees in the Japanese Style. Faber and Faber Ltd., London.

Stifter, R.1997. Greenery on the Roof: a Futuristic, Ecological Building Method, Hundertwasser, F., For a More Human Architecture in Harmony with Nature, Hundertwasser Architecture, Benedikt Taschen Berlag, GmbH, Cologne, p156-158.

Stutte, C. A. 1977. Plant Growth Regulators. American Chemical Society, Washington D. C.

Swarup, V. 1967. Garden Flowers. National Book Trust, New Delhi.

Swarup, V. 1984. Export of Ornamentals: Problems and Prospects. Indian Horticulture, 29 (2): 53-56.

Towmshend, D. 2007. Study on Green Roof application in Hong Kong. Architectural Services Limited. Urbis Limited.

Trivedi, D. 1975. Ikebana. Vikash Publishing House, Delhi.

Ulrich, R.S., 1984. "View from a Window May Influence Recovery from Surgery", Science.224, p 420-21.

Underwood, C. J. 1971. The Time Life Encyclopaedia of Gardening "Bulbs". Time Life Books, New York.

Went, F. W. and Thimann, K. V. 1937. Phytohormopnes. The Mcmillan Co., New York.

Wilson, G. 1999. An Urban Rooftop Integrated Microfarm for Mt Gravatt's Commercial Buildings; The Urban Agriculture Network- Westron Pacific Office.

Wong, N. 2003. Environmental benefits of Green Roofs. *Building and Environment*, 38 (3): 499-509.

GLOSSARY

Aberrant: Different from the normal.

Abnormal: Different from the usual or prevailing form or structure.

Abortion: Failure of development or imperfect development.

Abortive: Imperfectly developed or underdeveloped.

Abruptly pinnate: Pinnate but without terminal leaflet.

Abscission: The shedding of some part or structure as a leaf or flower at its base that break apart readily.

Accessory: Additional beyond the normal; extra.

Accrescent: Increasing in size after flowering, enlarging with age.

Aceriform : Similar to the leaf of a maple.

Acerose: Needlelike.

Achene: A dry one seeded fruit with a firm close fitting wall which does not open by any regular dehiscence.

Achlamydeous: Having neither calyx or corolla.

Acorn: The leathery fruit of an oak, containing a single large seed and enclosed basally in a cup formed from bracts.

Actinomorphic: Radially symmetrical, that is, capable of division by straight boundaries into three or more similar sections.

Active bud: A growing bud.

Aculeate: Covered with prickles.

Acuminate: With a long, tapering point set off rather abruptly from the main body.

Acute: With a pointed end forming an acute angle, that is, less than a right angle.

Adaxial: On the side towards the axis, as for example, the upper side of a leaf.

Adherent: Grown fast to a structure of a different bind, as for example, a stamen grown fast to a petal.

Adnation : Fusion with or attachment to another structure from the beginning of development.

Adventitious: A structure occurring in an unusual position as, for example, an adventitious root formed from a stem or a leaf.

Adventitious bud: A bud produced in a unusual or unexpected place, as for example near the point of injury of a stem or on leaf or a root.

Adventitious roots: Are those roots that arise from the aerial plant parts, underground stem or from old roots.

Adventitious shoots: Are those shoots that develop on roots or inter-nodally on stems.

Adventive: Said of an introduced plant beginning to spread into a new locality or region.

Aerial root: Roots exposed to the air, as those of tropical plants growing on the trees.

Aestival: Of the summer.

Aestivation: Arrangement of the young flower parts in the bud.

Agglomerate: Crowded into a dense cluster but not joined synonymus aggregate.

Alate : With a wing.

Alternate: With a single structure of each bind occurring at each level of the axis appearing to alternate on opposite sides of the axis but actually in a spiral arrangement.

Ament: A soft, usually scaly spike of small, apetalous, unisexual flowers, this usually falling as a single unit.

Amentiferous: With the flowers in aments i.e., catkins.

Amorphous: With no definite form.

Amplexicaul: Clasping the stem, that is, the base nearly surrounding it.

Ampliate: enlarged.

Anastomosing: Joining each other and forming a network, the term being applied to veins as the veins of the leaf.

Ancipital: Two edged.

Androecium: The male reproductive organs; in the flowering plants the stamens- a collective term for all those within a flower.

Androgynous: A term applied to an inflorescence which includes both staminate and pistillate flowers, the staminate ones being apical, the pistillate basal.

Androphore: A stalk or other supporting structure under stamens raised above their normal position in the flower.

Anemorphilous: With the pollen carried by wind.

Annual: A plant completing its life cycle in a year or less.

Annular: Ring like.

Annulus: A ring. In the ferns a crest like or other special structure on the sporangium.

Anther: The portion of the stamen which produces pollen.

Anther tube: A tube formed by coalescent anthers, as in the sunflower family.

Antheridium: A structure producing antherozoids, that is male gametes or sex cells.

Antherozoid: A male gamete (sex) cell of a plant.

Anthesis: The time when the flower expands and opens or the process of expansion and opening.

Anthocyanin: Any of a common class of pigments having colours ranging from labender to purple. These pigments are affected by the acidity or alkalinity of the cell sap, and they change colour in approximately the same way as litmus paper, tending towards red in an acid medium and blue in a basic medium. These pigments are water soluble and not associated with plastids.

Antipodal cells: Three cells at the end of the flowering plant megagametophyte opposite the egg.

Antrorse: Directed upward or forward.

Apetalous: Without petals.

Aphyllous: Without leaves.

Apical: Of the apex.

Apical placenta: A placenta at the distal (apical) end of the ovary.

Apiculate: Terminated by an abrupt, short, flexible point.

Apiculation: An abrupt, short, flexible point.

Apocarpous: With the carpels separate.

Apogamous: Developed without the joining of gametes, that is asexually.

Apomixes: In some species the embryo is not produced as a result of meiosis and fertilization, but form a cell in the embryo sac or surrounding nucellus which does not undergo meiosis but develops to form a zygote of same genetic makeup as the female parent.

Aquatic: Growing in water.

Arboreous: Of tree like form, that is with a main woody trunk.

Arborescent: Of large size and more or less tree like but without the clear distinction of a single trunk.

Archegonium: A flask shaped organ containing an egg, that is, female gamete or sex cell.

Arcuate: Forming a moderate curve or arc.

Areolate: Divided into small, marked-off spaces (Reticulate).

Areole: Diminutive of area; a small, clearly marked space. The term is used most frequently in reference to the small, special spine-bearing areas on the stem of a cactus.

Aristate: with a stiff bristle.

Articulate: with conspicuous segments or joints.

Artificial system: A system made up according to predetermined supposedly important characters.

Ascending: Arising at an oblique angle.

Aseptic: Absence of fungi, bacteria, viruses, mycoplasmas, or other microorganisms in cultures.

Asperous: Rough.

Assurgent: Ascending.

Altenuate: With a long, tapering point, this usually set off rather abruptly from the main body of the object (eg. a leaf blade).

Auricle: An appendage shaped like the lobe of a human ear.

Auriculate: Having an artricle.

Autogamy: When a flower is fertilized by its own pollen.

Awl-shaped: With a narrow flattened body tapering very gradually upward into a point (subulate).

Awn: A long stout or stiff bristle.

Awned: With an awn.

Axenic: Totally free from association with other organisms.

Axil: The adaxial angle between two organs, particularly the angle between the upper side of a leaf and the stem.

Axile: On the axis, as for example, said of placentae at or near the centre of an ovary.

Axillary: In the axil.

Axillary bud: A bud in a leaf axil.

Axillary flower: A flower in the axil of a leaf or a bract.

Auxin: Auxin is a generic term for compounds characterized by their capacity to induce elongation in shoot cells. They resemble indole-3-acetic acid in physiological action. Auxin may, and generally do, affect other processes besides elongation, but elongation is considered critical. Auxins are generally acids with an unsaturated cyclic nucleus or their derivatives.

Baccate: Berry like, that is, flushy or pulply.

Banner: The upper and usually largest petal in the papilionaceous corolla of a plant of the pea family. Known also as a standard or a vexillum.

Barbed: With a rigid barb like the barb of a fish hook.

Barbellate: Diminutive of barbed (Still smaller, barbellulate).

Barbulate: With a beared of fine hairs.

Bars of sanio: Special thickening on the walls of some xylem cells.

Basal leaves: Leaves at the base of an herbaceous plant arising from several nodes separated by exceedingly short internodes occurring at about ground level.

Basal placenta: A placenta at the basal end of the ovary.

Basifixed: Attached at the base.

Beaked: Ending in a firm elongated slender structure.

Beared: With long or stiff hairs.

Bidentate: With two teeth.

Biennial: Completing the life cycle in two years. Biennial plants usually produce only basal leaves above the ground the first year and both basal leaves and flowering stems the second.

Bifid: Forked, that is, ending in two parts.

Bilabiate: Two lipped. A bilabiate corolla has petals in two sets commonly with two in the upper and three in the lower.

Bilateral: Two sided.

Bilaterally symmetrical: Capable of division into only two similar sections, which are mirror images of each other.

Bilocular: With two cavities, as an ovary with two seed chambers.

Bipinnate: Pinnate and the primary leaflets again pinnate.

Bipinnatified: Pinnatified with the primary divisions again pinnatified.

Bisexual: With both sexes represented in the same individual or organ e.g., with stamens and pistils in the same flower.

Blade: The broad, usually flat part of a leaf.

Bloom: A usually waxy; whitish or bluish powder covering the surface of a leaf, stem, fruit or other organ.

Blossom end: The end of an inferior ovary and the surrounding floral cup which supports the flower parts or at fruiting time the calyx and remains of other flower parts.

Boss: A protrusion, as for example, a protuberance near the centre of the apophysis of a scale of a gymnosperm cone.

Bract: A leaf subtending a reproductive structure, such as a flower or a cluster of flowers or an ovuliferous scale. Usually the leaf is specialized and at least somewhat dissimilar to the foliage leaves.

Bracteate: With bracts.

Bracteolate: With bractlets.

Bracteole: Diminutive of bract, a mere scale.

Bractlet: A minor bract.

Branchlet: A small branch, that is one of the smallest degree.

Branch primordium: The lump of tissue which develops into a young branch.

Bristle: A stiff hair.

Bryophyta: The mosses, liverworts and anthocerotae.

Bud: A growing structure at the Tip of the stem or a branch, with the enclosing scale leaves or immature leaves; a young flower which has not yet opened. There are vegetative buds and flower buds, as described in the definition above.

Bulb: An underground bud covered by fleshy scales, the coating formed from the bases of leaves.

Bulbiferous: With bulbs.

Bulbils: A small bulb. The word is applied to bulb like structures produced on the stems, usually in the axils of leaves or sometimes in the places where flowers ordinarily occur.

Bulblets: A small underground bulb.

Bulbous: Bulblike.

Bullate: Blistered or puckered.

Caducous: Falling very early. In the poppy family the caduceus sepals fall away when the flower open.

Caespitose: Growing in tufts or mats.

Calcarate: With a spur.

Callosity: A thickened hard structure.

Callous: With the texture of a callus.

Callus: Production of new unspecializing cell from a part of the plant, growing as a result of injury or wounding.

Calyculate: With small bracts in a series below the flower, these resembling à calyx.

Calyptra: A cap, cover or lid.

Calyx: A cup; the sepals of a flower, the outermost series of flower parts. Each sepal has the same number of vascular traces as a leaf of the species. If there is doubt it may be distinguished by this character cf. petal.

Calyx tube: A tube formed from the lower portions of the sepals. The term has been used loosely for (a) a floral cup or floral tube regardless of its origin, (b) a floral cup or tube formed by coalescence and adnation of the bases of the sepals, petals and stamens, (c) a perianth tube of the type in the monocotyledons formed by edge to edge adnation of the adjacent sepals and petals together with the bases of the stamens (d) and the portion of a floral cup or tube above the area of adnation to an inferior ovary.

Cambium: A group of cells which possess the power of active growth and division and which is responsible for the production of old tissues in matured organs.

Campanulate: Bell shaped, that is, the shape of an inverted church bell i.e., rounded at the attachment and with a broad flaring rim.

Campylotropous: Descriptive of an ovule which curves in such a way that the micropyle is near the funiculus or stalk but the side of the ovule is not adnate to the funiculus.

Canaliculated: With lengthwise furrows or channels.

Cancellate: Appearing to be a lattice work.

Canescent: Grayish-white or hoary, densely covered with white or gray fine hairs, these usually short.

Capillary: Like an elongated delicate hair or thread.

Capitate: In a dense cluster or head.

Carina: A keel, literally like the keel of a boat. Sometimes said of a structure which simply is folded and creased and without a projecting keel on the crease.

Carpel: A specialized leaf which forms either all or part of a pistil.

Cartilaginous: With the texture of cartilage that is tough and firm but somewhat flexible.

Catkin: A soft, usually scaly spike or raceme of small apetalous unisexual flowers, the inflorescence usually falling as a single unit.

Caudate: With a talelike structures.

Caudex: A largely underground stem base which persists from year to year and each season produces leaves and flowering stem of short duration.

Caulescent: Having a well developed stem above ground as opposed to having only what appears to be the stalk of the individual flower or cluster of flowers.

Cell: The structural and functional unit of living organisms.

Cell culture: This term is used to denote the growing of cells in vitro including the culture of single cells. In cell cultures, the cell are no longer organized into tissues.

Centrifugal: Developing first at the centre and then gradually toward the outside.

Centripetal: Developing first at the outside and the gradually towards the centre.

Certified seed: Progeny of the registered seed that is produced in the largest volume and sold to the crop producers.

Chaff: Dry, membranous scales or bracts, that is, similar to the chaff which comes from a thrashing machine.

Chamber: A room. Applied to the cavities of an anther or an ovary.

Channeled: With lengthwise grooves, the grooves usually deep.

Chasmogamy: Pollination only after the opening of the flower.

Chimeras: When a mutation occurs within a single cell of a clone it initially produces an "islands" of mutant cells within a growing point of a stem. If successful, the plant then becomes a mixture of two different genotypes. This structural arrangement is known as a chimera.

Chlorophyll: The green colouring of most plants. A substance which aids in making the energy of light available to photosynthesis.

Chloroplast: Literally a green body, actually a solid body with chlorophyll in its outer part.

Chlorosis: A diseased condition shown by loss of green colour.

Choripetalous: With the petals separate or atleast with some of them separate from others.

Cilia: Hairs along the margin of a structure, placed like the eye-lashes on a human eyelid.

Ciliate: With cilia along the margin.

Cinereous: The colour of ashes.

Circinate: Coiled at the tip, as the young coiled leaf of a fern which uncoils gradually as it develops.

Circumscissile: Opening by a horizontal circular line, the top coming off like a lid.

Class: The next taxon below division; a group of related orders or sometimes a single order.

Clavate: Gradually enlarged upward after the manner of a base-ball bat or the traditional giants club, that is, either tapering gradually upward or with an enlarged knob at the summit.

Clavellate: Diminutive of clavate.

Claw: The narrow stalk at the base of a petal. This resembling the petiole of a leaf.

Cleft: Indented about half way or little more than half way to the base or to the midrib.

Cleistogamy: Self-pollination without the flower opening.

Cleistogamous: Self-fertilized in the bud stage or atleast without opening.

Climbing: Supported by clinging (Scandent).

Clonal propagation: A sexual reproduction of plants that are considered to be genetically uniform and originated from a single individual or explant.

Clone: Genetically uniform material derived from a single individual and propagated exclusively by vegetative means as cuttings, graftage or division.

Coalescence: The union of similar parts as for example, the petals of a flower.

Coherent: Grown fast together.

Colonial: In colonies. For the angiosperms used, primarily in reference to plants occurring in clumps connected by rhizomes.

Coloure: The failure of blossoms to set, resulting in a pre-matured drop.

Column: A slender aggregation of coalescent stamen. Filaments, as in some members of the mallow family.

Coma: A tuft of hairs on the end of a seed.

Commissure: The surface along which two or more locules are joined to each other.

Comose: With a coma.

Compatible: Ability of pollen to develop in the styles rapidly enough to reach the ovule in time to effect fertilization.

Compatibility: Of sex cells, the ability to unite and form a fertilized egg that can grow to maturity.

Complete flower: A flower with all the four usual series that is sepals, petals stamen and pistils.

Compound leaf: It is composed of two or more leaflets, a compound pistil is composed of two or more coalescent carpels.

Conduplicate: Folded together lengthwise.

Cone: A reproductive structure composed of an axis bearing sporophylls or other seed or pollen bearing structures.

Conglomerate: Densely aggregated; a cluster or a heap.

Coniferous: Cone bearing.

Conjugate: Lying together in pairs.

Connate: Joined from the beginning of development.

Connate perfoliate: Both connate and perfoliate.

Connective: The middle part of an anther connecting the two pollen sacs or two pairs of pollen sacs.

Connivent: Standing together. Stamens with their tips ending against each other are connivent.

Contorted: Twisted out of the usual form. Petals may be contorted in the bud.

Convolute: Rolled up lengthwise. Petals may be convolute in the bud.

Cordate: Of a conventional heart-shape, the length greater than the width, the petiole attached in the basal sinus; applied also to the basal indentation of a leaf or other structures.

Coriaceous: Leathery.

Corm: A bulblike structure formed by enargement of the stem base. It is sometime coated with one or more membranous layers.

Corneous: Horny.

Corolla: The petals of a flower, that is, the inner series (or several series) of the parianth. Each petal has usually a single vascular trace as does a stamen.

Corolla division: A division is longer than a lobe or part.

Corolla lobe: A lobe is longer then the tooth. Lobes may be applied in a broad sense to cover lobes, parts or divisions.

Corolla teeth: The separate tips of the individual petals of a sympetalous corolla.

Corolla tube: The hollow cylinder formed by coalescence of petals.

Corona: A small crown, the term being applied to special appendages of the corolla. These sometimes form a tube.

Coroniform: Shaped like a crown.

Corrugated: With many small folds or wrinkles.

Cortex: The layers of living cells outside the central stele but inside the outermost single layer of cells of a stem or a root.

Corymb: A flat topped cluster of flowers; fundamentally like a raceme but with the pedicels of the lower flowers longer and the pedicels of the upper flowers gradually shorter.

Corymbiform: In the form of a corymb.

Corymbose: Arranged in corymbs.

Costa: A rib or a promiment nerve.

Costate: Ribbed lengthwise.

Cotyledons: One of the first leaves developed in the embryo in the seed at the joining point of the hypocotyls and the epicotyl. Often food materials are stored in them.

Creeping: The stem growing along the ground and producing adventitious roots.

Crenate: With rounded teeth projecting at right angles to the edge of the leaves.

Crenulate: Diminutive of crenate.

Crested: With a crest, that is a projection at a prominent position such as the apex or the midrib of an organ.

Crisped: Ruffled, that is with the same bind of winding as in sinuate, but in the vertical plane instead of the horizontal.

Cross-pollination: Transfer of pollen grain from a flower of one variety to a flower of another variety.

Cross-compatible: The pollen of one variety 'A' is capable of functioning in the styles and fertilizing the ovules of variety 'B' (variety 'B', however, may not be cross-compatible with 'A').

Cross-incompatible: Variety 'A' produces functional sex cells, but its pollen tube grows too slowly in the styles of variety 'B' to effect fertilization. Variety 'A' may, however, serve as an effective pollinizer for some other varieties. (Variety 'B' mar serve as an effective pollinizer for variety 'A').

Cross-fertile: One variety 'A' is used as a pollinizer for another variety 'B' and 'B' produces fruit with viable seed.

Cross-fruitful: One variety 'A' is used as a pollinizer for another variety 'B' and 'B' produces a commercial crop.

Cross-pollination: The transfer of pollen from the anthers of a flower of one variety to the stigma of a flower of a different variety.

Cross-unfruitful: One variety 'A' is used as a pollinizer for another variety 'B' and 'B' fails to produce a commercial crop.

Cross-sterile: One variety 'A' is used as a pollinizer for another variety 'B' and 'B' fails to produce fruit with viable seed.

Cruciate, cruciform: Cross like.

Crustaceous: Hard and brittle in texture.

Cryptogames: An old term applied to the thallophytes, bryophytes and the pteridophytes, that is the plants which regularly reproduce with out formation of seeds.

Cucullate: Hood shaped

Culum: The hallow stem of a grass, the term being applied some times to ridges also.

Cuneate, cuneiform: Wedge shaped; essentially a narrow isosceles triangle with the distal corners rounded off. The petiole of a cuneate leaf is attached at the sharp angle.

Cupule: A little cup.

Cuspidate: With a sharp, firm point at the tip, as applied to leaves, the term indicates a point of firmer texture than the rest of the blade.

Cuticle: The waxy, more or less waterproof coating secreted by the cells of the epidermis of a leaf, stem or flower parts.

Cyathiform: Cup shaped.

Cyathium: A cuplike involucre enclosing flowers.

Cycle: A circle. Leaves or flower parts arranged in a single series at a single node or in a cycle.

Cyclic: Arranged in a cycle.

Cylindroidal: In approximately the shape of a cylinder.

Cyme: A broad, more or less flat-topped cluster of flowers.

Cymose: With cyme like cluster of flowers.

Cymule: Diminutive of cyme.

Cypsela: An achene which is attached to the enclosing floral cup or tube, that is, an achene formed from an inferior ovary.

Cytology: The study of cell. Often particular emphasis is placed upon the chromosomes.

Cytoplasm: The living substance outside the nucleus and inside the enclosing membrane.

Deciduous: Falling off at the end of each growing season.

Deciduous tree: Tree which shed their leaves during winter months to enable them to stand cold injury.

Declinate: Bending or curving downward or forward.

Declined: Bending over in one direction.

Decompound: More than one compound.

Decombent: Reclining except at the apex.

Decurrent: Leaf bases which continue along the stem as wings or lines.

Decussate: In opposite pairs with the alternate pairs projecting at right angles to each other.

Deflexed: Abruptly bent or turned downward.

Dehisce: The split open along definite lines.

Dehiscence: The process of splitting open at maturity.

Dehiscent: Splitting open along definite lines.

Deltoid: Of the shape of the greek letter delta, that is, an equilateral triangle, the attachment being in the middle of one side.

Dentate: With angular teeth projecting at right angles to the edge of the structure.

Denticulate: Diminutive of dentate.

Depauperate: Stunted, that is, very small.

Depressed: Flattened from above as if pushed downward.

Determinate: With a definite predetermined number of structures.

Diadelphous: In two brotherhoods, the term being applied to stamens coalescent in two sets.

Diandrous: With two stamens.

Dichasium: A cyme with two axis running in opposite directions, that is, the type of cyme formed in plants with opposite branching in the inflorescence.

Dichlamydeous: With both calyx and corolla.

Dichogamy: Insuring cross-pollination by the sexes being developed at different times.

Dichotomous: Forking, with two usually equal branches at each point of forking.

Dicotyledonous: With two cotyledons.

Dicliny: Male and female organ separate and in different flowers.

Didymous: Twin like, that is, occurring in pairs.

Didynamous: In two pairs, the pairs not being of the same length. The term is applied to stamen.

Diffuse: Spreading widely and diffusely in all directions.

Digitate: Resembling the fingers of a human hand, that is, with several similar structures arising at a common point.

Digynous: With two pistils.

Dimerous: With two members; the flower parts in two.

Dimidiate: With the appearance of being only half a structure.

Dimorphous: With two forms.

Dioecious: Unisexual, the male and female elements in different individuals.

Diploid: With 2n chromosomes per cell.

Diplostemonous: The stamens in two series, those of outer series alternating with the petals.

Dipterous: With two wings.

Disc, disk: In the compositae, the central portion of the compound receptacle bearing the disc flowers.

Disc flowers: One of the flowers with tubular corollas.

Disciform: Circular and flattened like disc.

Discoid: Resembling a disc.

Discrete: Separate.

Dissected: Divided into narrow segments.

Dissepiment: A portion dividing an ovary or a fruit into chambers.

Distichous: In two vertical series.

Distinct: Separate.

Diurnal: Occuring in the day time. The term is applied to the flowers which open in day light as opposed to the nocturnal flowers which open at night.

Divaricate: Spreading widely, that is, divergent.

Divergent: Spreading away from each other.

Divided: Indented essentially to the base or midrib.

Division: The highest rank of taxon in the plant kingdom, a group of related classes or some times a single class; a segment of a structure, such as leaf.

Dormant: Applied to buds when they are not actively growing and to plants when they are not in leaf.

Dorsal: On the outer surface of an organ, that is, the side away from the axis.

Dorsiventral: A structure having a clear differentiation of a back and front or upper and lower side.

Dorsoventral: The distance or measurement from the back of a structure to the front, that is from dorsal to ventral as opposed to lateral distance.

Double samara: A Samara with two locules and two wings.

Downy: Finely and softly pubescent.

Drainage area: The watershed or area into which the excess precipitation of a region drains.

Drupaceous: Druplike.

Echinate: covered with prickles.

Egg: A female gamete cell of a plant.

Effective bloom: The length of time the tree is in conspicuous blossom.

Ellipsoid, ellipsoidal: Elliptical in outline with three-dimensional body.

Elliptic, elliptical: In the form of an ellipse, that is, about one and one half times as long as broad, widest at the middle and rounded at both ends. A two dimensional figure.

Emarginate: With a shallow broad notch at the apex.

Embryo: The new plant enclosed in the seed. Its formation follows union of gametes.

Embryo culture: In vitro development or maintenance of isolated mature or immature embryos.

Embryogenesis: The process of embryo initiation and development.

Embryo sac: The cell in the ovule in which the embryo is formed.

Emersed: Above water.

Enation: An outgrowth from the superficial tisssues of the stem.

Endimic: Restricted in occurrence to aparticular geographical area.

Endosperm: A cell layer occurring in at least the immature seeds of flowering plants.

Ensiform: Sword like; in the form of sword.

Entire: without division or toothing of any bind.

Entomophilous: Insect pollinated.

Emphemeral: Lasting for a brief period.

Epicotyl: The portion of the embryo of a seed plant just above the cotyledons, the young stem.

Epigynous: The sepals, petals and stamens apparently upon the ovary, but actually growing from the edge of the floral cup, which is adnate to the ovary.

Epigynous disc: A disc within the floral cup and on top of the inferior ovary.

Epiphyte: A plant growing upon another plant but not parasitic upon it.

Equitant: With the leaves folded around a stem after the manner of the legs of a rider around a horse or some times with the leaves folded around each other in rows.

Errect: Standing upright.

Erose: With the margin appearing to have been gnawes.

Etiolated: White through failure to develop chlorophyll.

Euploid: The situation which exists when the nucleus of a cell contains exact multiples of the haploid number of chromosomes.

Even pinnate: Without a terminal leaflet.

Excentric: Off centre.

Excortis: A shelling off the bark of tree.

Excurrent: Projecting as for example, a leaf base which projects beyond the margin of the blade.

Exfoliating: Separating into thin layer.

Exocarp: The outer layer of the pericarp.

Explant: Tissue taken from its original site and transferred to an artifical medium for growth and maintenance.

Exserted: Projecting beyond the usual containing structure.

Extrose: Facing outward.

Falcate: In the shape of a scythe, that is curving, flat and tapering gradually to a point.

False partition: An ovary partition not formed by infolding of the edges of the carpel, growing from the middle of the placenta on the opposite side or formed by in growth of placentae.

Farinose: Mealy, that is composed of mealy granules or with granules on the surface.

Fasciate: Literally, in a bundle or bundled together, the term being applied as fascinated, to branches remaining parallel and grown abnormally together.

Fasciation: A deformity in which the stem becomes much flattened as a result of multiple terminal buds arranged in a single plane.

Fascicle: A bundle or cluster.

Fastigiate: Errect and close together.

Faveolate or favose: Resembling a honey comb.

Fecundation: The fusions of two gametes to form a new cell.

Fecundity: The ability of flowers to produce seeds that will germinate.

Female gamete: An egg; a female gamete cell.

Fenestrate: Perforated.

Ferruginous: Rust coloured.

Fertile: Productive, mean capable of producing fruit or spores. Sometimes a staminate flower is referred to as infertile or sterile because it produces no seed.

Fertility: The ability to set and mature fruit with viable seed.

Fertilization: The union of male germ cell, contained in the pollen grain, with the female germ cell, or egg, in the ovule.

Fibrillose: With fine fibres.

Fibrous root system: A root system with several major roots about equal and arising from approximately the same point.

Filament: A thread; the stalk of a stamen.

Filamentous: Composed of threads.

Filiform: Thread like, that is, long slender and cylindroidal.

Fimbriate: Fringed, that is resembling the fring on the sleeve of an early American buckskin shirt.

Fimbrillate: The diminutive of fimbriate.

Fimbriolate: With a very fine fringe.

Fistulose: Hollow and cylindroidal.

Flabellate: Fan shaped.

Flaccid: Weak.

Flagelliform: Whiplike or lash like.

Flates: They are shallow plastic, styrofoam, wooden or metal trays with drainage holes in the bottom. They are useful for germinating seeds or rooting cuttings, since they permit young plants to be moved easily.

Flexuous: Curved in first one direction, then the opposite.

Floccose: With tufts of wooly hair.

Flocculent: Diminutive of floccose.

Floral cup: A cup bearing on its rim the sepals, petals and stamens; originating as (a) a hypanthium. (b) a "calyx tube" formed by coalescence and adnation of the bases of the sepals, petals and stamens, or (c) a perianth tube of the type in the monocotyledons, the sepals and adjacent petals being adnate edge to edge.

Floral tube: An elongated, slender floral cup.

Floret: A small flower, the flower of a grass and the two immediately enclosing bracts, that is the lemma and palea.

Floricana: A canelike stem producing flowers.

Floriferous: Bearing flowers.

Flower: A complex strobilus formed at the end of a branch, including the receptacle (thalamus or torus) and bearing sepals, stamens, petals and pistils or some of these.

Flower bud: A bud which will develop into a flower, actually the young flower.

Flowering hormones: Are hormones which initiate the formation of floral primodia, or promote their development.

Flowering regulators: Are regulators which affect flowering.

Foliaceous: Leaflike.

Foliage bud: A bud containing new young leaves.

Foliage leaf: The green leaf of the mature plant.

Foliar: Relating to a leaf.

Foliate: Leaved, an example being 3-foliate or trifoliate.

Foliolate: With leaflets.

Foliose: Bearing many leaves.

Follicular: Of the nature of a follicle.

Forked: Dividing into branches which are nearly equal.

Foundation seeds: Progeny of breeders seed which is so handled as to maintain the highest standard of genetic identity and purity.

Foveolate: Pitted.

Free: Separate from other organs.

Friability: A term indicating the tendency for plant cells to separate from one another.

Frond: The leaf blade of a fern.

Frondose: Leafy, that is with frond like leaves.

Fruit: A matured ovary with its enclosed seeds and some times with attached external structures.

Fruitescent: Shrubby or becoming so at length.

Fruitful: A plant or variety that sets and matures a commercial crop of fruit.

Fruiticose: Distinctly woody, living over from year to year and attaining considerable size, with several main stems instead of a single trunk.

Fruit setting: A development of the ovary and adjacent tissues following the blossoming period.

Fugacious: Falling away early.

Fungus: A plant without chlorophyll and with no vascular tissue , stems or leaves. Plural fungi.

Funnelform: In the shape of a funnel.

Furcate: Forked.

Fusicous: Grayish-brown.

Fusiform: In the shape of a spindle, that is, widest at the middle and tapering gradually to each pointed end, the body being circular in cross section.

Galea: A hood formed from a portion of the parianth derived, for example, from the two upper petals coalascent indistinguishably into one or from the upper sepal.

Galeate: With a galea.

Gamete: A unisexual cell which must fuse with another gamete to produce a new individual.

Gamopetalous: With all the petals coalescent.

Gametophyte: The gamete producing generation, each cell with a chromosomes.

Geminiate: Equal or arranged in pairs.

Generative cell: A cell in the microgametophyte (or pollen grain) which may give rise directly or indirectly to male gamete cells or nuclei.

Genetics: The study of heredity.

Geniculate: Bent like the human knee.

Genus: A group of related species or sometimes a single species. Plural, genera.

Gibbous: Swollen or distended on one side.

Glabrate: At first hairy but latter becoming glabrous.

Glabrous: Not hairy.

Gladiate: Sword like.

Gland: A secreting organ.

Glandular: Bearing glands, small cellular organs secreting oils, tars, resins etc. often only the secretion is visible.

Glaucescent: More or less glaucous.

Glaucous: Covered with a white or bluish powder or bloom, this often composed of finely divided particles of wax. Ex. The bloom on a plum.

Globose, globular: Spheroidal.

Glochid: A sharp hair or bristle tipped with a barb.

Glochidiate: Barbed at the tip.

Glomerate: In compact clusters.

Glomerulate: Diminutive of glumerate.

Glomerule: A single cyme of sessile flowers forming a compact cluster. It may be distinguished from a head by blooming of the central flower first.

Glumaceous: Resembling a glume of a grass spikelet.

Glume: One of the two chaff like bractlets at the base of a grass spikelet. The glumes do not enclose flowers.

Glutinous: covered with sticky material.

Granulose: Covered by minute grains of hardened material.

Gregarious: In large colonies.

Growth hormones: A hormone which regulate growth.

Growth regulators: (Synonym: growth substances) are regulators which affect growth.

Gymnospermous: With the seeds naked, that is not enclosed in an ovary.

Gynandrium: A structure formed by adnation of stamens and pistil.

Gynandrous: With the stamen adhering to the pistils.

Gynecandrous: With staminate and pistillate flowers in the same inflorescence, the pistillate above and the staminate below.

Gynobase: An enlarged or elongated portion of the receptacle bearing the pistil.

Gynoecium: The pistil of a flower or its group of pistils.

Gynophore: A special stalk under a pistil.

Habit: The general appearance of a plant.

Habitate: The type of locality or the set of ecological conditions under which the plant grows.

Hair: A slender cellular projection.

Halberd-shaped: Hastate.

Halophyte: A plant growing in salty soil as for example an alkali flat or a salt water marsh.

Hamate: With a hook at the tip.

Haploid: With a chromosomes per cell.

Hastate: More or less sagittate (arrow head shaped) but with the divergent basal lobes.

Head: A cluster of sessile or essentially sessile flowers or fruits at the apex of a peduncle. Essentially a spike with a very short axis.

Helicoid: Spiral, like the shell of a turban snail.

Helicoid cyme: A coiled inflorescence. The main stem terminates in a flower and a single bud just below grows out as a stem but terminates also in a flower, the process being repeated many times and always in the same direction.

Herb: A non woody plant, at laeast one which is not woody above ground level.

Herbaceous: Not woody.

Hermaphrodite: Bisexual, that is, with stamens and pistils in the same flower.

Heterocarpous: Producing more than one kind of fruit.

Heterogamous: With more than one kind of flower.

Heterogeneous: Of various binds, that is, not all individuals the same.

Heteroploid: The term given to a cell culture when the cells comprising the culture possess nuclei containing chromosome numbers other than the diploid number. This ia a term used only to describe a culture and is not used to describe the individual cells. Thus, a heteroploid culture would be one which contains aneuploid cells.

Hilium: The point of attachment of the funiculus (Stalk) to the seed.

Hip (of a rose): A floral cup which usually becomes enlarged and fleshy at fruiting time. Thetrue fruits are achenes inside.

Hippocrepiform: Horse shoe shaped.

Hirsute: With fairly coarse more or less stiff hairs.

Hirsutulus: Slight hirsute.

Hispid: With rigid or stiff bristles or bristly hairs.

Hispidulous: Diminutive of hispid.

Hoary: Covered with short, dense, grayish white hairs, the surface of the stem, leaf or other structure therefore appearing white.

Homogamous: With only one kind of flower.

Homogeneous: With all members similar.

Hood: A hoodlike structure, often formed from a petal or a sepal or more than one of either.

Humifuse: Spreading on the ground.

Hyaline: Thin and membranous being transparent or translucent.

Hybrid: Produced by dissimilar parents.

Hydrophyte: An aquatic plant.

Hygroscopic: Changing form with changes of moisture content.

Hygroscopic coefficient: The percentage of soil water retained in contact with a saturated atmosphere and in the absence of any other source of moisture.

Hypanthium: A floral cup or tube developed by extra growth of the margin of the receptacle. An alternative adopted by some authors in use of hypanthium with the meaning of floral cup.

Hypocotyl: The portion of the axis of an embryo of a seed plant just below the cotyledon(s).

Hypogaeous: Below the ovary, that is, referring to flower parts which come directly from the receptacle and not from a floral cup or tube. A hypogynous flower is one which does not have a floral cup or tube.

Hypogynous disc: A flushy cushion of tissue growing from the receptacle below the ovary, often the stamens and sometimes the petals being attached to it.

Imbricate: overlapping like the shingles on a roof.

Imparipinnate: Odd pinnate.

Implexed: Tangled, interlacing.

Implicate: Woven in.

Inactive bud: A bud dormant either before the beginning of the growing season or through a longer period.

Incanous: Covered with white hairs.

Included: Not protruding beyond the normal surrounding structures.

Incompatible: Inability of viable pollen to develop in the styles rapidly enough to reach the ovule in time to effect fertilization.

Incompatibility: Of sex cells, the inability to unite and form a fertilized egg that can be grown to maturity.

Incomplete flower: A flower lacking one or more of the four usual series of structures, that is, sepals, petals, stamens or pistils.

Incrassate: Thickened.

Incumbent: Applied to a pair of cotyledons which lie with the back of one against the axis of the embryo.

Indehiscent: Not opening by splitting along regular lines or not opening at all.

Indeterminate: Of indefinite growth i.e., the size or number of organs to be produced not predetermined.

Indigenous: Native in a particular region.

Indument: A covering of hairs.

Induplicate: With the edges folded inward.

Indurate: Hardened.

Indusium: The membranous covering of a sorus of a pteridophyte.

Inferior: Below.

Inferior floral cup: The portion of a floral cup or tube adnate to the wall of an inferior ovary.

Infertile: Varieties 'A' and 'B' both produce fruit with viable when pollinated by each other.

Inflorescence: The flowering area or segment of a plant.

Integument: The outer coating of an ovule, a structure grown up from the sporophyll and surrounding the sporangium. The integument becomes the seedcoat.

Intercompatible: The pollen produced by either variety of a combination is capable of functioning in the styles and fertilizing the ovule of the other variety.

Interfruitful: Varieties 'A' and 'B' both produce commercial crops when pollinated by each other.

Interincompatible: Varieties 'A' and 'B' are unfruitful when pollinated by each other because the pollen tubes of each variety grow too slowly in the styles of the other to effect fertilization. Either variety may serve as an effective pollinizer for some other varieties.

Intersterile: Varieties 'A' and 'B' both fail to produce fruit with viable seed when pollinated by each other.

Interstock: It is a piece of stem inserted by means of two graft unions between the scion and the rootstock.

In vitro propagation: Propagation of plants in controlled, artificial environment, using plastic or glass cultures vessels, aseptic techniques, and a defined growing medium.

In vitro transformation: A heritable change, occurring in cells in culture, either intrinsically or from treatment with chemical carcinogens, oncogenic viruses, irradiation, etc., and leading to the acquisition of altered morphological, antigenic, neoplastic, proliferative, or other properties.

Involucel: The involucre of a secondary umbel.

Involucre: A series of bracts surrounding a flower cluster or some times a single flower.

Irregular: Used in botany to indicate a bilaterally symmetrical structure as for example, a bilaterally symmetrical flower.

Isomerous: With the members of the various series of flower parts of equal number.

Keel: A ridge along the outside of a fold, like the keel of a boat. The term is applied to the two coalescent lower petals of a papilionaceous corolla of the pea family.

Labiate: With lips, that is, two opposed structures as for example, the upper two petals as opposed to lower three petals in the mint family.

Lanolin: The natural fat of wool.

Latent bud: A bud, usually concealed, more than one year old, which may remain dormant indefinitely or may develop under certain conditions.

Lateral bud: One in a leaf axil.

Legume: A dry several seeded fruit formed from a single carpel and dehiscent on both margins.

Locular: Divided into locules.

Loculicidal: Dehiscent along the midrib of a carpel of an ovary containing more than one carpel and chamber.

Lodicule: One of the two small scales at the base of the grass flower.

Loment: A legume divided by constriction into a linear series of segments each containing one seed.

Male gamete: An antherozoid or a male gamete cell or nucleus.

Male nucleous: The male gamete of a flowering plant, that is, a single nucleus with the associated cytoplasm but with no cell wall.

Megagametophyte: A female gametophyte.

Megasporangium: A sporangium producing megaspore.

Megaspore: A larger type of spore developed by a plant with spores of two sizes or kinds.

Megasporophyll: A sporophyll bearing one or more megasporangia.

Mericloning: A popular term, not in scientific usage, referring to the in vitro vegetative propagation of orchids from excised shoot tips, axillary buds, or floral organs.

Meristem: A plant tissue in which the cells are capable of, under favourable growth conditions usually in process of active division, to produce new daughter cells.

Meristem culture: In vitro culture of a generally shiny dome-like structure measuring less than 0.1 mm in length when excised, most often excised from the shoot apex.

Meristemming: A popular term, not in scientific usage, referring to the in vitro clonal propagation of plants from various explant sources including shoot tips, leaf section and calli; shoot apical meristems are seldom used.

Meristemoid: Meristem-like cells located in areas of a plant or culture other than the meristem.

Metaxenia: The supposed direct influence of the pollen or pollen parent on the characteristics of the developing fruit.

Micropropagation: This term is synonymous with in vitro propagation.

Morphogenesis: The process of growth and development of differentiated structures.

Microspore: The smaller type of spore in a plant producing spores of two sizes.

Mixed bud: A bud containing both leaf primordial and rudimentary flowers.

Monoadelphous: In one botherhood; referring to stamens with their filaments coalescent into a single tube.

Monochlamydeous: With a single series in the perianth that is only the sepals.

Monoecious: The stamens and pistils in separate flowers borne on the same individual.

Naked bud: A bud not covered by special scales but only by the outer leaves.

Nocturnal: Occuring at night. The term is applied to flowers which open at night.

Nucellus: The sporangium enclosed in the ovule of a seed plant.

Nut: A hard, relatively large, indehiscent, 1 seeded fruit.

Nutlet: Diminutive of nut.

Nutrients: Are defined as materials which supply either energy or essential mineral elements.

Order: A tascon composed of related families or sometimes of a single family.

Organ culture: The maintenance or growth of organ primordial or the whole or parts of an organ in vitro in a way that may allow differentiation and preservation of the architecture and/ or function.

Organogenesis: The evolution, from dissociated cells, of a structure which shows natural organ form or function or both.

Osmosis: The passage of water through a semi-permeable membrane.

Ovary: In the flower, that portion of the female organ which contains the potential seeds (ovules). After fertilization it grows into the fruit.

Ovulate: Producing ovules.

Ovules: The potential seed before fertilization.

Panicle: A cluster of associated spikes racemes or corymbs.

Papilionaceous: Butterfly like.

Pappus: The specialized calyx of members of the sunflower family; composed of bristles or scales.

Parthenogenetic: Developing without fertilization

Partly inferior ovary: With only the basal portion of the ovary adnate to the floral cup.

Passage: The transfer or transplantation of cells, with or without dilution, from one culture vessel to another. It is understood that any time cells are transferred from one vessel to another, a certain portion of he cells may be lost and, therefore, dilution of cells, whether deliberate or not, may occur. This term is synonymous with the term "subculture".

Passage number: The number of times the cells in the culture have been subcultured or passaged. In descriptions of this process, the ratio or dilution of the cells should be stated so that the relative cultural "age" can be ascertained.

Peat: It consists of remains of a aquatic, marsh, bog or swamp vegetation which has been preserved under water in a partially decompose state.

Pectinate: Resembling a comb.

Pedicel: The internode below a flower.

Peduncle: The stalk of a cluster of flowers or the next to the last internode below a single flower.

Pentagynous: With five pistils.

Pentandrous: With five stamens.

Perfect: A flower having both functional pistils and functional stamens.

Perennation: A lasting state referring particularly to the persistence of fruit long after its usual season of maturity.

Perianth: A collective term for the calyx and the corolla.

Perianth tube: A tube formed by coalescence and adnation of the lower portions of the sepals and petals.

Pericarp: The wall of a matured ovary, that is, the wall of the fruit or the inner wall if the ovary is inferior.

Perigynium: A special sac which encloses the ovary of calyx.

Perigynous: Descriptive of the parts of a flower attached to a floral cup or tube which is not adnate to the ovary. A perigynous flower has a floral cup but the ovary is not adnate to it.

Perigynous disc: A disc adnate to the floral cup of a perigynous flower.

Perlite: It is a graywhite silicaceous material of volcanic origin, mined from larva flows.

Permanent wilting point: The amount of water in soils when rapidly growing plants fail to recover from wilting under condition of low transpiration.

Petal: One member of the series of flower parts forming the corolla.

Petaloid: Resembling a petal in colour and texture.

Photosynthesis: The process of combining in the presence of chlorophyll and light of carbon dioxide and water yielding glucose and oxygen.

Photosynthetic: Descriptive of a green portion of a plant capable of carrying on photosynthesis.

Pistil: The female organ of a flower.

Pistillate: Having pistils, that is, a flower which has pistils but no stamens.

Placenta: The tissue of an ovary which bears ovules or seeds.

(Plant) Hormones: (Synonym: phytohormones) are regulators produced by plants, which in low concentrations regulate plant physiological processes. Hormones usually move within the plants from a site of production to a site of action.

(Plant) Regulators: Are organic compounds, other than nutrients which in small amount promote, inhibit or otherwise modify any physiological process in plants.

Plating efficiency: The percentage of cells plated which give rise to colonies. The total number of cells in the inoculum, type of culture vessel and the environment conditions (medium, temperature, closed or open system, etc.) must always be stated. This term is often expressed as the percentage of individual cells in the vessel which give rise to colonies. If one is certain that each of the colonies arose from single cells, then one may properly apply the term "cloning efficiency".

Pollen: The spheroidal structures produced in an anther of a flower or in the microsporophyll of a gymnosperm. The pollen grains are microgametophytes developed from microspores.

Pollen sac: Pollen bearing cavity.

Pollen tube: A tube developed by a pollengrain and growing through the microphyle of an ovule where its contained cells or nuclei effect fertilization of the egg.

Pollination: The transfer of pollen to the stigma; or in a broad sense, the distribution of pollen. Pollination may be accomplished by insects, wind, gravity, water, birds and artificial methods derived by man.

Pollinizer: The variety (plant) used to furnish pollen. The male parent.

Polyadelphous: In several brotherhoods; with several groups of coalescent stamens.

Polyandrous: With an indefinite large number of stamens.

Polyembryony: Production of more than one embryo in a single ovule.

Polygamo-dioecious: With hermaphrodite and unisexual flowers on different individuals of the same species.

Polygamo-monoecious: Polygamous but in the main monoecious.

Polygamous: With bisexual and unisexual flowers on the same or different individuals of the species.

Polygynous: With a large indefinite number of pistils.

Polymorphic: With several or many forms.

Polyploid: With several to many times n chromosomes per cell.

Prickle: A sharp, pointed outgrowth from the superficial tissues of the stem, that is, from the epidermis or the cortex, as in a rose prickle. The structure is not associated with the conducting tissues at the centre of the stem.

Protandry: The pollen being discharged before the pistils are receptive.

Protogyny: The pistils being receptive before the anthers have ripe pollen.

Pruinose: Covered with a bloom, that is, finely divided particles of a waxy powder.

Protoplast: A plant cell without its outer retaining cell wall.

Protoplast fusion: Technique in which protoplasts are fused into a single cell.

Pruning: Means removing certain parts of the tree in order to modify and utilize its natural habits so that more and better fruit can be obtained at less cost over a longer period.

Pumice: Increases aeration and drainage in a propagation mix and can be used alone or mixed with peat moss.

Raceme: An inflorescence composed of pedicelled flowers arranged along an axis which elongates for an indefinite period. The lower flower blooms first and eventually the terminal bud forms the last flower.

Racemiform: In the form of a raceme.

Rachis: The axis of a pinnate leaf or of an inflorescence.

Ray: A pedicel within an umbel; a ray flower or its corolla.

Ray flower: In the sunflower family, one of the flowers with a ligulate corolla. The flattening is due to failure of complete coalescence between two petals of the sympetalous corolla.

Receptacle: The apical area beyond the pedicle, that is, the portion which bears flower parts. The receptacle consists of several or many nodes and short internodes.

Regular: Radially symmetrical.

Reproductive bud: A bud developing into a flower, cone or other pollen-, seed- or spore bearing structures.

Resting bud: An inactive bud.

Rockwool: This material is used as a rooting and growing medium.

Rouging: The removal of off-type plants or plants of other varieties.

Rosette: A condition in which the internodes are much shortened giving the leaves a bunched or clustered appearance.

Salverform: Descriptive of a sympetalous corolla with the slender basal tube abruptly expanded into a flat or saucer shaped upper portion.

Samara: A dry indehiscent fruit with a wing.

Sand: It consists of small rock particles 0.05-2.0 mm in diameter, formed as a result of weathering of various rocks, its mineral composition depending upon the type of rock.

Scape: A flowering stem which bears no leaves or only a small bract or a pair or whorl of bracts.

Schizocarp: A fruit which splits into one seeded sections (mericarp).

Scion: It is the short piece of detached, shoot containing several dormant buds which, when united with rootstock, comprises the upper portion of graft.

Scorpioid: Often used as descriptive of an inflorescence which is coiled in the bud stage as in the forget me not or fiddle neck. This is a helicoids cyme although it appears to be a spike or a raceme.

Seed: A mature ovule consisting of an integument (seed coat), an enclosed nucellus, the remains of the megagametophyte, the endosperm and embryo.

Seed dormancy: It is a condition where seeds will not germinate even when the environmental conditions (water, temperature and aeration) are permissive for germination. This not only prevents immediate germination but also regulates the time, conditions and place that germination will occur.

Self-fertile: The ability of a variety to produce fruits with viable seeds following self-pollination.

Self-pollination: The transfer of pollen from the anthers of a flower to one variety to the stigma of a flower of the same variety.

Self-sterile: The inability of a variety to produce fruit with viable seed following self-pollination. (Some varieties may be self-fruitful, even though they are self-sterile, because of their ability to produce parthenocarpic fruits.).

Self-unfruitful: A variety which is unable to set and mature a commercial crop of fruit with its own pollen (or as a result of parthenocarpic fruit development).

Sepal: One of the flower parts of the outer series, the sepal forming a calyx.

Septicidal: Descriptive of a fruit dehiscent through the partitious between the seed chambers.

Silique: The elongate capsular fruit of the mustard family which has two seed chambers separated by a false partition from the middle of one placenta to the middle of other. The false partition in this case results from presence of some fertile and some sterile carpels in the pistil.

Sod mulch: A method of charged soil management in which a permanent perennial crop is grown between the trees, mowed once or twice during the growing season and then allowed to remain on the ground.

Somaclonal variation: This type of genetic variation occurs when plant cells of certain species were grown in culture and new plant regenerated.

Somatic cell hybrid: The cell or plant resulting from the fusion of animal cells or plant protoplasts, respectively, derived from somatic cells.

Somatic hybridization: The in vitro fusion of animal cells or plant protoplasts derived from somatic cells which differ genetically.

Spadix: A spike with a fleshy or succulent axis, the flowers often partly embedded in the axis.

Spathe: A large bract enclosing an inflorescence at least when it is young. Spathes are either white or highly coloured but usually not green.

Species: A group of related varieties or often a single unit.

Spike: An inflorescence in which the sessile flowers are arranged along an axis. The basal flower blooms first, the last one formed is at the apex.

Spur: An elongated sac produced from a part of a flower as in the larkspur from a sepal or in the columbines from a petal.

Stamen: The pollen-producing structure of a flowering plant, consisting of an anther and of a filament.

Staminodium: A sterile stamen, that is, without an anther or at least not producing pollen.

Stem end: The basal portion of an inferior ovary at fruiting time, the point of attachment of the pedicel.

Stigma: The apical portion of a pistil i.e., the portion receptive to pollen. It is covered commonly with minute papillae, and it is sticky through production of a sugar solution in which the pollen grains germinate.

Stock or rootstock: It is the lower portion of the graft which develops into the root system of the grafted plants.

Style: the tubular upper or middle part of a pistil connecting the stigma and the ovary.

Subclass: A taxon of a rank between class and order.

Subspecies: A taxon of a rank between species and variety; a group of related varieties.

Substrain: A substrain can be derived from a strain by isolating a single cell or groups of cells having properties or markers not shared by all cells of the parent strain.

Sucker: A rhizome or a branch of a rhizome which comes to the surface and grows into a leafy shoot.

Sunburn: A killing of bark near the ground surface due to reflected heat rays, a form of sun scald.

Suspension culture: A type of culture in which cells, or aggregates of cells, multiply while suspended in liquid medium.

Sterility: The inability to set and mature fruit with viable seed. This failure may be due to non-function of the pollen, the ovule or both.

Syconium: An enlarged hollow receptacle bearing flowers and ultimately fruits inside.

Sympetalous: All the petals coalescent at least basally.

Syncarp: A structure composed of several fruits, these more or less coalescent as for example the fruits of pineapple or mulberry.

Syncarpous: With coalescent carpels.

Syngenesious: With anthers cohering in a circle.

Synsepalous: The sepals coalescent.

Taxon: A category used in classification as for example, a variety, a species, genus, family etc. Pural taxa.

Taxonomy: The principles of classification.

Tepal: A term used for sepals and petals which are similar and not easily distinguished from each other.

Terminal bud: Bud at the end of the stem or a branch.

Testa: The seedcoat, that is, the hardened mature integument.

Tetradynamous: Having four long and two short stamens. A condition found almost throughout the mustard family.

Tetragynous: With four pistils.

Throat: The opening of a sympetalous corolla or a synsepalous calyx, that is, the expanding part between the proper tube and the limb.

Thyrse: A densely congested panicle, the main axis indeterminate, the lateral typically determinate and, therefore, cymose. A mixed inflorescence.

Tissue: Groups of cells having common functions.

Tissue culture: The term used for range of procedures used to maintain and grow plant tissues and organs in aseptic culture.

Transpiration: The phenomenon of giving off water in form of vapours.

Tuber: A thickened short underground branch of the stem serving as a storage organ containing reserve food. Ex. potato.

Umbel: An inflorescence with the pedicles of the flower arising from approximately the same point. A compound umbel is umbal of umbels.

Unfruitful: A plant or variety that fails to set a commercial crop of fruit and mature it.

Unisexual: Of only one sex. Descriptive of a flower having only stamens or only pistils, not both, or of a gymnosperm producing only pollen or only ovules or of the gametophytes of pteridophyte bearing the reproductive organs of only one sex.

Utricle: A small, seeded more or less indehiscent fruit which appears to be inflated, that is, with a relatively thin pericarp more or less remote from the single seed. At maturity the utricle opens either irregularly or along a horizontal line.

Vascular cambium: It is a thin tissue located between the bark (periderm, cortex and phloem) and the wood (xylem).

Vermiculite: It is a micaceous mineral that expands markedly when heated. It is very light in weight, neutral in reaction with good buffering properties and insoluble in water.

Wind burn: A disorder of the leaves in which first their edges and later perhaps the entire leaf dries out and present a scorched appearance.

Xenia: The direct influence of foreign pollen on the part of the mother plant that develops into endosperm.

Zygomorphic: Bilaterally symmetrical. Often this is described as irregular, especially with reference to corollas.

Zygote: The fertilized egg, resulting from combining of the male and female gametes.

INDEX